© Bettina Strauss

About the Author

BARBARA MERTZ is the *New York Times* bestselling author of the popular Amelia Peabody mystery series, writing under the pen name Elizabeth Peters, and romantic suspense novels, writing as Barbara Michaels. She was born and brought up in Illinois, and earned her Ph.D. in Egyptology from the University of Chicago's famed Oriental Institute. Mertz was named a Grand Master by the Mystery Writers of America. She lives in a historic farmhouse in western Maryland.

www.mpmbooks.com

ALSO BY BARBARA MERTZ

NONFICTION

Temples, Tombs, and Hieroglyphs

FICTION

Writing as Elizabeth Peters
The Amelia Peabody Mystery Series

Crocodile on the Sandbank
The Curse of the Pharaohs
The Mummy Case
The Deeds of the Disturber
The Last Camel Died at Noon
The Snake, the Crocodile, and the Dog
The Hippopotamus Pool
Seeing a Large Cat
The Ape Who Guards the Balance
The Falcon at the Portal
He Shall Thunder in the Sky
Lord of the Silent
The Golden One
Children of the Storm
Guardian of the Horizon
The Serpent on the Crown
Tomb of the Golden Bird

RED LAND, BLACK LAND

Daily Life in Ancient Egypt

SECOND EDITION

BARBARA MERTZ

HARPER

NEW YORK • LONDON • TORONTO • SYDNEY

HARPER

This book was originally published by Coward-McCann in 1966 and republished by Dodd, Mead and Company in 1978.

A hardcover edition of this book was published in 2008 by William Morrow, an imprint of HarperCollins Publishers.

FIRST HARPER PAPERBACK PUBLISHED IN 2009.

The Library of Congress has catalogued the hardcover edition as follows:

Mertz, Barbara.
  Red land, black land : daily life in ancient Egypt / Barbara Mertz.
    p. cm.
  Originally published: New York : Coward-McCann, 1966.
  Includes bibliographical references and index.
  ISBN 978-0-06-125274-7
  1. Egypt—Civilization—To 332 B.C. I. Title.
  DT61.M54 2008
  932—dc22   2007036448

ISBN 978-0-06-125275-4 (pbk.)

09 10 11 12 13 WBC/RRD 10 9 8 7 6 5 4 3 2 1

For my mother and father

Contents

PART II THE WORLD OF THE DEAD

Foreword to the First Edition

This is not a book about ancient Egyptian culture; it is a book about ancient Egyptians. It might even be subtitled "How to Be an Ancient Egyptian," for, if properly studied, it will teach the reader how to make papyrus, how to build a pyramid, and how to dress, dine, and furnish a house in the Egyptian manner, among other matters of equal interest. The objects of our study are, for the most part, anonymous, but they are, or were, people—human beings—Egyptians. I have tried, therefore, to talk about them as people, not as featureless statistics or as the vague blur of humanity underlying such academic topics as Egyptian Literature or Egyptian Architecture. The reader will not find a chapter on Egyptian Literature in this book, although a good many literary works are discussed. He will not find a chapter on Architecture either, but houses, temples, and tombs will be described. We do have a longish chapter on Egyptian Religion; however, the chapter on Costume is almost as long, although it concerns itself with a subject which is decidedly frivolous compared to theology. Yet I suspect that a well-to-do Egyptian lady, like her descendants in other countries and other ages, sometimes spent as much time thinking about her clothing as about her gods.

I apologized, in another book, for what might strike a sensitive reader as a frivolous approach to ancient Egypt, but I do not really believe that an apology is necessary. The popular view of Egyptian civilization as dignified and austere is incorrect. It comes from the massive temples, the grisly mummies, the crumbled and ruined tombs. Yet the temples were once bright with paint and aglitter with gold; the mummies were men, women, and children who enjoyed life so much that they went to unusual extremes in the hope of perpetuating it; the tombs were Houses of Eternity, equipped with "every good and pure thing" for the enjoyment of life everlasting. We are not insulting the Egyptians or falsifying their view of the world if we catch a glimpse of them telling bawdy stories about the gods, getting drunk, writing sentimental poems to their sweetheart, or lecturing their bored children. If we laugh at them just a little, it will not diminish them; and if we fail to see that we are also laughing at ourselves, we are missing the best part of the joke.

Foreword to the Second Edition

In the forty-plus years since this book was written, it has been read by a good many people. I owe a great debt to these readers, some of whom went on to become professional Egyptologists, for helping to keep the book in print and for nagging me (in the kindest possible manner) to revise it. Since the original year of publication, hundreds of new books and thousands of new articles have appeared. The additions to one category are particularly striking: in the 1960s there were no books on the subject of Egyptian women. There are now quite a number of them, not to mention innumerable articles.

I won't claim I've read all the new material, but I have read a good deal of it. I have made many trips to Egypt and talked with a number of obliging Egyptologists. And yet, I still stick to what I said in the foreword to the first edition. The refinements, the new information, the new interpretations of old data, really haven't changed the picture as I see it. One may stress the differences between cultures such as our own and that of ancient Egypt, or one may insist on the fact that people ancient and modern, Western and Eastern, are basically much alike, with the same ambitions, dreams, and fears. It seems to me that in today's world it is all the more necessary to focus on the second approach.

Ancient Egyptian Chronology

Dating based on William Murnane, *The Penguin Guide to Ancient Egypt*, rev. ed. (Penguin Books, 1996).

Author's note: You will find different dates in different books; the further back in time, the greater the uncertainty. Chronologies are based on a number of sources, some more reliable than others. The general outline of dynasties comes from the Greek writer Manetho, who divided Egyptian history into families of rulers. Modern scholars have cast doubt on certain details, but the system has been in use so long that it would be inexpedient to change it.

You will sometimes encounter the terms C.E. (Common Era) and B.C.E. (Before the Common Era) instead of B.C. (Before Christ) and A.D. (Anno Domini). There is a reason for this, but I have been using the old terms too long to change.

ARCHAIC PERIOD: 3150–2686
Dynasty O: Scorpion, Aha, Narmer
Dynasty I: Unification; Menes, Djer, Djet, Den, Queen Merneith
Dynasty II: Peribsen, Khasekhemui

THE OLD KINGDOM: 2686–2181
Dynasty III: Step Pyramid; Djoser, Khaba, Huni
Dynasty IV: Pyramids of Dahshur, Medum, Giza; Snefru, Khufu,
     Khafre, Menkaure
Dynasty V: Userkaf, Sahure, Unis
Dynasty VI: Teti, Pepi I, Pepi II

FIRST INTERMEDIATE PERIOD: 2181–2040 — Breakdown of
     central government.
Dynasties VII–X. Some partially overlapping.

MIDDLE KINGDOM: 2040–1782 — Reunification.
Dynasty XI: Intefs and Mentuhoteps
Dynasty XII: Amenemhats and Senuserts, Queen Sobekneferu

SECOND INTERMEDIATE PERIOD: 1782–1570 — Breakdown of
     central government.
Dynasties XIII–XVI: Some overlapping. Hyksos
Dynasty XVII: Sekenenre Tao II, Kamose 1663–1570

NEW KINGDOM: 1570–1070 — Reunification.
Dynasty XVIII: Ahmose, Amenhoteps and Thutmoses, Queen
     Hatshepsut, Akhenaton, Tutankhamon, Ay, Horemhab
Dynasty XIX: Seti I, Ramses I and II, Merneptah, Queen Tausert
Dynasty XX: Ramses III–XI, Herihor

THIRD INTERMEDIATE PERIOD: 1070–525
Dynasty XXI: Smendes, Psusennes, Pinudjem
Dynasty XXII: Libyan Sheshonks, Osorkons, Takelot
Dynasties XXIII–XXIV: Libyan
Dynasty XXV: Cushite; Piankhi, Shabaka, Taharka
Dynasty XXVI: Psamtiks (3), Necho, Apries

LATE PERIOD: 525–332
Dynasty XXVII: First Persian
Dynasties XXVIII–XXIX: Egyptian dynasts
Dynasty XXX: Nectanabo I and II
Dynasty XXXI: Second Persian

PTOLEMAIC: Conquest by Alexander the Great, 332 B.C.
   Succeeded by Ptolemies and Cleopatras.

ROMAN: Conquest by Julius Caesar, 30 B.C. Egypt a Roman
   province.

List of Black-and-White Illustrations

PART I

THE WORLD
OF THE LIVING

One

PEOPLE OF THE TWO LANDS

May she flow away—she who comes in the darkness,
Who enters in furtively
With her nose behind her, her face turned backward—
Failing in that for which she came!
Have you come to kiss this child?
I will not let you kiss him!
Have you come to harm him?
I will not let you harm him!
Have you come to take him away?
I will not let you take him away from me!

K neeling on the bare earthen floor, the woman chants softly, lest she wake the child asleep in her arms. The little one-room hut is dark except for the dim red glow from the brazier, where

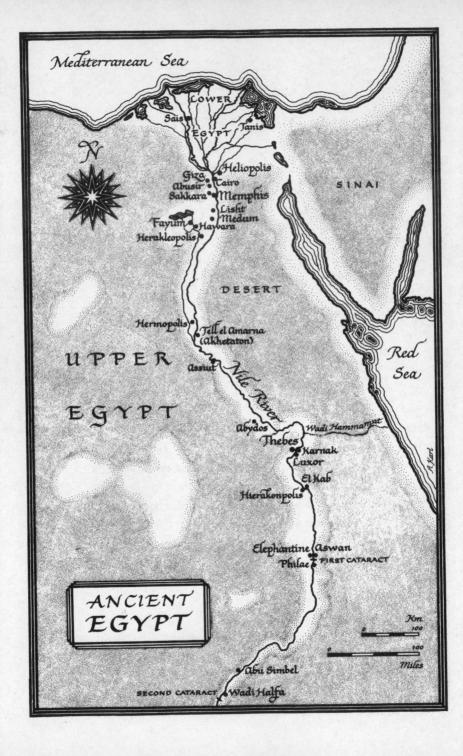

Mediterranean Sea

LOWER

Sais

EGYPT

Tanis

N

Heliopolis

Giza

Cairo

SINAI

Abusir

Sakkara

Memphis

Lisht

Fayum

Medum

Hawara

Herakleopolis

DESERT

Hermopolis

Tell el Amarna
(Akhetaton)

UPPER

Assiut

Nile River

Red
Sea

EGYPT

Abydos

Wadi Hammamat

Thebes

Karnak

Luxor

El Kab

Hierakonpolis

R. Karl

Elephantine

Aswan

Philae

FIRST CATARACT

ANCIENT
EGYPT

Km.
0   100

0   100

Miles

Abu Simbel

SECOND CATARACT   Wadi Halfa

the cooking fire still smolders. A last expiring flame leaps up and shows the crouching form more clearly: a slender brown girl with long black hair and dark eyes—eyes that dart glances half-defiant, half-apprehensive toward the door. It is closed and barred, but she can feel the dark pressing in—the dark from which "she with her face turned backward" may enter furtively, to steal the breath of the sleeping child.

I see this picture whenever I read the lines quoted above. They are singularly moving lines, even in translation; the original text was written several thousand years ago, in the ancient Egyptian language. Surely the night-demon is one of the most dreadful specters in the folklore of any people, with her head twisted about on her neck, and with the suggestion of melting shapelessness in the words "flow away." Like the old Scottish prayer against "ghosties and ghoulies and things that go bump in the night," this Egyptian spell carries a hint of diabolic danger which is all the more terrifying for never being made explicit.

There is another point of similarity between the Scottish poem and the Egyptian one. We quote the first as a joke nowadays, laughing and pretending to look nervously over our shoulders; but like its Egyptian counterpart, it was neither a joke nor an exercise in literature for its own sake. It was a charm—a prayer, if you will—against the powers of evil. In both examples we have first a description of the threatening forces. Then the counterspell is recited. In the Egyptian example, defensive measures take the form of powerful denials, made more potent by mounting repetition—"I will not let you kiss him! I will not let you harm him!"—and also by a recipe of magic herbs, which I have not quoted. In the Scottish prayer the invocation of defensive powers is simple—"Good Lord, deliver us."

Well, we mustn't press the comparison too far; it has no significance, except to show that many people, in many times and places, have been afraid of the dark and of that which may come out of the dark. What touches me most about this Egyptian prayer is that it is designed for the protection of children. There is no sphere of life in which man feels his vulnerability to the caprice of Fate more poignantly than in that which threatens his children; and at no time in his life is he more helpless than when he comes into it, naked and squalling. This book concerns itself with the daily life of the ancient Egyptians, so it is fitting that we should begin when the Egyptian began—at birth. Having pronounced the proper protective incantation, we may proceed to bring our fictitious baby into the world.

CHILDBIRTH

Once upon a time there was an Egyptian lady who attracted the interest of no less a personage than the great sun-god, Re. Perhaps the god's attentions were motivated not so much by the lady's charms as by his desire to produce three offspring who would eventually rule the land of Egypt. Yet the lady was only the wife of a humble priest of Re; his name was Rauser, and hers was Reddjetet, and . . .

One day it happened that Reddjetet felt the pains of labor; and her labor was hard. So the majesty of Re said to Isis, Nephthys, Meskhenet, Hekat, and Khnum, "Go on and deliver Reddjetet of the three children who are in her womb, and who will exercise the kingship in the entire land.

The informed reader will recognize in Isis and Nephthys two of the great goddesses of the Egyptian pantheon; they were the wife and sister of Osiris. Meskhenet was another goddess—a patroness of childbirth, appropriately enough. Khnum, the only male in the party, also had a role in creation. He was the potter who fashioned the bodies of newborn children, in clay, on his divine wheel. Heket assisted at the birth of the sun-god each morning, so she was a logical person to supervise the birth of his children.

The goddesses disguised themselves as dancing girls, with the lordly Khnum as their porter, and all five of them set out for the priest's house. They found the purported father-to-be in a pitiable state, which is described with concise eloquence by the Egyptian author: he was "sitting motionless, his clothing in disarray." To me, the priest is a most sympathetic character. Although he was desperately worried about his wife, he took the trouble to speak courteously to the itinerant entertainers: "You see, ladies, the mistress of the house is in labor; and her labor is hard." The dancing girls took up their cue. "Let us see her. We know how to facilitate a birth."

The father could not refuse the offer; Re, looking down from his golden boat, would see to that. Still, we have a feeling that it was a natural suggestion. The function of midwife was not a medical specialty. As in most pre-industrial societies, including that of medieval Europe, a woman in labor was probably attended by the other women in the house or the village, with a local "wise woman" on call in case the situation became complicated. Even a dancing girl might claim special skill in obstetrics, and the distracted husband's response is perfectly understandable. At that point he would have been willing to try anything and anybody. He gave the five divinities his permission, and they locked themselves up with the lady.

"Then Isis put herself before her, Nephthys behind her, and Hekat assisted the birth." In this case the assistance was mostly magical: potent spells pronounced by a divinity. After not one but three babies had been delivered, the goddesses came out to reassure the husband, who, overcome by gratitude, paid them with a sack of grain "in order to make beer."

Since the three babies were given, by Isis, the names of the first three kings of the Fifth Dynasty, one cannot help but suspect this pretty tale has a political element. The text doesn't tell us much about the actual process of childbirth. Fortunately there are a few other sources, so we know that the Egyptian mother gave birth squatting, her feet raised on bricks, supported fore and aft by two women of the household, while the midwife knelt in front of her ready to receive the child. The hieroglyphic sign meaning "to give birth" depicts her position; it is that of a kneeling, very pregnant woman, with the arms and head of the baby already out. The squatting position makes better sense in some ways than a recumbent position; the lady had the force of gravity to assist her.

Considering how often they were employed, it is surprising that until very recently we had no examples of these birth bricks, as they are called. Maybe the majority just wore out and were discarded; new mud bricks aren't that hard to make. However, a University of Pennsylvania Museum expedition at Abydos came across a single example— one of a pair, one must assume—that was elegantly painted with scenes of protective deities and a mother holding an infant. It measures fourteen by seven inches, and the top, say the excavators, was badly worn. I'm not surprised.

In poorer families one room of the house would be used when the day came, but there are references to and depictions of special birth pavilions—light, temporary garden buildings where a wealthier lady could enjoy fresh air and garden flowers. A number of houses in a village built for the workmen who toiled on the royal tombs have odd little structures in the front rooms—enclosed, raised platforms which have been identified by some scholars as "birth boxes." I remain dubious about this, simply because the houses were small and it would seem extravagant of space to set aside a particular place for a particularly limited activity. But maybe the "birth boxes" served other functions at other times.

One potential source of information has proved a disappointment; the medical papyri, though they include one of a specific gynecological nature, give no information about labor or the methods of the obstetrician. There are spells for "releasing a child from the belly of its mother" and a number of other helpful magical aids, but not much in the way of practical information.

It may seem surprising that the Egyptians, who preserved for us so many details of the activities of life and death, left so little information about the essentials preliminary to the first. Yet the seeming wealth of documentation is illusory; it is only rich by comparison with other pre-Greek societies. An Egyptologist can read, during his professional lifetime, every single document written by the ancient Egyptians—all the original source materials—and still have time to read most of the secondary sources. Admittedly it would keep him pretty busy, but a scholar in any field of modern history would be hard-pressed to do this for a period of thirty years, let alone three thousand. He probably couldn't even cover the source materials—the novelists and essayists, major and minor, the wills and other legal documents, the personal and business letters, the treaties and laws, the scientific treatises. . . .

I make this point, not to gloat over the thoroughness of the student of Egyptology, but to mourn for his limited sources. Books on ancient Egypt often give the reader a misleading impression, presenting hypotheses as if they were facts and possibilities as if they were certainties. Some of this is inevitable; one cannot explain in painful detail the evidential background for every statement. But the most reliable books are loaded with boring words like "probably" and "perhaps" and "possibly"; scholars avoid "maybe" for stylistic reasons, but it should be prefixed to at least 50 percent of the statements made in any book on Egypt—including this one.

We cannot conclude, when we know nothing about a particular facet of Egyptian culture, that it was either nonexistent or produced by some "lost science" or occult power. We are ignorant only because that particular body of information has not survived four thousand years of time, or because the Egyptians did not bother to tell us about it. Egyptian culture was literate, but it was not self-analytical, nor was writing a universal skill. The Egyptians were busy people; they had fields to sow and harvest and irrigate, pyramids to build, battles to fight, and tombs to equip; they preserved in writing only the things they needed to know, not all the matters which might be of interest to alien peoples in some unimaginable future. It is no wonder we know so little about childbirth; in fact, it is surprising that we know as much as we do.

THE PEOPLE IN ART

Having gotten our Egyptian into the world, we can now ask what sort of person he or she was. Habits and beliefs and mannerisms will emerge, let us hope, in future pages. We will restrict ourselves here to physical characteristics. But before describing the Egyptians as they look to us, it might be interesting to see them first through their own eyes. How did they want to look? What was the ideal physical type?

Paintings and sculptures give a good idea of the desired norm. In fact, the similarity of the types depicted, the lack of deviation, is astounding when you consider the number of centuries involved—from somewhere in the neighborhood of 3000 B.C. (give or take a few hundred years) down to the first century of our own era. The ladies are slim, so slender that their bodies look almost flat in profile from waist to knee. Rounded hips were evidently not admired; shapely breasts were. The ladies in the paintings have small but firm bosoms, and some of the mummies of older women, whose natural equipment had sagged under the relentless pressure of the years, were stuffed with wax or sawdust in the pectoral region to give the necessary curves. One late mummy, described by Grafton Elliot Smith in his classic book on mummification, had an entirely new body surface molded over the withered flesh in a kind of papier-mâché made of bandages and resinous paste. The breasts were beautifully modeled and tipped with copper buttons. This mummy is uniquely well made; Smith says, enthusiastically, that it resembles an exquisite statue of Venus.

The male physique which became the model for sculptors of kings and commoners was one which moderns would approve—very broad shoulders tapering down to a flat abdomen and lean flanks. When customers came to a sculptor to order statues of themselves or hired an artist to paint their forms on the walls of their tombs, it was in bodies like these that they expected to appear.

There are exceptions to this rule. Some of them are famous, known to every working Egyptologist, just because they are exceptions: the old blind harper, with his bent shoulders and wrinkled face; the emaciated herdsman, whose ribs stand out under his skin; the dwarf, sitting on a platform beside his normal-size wife, so that they appear to be approximately the same height. The art of the Amarna Period is exceptional too. We'll talk about that later. Some of the exceptions are superb pieces of the sculptor's or painter's art.

One of my favorites is the figure we call the "Sheikh el Beled." This means "Mayor of the Village," and the way in which the statue came by its name makes a nice little story.

The Mayor was found by Auguste Mariette, one of the great French

Egyptologists of the nineteenth century. For me, the names of Mariette and Gaston Maspero, like ham and eggs, always go together: Mariette, the founder of the Egyptian Antiquities Service, who established the regulations which restricted the plundering of tombs and temples by European excavators; and Maspero, his equally dedicated successor. Though Mariette had to supervise all the archaeological work carried on in Egypt in order to make sure the rules were being followed, he liked to do some digging of his own. One morning his workers were shoveling away when the head and shoulders of a statue came into sight. The statue was carefully freed from its covering; and as it was drawn out of the earth, a simultaneous gasp of recognition came from a dozen throats. "The Sheikh el Beled!" they cried with one accord.

One can easily believe, looking at the statue—which is now in the Cairo Museum—that it reminded the men of their mayor. It looks like someone I used to know too. The figure is life-sized, carved of wood and cunningly fitted together at the joints. The form is that of a man of middle age, rather portly, with a round face which combines joviality and firmness. He stands in the conventional Egyptian attitude, stepping forward, one foot before the other. One arm hangs at his side. The other hand holds a long walking stick which is obviously, despite his corpulence, designed for prestige rather than support. He is a man of dignity and of authority. The eyes of the figure are incredibly lifelike; they seem to stare back at the beholder, not with the expressionless blankness of wood but with calm curiosity. Indeed, the eyes are masterpieces of craftsmanship. The eye sockets are lined with copper, and the eyeballs are composites of inlaid pieces—opaque quartz for the white of the eye, rock crystal for the cornea, and a little round cylinder, filled with dark resin and sunken behind the crystal cornea, for the pupil. The statue is probably over four thousand years old. That it survived at all is due to the miracle of the dry Egyptian climate.

The Sheikh, whose real name was Ka-aper, is broader around the middle than at the shoulders; he certainly doesn't exemplify manly beauty, like the majority of the other male statues. But he is a handsome figure in his way. He is portly, not fat. Indeed, he is a joy to

Queen of Punt

behold. So is Hemiun, the vizier of the great king Khufu, who had the rolls of fat around his midsection faithfully reproduced. The same characteristic shows up with other high officials; it may have been a visual demonstration of leisure and wealth. But the great majority of Egyptians, male and female, are shown with youthful, well-shaped bodies and well-formed features. (The famous Queen of Punt, who is certainly shaped like a nightmare, is not an Egyptian; barbarians were not entitled to the same courtesies as were inhabitants of the great land of Egypt.)

Scholars who are specialists in Egyptian art have explained the reason for the persistence of the artistic norm. This involves profound speculations on Egyptian mass psychology, attitudes toward the universe, and the function of art—which served a magical rather than an aesthetic function. We'll go into this later. But it amuses me to wonder if there might not be another, more simpleminded reason in operation when an Egyptian merchant stalked into a sculptor's studio to order his mortuary statue. Who would choose to have his double chin and protruding belly immortalized when he can go down to posterity looking like Apollo? Of course, if you were a big man in the bureaucracy, you might prefer to show yourself as big around physically.

THE PROBLEM OF QUEEN TIYE

History is not a series of facts; it is a series of opinions and theories, some solidly based, some sheer nonsense, most more or less probable.

Unless a historian who is writing a book confines himself to a particular problem within a limited era of history, he cannot possibly explain all the evidence, pro and con, or give all the variant theories for every debatable problem. There are too many debatable problems! Yet it is important to remember how flimsy some of our historical reconstructions actually are, and it is interesting to see how some of them have developed.

We have been talking about a fairly basic point—the physical appearance of the ancient Egyptians. It is not an important point, in terms of cultural history, nor does it seem like a difficult one. Either you know what people looked like, or you don't know. Either you have mummies and skeletons, or you lack them. Either these people painted pictures and sculpted statues of themselves, or they didn't.

Physical remains and pictorial representations are the basic sources for the description of a human being. But the relative reliability of these sources may be quite different. A skeleton is finite and objective. It can tell us height, build, sex, and age. With a mummy we get more data—hair color and texture, skin color, body weight. Even this evidence is subject to variation because it must be interpreted by human beings. Read the learned discussions on the skeleton which was believed to be Akhenaton's if you doubt that two qualified physicians can disagree on anything as solid as bones.

The evidence derived from pictures and statues is extremely subjective. We have seen that the Egyptians didn't show themselves as they actually looked. Some scholars, not to mention the writers of popular books on Egypt (except this one) are inclined to see what they want to see. Usually they do this to fit some theory or other. Take the case of Queen Tiye, the commoner who rose to be King's Great Wife and mother of the heretic Akhenaton. She has been described as blue-eyed and fair, and as a dark-skinned Nubian.

It doesn't really matter whether Queen Tiye was blond or black or spotted with purple polka dots, and yet descriptions like these are vexing. They are not wild flights of fancy on the part of writers who are not specialists in the field; they are based on interpretations of professional Egyptologists. How, then, can they be so disparate?

The answer is obvious: because the learned authorities are talking about pictures, not people, and because their theories are influenced by unconscious preconceptions. Let's take the fair queens of Egypt to begin with. I discussed them in another book, but this point seems to require repetition. As far as I know, there never was a blond queen of Egypt. The famous Fourth Dynasty lady, Hetepheres, who was believed to be blond or redheaded, has been shown to be wearing a yellow head-cloth. Most mummies that have fair or red hair didn't have it in life; white and even dark hair reacts to the chemicals used in the embalming process. I should add, for the sake of strict accuracy, that certain neighboring peoples, particularly the Libyan tribes, could have had blue or gray eyes and fair hair. Interbreeding, which certainly went on, might occasionally turn up a redheaded Egyptian. One of the leading candidates is Ramses II. I can't help wondering how the experts can be so sure, since his hair was pure white by the time he died. The embalmers died it red, with henna.

The view that Queen Tiye was a Nubian is more popular than the blue-eyed version; although I hesitate to accuse scholars of succumbing to such obvious fallacies, I suspect that one reason for this belief is the wonderful little head in Berlin that is usually identified as that of Queen Tiye.

The personality suggested by this marvelous sculpture is not the kind you would want to live with permanently, nor make an enemy of. This impression may be unfair to the long-dead queen, but the impact of the head cannot be denied. Because it is so expert, so evocative, it makes a lasting impression. It is carved of black wood.

The real evidence about Tiye's ancestry is available—objective and indisputable. Not her mummy—at least I don't believe the woman's mummy from one of the royal caches is hers, though there was a huge sensation in Egyptological circles when this claim was made. It is based on electron analysis of the hair of the mummy in question and that of a lock of hair found in Tutankhamon's tomb, in a box bearing Tiye's name. The identification has been questioned by a number of people, on a number of different grounds. Believe me, it's too complicated to go into here.

However, we do have the mummies of both Tiye's parents, Yuya and Thuya, which were discovered by Theodore Davis in 1905. Davis was one of those enthusiastic millionaire amateurs who were not uncommon in the early days of Egyptology. Like Lord Carnarvon twenty years later, he spent his winters in the genial climate of Egypt and amused himself by excavating. From Maspero, head of the Antiquities Department, he obtained the firman, or concession, to dig in the Valley of the Kings. He paid for the work he conducted and was given in return any objects the Cairo Museum didn't want. Maspero was much more generous than some of his successors; the collection Davis left to the Metropolitan Museum at his death includes some remarkable pieces.

One must give credit to men like Davis for sponsoring such excavations. However . . . let's put it this way. Even his friends described Davis as "brusque and eccentric." The terms of his firman required that he have a professional Egyptologist on tap while he was digging in the Valley, but on several occasions he got around the professionals and their boss Maspero, presumably because he couldn't wait to see what was in the new tomb. Among the royal tombs he found were those of Thutmose IV, Hatshepsut, Siptah of the Twentieth Dynasty, and the cache containing the disputed mummy which has been successively identified as that of Queen Tiye, Akhenaton, and the latter's successor, Smenkhkare. This last discovery has been described, possibly by me, as one of the most aggravatingly botched excavations in the Valley of the Kings.

In January 1905, Davis was being supervised by James Quibell, the very competent Inspector for Upper Egypt. On February 5 Davis's men uncovered the top step of a rock cut stair. Davis sent for Arthur Weigall, who had replaced Quibell—the story has it that Quibell found the bossy American such a pain in the neck he asked for a transfer—and about a week later the steps were dug out and the top of the tomb doorway appeared. The excavators' excitement was dimmed by the discovery that the original seals on the door had been broken. Someone—thieves, undoubtedly—had been there before them.

They were in for a pleasant surprise. The funerary chamber lay just beyond the door, with no intervening passages. Within it were two sarcophagi, each holding nested coffins. All the lids were off; they had been flung aside, as if in guilty haste. The mummies lay exposed, their face wrappings torn off, within the innermost coffins. One "was the mummy of an old man of striking appearance and dignity. His splendid head and fine features bore a striking resemblance to Lincoln."

So wrote a contemporary observer, who was with Davis at the first moment of entry. The other mummy was that of a woman. "The face was serene and interesting, a low brow and eyes wide apart, and a curiously expressive, sensitive mouth."

The chamber was packed with wonders: boxes and furniture, a chariot, perfectly intact, the gleam of gold on the inner two coffins of the mummies, the blue faience ornaments. Thieves had tunneled into the tomb, but evidently they had been interrupted before they did much damage. Best of all, the inscriptions on the coffins and other articles had not been mutilated. The identity of the mummies was easily discovered. They were Yuya and Thuya, the parents of Queen Tiye.

Wonderful as the contents of the tomb were, the most important aspect of the discovery, for our present purposes, was the identity of the mummies. The descriptions quoted are accurate enough, if one allows for the sensitive imagination of the beholder. I lack this kind of imagination. I can't look at the wrinkled face of a mummy—leathery brown skin and shrunken lips, protruding teeth, sunken cheeks—and tell myself that the lady may, in life, have been the toast of ancient Thebes. The bones, the basic structure of beauty, still remain; one can describe a brow as oval and high, a set of teeth as even and white. But the mental picture disintegrates under the impact of the grisly face.

However, the mummy of Yuya, Tiye's father, isn't bad. Yuya, who was an officer of charioteers (hence the chariot in his tomb), was a tall man with strong features and a prominent hooked nose. Elliot Smith, the mummy expert of the period, examined both bodies and described the skull of Yuya as unusual. Smith thought he might have been a Semite—meaning that he came from Syria-Palestine, or points north. Thuya, the lady, was, in Smith's words, a typical Egyptian of her time and place.

There is no indication that Yuya was an immigrant to Egypt, except for the fact that his name is not always spelled the same way. That is sometimes a sign that the Egyptians couldn't decide on the proper rendering of a foreign-sounding name. I find this inconclusive evidence, one way or the other. If Yuya did move to Egypt from some other country, he must have arrived when he was fairly young; his career and titles seem to be consistent with those of any other Egyptian official. Nor would I insist on Smith's expertise. He was an excellent scholar in many ways, but he too had his favorite theories, and there is nothing more destructive of objective scholarship than a pet theory.

Yuya looks like an Egyptian to me. So does his wife. And so, therefore, must their daughter have been. However, as I am about to inform you, there was no such thing as a "typical Egyptian."

THE PEOPLE IN ACTUALITY

On the average they were shorter than we are; the women were about five feet tall, the men perhaps five feet five inches. Again, as always, we must note variations. Amenhotep II was several inches taller, but then he was a pharaoh, who got plenty to eat and had the best medical care available. (By our terms it wasn't much, but it was better than the peasants got.) Their skin color ranged from pale to dark to darker. Unless it has turned white with age, the hair of mummies is usually black or brown; it may be straight or it may wave. The features are regular, with narrow noses, although some mummies (including Yuya's) exhibit what I like to call the Thutmosid nose. It was like George Washington's.

At one time some anthropologists thought they could distinguish two main physical strains in Egypt. Predynastic Egyptians, we were told, were not the same people as the "Giza" men of the Third and Fourth Dynasties. The earliest Egyptians were dainty little people with small delicate faces; the men must have been slender, since the skeletons of males and females are indistinguishable, with none of the heavier bone formation which male skeletons usually exhibit. The only exceptions, among predynastic skeletons, are the people of Tasa, one of the very early predynastic cultures. They had square heads, coarser bones, more robust skeletons. (That word is not a particularly happy one to use in describing a skeleton, but it's the one the excavator used, and it does give you an idea.) The later people of Giza resemble the Tasian type. Dr. Douglas Derry, who was in his time one of the leading medical authorities on ancient Egypt, claimed that they also resembled the ruling class of the Twenty-Second Dynasty, which came from Libya.

You see the point, I'm sure. The great efflorescence of Egyptian culture that came to its head in the Fourth Dynasty was brought in by a group of people who differed from the little predynastic folk. This notion has now been pretty well abandoned, along with the assumption that every major cultural change had to be brought into the country by a new "race."

Egyptologists don't like to talk about race—not because it's a touchy subject (though it is) but because it didn't matter to the ancient Egyptians and because the whole subject is so burdened with conflicting definitions and irrational preconceptions. Eurocentrism—the notion that only the Indo-European peoples are capable of producing advanced civilization—pervaded nineteenth-century scholarship. European (including English and American) historians focused on the Greeks as the cultural ancestors of the only civilization that mattered—theirs—and resisted any suggestion that the monumental accomplishments of Egyptian culture could be attributed to "nonwhites." A reaction to this absurdity is understandable, and long overdue. But both action and reaction are irrelevant to an understanding of what the ancient Egyptians thought about the subject.

The concept of race would have been totally alien to them. Of course the Egyptians discriminated; doesn't everybody? Like most ancient (and many modern) peoples, they divided the world into two groups: us and them, "people" and "barbarians." When the texts refer to Cush, the land of Nubia to the south of Egypt, it is always as "wretched Cush." "Don't worry about the Asiatics," a Thirteenth Dynasty prince advised his son. "They are only Asiatics." But it is evident, from reliefs, inscriptions, and actual mummies, that they did not discriminate on the basis of color. The skin color that painters usually used for men is a reddish brown. Women were depicted as lighter in complexion, perhaps because they didn't spend so much time out of doors. Some individuals are shown with black skins. I cannot recall a single example of the words "black," "brown," or "white" being used in an Egyptian text to describe a person. The "Black Land," Kemet, referred to the rich fertile soil, not the people who farmed it.

Neither color nor "previous condition of servitude" prevented an individual from becoming "one of us." Slaves sometimes married into the family or were adopted. Some persons of foreign origin attained high rank, including that of vizier, and one of Thutmose III's "sole companions" was Nubian or Cushite. He was awarded the high honor of a burial in the Valley of the Kings, and his well-preserved mummy is that of a young man with Nubian characteristics. In his funerary scroll, he is shown with dark brown skin instead of the conventional reddish brown.

Foreigners became Egyptians when they learned the language and adopted the customs of the country. When, around 730 B.C., the Nubian kings invaded Egypt and started a new dynasty, they claimed to be restoring "maat," the proper order, and considered themselves to be the legitimate inheritors of Egyptian kingship.

And they were. People from the south had been migrating into Egypt and intermarrying with the Egyptians who already lived there for countless generations. Most populations, ancient and modern, are mixed. I was delighted by a recent article describing a small skeleton as showing a combination of Cro-Magnon and Neanderthal characteristics. If it's true, it means that the "superior" Cro-Magnons didn't exterminate the Neanderthals, but interbred with them, and that even back in Paleolithic times the mingling of races was well under way. No group remains "pure" for long unless it is completely isolated, and if it gets too "pure" it will commit racial suicide through inbreeding. Egyptian civilization was produced by a mixture of peoples and cultures and racial strains. In the south the Egyptians intermingled with the people of Africa; in the north they did the same with the "Asiatics" or anybody else who happened to wander into the Delta.

The Egyptian language is a mixture too. Egyptian isn't Hamitic (African) or Semitic; it has both elements. It is also impossible to describe cultural traits in simplistic terms. There is no single "African culture." The long rich history of that huge continent, the enormous diversity of ethnic and societal groups, cannot be reduced to a single adjective. Egyptian civilization was not Mediterranean or African, Semitic or Hamitic, black or white, but all of them. It was, in short, Egyptian.

Two

THE RED AND BLACK LANDS

THE TWO LANDS

The world into which the Egyptian baby emerged was a narrow one, especially in the physical sense; the Valley of the Nile is some six hundred miles long and on average about ten miles wide. Pharaonic Egypt consisted of the elongated valley and the triangular delta, where the river breaks up into several branches before it reaches the Mediterranean Sea. The two parts of Egypt are very different in physical geography, and the Egyptians always thought of them as distinct areas. Before the First Dynasty, when Egypt emerges into historic times as a united nation under a single king, the Delta and the Valley were probably separate kingdoms. Even after the unification there are constant references to what must once have been separate entities.

The king of Egypt wore two hats—literally. His Double Crown was a combination of the White Crown of Upper Egypt and the Red Crown of Lower Egypt. The duality of the monarchy is indicated by many other signs: the two goddesses, Nekhbet of the south and Buto of the north, protected the king; and his titles include "King of Upper and Lower Egypt" and "Lord of the Two Lands." We could go on, but this is enough to indicate why we feel we are safe in assuming that, at some point, there was political separation as well as topographical difference between Upper and Lower Egypt.

The Two Lands were the areas we call Upper Egypt and Lower Egypt, corresponding, roughly, to the Valley and the Delta. (The Nile flows from south to north, so Upper Egypt is "under" Lower Egypt on a normal map.) You may encounter a reference to Middle Egypt, meaning the area between Cairo and Assiut, but the threefold division was not natural to the Egyptians. They apparently enjoyed parallels, for in addition to the contrast between Upper and Lower Egypt they emphasized the difference between the Red Land and the Black.

The Black Land was Egypt, and anyone who has ever visited the Nile Valley can understand why the Egyptians chose this name for their own land, in comparison with the Red Land of the desert. On either side of the Nile there is a strip of rich, dark soil which, before the construction of the Aswan dams, was fertilized annually by the inundation of the river. The Black Land ends so abruptly that it is as if a divine finger had drawn a line down the length of the land, decreeing: on this side life, the green of growing crops; on that side, death and sterility in the lifeless sand. The sterility which begins within the Valley itself extends on, up and out, over the cliffs and into the two deserts of Libya and Arabia, which border Egypt on east and west.

For the Egyptians, the desert was a place of abhorrence. There dwelt the wretched Bedouin, the wanderers who did not know the gods; there the traveler found heat and thirst and misery. Yet without the Red Land, Egypt as we know it would never have existed. From the barren plateaus the Egyptians drew the gold which made them an object of envy among the other ancient peoples of the Near East and gave them the power that comes from wealth. In the Red Land of the desert they found copper, the source of the tools that built the pyramids and the weapons that helped them conquer an empire. And on the sands that bordered the Black Land, below the cliffs, they built the temples and tombs that have survived to tell us of the splendor that was Egypt. The rich black soil the Egyptians prized so highly gives life to the ephemeral things that survive for one season; the sterile desert sand has preserved not only stone but such frail objects as textiles and papyrus and human flesh. Ancient Egypt was the product of both Black Land and Red Land, though its people called it Kemet, the Black.

The Delta region was all black land—flat, green, and swampy. Artifacts, including mummies, don't survive as well in damp soil as in dry sand. Thus, we know less about Lower Egypt than we do about the narrow ribbon of valley. However, a number of expeditions have been working in this difficult area, where the water table is often so high that pumps must work continually to keep the lower levels of excavation dry. They have come up with some interesting new information.

In the western Delta was the predynastic northern capital, Buto, "the place of the Throne." Its goddess, the cobra, later became one of the two protective powers that guarded the king. South of Buto was Sais, with its sacred lake, the home of the goddess Neith. Farther east, almost in the center of the Delta, lay Busiris, where Osiris lived before he moved south to Abydos, in Upper Egypt. Bubastis, southeast of Busiris, should be an object of interest to all cat fanciers, since it was here that the feline-headed goddess Bastet had her chief shrine. North and east of Bubastis lay Mendes, home of the sacred ram, and directly east of that city was Tanis, on the salty plain south of Lake Menzalah. It was not so old a city as Sais or Buto. For a time scholars believed Tanis could be identified with Avaris, the stronghold of the Hyksos, who invaded Egypt during the Second Intermediate Period and took over the northern part of the country. Recent excavation by a team from the University of Vienna has proved that the Hyksos capital was someplace else—a site called Tell el Dab'a, in the eastern Delta. Tanis was an important city, though, and the capital of Egypt in the late dynasties. A French expedition working there at the beginning of World War II found royal tombs of the Twenty-First and Twenty-Second Dynasties,

with treasures second only to those of Tutankhamon. In its neighborhood the Ramesside kings built temples and pleasure palaces. One
source of pleasure, surely, was the fine wine of the Tanis area, and that
of Inet, south of Tanis.

The northeast Delta was famous for wine in ancient times, and it
also provided pasturage for the great herds of the king and the gods.
Great stretches of the region must have been pure swamp, filled with
the pretty, feathery papyrus and with reeds which grew higher than
a man's head. The reeds sheltered geese and duck and other fowl,
including ibis and heron. There were even hippopotami there in
pharaonic times, although these animals have now vanished from
Egypt proper, along with crocodiles. The Delta cities and villages were
often raised on hillocks or man-made eminences. The area is wet today, and it may have been wetter in ancient times. Now there are two
main exits for the river, the Damietta and Rosetta Mouths. In the
time of Herodotus there were no fewer than seven mouths, and between the main branches there were streams and canals and lakes.

It is a pity we don't know more about the Delta, with its handsome
palaces and temples, its prized vintages, its herds and wildfowl and
fields. We have had to be content with a hasty, bird's-eye survey of the
area. Now let us compensate by viewing Upper Egypt in more detail.
Naturally, we will go by boat. It is still the pleasantest way of seeing
Egypt, and in ancient times it was the only practical way.

We cast off from the docks at Men-nefer, Memphis, before dawn
on a fine summer morning in the fifty-second year of the Lord of the
Two Lands Usermaatre Setepenre Ramses Meriamon—whom later generations will know, more conveniently, as Ramses II. We have the
king's permission to hitch a ride, and such permission is necessary because the ship and its cargo belong to him, as does almost everything
in Egypt that doesn't belong to the gods—grain, temples, animals, and
men. The voyage is not a commercial enterprise for profit. The boat
carries wine of the king's vineyards of Inet to be delivered to the god
Khnum of Elephantine, and to the god's priests, who will probably
enjoy it more than he does. Along the way we will stop to drop off a
few jars at certain cities especially favored by the king.

The skies are a pale brightening blue as we lean against the rail, yawning, and look back to see the stately triangles of the Giza pyramids outlined on the horizon. Above our heads the great sails swell and grow taut; boats coming downstream to Memphis go with the current, but we must depend on the north wind for power. Luckily it is almost always blowing from that direction. We pick up speed, leaving Memphis behind—the White Wall, the first capital of united Egypt, which has stood at the junction of the Two Lands since the time of Menes the Unifier. From afar we can see the pylon gate of the temple of Ptah rising high above the massed greenery of palms and tamarisks that beautifies its courts.

The light grows stronger; then the glowing disk of the sun, Re-Harakhte, soars on falcon wings up over the rim of the world. His beams illumine the mighty bulk of the Step Pyramid, marking the old cemetery of Sakkara. Across the river, on our left, the black holes of the limestone quarries at Masarah are conspicuous against the pale gold of the cliffs. From these quarries came the stones which smoothed the slopes of the pyramids of Giza, and still the pharaohs delve into the heart of the hills to extract blocks for their temples and shrines.

The sun is high when we pass the Dahshur pyramids; their slopes shine golden in the light. At Medum we see the last of the big pyramid tombs of the Old Kingdom. It is a landmark for miles around. Still pyramid-shaped, it will not remain so much longer. The collapse of its sides has already begun, and in the twenty-first century it will look like a tall, stepped tower.

Near Medum we have to stop and tie up for the night. Nothing short of a dying mother or a threat to the crown could make a captain sail his craft in the darkness. There are too many sandbars, for one thing, and the spiritual dangers are equally grave. The dead wander at night—the ones with their faces turned backwards.

The captain has invited us to dine with him on the deck. It is a pleasant spot, with the cool night breeze touching our faces and the glitter of stars overhead. The captain apologizes for the meal—just rough sailor's food—but we find it more than ample. A roast duck, onions and radishes, fresh baked bread from the village where we lie at anchor, and fruit to finish up with—dates and apricots and figs. And— can it be?—wine of Inet!

The captain is surprised and a bit hurt when we mention the wine, although we do so tactfully. Certainly it's wine of Inet. Would you expect him to travel six hundred miles with that nectar in the hold and not have so much as a taste? He shrugs, throwing out his hands in a gesture which must have been born with the human race. A little wine here and there will never be missed; everyone expects that sort of thing, it's the custom. He is an honest man; he won't sell a quarter of the cargo on the side, with a share of the profits to the scribe who checks the king's accounts at the end of the trip. None of that sort of thing for him! Indeed, it is not too safe at this point in history, for Usermaatre (may he live, prosper, and be healthy!) is not patient with trifling of that nature. In past times, the captain has heard, such things were done with impunity. The good old days . . . but who is going to make a fuss over a jar or two? It is excellent wine, isn't it? We agree, and empty another cup, safe in the knowledge that if anyone is going to suffer for the missing wine it won't be us.

Next day we pass the entrance to the Fayum. If we could see that far—which we can't—we would behold a wide lake surrounded by green fields and temples, towns, and palaces. The wonder of the Fayum area is the Labyrinth, as it will be called by a Greek named Strabo a thousand years from now. The captain knows it as the temple of Amenemhat, an ancient king; it contains two thousand rooms built of monolithic slabs of stone. The Fayum is like a big oasis, attached to the Nile by a tributary which will be called the Bahr Yusuf—Joseph's Canal—to commemorate a man and a series of events of which Egyptian records hold not the slightest trace. Is this because Joseph never existed, except in the poetic imaginations of the Hebrews? It's a great story, from the coat of many colors to the final triumph of Joseph as right-hand man of pharaoh, but there is no archaeological evidence for it. Ramses II is believed by some to have been the pharaoh of the Exodus. There's no evidence for that either, but if an evil spirit appeared and offered a biblical scholar the chance to take a trip like this one in exchange for his immortal soul, many of them, I imagine, would be sorely tempted.

One hundred and eighty miles south of Memphis, we pull into the docks at Beni Hassan, our first real stop, to drop off a few jars of wine. The local prince is partial to Delta wine, and he is a close friend of the king's. They shared many a jar on the Kadesh campaign. The town is on the east bank, and up in the cliffs behind it there are tombs, already ancient, which archaeologists of future generations will cherish tenderly. The prince is not at home just now; he's off in the desert hunting, so we are not invited to drop in for a drink. The captain is anxious to get on, so as soon as the prince's porters have carried off the jars we set sail again.

Next day we pass a spot where the eastern cliffs fall back, leaving a fertile cup of land along the river. We crowd to the side and stare; the sailors whisper among themselves and finger the amulets hung around their necks on bits of string. There is not much to see now, only ruined walls and heaps of stone. But once this was a city, the capital of the arch-heretic who tried to defy the king of the gods himself. He met the fate he deserved, that criminal of Akhetaton. Even his name is forbidden now, so we don't mention it, or that of his more famous son-in-law, Tutankhamon.

Just below Akhetaton, which we know better as Tell el Amarna, we are conscious of a tightening of tension on board. The captain comes out from under his shelter and stands alert in the prow, eyes sweeping the river. The oars are manned. Then we see that the cliffs which bound the river on the east have moved in. They form a sheer wall down into the water, and from countless holes in the rock an army of birds emerges, fluttering and screaming. This is one of the worst spots on the river, where gusts of wind dropping down the cliffs seize the boat and whirl it into hidden sandbars. The oars dig in, at a shouted command, and we swing away from the cliffs, missing a sandbar by inches. There are twenty miles of this sort of thing, and when we emerge from the narrows of the Gebel Abu Feda (a name, of course, which our captain has never heard of), we are ready to stop for the night. The captain took a chance coming through so late; twilight falls as we drop anchor and prepare the evening meal.

Eighty miles from Beni Hassan, over two hundred and fifty from

Memphis, and we are approaching Assiut. We have been on the way for over ten days now, and we are less than halfway to Elephantine. Assiut is a great city whose rulers once came close to being kings of Egypt, and the prince of Assiut is still an important nobleman. Perhaps if we reach the city before nightfall we will have time for a visit to the tombs of his ancestors, up in the cliffs.

Date palms and sycamores, pomegranate and persea, fields of flax and wheat—it is through a green, fertile district that we pass on from Assiut, reaching the holy city of Abydos two weeks after leaving Memphis. Osiris himself lies buried here, and the waters are crowded with boats. Some are barges, bringing stone for the great temple Ramses is building, but most are carrying pilgrims to the shrine of Osiris— live pilgrims and dead ones. A funeral boat, with a gilded mummy case on deck under an awning, cuts under our prow, and the captain, forgetting respect for the dead, hurls a string of curses at the sweating rowers. Then he steps to the side and makes an obeisance and says a prayer or two in the general direction of the Great Temple. He will make this journey again one day, in the same shape as the Osiris on the boat he nearly ran down—if he can save enough to pay for the pilgrimage.

When we reach Hu (which the Greeks will call Diospolis Parva) the perpetual low undercurrent of grumbling which marks the Egyptian sailor rises to an audible growl. We have had stretches before where the men had to man the oars, not only in the narrows but in spots where the river turned east or west for a short distance. Here begins the great bend, going almost due east for thirty miles and then turning back on itself for another thirty miles westward. There will be blisters even on the sailors' callused hands three days from now.

The last of the cities on the eastward section of the bend is Denderah, the site of the Hathor temple. In the twenty-first century A.D., men will travel a long way to visit the Temple of Denderah, but they will see only a graceless, late version of the wonder we now behold—a shrine built by Thutmose III, the great conqueror of the Eighteenth Dynasty, after a plan handed down from the time of Khufu.

Past the cities of Coptos and Kus and Nagadah, still laboriously rowing; and then we are in the long westward stretch, and ahead of us, red in the sunset, rise the obelisks and pylons of Thebes. The capitals of Egypt's present kings lie far to the north, in Memphis and Tanis, but they still come here for burial, where the capital of the king of the gods will always remain. The captain calls it Waset, but the Greeks will give it the name that endures—Thebes of the Hundred Gates, with its massive temples of Karnak and Luxor. A little farther, and we can see both temples; the gold-tipped flagstaffs before the painted pylons bear scarlet banners that flutter bravely in the evening breeze. As we move in toward the docks on the east bank the panorama of west Thebes, City of the Dead, glides into view: first the giant seated statues flanking the handsome mortuary temple of Amenhotep III, then the temple of our own Ramses, looking raw and new against the weathered cliffs. It makes a brave show, however, even in comparison with the other rich temples that run in a colorful line along the western desert. In a sheltered bay there is one structure that holds the eye, among all the other marvels—a temple of sweeping colonnades and soaring ramps. This temple is dedicated to Amon and Hathor and to the Thutmosid kings, says the captain, and he ought to know; he is a widely traveled man and has visited many of the temples himself. We nod politely; but we, travelers from a world distant in time as well as in space, for once know better than the native of the era of Ramses Usermaatre. This was the temple of Hatshepsut, the woman who dared to be king. Her name is not mentioned in the king lists. Her cartouches and her form have been cut out and covered over on the walls of her own temple. It will remain for archaeologists of a future day to bring her back to life.

It is still a few hours before dark, but the captain decides to lie over at Thebes till morning. He is an indulgent captain, for he lets the men go ashore. We seize the opportunity too and go up to pay our respects to Amon—a sheep, perhaps, to be offered at the sunset service. After our religious obligations are fulfilled we can visit the town. We owe it to ourselves to see the nightlife of this great city of the past. There is not time to visit the tombs on the west bank, even if we were allowed to do so. The Valley of the Kings is guarded, and inquisitive visitors are regarded with suspicion.

Unfortunately the sailors find the nightlife of Thebes equally fascinating, though they lack our antiquarian bent. In the morning they
are sleepy and disagreeable, and two of them never show up at all. The
captain comments on their ancestors and personal habits, hires two of
the hangers-on around the dock, and we set sail, only an hour behind
schedule.

The men have another ten or fifteen miles of rowing ahead of them,
but we leisured tourists can lean over the boat's side and watch the obelisks of Karnak fade into the distance. Before long we are passing Hermonthis, also on the Theban plain. Montu lives here, Montu the war
god. Then at last we round the far bend and head south under a stiff
breeze. The pace seems like flying after the hard days of rowing; two
days after leaving Thebes we pass the twin cities, El Kab with the
remains of its ancient wall and Hierakonpolis on the opposite side of
the river. They are very old cities indeed, dating back to the time of the
primeval kings. A little farther on is Edfu, one of the sanctuaries of Horus. As at Denderah, we now see something finer than the Ptolemaic
temple which will one day attract hordes of tourists; this is the original,
designed by the great Imhotep himself, who erected the Step Pyramid.
His plan has been cherished and preserved by all succeeding kings.

Two more days, and we approach Silsileh, sacred to Sobek the
crocodile god. There is a good reason for being polite to crocodiles
here. The plateaus of the northern part of Egypt are limestone rock,
which changes to sandstone near Silsileh, where the river cliffs come
together like the pylons of a giant gateway. Whirlpools, rocks, and
sandbars make this into a treacherous stretch; often in the past boats
have struck and capsized. Then the proper prayers to Sobek might
have paid dividends. Gape as we may, we see no crocodiles; they have
become scarce in past generations. But as the captain pessimistically
remarks, you usually don't see them until it's too late.

There is another small bend, and a group of islands, at Kom Ombo,
which will be a favorite tourist spot in a few thousand years; from
there we have a straight stretch twenty-five miles long into Elephantine. The scenery makes a wonderful close to this part of our trip.
Straight ahead is the end of the island of Elephantine, with a cluster of

houses around the temple, which is on the high point at the south end of the island. The sandstone cliffs begin to show outbreaks of granite, and granite boulders protrude above the brown water of the river.

The house of the prince is on the island—his earthly house. His House of Eternity is being built for him in the north, so he can lie near his royal master. But there are tombs high in the western cliffs across from the island; we can see them, if the sun is right, as rectangular black holes against the cliff face. If we feel like it, we can climb the cliff and walk right in; these Houses of Eternity are empty now. Perhaps the prince of Elephantine, who is also vizier of Cush, is wise to locate his own tomb in the capital where the cemeteries are guarded against thieves. His predecessors, the owners of the empty tombs, however, were not men who leaned on someone else for protection. Explorers and adventurers, they set out for the next world just as they had ventured into the wild jungles of inner Africa—alone, leading instead of following. We can read about their exploits if we like; they are carved on the walls of their tombs, and in perfectly good Egyptian too. Some of the words are a little odd, old-fashioned, but any literate person can read them. There is a lot to see at Elephantine: the granite quarries; the two holes out of which the Nile flows; and on the island of Sehel, to the south, the Nilometer, which measures the height of the inundation, so important to the prosperity of the nation.

NUBIA AND THE DESERTS

Elephantine is the border between Egypt proper and the land of Nubia; the boundary is marked by a particularly nasty cataract region filled with granite rocks. To get to Nubia we go overland for a few miles and join our boat, which has been towed over the rocks, below the cataract. We get on board opposite a big island which will one day be called Philae.

The next part of the trip is not as interesting; the land is poor and not so green with growing crops. Insofar as the monuments go, however, we might still be in Egypt. We pass temples built in the traditional style at half a dozen places, and at least half of them were built by Ramses, a not immodest pharaoh. His most impressive enterprise is at Abu Simbel, which we reach on the eighth day after leaving Aswan. The temple itself is cut into the rock; on the facade are four enormous statues of Ramses, sixty-six feet high.

One of the passengers on our boat is a scribe, who will leave us at Abu Simbel. He carries a bag of scrolls with the texts which he is going to copy onto the walls of the temple, and he tells us that the king wants to revise—once again—the inscriptions that describe his great victories over the Hittites, that presumptuous group of people far away in the north. The scribe is a middle-aged man, run to fat a trifle around the waistline, as scribes usually are; his face has the blank amiability of the trained bureaucrat of any age. But we think we see a twitch at the corner of his mouth as he refers, respectfully, to the king's famous victory. We too know a few things about the battle of Kadesh, but we are just as tactful as the scribe.

To purists the statues at Abu Simbel seem too big, and rather stumpy. The facade of the temple looks overloaded, with the four colossi, a complicated sculptured group over the doorway, and a row of carved apes on top of the whole thing. It is impressive, though, in keeping with the ambitions of the king. The smaller, adjoining temple is dedicated to the king's wife, Nefertari, but hers is not the only image to appear there. You can guess who predominates. Beautiful or not, it is certainly solid. As the captain says, it will surely endure as long as the pyramids of Giza.

A further two days' travel brings us to the Second Cataract, where the river descends in a series of rapids and a chaos of glistening black boulders, wet with foam. Above the gorge is our destination, and it is quite a sight: a massive fort, with battlements and ramparts. Our messages are for the commander of Buhen, where we are welcomed by a crowd which consists of most of the inhabitants of the fort. It is a dull life, and they are always glad to see someone from home.

Buhen is a good place to stop on this trip, for it marks the end of the area which has been under Egyptian control for so long that it is Egyptian in manners and customs—Lower Nubia, or Wawat, as it was known in those days. Anyhow, the rapids of the Second Cataract are dangerous; few vessels attempt to pass them. There are forty miles of rapids, with more forts along the way. The region to the south, Upper Nubia, or Cush, was invaded by several warrior pharaohs, but it refused to stay conquered. We decide not to go on; we are five hundred years too early for the pyramids of Napata and Meroe, which will be built by the descendants of the wretched Cushites whom the commander of Buhen has just mentioned with such sneering condescension. He seems like a pleasant fellow; we need not tell him that within a few centuries the wretched Cushites will be on their way north to take over the throne of Egypt.

We have seen most of the Black Land now, and without so much as leaving the deck of the ship. Boat travel is pleasant; but as we turn from the Black Land to a quick survey of the Red, we can be thankful that our journey is only an imaginary one. We are going into the desert, and that requires fortitude.

The deserts—the Libyan on the west and the Arabian on the east—are high above the valley. In prehistoric times the river cut its way through a plateau which is composed of limestone in the north and sandstone in the south, so that by the pharaonic period, as today, the valley lay at the bottom of a trench whose cliffs are several hundred feet high.

If we were going into the eastern desert with the ancient Egyptians, we would probably backtrack down the Nile to Coptos, which lies on the eastward bend where the river comes closest to the Red Sea. Here we would fit out a caravan of donkeys—the camel will not be known for a long time yet—and start out along the Wadi Hammamat, heading due east.

The eastern plateau is full of these wadis, which are like small canyons or arroyos, and we follow them when we can. There are wells along this particular wadi, which has been a traveled route for millennia. Even so, it is a dreadful trip. The landscape is as barren and dead as a scene on the moon; high mountains parallel the coast, and at one point in our route we have to climb over a pass that rises to 2,500 feet above sea level. The sun is baking hot, and the short-lived spring flowers, products of the winter rains, have long since died. Remembering the cool gardens around the prince's palace in Coptos, we wipe our streaming brows and wonder why anyone but a madman would venture into these purgatorial rocks. The clue lies, in part, in the ancient name of Coptos. It was called Nebet, and "Nebet" means "the Golden Place."

Some of the gold that made Egypt great among the nations came from Nubia, but a goodly share of it was found in the desert east of Egypt proper. Some of the gold is still there. Corporations to rework the ancient mines were formed in the last century of our era, but the effort had to be abandoned after a few years because the ores were not worth the expense of extraction. This problem would not have worried the Egyptians; if they wanted something they were willing to put forth a degree of energy which we would consider prohibitive—as witness the pyramids. Perhaps, too, they got all the richer ores and left the rest.

In the Museum at Turin there is a particularly fascinating papyrus, perhaps the oldest treasure map in the world. It may have been drawn at about the time of this imaginary journey to ancient Egypt, and it shows the location of some of the gold mines of the eastern desert. Archaeologists are not sure which mines were meant, but they may have been the very mines that lie along the Hammamat route. These mines, those of Fawakir, are almost on Egypt's front doorstep compared with some of the others. At some of the desolate, isolated sites there are ruins of ancient camps—stalls for cattle and for the miserable human cattle who worked the mines, barracks for the troops who kept them at a job none of them would have endured unless they had been forced to do it. Perhaps only criminals and prisoners of war were sent to these godforsaken spots; it would have been punishment to suit any crime.

There are jewels in this desert as well as gold—garnets, agate, chalcedony, jasper, rock crystal, carnelian—all prized by the Egyptians for ornaments. Apparently the ancients never discovered the beryls and emeralds, which were found later.

Hard stone was quarried in this barren landscape. True, all stones are hard, but some, I am told, are a lot harder than others. The limestone and sandstone of the valley cliffs, from which most temples were

Ancient map of gold-mining area

constructed, are soft stones. The Egyptians wanted finer material for special objects, such as the sarcophagus that held a king's body and the statue that depicted his divine form. At Aswan they quarried red and black granite, from a quarry northeast of Cairo they obtained quartzite, and from the Wadi Hammamat they got the "beautiful bekhen stone," a gray-blue graywacke prized for the mirrorlike polish it could take. Flint also came from the desert; the ancient mines have been located.

Under its forbidding surface, the desert was a treasure house. But the Egyptians had still another motive for venturing into it. Through the Wadi Hammamat, ancient caravans made their way to the Red Sea, and from ports on the coast they set sail on trading expeditions south to Africa. The products of the mysterious country the Egyptians called "God's Land" are as poetic as the name itself—apes and ivory, gold and ebony, panther skins, ostrich feathers, frankincense and myrrh. The strange little dancing dwarfs, who made such popular royal "pets," also came from God's Land. We don't know precisely where this exotic country was located, but we think it was somewhere near modern Somaliland.

Having made one jump from Elephantine to Coptos, let us make another one northward, to where the Delta spreads out green arms to east and west. The desert east of the Delta merges into the peninsula of Sinai, also a source of wealth and a high road to distant lands.

The discovery of how to mine and work copper was one of the great advances of early Egyptian culture. The pyramids were built with copper tools. There are a number of ancient mines in Sinai, most of them in the south of the peninsula. Some of the copper which was so essential to Egypt must have come from the eastern desert, although inscriptional evidence is scarce. It is also scarce with regard to the copper mines of Sinai, but it is a safe assumption that the Egyptians got a good deal of this essential mineral there. The miners who worked at Magharah and Serabit el Khadim in the Sinai left numerous inscriptions scratched on the rocks nearby, but these workmen were after turquoise. This semiprecious stone, popular in jewelry from the earliest times, was sacred to the goddess Hathor, one of whose epithets was Lady of Turquoise.

The rocky, sandy roads of northern Sinai led into Asia. The Egyptians got tin and silver, amber and lapis lazuli from the East, not to mention the famous cedar of Lebanon. Under the empire, when they conquered—and were conquered—they also acquired slaves, mercenary soldiers, cattle, and miscellaneous booty. Unfortunately, roads go two ways—if the Egyptians could get out, the Asiatics could get in. They could not get in so easily, since the Egyptians guarded the paths; by garrisoning the few wells they could pretty well control the goings and comings of the "wretched Asiatics." Still, the Asiatics came, and at certain periods they came in a flood instead of a trickle. The hated Hyksos were Asiatics who brought to Egypt a national humiliation which was not wiped out until the warrior kings of the Eighteenth Dynasty drove the invaders back out into the deserts from which they had come. Even from the invaders the Egyptians got new and useful ideas, and at all periods contacts with the other civilized powers of the Near East—Sumer, Babylon, Assyria, Mitanni, Hatti—led to important developments in Egyptian history and culture. The other great civilized powers with whom Egypt had trade relations were off in the middle of the "Great Green"— Crete, Cyprus, and, later, the Mycenean civilization.

The desert on the west of Egypt, the one we call the Libyan, was not so exciting as the eastern desert. It had some valuable minerals, notably diorite and amethyst, but its most distinguishing characteristic was the string of oases that ran in a line roughly paralleling the Nile. There are six oases, five of which were controlled by the ancient Egyptians. Kharga, the "southern oasis," was one of the most important; it was famous for wine, as was Bahriyah, the "northern oasis." Perhaps the most useful was the Wadi Natrun, the source of natron, the salt used by the Egyptians in embalming. Far to the northwest of the Wadi Natrun lay Siwa, the only one of the group which was probably not under Egyptian control until late. This was where Alexander the Great went to be recognized as king of Egypt by the great god Amon.

The water which makes the oases possible comes up in pools or springs, some of them thermal in nature. There is so much water that, ironically, the oases used to be quite unhealthy because of malarial fevers. Perhaps the ancient Egyptians were more skillful at handling their water supply than were the Arabs of the nineteenth century A.D., but it is interesting to note that the oases were dumping grounds for undesirables in pharaonic times—political enemies and criminals were exiled to them. The isolation of the oases did make them good prisons without bars; once you were there, there you stayed unless you could bribe the soldiers of the desert patrol to look the other way while you loaded a donkey caravan with food and water. But if the places were as unhealthy in ancient times as they were a century ago, they might also have been a slow sentence of death for anyone the king wanted to get rid of.

The original inhabitants of the oases may have been the wandering tribes the Egyptians called the Tjemehu and Tjehenu. These people had to live somewhere, and there is no place else to live in that area; a few days away from the oases the great sand sea of the Sahara begins. Other nomads lived up north, near the western side of the Delta. They were relatively primitive peoples compared with the Egyptians, who were constantly having to go out and "chastise" them. Living where and as they did, we can hardly blame the Libyan tribes for occasionally raiding one of the oases or a western Delta village. Eventually some of them migrated into Egypt itself and became "Egyptianized."

In our armchair sail up the Nile, we have seen more of Egypt than most ancient Egyptians did. Even if they were adventurous travelers who had gone all the way from Coptos to Memphis, or Amarna to Elephantine, they still saw the same eternally unchanging landscape— the river and the valley, the high cliffs, the desert and the sown. In the heyday of the empire a commoner might see exotic foreign lands, but usually as a soldier. And even if he did not leave his bones in the unconsecrated soil of Asia or Cush, the Egyptian hated every minute away from home. For him the world was small and serene, and blessedly predictable; and that was just the way he wanted it to be.

Three

"BELOVED OF HIS FATHER
AND MOTHER"

CHILDREN

When an Egyptian nobleman went hunting, he took the whole family along. The gentleman in our jacket illustration is Nebamon, an official of the Eighteenth Dynasty; his little girl squats at his feet and his wife, beautifully and inappropriately dressed, stands behind him, in a pose which looks as if it would cause the light papyrus skiff to tip over. Nebamon has draped some of the lotus flowers his child is picking over one shoulder; one can almost hear the high, childish voice insisting. "They look pretty there, Daddy!" In one hand he holds the live ducks which act as decoys, and in the other he wields a throw stick shaped like a serpent. Even the family cat is there, grabbing a duck as it takes wing in a futile attempt to escape. Under the boat the fish swim placidly along in a line, and to the left we see the tall reeds and flowers of the swamp.

This is a very popular scene in tombs of the Old Kingdom. Another nobleman named Menna had three children, two girls and a boy, and the entire family—wife, boy, and girls—accompanied their father on the expedition.

Egyptian fathers may have preferred sons for practical reasons; only a boy could play the part of Horus, the dutiful son, when the sad hour of making offerings to his deceased father came around. But there is no reason to suppose that men were not equally fond of their daughters. To take little girls along on a duck-hunting trip is a sign of affection which few modern fathers would be willing to emulate.

I should add that some scholars interpret scenes like these as having a purely ritual function; they are artistic fictions, and almost every element of the painting has some mystical significance or other. Certain details almost certainly are imaginary; it's unlikely that anyone in any era would go hunting in such impractical garments, but it seems to me to be going a bit overboard to suggest that hunting scenes have no basis in reality. Men liked to hunt for pleasure. They still do.

If one may judge him by the reliefs that have survived, Akhenaton, the heretic pharaoh, was one of the most affectionate fathers in ancient Egypt. He may or may not have had sons; they may or may not have been born of his beautiful wife Nefertiti. There is no doubt of the parentage of his six daughters. "King's daughter, of his body, born of the Great Royal Wife," they are called. I can't help suspecting that they were rather spoiled. Wherever he went, they went too—to the temple to worship Aton, to state banquets, to ceremonies honoring virtuous officials. When Akhenaton and Nefertiti drove out in their chariot, the girls came along in their own chariots, or in that of their parents. In one such scene, we observe that Akhenaton has turned to give his pretty wife an affectionate kiss, and one of the girls, riding with them in their chariot, takes advantage of her parents' distraction to stir up the horses with a stick. (I cannot imagine what the symbolic significance of that gesture might be, but some Egyptologist may yet come up with one.) Akhenaton lost one of his daughters when she was still quite young. On the walls of the royal tomb where the child was buried, he had himself depicted in attitudes of frenzied mourning which no other king employed.

Another extremely successful royal father—if one measures success in terms of quantity—was Ramses II. He is reputed to have had more than one hundred children. Rows of them, male and female, march along the walls of many of his temples. This was an unusual gesture, since as a rule royal children, especially sons, were not shown during the lifetime of their father. One cannot help but suspect, however, that Ramses was motivated not so much by paternal affection as by macho conceit. (That is a subjective statement, which the informed reader should ignore.)

The formal attitudes to which Egyptian art was usually restricted do not often allow intimate family scenes. We know, however, that family life was close and warm. Among the most honorable epithets a man could claim when he inscribed his dignities on his tomb stela was the one we have chosen as the title of this chapter: beloved by his mother and father.

Children led a fairly carefree existence when they were small. What did they play with? Sticks and stones and mud, and bits of broken pottery probably, as modern children did before television and merchandising turned them into brainwashed consumers. Some ancient toys have survived—tops, miniature weapons, and several elaborate mechanical toys. One of these has a row of little dancing dwarfs on a platform; they are made to jog up and down by pulling a string. An expensive toy, this one, for some nobleman's son—who probably left it lying in the dust after five minutes and went back to his mud pies. Another mechanical toy was a cat. A string made the jaws move up and down.

You can find Egyptian dolls in many museum collections, but they may not have been children's toys. Some obviously are not; they are little naked female figures which were once called "magical concubines" but which are now considered to be symbols of regeneration and rebirth. Other dolls are very crude, just paddle-shaped chunks of wood with roughly painted features and a mop of clay curls. Since these have also been found in tombs, they may have had magical significance. But one suspects that female children would demand a "baby" to play with, and Egyptian girls may have played with these unprepossessing specimens whatever their original purpose.

Swimming must have been a popular sport for children. The houses of wealthy nobles boasted garden pools, and the villagers had the Nile or a handy canal. The youngsters played ball; the object they used was similar to a modern baseball, made of hide stitched together and stuffed. Races and wrestling matches were popular with the boys, dancing and playing house with the girls. Some games are shown in the tomb reliefs; one is played by four children, two mounted on the backs of two others, with a ball flying back and forth between the two riders. The point of this game is not hard to discover; it looks like fun too, for the young and agile. In another game, one boy stands in the center with four or five others hanging on to his arms and forming a circle. This one is called "Going Around Four Times," but we do not know its rules.

HOUSEHOLD PETS

Egypt was probably the original home of *Felis catus*, the domesticated cat. The wild variety from which our alley cats (excuse me, "domestic shorthairs") ultimately derive is *Felis sylvestris lybica*, the African wildcat, basically sand-colored with tabbylike stripes. The Egyptians discovered the usefulness of this delightful creature at an early stage, perhaps in connection with their cultivation of grain. Wherever there are granaries there will be rodents, and no man-made mousetrap is as effective as a cooperative cat. With the subtle presumption of the breed, Egyptian cats soon made their way out of the granary and into the house, ending up in a favorite feline position under their owner's chair.

A popular Egyptian goddess, Bastet, was cat-headed, which is in itself no sign of distinction, since many animal species were connected

A cat under its owner's chair

with one divinity or another. Not all cats were sacred animals, but there were sacred cats at Bubastis, where Bastet had her principal shrine. Mummified cats have been found in large numbers; I regret to say that the majority appear to have been deliberately done in, presumably as an offering to the goddess in question. (Don't ask me to explain the logic of this.)

The beauty of the cat's graceful body must have appealed to Egyptian sculptors because there are a lot of cat figurines, ranging in size from little ones which could be worn as amulets up to nearly full-size statues. In the latter the curves of the back and flanks and the proud pointed face are beautifully modeled. In all the representations we have, the cat in question looks sleek and well tended.

Certainly some cats were beloved household pets. They are shown in a number of tomb reliefs; those that depict them retrieving birds for their owner must be wishful thinking, since cats are not easily trained. In other paintings the cat isn't even pretending to be useful. Wearing an elegant gold collar and perhaps an earring, it hangs around the dining tables. One of my favorite scenes shows the mother cat under the chair of the tomb owner's wife, glaring full-face at the beholder— an unusual feature, since people and animals are almost always shown in profile. On the knee of the husband, Ipuy, sits a kitten which is apparently clawing at the sleeve of his elegant pleated robe. Once again I should point out that some scholars believe the cats have a purely

A hunting cat

ritual significance. The cat goddess Bastet was related to Hathor, goddess of love and beauty, and cats are more often associated with women than with men. But I'd like to have someone explain the ritual significance of the spoiled kitten. It seems simpler to me to assume that Ipuy just liked cats.

Then there is the handsome sarcophagus of the cat who belonged to Prince Thutmose, son of the magnificent Amenhotep III, and high priest of Ptah at Memphis. Her name was Ta-miut, the Female Cat, or as we might say, Miss Kitty. Thutmose may not have been good at picking original names, but he certainly loved his cat. On the long sides of the little stone box Miss Kitty is shown sitting in front of a table heaped with offerings, and the text refers to her as the "Osiris Ta-miut, true of voice before the Great God." This is a unique and astonishing object—a deliberate imitation of the mortuary texts and scenes used for human beings, giving the cat the same promise of immortality.

One can't help wondering what the priests of Ptah thought of it. Was Prince Thutmose attempting to start a cult of the cat, like that of the sacred Apis bulls, who were carefully tended in life and buried in magificent sarcophagi after they died? His father is believed to have begun the burials of the sacred bulls, but if Thutmose had something similar in mind, the idea never caught on.

If one were given to baseless speculation one might also wonder whether Thutmose was displaying the same contempt for the old gods and their traditions as did his brother Akhenaton. That would be going too far, even for me, but I must differ with the scholar who deduced that Thutmose must have died young, since no grown man would lavish such affection on a cat. (He is probably a dog person.) The sidelock shown in several representations of the prince does not, as in other cases, indicate youth. It was one of the designations of the High Priest of Ptah.

There is a formula for removing poison from a cat who has been stung by a scorpion. It comes from a very late text, but the formula is similar to medical prescriptions of all periods and, like most Egyptian medical prescriptions, it relies heavily on what we would call magic. "Oh, Re, come to your daughter," it begins, "whom a scorpion has stung on a lonely road. Her cries reach heaven; harken on your way! She has used her mouth against it [sucked the wound] but lo, the poison is in her limbs." Re says he will come to the cat's aid, and then, to make sure, each part of the animal is placed under the protection of a particular god. "Oh cat, your head is the head of Re; oh cat, your nose is the nose of Thoth . . ." and so on. After this, there is the more practical recommendation that a tourniquet be applied.

We must mention that the Egyptian word for "cat" was spelled "miw." How it was vocalized we may safely leave to the imagination of any cat-owning reader.

Dogs seem to have been domesticated early, in many parts of the world. By the time they make their appearance in Egyptian reliefs, there were already several breeds differentiated. One is a lanky, long-legged greyhound type, probably related to the saluki hounds of Africa, which are still used for hunting. Another looks something like a short-haired terrier, except for the peculiar blob on the end of its tail, which is not found in any known species and which may have been some Egyptian dog-lover's idea of a pretty decoration. The most charming of

Egyptian dogs

the Egyptian dogs of my acquaintance is a little female with the bandy legs, sausage body, and long muzzle of a dachshund. The ears are different, however.

While dogs appear in numerous paintings and reliefs, as house pets and hunting companions, they were not a popular subject for sculpture. There may, or may not, be some relation to the fact that dogs were not sacred animals, like cats or baboons or crocodiles. It has been suggested that the god Anubis, who presided over mummification and led the soul of the deceased into the hall of judgment, had the head of a wild dog, not a jackal, as was once believed. Both animals hang around cemeteries. Anubis looks like a jackal to me, but some scholars use the word "canid-headed" just to be on the safe side. There are certainly plenty of statues of Anubis, including the one found in Tutankhamon's tomb. It has also been suggested that the peculiar creature known as the "Set-animal" was a dog. It does look something like a greyhound, but there are confusing details. I think he's a composite. Yes, he has a long muzzle, but just look at those ears—and that tail!

Modern dog-lovers claim that canines are more lovable than cats. The Egyptians also praised their dogs for faithfulness and obedience, but several inscriptions use the noun to suggest servility. One can't imagine a conquered enemy telling the king, "We are your cats."

Perhaps the most famous ancient dogs belonged to a budding pharaoh of pre–Middle Kingdom Thebes. His name was Wahankh, and on his tomb stela he had five dogs shown with him. Possibly he hoped, in this way, to insure their affectionate companionship in the next world. All the dogs had names written next to them; three have been translated as "the Gazelle," "the Black One," and "the Cook-pot" (?). The last one is questionable, but it is not hard to think of an explanation for it. Cooking pots are full of food, and this dog may have had a hearty appetite. One enterprising researcher compiled a list of approximately seventy names given to dogs—which was quite a distinction in ancient Egypt, since a name had magical significance.

There are some dog cemeteries, and we have a rather nice dog mummy—if one may use the word "nice" in this context. At the present time he resides in the Cairo Museum, but he was found in a tomb in the Valley of the Kings. Three such small tombs contained animals that may have been household pets of a single pharaoh—the dog, five monkeys, a baboon, three ducks, and one ibis.

Or maybe they had a ritual purpose.

Baboons and monkeys were extinct in Egypt by the New Kingdom. They were imported from Nubia and points south. Baboons may have had—right—a ritual significance, being sacred to the god Thoth, but some were certainly pets. One was mummified and buried in the coffin of her owner, the princess and god's wife Maatkare. (Until a recent X-ray examination identified the small bundle as a female baboon, scholars assumed that it was the supposedly celibate lady's baby and that she had died in childbirth. *Honi soit qui mal y pense.*)

There are a few pictures of monkeys squatting morosely under the master's chair, in the position more commonly occupied by the family cat. A more cheerful picture shows several monkeys hand in hand with children. One of my favorite pet scenes has a cat, a goose, and a monkey. The monkey is swinging gaily from the rung of a chair; cat and goose are in a loving embrace, with the cat's paw wrapped around the neck of the goose. The fowl seems to have doubts as to its friend's intentions; its eye has a terrified glare and its feet are off the ground, as if it were trying to fly. I wish I could reproduce this scene, but some ancient vandal removed the cat's head and spoiled the picture. Only the tips of the ears and the ends of the whiskers remain—enough, however, to clear the cat of the suspicion we might otherwise entertain, from the goose's agitation, that her jaws are buried in her companion's neck.

Many other animals were domesticated, but we cannot always say which ones were regarded as pets. Horses might be included in this select category; they were relatively rare beasts. Senenmut, the close friend of Queen Hatshepsut, had a little mare mummified and buried near his tomb. He may have been an animal-lover, since his pet ape was also buried nearby. The Nubian kings of the Twenty-Fifth Dynasty were great horse fanciers. One unfortunate Egyptian prince, whose city was besieged and conquered by Piye (formerly known as Piankhi), the first of the Nubian dynasty, almost lost his head when the conqueror discovered that the horses in the princely stable had suffered from the long siege. Piye expressed himself as more distressed by the discomfort of the horses than by anything else—including, one presumes, the near-starvation of the citizens of the town and the death and mutilation of soldiers of both sides. I am an animal-lover myself, but I find this attitude somewhat exaggerated. It is not unique to ancient Egypt, however.

Perhaps these were the only animals that could actually be called pets; but I am sure that the children of ancient Egypt enjoyed playing with the other animals, especially the young ones. The Egyptians did not employ the camel; their beast of burden was the donkey. For food they raised goats and pigs and cattle of various kinds, including some wild varieties. Gazelles and ibexes were domesticated, and the young of these species must have appealed to the young humans. Baby ducks and geese would have had their admirers too. But there were no baby chicks; the domestic fowl was unknown in pharaonic Egypt, except as a rare and exotic import.

GROWING UP

When they were very little, children didn't have to bother with clothing. Considering the Egyptian climate and the habits of children, this was an admirable idea. Older children wore clothing like that of their parents, a kilt for boys, a simple linen dress for girls. The girls let their hair hang loose or braided it into pigtails, but boys had an unusual coiffure—the head was shaved except for one long lock on the side, which was braided.

The distinctive sidelock is known from the reliefs, and it was actually found on a mummy, that of a boy about eleven years old. He had not been circumcised. Circumcision seems to have been standard practice, but there are some odd exceptions, including at least two pharaohs. However, this boy was still young. There may have been a ceremony marking a boy's coming of age, when the sidelock was ceremonially cut off and the act of circumcision performed. One text mentions a mass circumcision of 120 men and adds that none of them hit out or was hit, none scratched or was scratched! Such mass puberty rites are known in many cultures, and manly indifference to pain is expected of the initiates.

If there were corresponding ceremonies for girls we know nothing about them. Certainly there is no evidence of female circumcision, in the texts or on the mummies. Perhaps the onset of menstruation signaled a girl's arrival at womanhood.

There is no proof that the cutting of the sidelock was part of the coming-of-age ritual, but it was one of the things that separated the men from the boys. The "sidelock of youth" is often mentioned in the texts, and men refer to the carefree days of boyhood as the time "before I had cut off the sidelock."

After the ceremony the boy was no longer a boy, nor was he that modern artificiality, a teenager. He was a man, and ready for adult responsibilities. Until relatively recent times, and in most cultures, children entered into adulthood at an age which may seem scandalously young to us. They didn't have any time to waste. Life was short and hazardous. In pharaonic Egypt the average life span was thirty to forty years. Some people, primarily kings, lived much longer. Pepi II, who came to the throne as a child, is said to have reigned for ninety-five years. You can take this or leave it, but Ramses II, to mention another long-lived king, was well over ninety when he died, as his mummy indicates.

Even before the formal achievement of maturity, children started working—girls in the house, helping their mothers with household chores and the care of younger children, boys learning the tricks of their fathers' trades. The fact is, we don't know much about the lives of the peasants, all of whom were illiterate and few of whom could afford tombs or other lasting monuments. When we talk about careers or professions we are talking about the small percentage of people who did leave such records—the skilled workmen, members of the professional class, and the nobility. However, even those records are scantier than we would like.

Several "autobiographies" have come down to us. Some shed an interesting light on "career tracks" for officials, but none offer any information about the ages at which these events occurred. The Egyptians dated events, when they bothered to date them at all, by the years of a particular king's reign. One event that was never recorded was the year of an individual's birth—and I mean any individual, king, commoner, or prince. Such information would settle a number of the arguments that still rage about the relationships of the royal families and would also enable us to state when an individual was considered old enough for marriage. It's absolutely maddening to modern scholars.

Setting up a household was a proper adult activity. A man needed to beget sons to carry out his funeral ceremonies and see that his spirit was provided with food and drink. This is the formal reasoning, but it would be absurd to suppose that it was the only reason why the ancient Egyptians got married. We don't know how often marriages were arranged by parents, but there was no seclusion of the female, and in some cases at least a boy and girl married because they had fallen in love.

Egyptian love poetry dates from a relatively late period, but we need not conclude that the state of mind it describes so eloquently only occurred after, let us say, 1200 B.C. It is a state of mind which we find quite familiar, expressed in figures of speech which sound ridiculous only to those who have never experienced the emotion in question themselves.

It is up to the boy to make his feelings known first; the girl remains modest and shy until he does so:

> I met Mehi driving in his chariot, with his companions.
> I don't know how to get out of his way!
> Shall I pass casually by him?
> The river is the same as the road [to me].
> I don't know where to put my feet!

Seeing the unaware object of her adoration, the girl dares not betray her love; in her efforts to appear calm and unconcerned she can hardly see where she is walking. But once she knows she is beloved, she voices her longing passionately:

> Oh, that you would come to your sister
> Like a stallion of the king,
> Chosen from among a thousand horses,
> The finest of the stable!

The boy suffers from the same pains and exultations that vex a modern hero of romantic fiction. When his beloved returns his love, he indulges in boastful fantasies:

> The love of the sister is on yonder bank;
> The river lies between us . . .
> and a crocodile lurks on the sandbank.
> But I go into the water, and I brave the waves,

And my heart is strong in the flood.
The water is like land to my feet,
The love of her strengthens me.
It makes a water-magic for me!

When she leaves him, he sinks into a decline:

For seven days I have not seen the sister.
And sickness has overcome me.
My body has become heavy.
If the chief physicians come to me,
My heart is not satisfied with their medicines.
The magicians, there is no help in them.
My malady will not be diagnosed.
When I see her, then will I be well;
When she opens her eyes, my body is rejuvenated.
When she speaks, I am strong,
When I embrace her, she banishes evil from me.
But—it has been seven days since she left me.

These poems express romantic love. No doubt physical union is the culmination both lovers desire, but it is not the only aspect of love that interests them. Both the chagrin and the plaisir d'amour are admirably expressed. The mere presence of the beloved is enough to transport boy or girl, and a kiss makes them think they are in an earthly paradise of perfume and incense. One young man remarks ecstatically,

When I kiss her, and her lips are open,
Then I am happy even without beer!

Intoxicated with love, in other words. I remember reading somewhere that the Egyptians did not kiss, but rubbed noses. It's another example of careless thinking. The verb translated as "kiss" is determined by the drawing of the upper half of the face, whose most prominent feature is admittedly the nose, and in some reliefs two people are shown familiarly "nose to nose." I suppose we would use the mouth sign for kissing if we wrote with pictures, but it isn't difficult to understand why the Egyptians did not attempt to depict osculation. It would have been tricky for an Egyptian artist to show two faces in such close contact as kissing demands; nose to nose was as close as he could get his lovers without overlapping the nasal members, which would have been against the rules. There are some depictions of actual kisses, mouth to mouth; most come from the Amarna Period, when the rules were relaxed in many respects. Certain of the Amarna reliefs show the royal couple in romantic poses. In one case Nefertiti's head is tipped back, and it is obvious that lips, not noses, are about to meet. In another relief she presses her lips to those of one of her daughters.

The Egyptians even admitted the possibility of that fictional device, love at first sight. Ramses II fell in love with his bride, the princess of Mitanni, the moment he set eyes on her, "because she was more beautiful than anything." And in one of the nicest of all Egyptian stories, the princess . . . but let's take it in its proper order.

"Once upon a time there was a king who had no son. So His Majesty asked the gods to give him a son, and they ordered that one be born to him. He lay that night with his wife, and she became pregnant. And when she had fulfilled the months of bearing, behold, a son was born. Then came the Seven Hathors [a cross between the Fates and the good fairies] to settle his destiny. They said: 'He will die by the crocodile, or by the snake, or else by the dog.'

"The people who were near the child heard, and they reported to His Majesty. So His Majesty's heart became very sad. And His Majesty caused to be built, on a desert plateau, a house of stone equipped with servants and every good thing from the palace—because the boy was not supposed to go outside the house.

"When the boy grew up, being, one day, out on the terrace, he saw a dog following a man who was walking along the road. So he said to his servant, who was with him, 'What is that thing walking behind the man who is going on the road?' He (the servant) answered: 'It is a dog.' And the boy said, 'Let someone bring me one.' Then the servant reported these words to His Majesty, and His Majesty said, 'Let one bring just a little dog, so that he won't be sad.' And so they brought him the dog."

Reaching manhood, the boy chafes at his imprisonment and finally persuades his father to let him go, arguing that the will of the gods will be fulfilled whatever he does. Equipped in style, he sets out on his travels and ends up in Naharin, where he finds an interesting situation. "The king of Naharin had no child, except one daughter, for whom he had built a house whose window was seventy feet above the ground. He called all the sons of the princes of Syria and said to them: 'The one who reaches my daughter's window, to him will I give her as wife.'"

The prince, newly arrived, is welcomed by the Syrian boys because of his beauty and because of the sad tale he tells; concealing his birth, he says that a new stepmother made life at home miserable for him. He asks them what they are doing, jumping up at the high tower all day long, and they explain the situation. "And he said to them, 'Oh, if my feet didn't bother me, I would jump with you.' So they went to jump, as was their daily custom, while the young prince remained aloof, to watch. And the princess of Naharin saw him.

"Now after several days had passed, the young prince went to jump with the sons of the princes. He jumped—and he reached the window of the princess of Naharin! She kissed him, and embraced him in all his limbs. They (the onlookers) went to tell her father . . . who asked, 'Is it the son of one of the princes?' They answered, 'It is the son of an officer who has come from Egypt, running away from his stepmother.'

"So the king of Naharin flew into a great rage, and said, 'Shall I give my daughter to a fugitive from Egypt? Let him go back!' And they went to tell him: 'You must return to the place from which you have come!' But the young girl seized him, saying: 'By Re-Harakhte, if they take him away from me I will stop eating, I will stop drinking, I will die at once!' So the messenger went back and told her father all that she had said. And her father sent men to kill him where he was. But the young girl said: 'By Re, if you kill him, when the sun sets I will be dead! I will not survive him a single hour!'"

"Beloved of His Father and Mother"   55

Naturally the king of Naharin has to give in to his infatuated and headstrong daughter; he too is impressed by the boy's beauty and royal manner. So the prince and the girl who fell in love with him at first sight are married. When the prince tells his bride of the destiny foretold by the Seven Hathors, she urges him to get rid of his dog; but he replies that he has raised the animal from a puppy and can't part with him. By her watchful devotion the wife saves the prince from his first fate, the serpent; but later he is frightened by his dog, and in fleeing from the pet he runs straight into the jaws of the crocodile. The beast presents him with an "out." If the prince will fight a water-spirit with whom the crocodile has been vainly struggling for months, he can go free.

Just at this desperate moment the manuscript breaks off; it is one of the most exasperating breaks in Egyptological literature, because we cannot be sure whether the prince escapes the snake and the crocodile only to fall victim to his own cherished pet, or whether the dog is allowed to be his salvation rather than his doom. I incline toward the latter ending, not only because I am an optimist, but because the Egyptians were optimists too; most tales of this type have happy endings. The astute reader will recognize a number of familiar elements in this story, which is less famous than I think it deserves to be. Not only do we have the immediate passion of the princess for the prince—standard emotional fare in Western fairy tales—but the disguised prince, the princess in the inaccessible tower, whose hand is to be the reward of prowess, the threatened doom, and the father's attempt to avert it by secluding the boy. All these are elements in a dozen well-known European stories. It makes us wonder where the origins of our own folklore are to be found. And yet, from the early centuries of the Christian era up to the middle of the nineteenth century, there was not a single man on earth who could read "The Doomed Prince," as our story is called. How then did bits of it get into "Rapunzel," "The Princess on the Glass Hill," and the others? Or are we dealing with basic human psychological traits or Jungian archetypes?

It seems clear, from references in the poetry and other sources, that there was no moral prohibition against physical love between young unmarried persons, nor was there any stigma attached to children born out of wedlock. What about incest and homosexuality? It is safe to say that the Egyptians didn't share modern taboos about such things; they didn't share a lot of our prejudices. We will talk about brother-sister marriages in the next chapter, but the question of relations between members of the same sex is still being debated.

In the "Declaration of Innocence," made by an individual claiming moral virtue when he or she faces the tribunal of the gods, there is a denial of having "copulated" improperly—whatever that may mean. With a goat? Naturally, some Victorian scholars interpreted this as a reference to homosexuality—they were always looking for "deviations" from their rigidly narrow code—but the text does not say that. A Fifth Dynasty tomb at Sakkara belongs to two men, officials of the court. Though both had wives and children, they are shown in their joint tomb in attitudes more commonly found between husband and wife, including one "nose-to-nose" embrace. Were these men lovers? Your guess is as good as mine, though I think the evidence points in that direction. If such is the case, it is a strong indication that such relationships were accepted. There is nothing more public or indicative of a strong commitment than a shared tomb. I know of at least one other tomb that belonged to two men, a craftsman and his apprentice.

It should be added that, as was the case with husband and wife, the attitudes and positions in question are quite proper, and without overt sexual overtones. What some of us would call erotica and others would call pornography is rare in Egyptian art. When I was a student there were rumors of "dirty" statues hidden in the dark recesses of the Oriental Institute basement, but none of us ever got a look at them (yes, we tried). Times have changed; several such statuettes are now on exhibit in various museums (no, I won't tell you which ones), and an erotic papyrus has been published. In its directness and lack of artistic merit it is somewhat reminiscent of the scenes in a certain house in Pompeii, where in my time women weren't admitted. (But the guides would sell a lady a set of postcards if she asked nicely—i.e., didn't refuse.)

Egyptologists can find religious or allegorical implications in practically everything, and perhaps the erotic papyrus has them, but you couldn't prove it by me. Satire it well may be, as is almost certainly the case of a graffito in a grotto near Deir el Bahri. It depicts two people who are believed by some to represent Queen Hatshepsut and her faithful architect Senenmut. I leave the pose to the imagination of the reader.

Four

LADY OF THE HOUSE

THE EGYPTIAN WOMAN

Someone, I think it was Dr. Margaret Murray, once said that a country's state of civilization could be judged by the position of its women. The higher the culture, the more honored were its female members.

Much as I would like to support this admirable idea, I am afraid that it falls apart at the first critical prod. To take a single example: the outburst of creative genius that took place in Periclean Athens puts that culture high up on any list of great civilizations, and in no ancient culture, perhaps, have women been held so cheap as they were in the age of Sophocles, Socrates, and Phidias. The rule was not even "Kinder, Küchen, und Kirche," for women were not encouraged to hang around the temples.

If you look up "Women of Ancient Egypt" in any bibliography, you will find hundreds of articles, dozens of books and dissertations, and at least two exhibition catalog—all of them dated within the past forty years. Admittedly my memory isn't what it once was, but I cannot recall a single book devoted to the subject before 1960. What prompted this sudden outburst of interest? The women's movement; not only the insistence on curricula that focused on female activities and accomplishments, but the increasing number of women professors and museum curators.

Some people feel that a separate field of women's studies is unfair. There isn't any corresponding field of men's studies, is there?

No, there isn't, and for a very good reason. Scholarly disciplines and studies have always focused on the accomplishments of men. This was certainly true of the early days of Egyptology. The assumption, not surprising in male Victorian scholars, that ancient Egyptian women were completely illiterate, subservient, and powerless (except for a few bizarre and perverse females like Hatshepsut) has been challenged and found to be inaccurate.

Naturally, there is a great deal of disagreement even among women scholars about the position of women in ancient Egypt. Some insist that women's roles were limited; others point out the relative freedom they enjoyed. In a way this is like saying a glass is half empty or half full. I belong to the half-full school. Compared to the women of classical Greece or of Victorian England, Egyptian females weren't bad off.

Admittedly, their career opportunities were limited. We know which sex did what from several sources: tomb inscriptions that mention the occupation of the owner, the charming servant statues that show people engaged in various jobs around the estate, and the reliefs and paintings that do the same. None of them depict women painting tombs or making furniture or engaging in any of the other crafts; there were even professional male bakers and brewers, though it's a safe assumption that lower-class women performed these chores for their own families.

The scribal professions required literacy, and it is unlikely that many women learned to read or write. I believe some of them did, not in school, but from private tutors or family members. Letters from women may have been dictated to professional scribes, but we have two "scribal palettes" that belonged to females. They were princesses, and Amarna princessess at that, but I can think of no reason why the girls would own such a thing unless they knew how to use it.

A few occupations seem to have been restricted to women. The professional mourners who followed the mummy to the tomb, weeping long strings of tears and tearing their garments, were female, and in some cases they were accompanied by a little girl apprentice, carrying on as dramatically as her elders. For obvious reasons, the occupation of wet nurse was also strictly female. It could be a position of some importance if the infant happened to be royal, and it rated a special title. Whether such nurses were resorted to only in cases of the mother's death or inability to supply infant nourishment, or whether upper-class women preferred not to nurse their own children, we don't know.

Women were also weavers, supplying their own households and entitled to use the excess fabric for purposes of barter. Each temple had its corps of women attendants. The commonest title of the temple women was "Singer"; they formed a choir of musicians and dancers, who performed for the god's amusement.

Female singers, dancers, and musicians are depicted entertaining guests at private banquets. The girls—most of whom were young and pretty—may not have been professionals who worked for pay; they may have been household servants or slaves. In one story, however, a group of itinerant female musicians is mentioned in such a way as to suggest that they were familiar figures.

There are some examples of women holding high position. We know of female treasurers and officials, and even a vizier—the highest position under the king. One woman held the fascinating title of "Overseer of Doctors." Were these women doctors? Was she a practicing physician? Nobody knows for sure. The rarity of such titles indicates that they were exceptions to the general rule of male domination of the professions and crafts, but that they occurred at all is another "half-full" sign. How many women presidents of the United States have there been?

Sometimes a woman might serve as her husband's surrogate when he was absent, and I feel quite certain that a lady of strong character could extend her influence over her husband's business. But, for the most part, woman's place was in the home.

> If you are a man of standing, you should establish your household and love your wife at home, as is proper. Fill her belly and clothe her back; ointment is the prescription for her body. Make her heart glad as long as you live—she is a profitable field for her lord. You should not judge her, or let her gain control. . . . Let her heart be soothed through what may accrue to you; it means keeping her long in your house.

That's the way to treat a wife, according to Ptahhotep, the Old Kingdom sage who left a book of advice for posterity. We can hardly picture him offering to wade across a river filled with crocodiles for his lady's sake, or sinking into a decline when she went to spend a week with her parents. Ptahhotep wrote during the Old Kingdom, and the love songs come from a period a thousand years later, but I suspect that the difference in tone is not the result of cultural change but of the change from romantic love to practical marriage. The words of a later sage, more nearly contemporary with the love songs, are more sentimental, but no more romantic:

> When you are a young man and take yourself a wife and are settled in your house, remember how your mother gave birth to you, and all her raising of you besides. Do not let her blame you, so that she lifts her hands to god and he hears her lamentations . . . . Do not supervise your wife in her house if you know that she is capable; don't say to her, "Where is it? Get it for us!" when she has [already] put it in the [most] useful place. Watch and be silent, so that you may recognize her talents.

The last sentences imply a high degree of sensitivity on the wise old gentleman's part; few men realize how annoying it is to be "heckled" about details of household management!

If there is no romance in Ptahhotep, there is another element which is very pleasant. Although the husband should be the master, his supremacy should be established by fairness and consideration, not by brute force. One has the feeling that the sage would have considered wife-beating too crude even to mention, although it may have occurred. There is a suavity and subtlety about many aspects of Egyptian culture, including the relations between man and wife—not the tortuous subtlety which Westerners consider typical of the Near East, but sophistication, even refinement.

Victorian scholars, who began the modern study of Egyptology, often read their own prejudices into the interpretation of those customs. Polygamy, concubinage, and harems were favorite topics; the Victorians, whose private activities weren't nearly as proper as their public images, enjoyed feeling morally superior to the heathen savages who practiced these perversions, even as they took a prurient interest in discussing them. More recent scholarship has shed a different light on these customs.

It seems likely that polygamy was not as common as was once believed. A man might have several wives, but did he have them serially or simultaneously? Death or divorce could open up the position to another lady. The word that is usually translated as "concubine" may mean something quite different from our modern notion of that term. Here again the evidence is confusing because the Egyptians didn't bother to explain what they meant.

The word "hemet" means wife. So, at some periods, did the word "senet," which also means sister. We think that the designation of the first or chief wife was "lady (or mistress) of the house." (In the days of door-to-door salesmen, they used to inquire after me with that title, and I was always tempted to greet one of them in Egyptian.) But the words translated as "wife" and "concubine" are occasionally used interchangeably, so what does that mean? Most probably that the "concubine" wasn't a "love-slave," but a woman who had status of some kind.

As for "harem," it should probably be read as "women's [...]
There was no seclusion of the female, no veils, no eunuc[...]
houses didn't have separate areas for women; some did; but the dwell-
ers therein were free to come and go as they liked. Kings certainly did
have multiple wives and large numbers of women hanging around the
palace—palaces, rather, since a responsible monarch traveled a lot
and he may have kept a separate entourage in various places.

We know very little about the ceremony of marriage, but most authorities agree that it was unimpressive, if indeed it existed. Evidently a
man simply built a house and invited a woman to share it; when she
moved in, the couple was considered to be married. Some sort of legal
settlement may have been drawn up, but there are no traces of religious
rites. Marriage was not for eternity. We cannot unequivocally state
what the grounds for divorce might have been; by the Late Period, from
which most of the documents relating to this subject come, simple in-
compatability might do the job. "If I repudiate you, if I take a dislike to
you and want someone else. . . ."

There was one serious crime against marriage—infidelity. As I
mentioned earlier, the Egyptians seem to have been amiably broad-
minded (or indifferent) about premarital sex, but several stories suggest that adultery, for the wife at least, was a dangerous game. There is
one such story about a great magician and his faithless wife. The lady
must have been sorely tempted to take chances with a man of her
husband's profession; of course, the seer found out what she was up to.
Her lover was given to a crocodile that, presumably, did something
unpleasant to him. By the king's command, the wife was burned alive.
In another story the erring wife—who was not guilty of actual adultery, but only of aspiring to it—was killed by her husband and thrown
to the dogs.

The literature unfortunately gives us no examples of what happened to unfaithful husbands, but it is evident that promiscuity, before
and after marriage, was frowned upon. We have already noted the punishment of the lover of the magician's wife. The Wisdom Literature
does not neglect the subject. Says Ptahhotep: "If you want to make
friendship last, in a house to which you have access as son, brother, or

friend . . . beware of approaching the women. . . . Do not do it . . . it really is an abomination." A later sage, Ani, warns: "Be on guard against a woman from abroad, one who is not known in her town. Do not stare at her when she passes by; do not 'know' her—a deep water, whose windings one does not know, a woman who is far away from her husband. . . . It is a great crime, [deserving] of death."

Even so, adultery was a private misdemeanor, not a state crime. Some marriage settlements deprive a woman of her property rights if she is caught carrying on with a man other than her husband, and there is a rather entertaining piece of advice in one of the so-called Wisdom Texts for a man who may be tempted to stray: "He who makes love to a married woman is killed on her doorstep" (presumably by the cuckolded husband). The sage does not recommend that the husband take this drastic revenge; instead, "if you find your wife with her lover, get yourself a bride to suit you." So the horrendous fates may have been purely for literary effect.

The greatest complication about divorce, whatever the grounds, had to do with property, and it is in this area that the Egyptian woman was far ahead of her time. The marriage settlements that have survived indicate that she controlled her own possessions, those acquired by inheritance or by her own diligence, and that in the case of divorce she was entitled to a percentage of the assets that had been acquired by the couple. Divorce involved certain financial penalties, depending on which party inititated it. Happily married men might settle property on their wives, and women could pass their property on to anyone they liked. One irritated old lady disinherited several of her children because they hadn't taken proper care of her.

The importance of a woman's ability to own property can hardly be overstated. Financial independence is, and has always been, the foundation on which all other rights of women must be based, and it was a right not obtained by married women in England and America— those great democracies—until the late nineteenth century A.D.

One wonders how many happy, independent spinsters there were in ancient Egypt. . . . Well, probably not many. Marriage was the desired goal of both men and women, and usually a man and wife expected to live together in "the West" just as they lived together in life. Some of the tomb statues which show husband and wife seated side by side, facing eternity with smiling faces and arms embracing one another, are attractive testimonials to the fact that affection did not always end with death or marriage.

Women were equal to men in their chance of immortality too, and that was a very important "right" to an Egyptian. Like her husband and father, a woman could become an Osiris, receive offerings, and even furnish a tomb. Usually a wife shared her husband's "House of Eternity," but there are a number of tombs, not all of them royal, designed solely for women, and hundreds of women's coffins, ushebtis, "Books of the Dead," and other funerary equipment. Oddly enough, the husband almost never appears in his wife's tomb, and in some male tombs the wife is replaced by the chap's mother. It will not surprise you to hear that Egyptologists are still arguing about the reasons.

A woman gained additional prestige when she became a mother. Sons were supposed to honor and care for their mothers, and the tomb inscriptions of the late Old Kingdom and First Intermediate Period, which listed the writer's claims to virtue, commonly mentioned that he was loved by his mother. Strangely enough, none of these inscriptions mentions the wife. A man is praised and loved by his parents, children, and brothers and sisters, but never, so far as I know, by his wife. It is an unexpected omission, and one whose implications, if any, are difficult to explain.

We have seen what the rights of women were. What were their obligations? "To be a fertile field for their lords" for one thing—to present them with children, preferably sons. Although other duties are seldom specifically named, naturally a wife was expected to tend to her husband's comfort, prepare his food, keep his house and clothing in order, and be a good mother to his children. If her husband was a farmer she helped in the fields; wives of officials and "businessmen" often managed their husbands' affairs when the men had to leave home temporarily. In the humbler households women were kept busy grinding grain, baking bread and brewing beer, weaving and making clothing. However, nobody expected them to fix electrical appliances, unstop a drain, discuss politics, drive a car, or be an expert on dietetics, child psychology, interior decoration, bridge, and educational theory.

One of the truisms about ancient Egypt that everybody seems to believe is that brother-sister marriages were practiced. I am generally suspicious of truisms, and it was with great pleasure that I found that this one is indeed suspect. Some years ago the assumption was reexamined by Jaroslav Černy; his name deserves mention not only because he was willing to challenge a long-held generalization, but because he had the patience to plow through hundreds of inscriptions looking for examples. The job was made even more difficult because of the Egyptians' vagueness about relationships. The most misleading of their habits, which may have led to the formation of the brother-sister theory in the first place, was that they did not always use "sister" in its literal meaning. By the Eighteenth Dynasty, if not before, it had come to mean "wife" as well, and in the love poems it is a synonym for "beloved." The only way we can be sure that man and wife are also brother and sister is when the parents of both are named. This ideal case does not occur very often. Still, Černy found enough examples to make a good sampling, and the results were startling. His Middle Kingdom examples produced several possible cases of brother-sister marriage; but one of these depends on the assumption that "sister" was not used to mean "wife" before the Eighteenth Dynasty. The other cases are those of a man and wife who had mothers with the same name—a name which was very common during the period. Černy found no cases of brother-sister marriage in the Eighteenth Dynasty. We cannot conclude from this that they did not occur, since we do not have enough data to check every known Egyptian marriage. But if marriages between siblings were legal, they were very uncommon—which is in direct opposition to the popular theory.

Commoners, then, usually didn't marry their sisters. Kings certainly did—not always, but often. Why?

THE QUEEN

Another of those once-popular theories that is now discredited concerns the role of the queen in the inheritance of the throne. The traditional theory argued that the queen could not reign, but that the right to reign could only be obtained through marriage with an "heiress" princess.

You will still find this explanation repeated in some books written about Egypt. So wide was its acceptance that it is almost impossible to find out how it ever began. Certainly by the 1890s, when Sir James Frazer was compiling *The Golden Bough*, he wrote that "Mr. William Petrie assured me that all Egyptologists accepted the doctrine of royal descent through the female."

Sir James was interested because he and other anthropologists had just discovered the primitive matriarchy. The idea was that most, if not all, societies were originally ruled by women. The mother goddess, symbol of fertility, was the top deity, and the mother was the head of the family, possibly even of the tribe. All this happened in the dawn of history, before written records; by the time the great civilizations arose men had rebelled and taken over. But traces of the old order of things survived in religious practices, inheritance, kinship terms, and so on.

At first glance this theory seems reasonable. The physical relationship between mother and child is obvious, but the father's role may be obscure. In the early part of the twentieth century A.D. there were tribes in Australia who did not know anything about the male role in conception. Babies were brought by spirits. Europeans found this naive doctrine highly amusing, and Frazer tells one pathetic story about an Australian whose wife had just borne a child after he had been away from home for a year. He couldn't understand why the Europeans for whom he worked kept snickering.

In all fairness, we must admit that the paternal role in conception is not the sort of conclusion that leaps to mind on the basis of the evidence. Some married women never conceive, and some girls who deny all contact with men do. The time between conception and parturition is great; it is five months before the embryo shows signs of life, and "quickening" might be the first indication a neolithic female had of her pregnancy. There would be no reason to connect conception with intercourse any more than with eating, sleeping, or planting taro; and, in fact, it is a wonder that so many people did eventually figure out the connection, without any knowledge of the physiological processes involved. We need not strain our credulity too much to admit that possibly primitive man did not know who his father was.

But it is a long jump from such an admission—which is not based on any concrete evidence from prehistoric cultures—to a conclusion that such cultures were matriarchies. Even if a man only knew his mother, he would not necessarily want to make her chief. Physical and political power do not need to be related to genealogy.

The brutal truth is that men have always been stronger than women. In primitive times, before agriculture, men were the hunters, who produced the food on which the very existence of the family or tribe depended. Childbearing, in such cultures, was not an asset to a female, but a positive handicap. For several months each year she was slow on her feet, sluggish, and clumsy. The baby picked its own time to be born—as it still does—and this might be a very inconvenient time: on the march, during a war, or right in the middle of the harvest. Admitting that primitive women may have been tougher than their spoiled modern descendants and took little time out to bear the child, they had to take some time; we can fancy the skin-clad husband stamping up and down as the tribe gets farther ahead, looking impatiently at the sun moving up the sky and yelling to his mate to hurry up! Childbirth is also a perilous time. The mortality rate may not have been as high in Neanderthal times as it was in eighteenth-century Europe, when ignorant physicians brought the germs of puerperal fever into the wards from the dissecting room, but childbirth has always had risks, and in the days before antisepsis and surgery a lot of women died. I may be prejudiced, but it seems to me that a pregnant chief would not be an asset to any tribe, particularly a tribe of wandering hunters.

It might be postulated that women only came into their own with the advent of agriculture. The first farmers might have been female, and some bright Neolithic husband might have seen the connection between the fertility of the earth and that of his wife. This could conceivably lead to a deification, if not of women, of the female principle. But the oldest statues which have been thought to be those of a mother goddess come from Paleolithic, not Neolithic, levels; so we get back to the caveman, leaning over his wife, his eyes misted and his mouth trembling, as she smiles up at him and presents him with his son. . . .

No, it won't do. Let us leave this fooling and say simply that anthropologists no longer accept the blanket theory of primitive matriarchies. So we can't quote the general thesis to support what looks like a survival of matriarchal conditions in Egypt.

In fact, when we examine the evidence from Egypt we find that the theory of inheritance through the female can only be supported by a series of unreasonable exceptions and explanations. The heiress must, by necessity, have been the daughter of a king and the previous heiress, who ought logically to have been the king's chief wife.

If these assumptions are correct (and nobody can prove they are), the theory simply doesn't work. There are too many exceptions. I will not weary the reader by detailing them, but if he knows anything about Egyptian history he can probably think of a few exceptions himself. (Tiye and Nefertiti, the mother and wife of Akhenaton, are conspicuous examples of great king's wives who were not king's daughters.) One or two exceptions may prove the rule, but too many exceptions mean that we need a new rule.

Like, for instance, what? I believe I can claim to be one of the first who questioned the conventional heiress theory; now that it has been dismissed in toto by the majority of scholars, natural perversity leads me to think there may be something to it after all.

Just kidding. However, it is simply not true that royal women had no claim whatsoever to the throne. The number of ruling queens is proof of that. Here's a trick question for you Egyptology buffs. How many reigning queens were there? Cleopatra, of course; everybody knows about her. But who else?

If you believe you know, you are smarter than I am. Hatshepsut is another indubitable example; we'll get to her in due course. However, at least five other women are contenders for that distinction. One trouble is that we know very little about some of the ladies. A First Dynasty queen had two big fancy tombs. Is that evidence of independent reign? Another queen-king is known only from Greek sources, and they repeat improbable legends along with possible facts. If the Greeks can be believed, this woman, Nitokris, was the last "king" of the Old Kingdom before it broke up into anarchy. Well, said male scholars of the not-too-distant past, no wonder chaos promptly ensued! Another reigning queen, Sobekneferu, was the last ruler of the Middle Kingdom. Well, no wonder . . . ! As Sir Alan Gardiner remarked, "So abnormal a situation contained the seeds of disaster." Sobekneferu is actually the first indisputable example of a queen-king, but we know almost nothing about her.

How many does that make? Five, if you include Nitokris and the First Dynasty queen, which I wouldn't—not enough evidence. Then there was Nefertiti. Maybe. The argument as to whether she was her husband's co-regent and identical with a seemingly male ruler named Smenkhkare still rages, and although I have strong opinions on the subject this is not the place to discuss them.

I'll get to the last example, Tausert, later.

Some queens may have acted as regent for infant sons, but that in itself is another indication that royal women had a certain status. Some cultures would insist on a male regent, the child's uncle or other kin. The inheritance of the throne in ancient Egypt can be explained by the simplest notion of royal succession—that the king was succeeded by the oldest surviving son of his chief wife. If the chief wife bore only daughters, the son of a secondary wife was next in line. If a king died without male issue of any kind, he might have designated a successor, or, particularly in cases of sudden death, the throne would be up for grabs by the strongest or most influential of his courtiers, some of whom might be distant relatives of the royal house. In many cases the designated heir ended up marrying a king's daughter. It may not have been necessary for him to do so in order to claim the throne, but it apparently struck a lot of people as a good idea, supposing such a lady was available.

A particularly interesting case is that of Ankhesenamon, the widow of Tutankhamon, who died, poor boy, before he was twenty. Two small fetuses were buried in his tomb—both girls, both premature, both suffering, according to the latest diagnosis, from spina bifida. There is no doubt that Tutankhamon died without a male heir. His widow said so, flat out, when she took the incredible step of writing a letter to a foreign ruler asking for one of his sons to become her husband and king of Egypt.

It's one of the most fascinating, mysterious, and—of course—hotly debated issues in Egyptian history. The Egyptians and the Hittites had had a number of run-ins; both were competing for control of the Syrian city-states. Why would this girl—she was only a few years older than her husband—write to an enemy of Egypt offering the throne to his son? What made her believe she could get away with it?

She didn't get away with it. The Hittite prince died, or was killed, on his way to Egypt, or maybe after he arrived there, and Tutankhamon's successor was an elderly official, and Ankhesenamon is never heard of again—except on one interesting object: a ring bezel, where her name and that of Tutankhamon's successor, Ay, appear side by side. Does this indicate he married her? If he did, he dumped her for another queen almost at once.

I feel sure the reader gets the point of this somewhat elongated digression. Ankhesenamon was the last survivor of the Amarna royal house. In lieu of male heirs, did she and her supporters believe she had a claim that could be passed on through marriage? It certainly appears that way, and the fact that Ay apparently felt it necessary to marry her substantiates the idea.

Incidentally, you will find some scholars who claim the Egyptian queen in question was not Ankhsenamon, but her mother, Nefertiti. The confusion arises in part from the fact that the only record of this transaction is in the Hittite annals, and that the Hittite versions of Egyptian names are open to question. Not in my mind, however.

At all periods the queens of Egypt were the First Ladies of the land. In the First Dynasty there were tombs as big and elaborate as those of the kings of that distant period which were designed for the royal wives. The pyramid builders made little pyramids for their queens—and the relative sizes of the monuments suggest that, however important the queen might be with regard to other women, by that time she was distinctly smaller than the king. The queen's titles of this period are indicative of high rank and power; one of them is almost impossible to translate literally, but a reasonable compromise between sense and grammar might go like this: "She for Whom Anything She Says Is Done." Impressive, if true!

Though kings might have, and clearly did have, a number of wives, one of them was preeminent. By the Eighteenth Dynasty she held the title which is translated "Great Royal Wife," or "King's Great Wife." It is, perhaps coincidentally, at this period that we see an increase in the prominence of the queen. The royal women of the Theban house that united Egypt after the Hyksos invasion must have been remarkable individuals; they were cherished by their husbands and sons, and even grandsons, and they sometimes exercised real power.

The rise of the royal women culminated in Hatshepsut, the female king, who mounted the throne beside her young nephew and wielded the scepters for over twenty years. Although she may have begun as regent for a youthful heir, Thutmose III was, at the very least, in his late twenties before he took over as sole monarch. It is hard to see such a vigorous man—one of Egypt's great warrior kings—putting up with the dominance of his aunt all those years; in theory they may have been co-rulers, but Thutmose was definitely Number Two. (Bear in mind that the Egyptians didn't think of people as adolescents or teenagers; when a boy reached puberty he was a man, and ready for adult responsibilities.) Hatshepsut's violation of tradition lay in the fact that she ruled, not as a queen, but as a king. Obviously the reigning monarch of Egypt had to be male; the titles, laudatory inscriptions, and ceremonies were all designed for men, and they were so deeply rooted in tradition and dogma that it was easier for a woman to change her sex—ritually speaking—than change the titles. There are a number of theories as to how Hatshepsut managed to hang on to power with a young, virile, adult, male heir on the scene, but at the very least her success indicates that a woman could rule Egypt, under certain conditions.

A century later Amenhotep III married a commoner—at least she wasn't a king's daughter—and his attitude toward Tiye deserves the word "uxorious." Letters from foreign potentates during this period make it clear that Tiye had a hand, potent if unofficial, in affairs of state, and she ruled supreme in the harem, taking precedence over kings' daughters and noblewomen. Her son, Akhenaton, not only continued to pay her homage but raised his own wife to a high position. Nefertiti was so beautiful, if we can believe the evidence of the statues which have come down to us, that Akhenaton's infatuation is understandable; but by the same evidence, Tiye was no beauty. Maybe she had "it," or "sex appeal," or the Egyptian equivalent. This interpretation is not accepted by the majority of Egyptologists, who want to find "logical" reasons for people's actions; they explain Tiye's power by making her a member of an influential noble family. It's a reasonable theory, but the proof is, to say the least, tenuous.

As I mentioned, Nefertiti is believed by some to have assumed kingly titles. She certainly acted like a king in a number of ways; there are even reliefs showing her bashing a captive over the head in conventional pharaonic style. That has to mean something, but don't ask me what. The jury is still out on the question of Nefertiti's kingship.

After the Amarna heresy, the queen's role became less active, except for another woman, Tausert, who sometimes has the title of "King." She ruled during the Nineteenth Dynasty, at a time of dynastic and political confusion. We know very little about Tausert; the only point of interest is that she probably was not a king's daughter. Some Egyptologists proceed, blandly, to remark that Tausert must have been the heiress, because she took the throne. This is one of those nasty circular arguments; Tausert's case is one of several that cast doubt on the theory of the heiress queen. If Tausert was not of royal birth, her assumption of the throne is quite remarkable, since she had no hereditary claim to partially balance the handicap of her sex. But don't ask me how she did it, because I don't know.

During the late dynasties, certain royal women acquired a new position which probably implied a certain degree of political power. This position was signified by the title of "God's Wife," which was originally a religious title belonging to queens of the New Kingdom. Presumably it referred to the intimate relations of the queen with the god Amon, who was the real father of her royal son. The later princesses who held the same title may also have been brides of Amon-Re, but they did not present him with offspring. They lived in Thebes, where they assumed some of the powers of the high priests of Amon. Since the capital of Egypt during this period was in the Delta, the king thus secured a valuable viceroy in the south—all the more valuable because she could rule as his representative, but never as pharaoh. The God's Wife, also known as "the Adorer of the God" and "the God's Hand," may or may not have been celibate, but the office was passed on by adoption, not by birth. When a new king ascended the throne he sent his daughter to Thebes, where she was adopted by the current God's Wife, whom, in due time, she succeeded.

The God's Wife may have gained her title because of her relationship to Amon, but the title of "God's Mother," which the queen occasionally bore, probably refers to the divine king. The king was a god in several senses; he was not only Horus himself, he was also the son of Re and, later, the son of Amon. The Egyptians were not worried by such apparent contradictions. Re and Amon might be regarded as manifestations of the same supernatural force, and Amon was certainly the king's divine father; two separate sets of reliefs make his paternity very clear. Although the god came to visit the queen in the form of her mortal husband, he was careful to announce his true identity, which naturally pleased her very much.

Queen or commoner, the Egyptian woman had a relatively pleasant life. Even in our "civilized" modern world, many women in many countries have fewer rights. The Egyptians were a "civilized" people in the looser meaning of that much abused word—urbane, amiable, fair-minded. We need not explain why they were nice to their wives; indeed—if I may be permitted some slight feminine bias—we ought to explain why other people are not nice to theirs. The notion of the primitive matriarchy seems to have blossomed in the depths of the nineteenth century, when women were described as sexless angels and treated like feebleminded children; perhaps this theory was the only way in which the bearded scholars of Victorian England could account for the peculiar customs they observed in other, inferior cultures.

Five

"CLOTHE HER BACK"

CLOTHING

Women aren't the only ones who are fashion-conscious. Until relatively recent times men were as fond of bright colors and sparkling ornaments, and spent as much on their attire as did their wives and daughters. It need not be pointed out that fashion is arbitrary; some of the styles of even the recent past look hilariously funny to us, and the haute couture of alien cultures may seem actually grotesque.

By our standards, Egyptian female costume and makeup look just alien enough to be exotic. Essentially the only material used for clothing was linen; cotton and silk were not known until much later, and although wool was sometimes used for clothing, it was uncommon. A lot of variety was possible with linen, however. Egyptian weavers were skillful, and the cloth they produced ranged from a coarse canvas texture to the most delicate, semitransparent gauze.

The Egyptian lady's version of our "good basic black dress," suitable for all occasions, was a form-fitting garment which went from below the breasts down to the ankles. Wide straps ran over the shoulders, covering the bosom but leaving a deep décolletage.

This dress is often worn by women in statues and painted reliefs, but the casual observer might not recognize it at once, owing to the conventions of Egyptian drawing, which have trouble with female anatomy. Usually one breast is shown in profile and the other is indicated only by a neat round nipple in some arbitrarily selected spot. The straps of the dress, however, are shown in front view, so that they look like the topless bathing suit straps of a few years ago. We know they weren't actually worn that way by the statues which show the same garment. In both statues and paintings it is sometimes hard to make out the dress at all, except as a pair of straps and an incised line

Left: *Basic woman's dress of the Old Kingdom*
Right: *Elaborate woman's gown of the New Kingdom*

for the hem. The dress must have been designed to fit the figure as tightly as possible, and it may have been stylish to make it of thin material. A becoming style for the slim and graceful, but I wonder how plump ladies felt about it? They could at least cover themselves with a mantle, which would have been comfortable on cool evenings. It could be draped to suit the fancy of the owner—over one shoulder and under the other arm, or wrapped around the shoulders like a shawl or a stole.

In later periods, coincident with the growing sophistication of society in general, another style came into fashion among the well-to-do. This was a robe made of the sheerest linen obtainable and covered with delicate accordion pleats. Over the shoulders went a capelike affair whose ends were crossed and tied on the breast; it gave the effect of wide, elbow-length sleeves, also narrowly pleated. Alas, there was still no relief for the full-figured female. Not only were these robes transparently thin, but they were open in front from breast to ankle, and they hung free unless confined at the waist by a bright embroidered or gold-ornamented sash. The ends of the sash hung down almost to the floor. Under the robe a modest lady might wear a shift like the older-style dress, but some of them seem to have worn nothing at all.

There has probably never been any period in which formal male attire was so drab as it is today, when changes in fashion are limited to the number of buttons on a coat or the width of a lapel. The modern masculine contempt for fashion as something which should concern only women is uncommon; I suspect that in Egypt men commented approvingly on Setnakhte's new collar and asked Amenhotep where he got his kilt pleated. The kilt or short skirt was the basic costume for men, but the kilt was capable of fascinating variations. Basically it was just a rectangle of linen, knee-length, which was wrapped around the waist and anchored in front by knots or sashes or by a simple overlap and tuck-in. Then some Egyptian Beau Brummell decided to have his kilt pleated; a rival lengthened the material and arranged the long overlapping end in a series of folds, fastened in front so that it fell like a pleated apron over the front of the thighs. One variant shortened the ends and brought them up in a sharp curve to meet at the waist;

Commoner   Noble, with shirt and   Pharaoh, with elaborate
              transparent overskirt   sash and blue crown

A man's kilt—various types

the resultant gap in front was filled in by a stiffened piece of material like a phallic sheath. The so-called bag tunic was a piece of cloth folded over and sewed up the sides, leaving open slits for the arms and a hole cut out for the head. Both sexes wore cloaks and mantles. Winter nights in Egypt can be chilly, even in the south.

The man's elaborate robe, corresponding to the later woman's dress, was like that of his wife: sheer, accordion-pleated, and long. He might also wear a two-piece outfit consisting of a pleated skirt and a plain shirt with wide, pleated sleeves. The shirt was collarless and tied at the neck.

There are many variations in the standard costume, some of them depending on the occupation of the wearer. Field-workers, men and women alike, wore only a loincloth or short kilt. The graceful acrobats and the dainty little serving girls who waited on guests at parties were adorned only with narrow girdles and strings of beads. Men's working

Vizier   *Costume of a Sem priest*

costumes varied even more; some could almost be called uniforms. The vizier affected a straight, unpleated robe which fell from below the armpits to the ankles; it was held up by narrow tapes around the neck. Sailors, and perhaps sportsmen, seem to have preferred an odd nether garment made of leather cut into an openwork, weblike pattern, with a solid patch left on the seat. Priests wore various ornaments to indicate rank; the most picturesque uniform was that of the Sem priest, a leopard skin arranged so that the snarling head lay on his breast.

Although most people went barefoot, they did wear sandals when they got dressed up. Even the poorer classes could afford papyrus sandals, but of course they didn't last long; leather was more practical. The gold and silver shoes, of which a few examples have been found, were probably only for funerary use. They certainly would have been hideously uncomfortable in the hot climate of Egypt—but then, people are notoriously willing to suffer in order to be beautiful.

These descriptions of costume come from painting and sculpture.

The marvelous climate of Egypt preserves fragile materials remarkably well, but, as it happens, mummies were usually buried with no covering except the mummy wrappings. However, we do have a surprising number of garments which were actually worn, and these shed some interesting sidelights on the fashion story told by the monuments.

The oldest surviving dress in the world comes from a First Dynasty tomb at Tarkhan. It is almost five thousand years old. Sir William Flinders Petrie, who excavated the mastaba in question, didn't recognize the garment for what it was, but one of Petrie's greatest talents was that he saved things other excavators would have thrown away. Years later someone found the dress in a pile of dirty linen rags Petrie had brought back from Tarkhan, and it was carefully restored. (Can you imagine ironing the pleats in a dress five thousand years old?!) Sleeves and yoke were intricately knife-pleated, and the skirt was a separate piece, sewn to the yoke.

Two other garments are somewhat unusual. They consist of a network of colored beads, arranged in symmetrical patterns. Dresses like these are shown in some reliefs and sculptures; they are worn by goddesses and by servant girls. The ones in question had to be painstakingly reconstructed, since the thread holding the beads in place had rotted, and I wish I had the space to describe the expertise and patience necessary for this job. Suffice it to say that they are now on display, one in University College, London, and the other in the Boston Museum of Fine Arts.

Dresses like these, which were more common than was formerly believed, were usually worn over a simple linen sheath. If they were worn without anything under them they would certainly deserve the adjective "erotic," at least in our terms. I'm not prepared to assert what the ancient Egyptians considered erotic, but there is one text which describes Good King Snefru, bored as kings sometimes get, deciding to take a row around the lake. Naturally he didn't do the rowing; he ordered his courtier to collect twenty good-looking girls and added, "Give nets to these women in place of their clothes." Were these "nets" made of open weave linen—there are several examples of such fabric—or were they bead-nets like the ones we have mentioned? In either case, jolly old Snefru must have enjoyed himself a good deal. But the bead dresses would have been hard to sit on.

Perhaps we never realized how extensive and elaborate a royal Egyptian wardrobe could be until Tutankhamon's tomb was discovered by Lord Carnarvon and Howard Carter. The gold coffins and mask, the shrines, the jewelry, have obscured some of the less conspicuous but equally important objects. Among these were garments once worn by Tutankhamon and packed carefully into chests and boxes so that he would be just as fashionable in the world of the dead.

One of the first objects to catch the eyes of the excited discoverers of Tutankhamon was a gorgeous painted chest, with scenes of the king hunting and fighting in battle. It is so beautiful that one forgets it was not an object in itself. It was, of course, a container, and it contained many things: four pairs of sandals, a head rest, robes, a glove, an archer's gauntlet, caps, loincloths, and other pieces of material. Carter's description of the way this chest was handled, after being tenderly removed from the tomb, is an example of the varieties of expertise necessary to archaeologists, and also an explanation of why it took him years to clear four small rooms.

When he first opened the chest, Carter found a pair of sandals on top and, to the left of them, a crumpled bundle which his expert eye immediately recognized as a royal robe. Its surface was entirely covered with a network of faience beads, arranged in squares with a gold sequin filling in each alternate square. The robe was bordered with bands of tiny colored glass beads, arranged in patterns. The patterns could still be seen, but all the thread which had held the beads in place had rotted away, and the slightest movement was sufficient to jar the loosened beads into a meaningless jumble.

How on earth, Carter wondered, could he get this unique object out of the chest without losing the design of the beads? Tutankhamon's tomb was not, strictly speaking, untouched; it had been entered by robbers in antiquity, and although they left a lot, they pulled everything out of the chests and boxes in their search for portable loot. This robe had been tossed onto the floor, and when the priestly restorers came to straighten up the tomb they did not fold the garment neatly, but wadded it up and jammed it into the box. The cloth which looked so solid fell apart under Carter's careful fingers when he touched it. He might have stiffened the cloth and fixed the beads in place by means of wax or some other substance, but then he might not have been able to unstiffen it in order to see what the underneath portions of the robe were like. Something had to go, either cloth or pattern, and Carter decided to sacrifice the cloth. He picked it out, fragment by rotting fragment, and removed the decoration in its original pattern.

Once this tedious task was finished, Carter was not even halfway through with the chest. Luckily the sandals were in good condition and could easily be removed. Under them and the robe was a second layer—three pairs of sandals made of leather elaborately decorated with gold. Two pairs were of the type that some of us still wear during the summer, with one strap coming up between the toes to join a band encircling the instep. In one pair of Tutankhamon's sandals the thong was made in the shape of a lotus. The stem was inlaid with tiny bits of gem material, and the flower was attached to the wide side straps, which were gracefully curved and beautifully inlaid. The third set of footwear was a pair of slippers; heelless, they had leather toes and sides covered with little golden sequins.

Under the sandals Carter found a sadly decayed mass which was beyond hope of preservation. He thought there were at least seven different garments tangled up in the bundle, all covered with spangles and sequins and rosettes of precious metal.

Two other robes, bundled hastily into another box in the Annex of the tomb, had resisted time and decay somewhat better. Carter believed them to be ceremonial garments. Both were shaped like long, loose vestments, with rich, tapestry-woven decoration and fringe. One had needlework of palmettes, desert flowers and animals in a broad pattern at the hem and at the neck opening. Another was covered with colored rosettes, flowers, and cartouches woven into the fabric, and its neck opening had the shape of a falcon with outspread wings.

So far as I know, there is no relief which shows a king wearing a garment like these robes, or heelless slippers like Tutankhamon's. Some statues depict men and women wearing embroidered or woven robes, but these are rare. We wonder, therefore, whether the representations tell the whole story. Maybe the colorful woven garments had a specific function (ritual! what else?), and maybe they didn't. The conventions of Egyptian art limited poses and attitudes, so perhaps they limited clothing styles as well. We can't even be sure that the paintings are literally accurate; the case of the ladies' shoulder straps is a case in point. With this in mind, some authorities have suggested that women's dresses were neither so tight nor so sheer as the paintings suggest. We can't be sure, of course, but I see no reason why they should not have been both tight and sheer. The Egyptians had no complexes about nakedness. They may not have been the first nudists—as, I believe, some nudist magazine has suggested— because nudism, in the modern sense, implies self-conscious violation of the society's customs. Normally, the sexual organs of adults, male and female, were covered—Tutanhkamon's "underwear" consisted of triangular loincloths—but the rest of the body was exposed whenever weather or convenience made this comfortable. Generally speaking, the richer you were, the more clothes you wore, at least in public.

COIFFURES

When we talk about hairstyles we are also talking about wigs. They were worn by both men and women. Most were of human hair. Actual wigs have been found, and in some of the statues and paintings you can see the owner's real hair under the wig if you look closely. Ladies usually wore their black hair long, although some female heads from the earlier dynasties display a "mannish" short haircut. A popular and becoming style was to let the long hair hang loose, thick and waving, from under a fillet or wreath of flowers; the "tripartite" coiffure separated the hair into three sections, two of which were drawn forward over the shoulders, with the rest hanging down the back.

During the New Kingdom, elaboration in clothing was accompanied by increasingly fancy coiffures. Most of the hairdos shown in tombs must have been wigs; it would have taken hours to produce all those curls and braids and ringlets. Some of the styles are enormously

Styles of men—Old Kingdom

Styles of women—Old Kingdom

Typical man's hairstyle of the
Middle Kingdom

Woman's hairstyle of the Middle
Kingdom, front and back views

Hairstyles of the Old and Middle Kingdoms

puffed, like the bouffant hairdos of today. But the Egyptian lady's coiffure was all hair, not air. When her own locks were inadequate they
were padded out with hairpieces, and when she tired of black or brown
hair she could dye it red with henna.

In the "classical" time of the Old Kingdom, men often wore a simple short cut like the one prevalent today. Other popular styles were
the long, shoulder-length bob and the short cap of tight curls set in
formal rows. The characteristic Middle Kingdom style was the "shawl-
shape," with bangs across the forehead and the long side hair cut to
points in front. In the New Kingdom a new coiffure swept the country,
at least among noblemen. It was cut in two layers. The top consisted of
long, thin sausage curls or tightly crimped locks, and the under layer
was made up of rows of shorter curls or marcelled waves hanging to the
shoulders.

Hairstyles of the New Kingdom

Styles of men

Styles of women

During the late Eighteenth Dynasty this marcelled men's wig came in two varieties, long and short. The short "Nubian" type, as it is called, consisted of tight curls that covered the head like a cap. It was also worn by women, including the ladies of Akhenaton's court. (This is one of the reasons why some of the sculptured heads of the period are very hard to identify.) It has been suggested that the adoption of male styles by women was another of the "degenerate" customs which some scholars like to find in the heretic Akhenaton and his family. We are somewhat degenerate ourselves, so the hairstyles popular with some of our young people may tend to prove this thesis. However, the ladies of the Fourth Dynasty—a period of classic dignity, with no discernibly nasty habits—also favored a mannish haircut upon occasion. Also, while fashions in clothing and hairstyles may be bound up with cultural progress and cultural decline, I have yet to see anyone prove it.

I suspect the reliefs do not tell all there is to be told about hairstyles. This suspicion is based on the mummy of a middle-aged woman who was found among the royal mummies of Deir el Bahri. She has the most extraordinary hairdo for an Egyptian woman. One cannot expect a mummy's hair to remain perfectly set, but judging from its present condition the lady wore an upswept hairstyle with sausage curls on top and waves over the ears. It is very "un-Egyptian," and I know of nothing like it in the pictorial representations.

As a rule, facial hair was not cultivated by the Egyptian male— nor, I hardly need say, by the female. At certain periods neat little mustaches were worn, and sometimes beards seem to have been fashionable. But the Egyptian gentleman, and peasant, was usually clean-shaven. The long stiff beards worn by kings for ceremonial reasons were artificial.

Upswept hairdo on the mummy of a woman

JEWELRY AND COSMETICS

Although some robes and dresses were woven in colors, the Egyptians usually preferred to wear white clothing and depended on their orna-ments for color. Egyptian jewelry is marvelous; the craftsmen of the earliest periods had attained real excellence. Inlay, embossing, filigree, gilding, and plating—they could do most of the things modern jewel-ers can do. One of their supreme achievements was granulated gold work, in which tiny spherical grains of gold are fused onto the golden background. They also excelled at a technique which looks like clois-onne: instead of enamel, bits of precious stones, faience, or glass were set into cells outlined by thin gold strips.

The gems used in jewelry were semiprecious stones; except for an isolated case of pearls, none of the precious stones were known to the ancient Egyptians, although emeralds do occur in the eastern desert. Carnelian, turquoise, garnet, feldspar, rock crystal, obsidian, and lapis lazuli were favored. The most useful and ubiquitous material used for jewelry—and other objects—was faience. This is the same name used for the glazed pottery of Renaissance Italy, but it isn't the same stuff. Egyptian faience is made of ground quartz mixed with various other things, including a colorant, and molded into the desired shape. When the object was fired, the colorant rose to the surface in a brilliant glaze. Blue-green, in imitation of turquoise, was the most popular color, but not the only one.

The main metals used in jewelry were copper and gold—copper for the commoner, gold for the nobly born. Both were readily available to the ancient Egyptians, from desert mines and from Nubia. Silver was not; it is rare in Egyptian jewelry, and possibly more valuable. The gold was used as found, without refining, so it varies in purity; it is for this reason that much ancient gold is colored. The shades range from gray to reddish-brown and owe their coloring to mixtures of silver or copper or iron. The best known of these natural alloys is electrum, a blend of silver and gold, which comes out a pale yellow. Being harder than gold, it was often used for jewelry, and the Egyptians probably got it in its natural state from veins in the desert. There is one variety of colored gold which appears to be deliberate—a handsome rose-pink. This red-gold has been described as the product of one of those "lost Egyptian sciences" which people are fond of discovering; but actually it has been reproduced by modern scientists. The color is due to iron.

Luckily we do not have to depend on pictorial representations for our knowledge of ornaments; it would be very limited if we did. A surprising amount of jewelry has survived from ancient Egypt. Of course there was a lot of it to begin with, and it was made of imperishable materials. On the other hand, it was the most sought-after loot of the tomb robbers. What we have is probably only a tiny percentage of the total, but much of it is incredibly beautiful.

The most common ornament was the wide flexible collar, made of concentric rows of beads, some of which might be shaped like animals or flowers or leaves. It covered the front of the wearer's body from the base of the neck to the middle of the breast, and since it was made of bright colors, it formed an important part of the overall costume. Instead of a collar, necklaces or pendants might be worn. The simple bead necklaces, strung on cord, which were brought home by tourists before the start of the last century are probably authentic; they had been found in such numbers that it was easier to sell the ancient ones than make fakes. (This is no longer the case; caveat emptor, if you are in Egypt.) The beads are usually of faience. Pendants, hung on cord or gold, depending on the wearer's income, ranged from faience amulets in the shape of gods or magical hieroglyphs to elaborate cloisonne pieces which had a whole miniature scene done in relief. Then there were bracelets, some flexible rows of beads, some rigid, of copper or gold. Earrings were worn by women and boys and sometimes by men; diadems and fillets held back the hair, and gold ribbons or rings confined long curls. Girdles, anklets, finger rings of all types—the variety is endless.

The prettiest jewelry ever found in Egypt belonged to a princess of the Twelfth Dynasty named Khnumit. The crown is made of gold with insets of lapis blue, orange-red carnelian, red jasper, and green feldspar. Another crown was one of the daintiest ever worn by any princess of any country: it consisted of very fine gold threads, set at random with tiny flowers of red and blue. At intervals the golden strands were caught together by a cruciform shape made up of four papyrus flowers. The designs are exquisitely simple. The princess's necklaces were plain gold chains with various pendants. Some of the latter, such as the large pendant stars and the butterfly, are covered with the delicate granulated gold work at which Egyptian jewelers excelled. One piece is unusual—a medallion hanging from the open-worked, granulated rosettes. On a pale blue background a miniature white bull with black spots was painted; the picture was then set in a gold frame and covered with a thin piece of rock crystal.

Khnumit's jewelry has been described as "un-Egyptian," perhaps because of its very simplicity. But the workmanship is typically Egyptian, exemplifying the high degree of skill which craftsmen had attained by the Twelfth Dynasty, and which was never surpassed. The miniature painting is uncommon; a Cretan origin has been suggested for the little bull, but he reminds me unmistakably of a certain Egyptian hieroglyph. I wonder, though, what was in the princess's mind when she ordered this piece? Could it have had a personal meaning for her?

There are several other elegant parures of Middle Kingdom princesses in various museums, and later periods are also well represented. The most extensive and most famous personal collection is certainly that of Tutankhamon.

When we view this collection, filling case after case in the Cairo Museum, we ought to remember that according to the excavator it is only a part of what was originally buried with the king. Being small and extremely valuable for its size, jewelry would have been among the first things the thieves who broke into the tomb looked for, and Carter was sure that they had made off with quite a bit of it. Neat dockets written on the storage chests listed the objects which were supposed to be in them, and Carter estimated that some of the jewel boxes had lost at least 60 percent of their contents. He actually found one group of heavy gold rings tied loosely in a cloth and lying on the floor of the Antechamber—mute evidence not only of the robbery but of its interruption, perhaps by necropolis police.

The earrings and pendants and pectorals worn by the young king may strike us as extremely ornate compared with earlier designs. However, similarly crowded designs are found in the Twelfth Dynasty; some of the pectorals owned by the princesses have everything in them but the kitchen sink. And Tutankhamon possessed some pieces of jewelry which compare favorably with the elegant simplicity of earlier designs. The hilts of his daggers, which have to be considered examples of the jeweler's craft, are beautiful by any standards, and so are some of his rings and one of his diadems. The pectorals and pendants do compensate for their heavy designs by the skill of the workmanship and the lavishness of color and material. The colors may sound garish when we describe them—dark blue lapis, orange-red carnelian, turquoise, amethyst, green feldspar—but they were made up into remarkably harmonious combinations, especially when separated by the thin gold lines of the cloisons, or cells, into which the stones were set. Comparisons are odious, and we can't really generalize about differences between Twelfth and Eighteenth Dynasty jewelry. All I can say is that while I admire Tutankhamon's jewels, I would wear Princess Khnumit's if I could get my hands on them.

Although Tutankhamon and the princesses have handed down to us several diadems or simple crowns, none of the formal crowns known from the paintings have survived. The king wore the tall white crown or the basket-shaped Red Crown, which rose to a point in the back, or else he wore the two combined. The blue battle crown may have been a war helmet originally. It seems to have been shaped of stiffened leather. Some of the crowns worn for ceremonial occasions were extremely complex; each element had, of course, a symbolic significance. One does wonder how on earth the unfortunate monarch could keep the thing on his head. Much more comfortable was the nemes headdress, made of striped linen, with lappets hanging down in front. With any or all of these the king would wear a piece of jewelry unique to royalty—the uraeus serpent, symbol of the goddess of Lower Egypt, which was fixed to the brow of the crown. Though we don't have the crowns, we have a couple of uraei, and they are gorgeous—solid gold, inlaid, and enameled.

And that's all I'm going to say about the symbolism of Egyptian jewelry.

The queens' crowns were just as fancy, although once again we

Red crown   White crown   Double crown   Blue battle crown

Nemes headdress   Afnet headdress   Atef crown

Crowns of the king

know them only from reliefs and statues. Nefertiti's tall blue crown is well known from her bust; she preferred this type, which covered all of her hair. (I wonder if she had bad hair days?) She was the only queen to have worn it. The most popular type was the vulture crown, made of gold and inlaid with bits of colored stone in the wonderful Egyptian technique which looks like cloisonne. On top of this the queen might wear the tall plumes and moon disk of Hathor, modeled in gold. There were other crowns, some as complicated as those of the king, and probably just as inconvenient to wear.

To complete the picture of ravishing beauty, the Egyptian lady had only to make up her face. At her toilet table—which was not a table, but a low chest—she had metal mirrors, pots and jars for cosmetics, tweezers, razors, and combs. Most of her time and attention was lav-

| Early form of vulture crown | Later form of same crown with plumes | Moon disk and horns crown | Tall blue crown of Nefertiti |

Crowns of the queen

ished on her eyes. Black eye paint, called kohl, is still used in the Near East, but it is now made of soot; the ancient equivalent was green (malachite) or gray (galena). These minerals were ground and made into a paste, which was applied in heavy lines over the eyebrows and around the eyes by means of a little wooden or bone rod or by that handy implement, the finger. Rouge, in the form of red ochre, was used, and there is one picture of a lady applying it to her lips—with a brush. Some of the nice little pots and jars on the lady's dressing table probably held ointments. The Egyptians were fond of oiling themselves—understandably so, in a climate so hot and dry as theirs—and their perfumes were not true perfume, which has an alcohol base, but scented oils. Myrrh and sweet-smelling resin were used to make the lady smell nice, but she also used flower scents, such as "perfume of lily." These beauty aids might be kept in a prettily designed and decorated cosmetic box.

It should be added, however, that one of the fanciest of these boxes, complete with a linen-lined cavity for a mirror, belonged to a man.

Six

"COME, TELL ME HOW YOU LIVE"

TOWNS AND HOUSES

One of the most fascinating sites in the Theban area is tucked away in a little valley west of Medinet Habu and south of Deir el Bahri. It doesn't look like much: row upon row of dark mud brick and stone chip walls, arranged in a sort of grid. There are tombs on the hillside, some of them beautifully decorated; there is a temple, but it's not high on anybody's list. The interest of the site is in those mud-brick walls—the remains of a town, inhabited by craftsmen and artists.

In the early days of archaeology it was the tombs that interested excavators and collectors. The city site was not investigated properly until the Institut Français d'Archéologie Orientale, under Bernard Bruyère, tackled it. He worked there for over twenty years, and he mentions that, at the beginning of the last century, a visitor to Deir el Medina might have seen houses with their walls still intact and tombs still capped by the little pyramids which were characteristic of the period. By the time he arrived it was all gone, wrecked by amateur archaeologists and by some professionals who did not know their trade well enough. "The passion for antiquity destroyed what the centuries had spared."

Deir el Medina is not as well known as some of the other tourist spots, yet it is an extremely important place—one of the few town sites found in Egypt. Unlike tombs, houses were built of perishable materials, and many of the most important ancient cities are hidden under modern villages. Therefore, the town sites we have found are vital, rounding out a picture of Egyptian culture still heavily biased by mortuary material. Deir el Medina has produced more useful information about town life than any other such site. It yielded masses of ostraca and papyri, including literary works, lists of supplies, rude letters, and irritable complaints. These artifacts give unique insights into the activities and interests of a group of average men and women of the Nineteenth and Twentieth Dynasties.

The isolation of Deir el Medina explains in part why it was spared for so long. It lies in a hidden valley behind a spur of the desert cliffs, away from the regular tourist routes. The area is desolate and inhospitable; there is not even a water supply at the village. We might wonder why a town was ever located there. The answer lies in another valley, not far distant from Deir el Medina. The inhabitants of the village were necropolis workers—the stonemasons, scribes, and other craftsmen who constructed and decorated the tombs in the Valley of the Kings.

The town was probably founded in the early Eighteenth Dynasty when the first royal tomb was begun in the Valley, and it was inhabited for roughly 400 years. A wall surrounded the site, and a single gate led into the main street, which was straight and only four or five feet wide. The houses, built of mud brick and limestone chips, faced directly on the street. Most of them were small, having on the average only four rooms. The room facing the street had no windows, except for small gratings high up near the roof. Behind was an all-purpose room in which the family slept, dined, worked, and entertained; columns supported the ceiling, which was higher than that of the neighboring rooms and which thus allowed light to penetrate through clerestory-style windows. There was usually a raised platform in this room, to serve as a couch and/or bed platform—or a birth box? Behind the main room were two smaller chambers. One was the kitchen and one a storeroom or extra bedroom. Most of the houses had basements, for storage, reached by stairs from the main room. Other stairs led up to the roof, which was flat and served as extra living space. There wasn't much privacy to be had in these smallish houses, for family units might include grandma, auntie, and other undefined relatives in addition to parents and children.

Not very glamorous, but on the whole not bad. A good many people in today's world live in less salubrious surroundings. However, we would probably prefer a nobleman's villa, as the Egyptians did if they could afford one. Our model comes from Tell el Amarna, which was the onetime, if short-lived, capital of Egypt. Most of the excavators of Amarna have pointed out that the name is incorrect; it is a misunderstanding of the names of two of the modern villages at the site. However, it has been used for so long that it has acquired a meaning, whether it had one originally or not, and I would rather use it than the ancient name, Akhetaton, which is confusingly like the name of its founder, Akhenaton.

Amarna was not a walled city, being bounded by the river on one side and the valley cliffs on the other. The modern road runs along the same route as the main street of the ancient city, called the "Royal Road." Along this street the city mushroomed into three major subdivisions. The central section contained the public buildings and the Great Temple, and a palace which the king and his family occupied on ceremonial occasions, leaning out the "Window of Appearance" to receive the plaudits of the crowd and present awards to deserving officials. A southern section was primarily residential, containing some of the largest and most elegant villas. The northern suburb included a couple of palaces. There was also a workmen's village, similar in function and general design to Deir el Medina, but much smaller, since it was occupied for such a short time.

Since the site had never been inhabited before Akhenaton's time, his chief courtiers could lay out elegant houses with ample grounds around them. The house itself was sprawling and one-storied. Set on a low platform, it was approached by steps or ramps. The main entrance led into a reception hall with painted wooden columns. Behind it was a central hall, a sort of family room, with columns, a brazier for heat on cool evenings, and a built-in divan along one wall. The private quarters of the family were little suites separated from the public part of the house. Some had small private sitting rooms. There were bedrooms, identified by the raised platforms on which the beds were placed, and a bathroom with stone or plaster walls. The bather stood on a stone slab with a low coping and the water drained off through a hole in the floor. Since there were no closets, storage space was provided by a separate room with rows of shelves. The amenities of the villa included a lavatory—a small, walled-off space with a seat supported by bricks and a removable vessel underneath.

An important part of a wealthy man's estate was his garden. Ideally it featured a pool, surrounded by carefully tended trees and flowers. To spend the day sitting or reclining in the shade of leafy branches, surrounded by sweet scents, and dreamily contemplating the limpid surface of a pool is, as gardeners lucky enough to possess these things know, one of the highest pleasures in life—particularly when you are watching someone else do the work. Several paintings show gardeners watering the plants; they are obviously servants, and some have been so busy that they haven't had time to shave.

Flowers were favored offerings to the gods; they were also used for funerary bouquets and wreaths. Perhaps the most-loved flower of all was the one erroneously, but commonly, referred to as the lotus. It was not a true lotus, but a water lily, and there were two varieties, blue and white—*nymphaea lotus* and *nymphaea caerulea*, to give them their scientific names. The lotus proper is a member of another family, Nelumbo, and it is quite different in appearance and habit. However, the word has been in use for so long that it would be pedantic to insist on calling the flower a lily.

From wreaths found in burials, such as those of Tutankhamon, we can identify poppies, cornflowers, and other blossoms, as well as leaves of the olive and willow. The brilliant scarlet poppy and vivid blue cornflower were often combined with a bright yellow fruit, possibly that of the persea trea, possibly that of the mandrake, to form a spectacular color combination. The mandrake is not the kind of plant you want to fool with; not only is it poisonous, but according to medieval herbals, it screams when it is uprooted. It has not actually been found in Egypt, so maybe the pretty yellow fruits are those of the persea.

You will not find roses mentioned in any of the books on Egyptian flowers, but the plant was known in Egypt by the Roman period. In tombs of that time Petrie found wreaths that included rosebuds, some of which actually opened when they were put in water. They are described as "red" roses, but they have been identified with the Rose of Abyssinia, and the modern variety is not red, but pink.

The above is a totally irrelevant interpolation, for which I do not apologize. I like roses and I have the Rose of Abyssinia (or *Rosa sacra*) in my garden. That's how I know it is pink.

If a nobleman's villa and garden don't satisfy you, we will offer a royal palace. Not many of them have survived, since they were built of the same brick and wood that constituted private dwellings. The plans of the Amarna palaces are known, but an even more interesting example is the palace of Amenhotep III, Akhenaton's father, on the west bank at Thebes. The site is called Malkata.

Amenhotep's palace was almost a city in itself; it consisted of four separate royal residences, a temple, a workers' village, and a series of houses for officials. Possibly one palace was the king's and the others belonged to the queens and crown prince. Amenhotep III had two important wives and a son who turned out to be Akhenaton, so the theory is neatly tempting, but of course we don't know whether it is true or not. Let's take a look at the building which has been called the King's Palace.

At the northern end were three audience halls, two big and one small. Each had a dais for the throne, and the largest was reached by a wide corridor, the main entrance to the palace. The king's private apartments consisted of a long columned hall with a throne room behind it. Behind the throne room was the king's suite, consisting of bedroom, bath, and robing room. Archaeological evidence indicates that it had two stories. On either side of the long hall there were four suites of rooms—for ladies of the harem?—each consisting of a storeroom with shelves, a robing room with more shelves, a bedroom, a parlor, and a bath.

The glory of the palace was not only its spaciousness but its decoration. Floors, ceilings, and walls were painted in brilliant colors, and with a naturalistic skill which reached its height at this period. A favorite motif for floors was a pool, surrounded by plants and water birds, and filled with fishes, lilies, and swimming ducks. Ceilings had grape trellises or flying birds; walls might be adorned with animals or graceful court ladies. In the king's bedroom there were prancing figures of the odd little dwarf god Bes, who was a popular household deity. Even the brick supports for the shelves were painted with papyrus plants and animals. The decoration of the throne rooms was more formal—figures of the king and of kneeling captives. The wooden columns which supported the ceilings of some rooms were made in the graceful shapes of plants, papyrus or lotus, and they also were brightly painted. No greater contrast to the general view of Egyptian architecture—grim, gray, and monolithic—could possibly be imagined than these palaces, aglow with color and alive with the fluttering of birds' wings.

We have had a small sampling of Egyptian houses, from the humble dwellings of workers to the abode of the king himself, but it should be pointed out that even the humbler abodes were those of craftsmen, who were several steps up the social scale from the peasants. Deir el Medina and the workmen's village at Amarna were planned and constructed by the government. There were similar towns at other sites— more of them than was once realized, since people keep finding new ones—designed for a similar purpose: the construction and maintainance of the royal tombs. At Giza, near the Great Pyramid, some structures were evidently food production centers, since bread and beer and, in this case, fish were part of the workers' pay. An additional perk was the right to build a tomb. Dr. Zahi Hawass has found dozens of the workers' tombs at Giza, and the people of Deir el Medina built theirs on the hillside near the village. (Excavators have recently identified a possible commoners' cemetery at el-Amarna. Stay tuned.) The hamlets of lower-class folks probably grew at random and were built of even more perishable materials—and were even less comfortable.

Although the above examples may be considered "typical" in a broad sense, others do show different features. The Malkata palace, which was similar to those of Amarna, particularly in decoration, may have been exceptional; this was an exceptional period, particularly in art. Plant columns were always popular, even in private homes, but the walls, floors, and ceilings of earlier palaces were probably painted with more formal designs or covered with woven matting. Egyptian animal and bird figures are always quite charming, but animal forms of the Amarna Period have a liveliness which is lacking in earlier times. We have no evidence that such motifs, appropriate and lovely as they are, were used in earlier palaces.

One important difference between the Amarna villas and those of other periods must be noted: there were no separate women's quarters at Amarna. Other well-to-do houses give the mistress her own suite, separate from that of the master. At Amarna, husband and wife apparently occupied the same suite. What does this mean? We could make some pretty generalizations about the changed position of women under the iconoclastic, uxorious Akhenaton, but they would only be guesses.

Villas and palaces are unusual in one important aspect—their spaciousness. The king naturally took all the room he wanted, and the villas were country houses. A town house, even one belonging to a nobleman, was more cramped because Egyptian cities were limited in space; they had to encroach as little as possible on the precious black soil used for crops. We think that houses in a city such as Thebes were several stories in height. Except in rare cases there would be no land available for gardens or "front yards," so the family had to take their airings on the roof, which was often surrounded by screens of matting.

I imagine most of us could endure living at a place like the Malkata palace; we wouldn't even mind the absence of plumbing if we had slaves to run back and forth carrying water jars and the ancient equivalent of chamber pots. The cramped quarters of the workmen's village might not appeal so much. Even the humbler houses, however, were well adapted to the Egyptian climate and customs. The main features of the climate are its rainlessness and its brilliant sunshine, with resultant heat. The sun-dried brick of which most houses were built was perfectly adequate in a rainless area; sloping roofs were unnecessary. Thus, a cheap, easy source of building material was readily available, and the flat roofs could be used as terraces, which would be an agreeable addition to city houses. To keep the houses cool, sunlight was excluded as much as possible; windows were few, high, and small. Walls were thick—twenty inches in the Deir el Medina houses—and there were ventilators on the roofs to catch the prevalent north wind. The city houses were limited in space, so cooking had to be done in the house itself, but whenever possible the kitchens were outside, in separate buildings. Other outbuildings on a country estate included servants' quarters and pens for animals, buildings for brewing, baking, and weaving, and a butchers' shop. It was a small economic unit in itself.

FURNITURE AND HOUSEHOLD EQUIPMENT

The Egyptians did not clutter up their houses with furniture, but some of the pieces which have survived are elegant enough to stand comparison with fine modern work. In fact, they are better looking than a lot of my furniture. Like their friends the jewelers, Egyptian carpenters had reason to be proud of their skill, all the more so because of the materials they had to work with. Egypt is poor in large trees, and early in pharaonic times she began importing cedar from the Lebanon for fine woodworking. Such imports were expensive, of course, so Egyptian carpenters had to learn to work, for the most part, with their scrubby native trees— sycamore fig, acacia, tamarisk, sidder, and willow. Mortise and tenon joints, dovetailing, and wooden pegs joined together the small planks which were obtained from these local trees. The tools were of copper; they included chisels, adzes, axes, and drills. Saws were of the "pull" type, with the teeth set toward the handle. I do very little sawing myself, but I understand that our saws are "push" saws, with the teeth set away from the handle. We usually lay the wood to be cut with a saw on a table or sawhorse, but the Egyptians tied theirs to a post and cut down from the top, this being the best position for using their pull saws. When the wood was cut and jointed it was "planed" by a lump of stone.

Softened as we are by our Posturepedic inner-spring mattresses, most of us would find Egyptian beds uncomfortable. They had wooden frames and springs of woven cord or leather strips. Most were higher at the head than at the foot, so they had a footboard—but no headboard— to keep the sleeper from sliding gently down onto the floor. Over the springs were placed pads of folded linen, with sheets of the same material as the covering. I imagine these beds were as comfortable as our camp beds, but the item that would finish most of us was the pillow, which was not a pillow at all but a headrest of shoulder height, with a support curved to fit the neck. I have always wondered whether the Egyptians didn't use cushions with these devices of torture, but I know of no examples, and apparently the headrest is not as painful as it looks once you get accustomed to it. Other peoples use them, and a modern archaeologist, Herbert E. Winlock, remarked that they were surprisingly comfortable after some little practice, "if you didn't pinch

Bed

your ear." Another intrepid scholar, who must have tried the darned thing himself, claimed that a headrest was okay if you were lying on your side. Rather him than me. . . .

There was very little in the bedroom besides the bed—only a few boxes and baskets for clothing. Most of these containers, though, were kept on the shelves of the storeroom next to the bedroom, if the house boasted such an arrangement. Women kept their toilet articles in a chest or a basket, and perhaps these were placed on low tables when the lady made up her face. Some storage chests could be provided with legs, forming a sort of stand. There were several such objects in Tutankhamon's tomb, and one of them is a particularly handsome piece of furniture; someday I intend to have it copied. Unlike many of Tutankhamon's possessions, it is of simple design, but the proportions and the row of ornamental hieroglyphs are quite elegant. Tutankhamon had some chests which are real objets d'art, especially the one painted with scenes of hunting and warfare, but of course they are not typical of those ordinarily used. Plainer wooden boxes and woven baskets were more common. Some had lids which could be tied on and—if

Chairs and stool

the owner was of a suspicious nature—sealed with a blob of clay that covered the knot. The boxes were often ingeniously designed, with separate compartments for different articles. One had a shallow space under the lid for a mirror, with supporting pieces set in to hold the handle and keep the mirror from banging around when the box was moved. The hollow interior of the box held pots for unguents and perfumes.

Living room furniture consisted of chairs, stools, and tables. The common people squatted on the floor or on the built-in divan; wealthier folk naturally had more furniture. Chairs exhibit a wide variety of forms, having long legs and short legs, arms or no arms, but most of them seem broad by our standards, especially for the slender Egyptians of the reliefs. The most gorgeous chair we have is one belonging to Tutankhamon; it was probably a throne rather than a household item, and it is inlaid with hundreds of little pieces of ebony, ivory, and colored wood. Stools usually had short legs and seats of woven rushes. There were no dining tables seating twenty-four, not even in the king's palace. At banquets each guest or pair of guests had his own little table. Although most people went to bed at sunset, they did have lamps—containers filled with oil, with a wick.

A remarkable discovery made by an Italian expedition digging at Deir el Medina in 1906 gives an accurate picture of what a well-to-do couple of the Eighteenth Dynasty considered necessary for comfortable living, in this world and the next. The tomb is unique; all others, even those of Tutankhamon and Yuya and Thuya, had been broken into by thieves at least once, but Kha and his wife Merit had not been disturbed since they were laid to rest approximately three thousand years before Ernesto Schiaparelli found them, with the wooden door of the tomb still in place.

In addition to the tables, stools, baskets, chairs, and beds we have mentioned, Kha's tomb contained large quantities of linen—sheets, tunics, and loincloths. Linens were among the first things taken by tomb robbers, since they could be recycled immediately and couldn't be traced back to the tomb owners. Kha and Merit also had toilet articles and vessels of pottery, metal, and stone, storage chests, food of all kinds. . . . A complete listing would take several pages. Kha and Merit definitely did take it with them. Among the other objects (which included their coffins and mummies) were two unusual items: lamp stands as tall as modern floor lamps.

Tutankhamon's furniture was a lot fancier than anything a commoner would own. One of his lamps is made of calcite (we used to call it alabaster) and it has a scene painted on the inside. It only shows up when the lamp is lit. His head rests are all decorated. Even the simplest are prettily colored, and except for the gold band around the "neck," they would not be beyond the means of a moderately well-to-do tradesman. One head rest was ivory, with carved heads of the grotesque god of the bedchamber, Bes, on either end, and with the legs ending in graceful stylized duck's heads.

The imaginative talents of the artisan show up most clearly in the objects we might lump together under the heading of toilet articles. Mirrors were circles of polished metal with handles cunningly carved into the shape of an animal or a lotus flower or a slim naked girl. The little ointment spoons may be seen in many museum collections. The covered, spoon-shaped space which held the ointment might be made in the form

Headrest of Tutankhamon

of a duck, with a swimming girl for a handle. Even the humble baskets of the poor were finely made, with strips of colored grass woven in to form patterns. The Egyptians were very much aware of natural beauty, and their ornamental designs reflect this awareness, making frequent use of plant and animal forms and graceful poses of the human body.

Although the furniture was scanty, the interior of an Egyptian house was cheerful and colorful. Woven mats were used as floor coverings, wall hangings, or even ceiling covers. As we have seen, some surfaces were painted.

Kitchen furniture was limited to utensils and the indispensable oven. Strange as it may seem, the Egyptian housewife cooked without any "counter space" at all. She squatted on the ground when she ground grain, and apparently she stayed there while she mixed and kneaded her bread. Her oven was a pottery shell about thirty inches high, with two doors, one at floor level for fire building and another, fitted with a lid, on top. The fire was allowed to die down into a bed of coals before the bread was put in, via the top hole, onto a shelf about a third of the way up. The housewife could cook on top of the stove or on a brazier. She probably dunked the dishes in the river and scoured them with sand, but no painting or model has preserved this homely detail.

Some kitchens had niches built into the wall for storage, but otherwise pots and jars just stood in rows along the walls. The Egyptians made good pottery in a variety of shapes—bowls and jars, spouted jugs, pots with handles. The material was the useful Nile mud, which produced a reddish-brown pottery. From the area near Qena in Upper Egypt came a special type of light-colored clay which made especially handsome pots.

And that is all I intend to say about pottery. A detailed description of types would only interest a specialist, and to be candid, Egyptian pottery of the historic period is not exciting. It was well made and nicely shaped, but there were few types as attractive as the painted wares of other Near Eastern countries. The buff and pale blue "Malkata" pottery is easy to spot and very attractive, but most was utilitarian, meant for the prosaic functions of the household. Luxury ware was not made of clay. In the earliest dynasties the best tableware, the vessels designed for the service of the gods and the royal dead, was laboriously shaped out of stone—alabaster, marble, porphyry, limestone, rock crystal, even basalt. I don't know which is more impressive, the sheer number of these stone vessels or the wonderful skill with which they were made. Walter Emery found over 1,500 stone vessels in a single First Dynasty tomb at Sakkara. The finest of the stoneware comes from the first three dynasties, and it is cut with such skill and accuracy that the walls are sometimes as thin as those of a modern dinner plate.

Metal vessels appear as early as the First Dynasty, and eventually royalty dined off gold and silver. A hoard of such vessels was found by Pierre Montet in the royal tombs of the Twenty-First Dynasty at Tanis; even as far back as the Fourth Dynasty, Queen Hetepheres I owned a gold drinking cup and several small bowls of the same metal.

The Egyptians also used glass. It seems to have appeared rather suddenly, around the time of the Eighteenth Dynasty. Unlike modern glass, it was not transparent; the opacity is due to the incomplete fusion of the materials. Apparently glass vases were made on a clay core which was dipped into the molten glass and then twirled rapidly to distribute the glass evenly. The hot material could be colored and rolled out into thin rods. When these were wound around a vase and dragged up and down, they produced the wavy effect which is so common in Egyptian glassware. Glass vessels are not often found, possibly because of the fragility of the material, and possibly because much of the glass made in the factories of Thebes and Tell el Amarna was used for jewelry, in the form of beads or inlay.

FOOD AND ENTERTAINMENT

What did the Egyptians eat out of all those pots? Quite a variety of things, if they could afford them. Bread was the staple food. Some loaves have survived to the present day; they are like rock, the stalest bread you can imagine. The yeast used was a wild variety, relatively impure, although one specimen from an Eighteenth Dynasty tomb turned out, upon analysis, to be as pure as modern yeast. We know about the yeast from beer, not from bread itself. There are no actual pots of that beverage still around, but it was possible to analyze it from the dried residue left in the bottoms of jars.

"A thousand [loaves] of bread, a thousand [jars] of beer"—so the Egyptian mortuary formulas began when they listed the food items desired in the next world. The two staples of the Egyptian diet are connected in another way, for both went through the same initial process. When the dough had been mixed and shaped into loaves, they were left to rise. If the housewife wanted bread she popped the pans (pots) into the oven. If she wanted beer, she crumbled the loaves and mixed them with water to form a mash. This "sat" for a few days till it fermented; it was then strained and poured off into jars. A similar beverage, called bouza, is still being made today, with added ingredients to suit modern tastes. It has an alcoholic content of about 7 percent. Recently someone came up with a so-called version of ancient beer, called King Tut's. I have not sampled it. It costs about $150 per bottle, when you can get it.

We know quite a lot about the ancient Egyptian diet, not only from painted and carved reliefs, but from excavation and from actual foodstuffs left in tombs for the benefit of the dead person. Meat was probably scarce in poor households, but well-to-do families raised cattle and such exotic animals as oryxes and gazelles for food. They also domesticated pigs and sheep. One of the many inaccuracies perpetuated by Greek historians like Herodotus was that these animals, especially pigs, were considered unclean by the ancient Egyptians. Maybe they were in some religious contexts, but a lot of pig bones have been found near village sites, and swine are mentioned in some lists of offerings. Fowl, including geese and ducks, had been domesticated; they were also available to hunters, like certain other animals. Chickens were not raised in pharaonic times; though Thutmose III brought back a few of these exotic creatures from one of his Syrian campaigns, no chicken bones have been found that date before the fourth century B.C. Thutmose's chickens appear to have been roosters, which may explain why the breed didn't survive.

Diodorus, another of those old Greek travelers, claimed that fish were also unclean. Again, the prohibition, if it existed at all, may have extended only to members of certain priesthoods; certainly the Egyptians of earlier periods ate a lot of fish—and why not? The Nile was full of the creatures, and they are excellent sources of protein. Milk and the cheese made from it were also consumed.

The main source of protein, at least for the poorer classes, came from legumes—beans, lentils, chickpeas. Their diet was heavy on vegetables, primarily onions and garlic, radishes and lettuce. The last named was considered an aphrodisiac. To the best of my knowledge it isn't, but it is very good for you.

The diet of a wealthy nobleman was extensive. Beef and mutton, goose, duck, and other birds were prepared in various ways. Honey was the main sweetener, sugar being unknown, and—I was really happy for the Egyptians when I learned this—they had carob, which is also a sweetener and the closest the ancient Old World ever came to chocolate. Fruit, including dates, figs, melon, and grapes, was popular. Grapes could be dried into raisins or used for wine. The sophisticated Egyptian of the New Kingdom had developed quite a taste for fine wines. Jars were labeled, not only with the year of the vintage, but with the vineyard of origin, and certain wines were prized above others.

We don't know much about how all these foods were prepared. Meat was usually grilled or roasted, lentils must have been stewed, and different kinds of bread and rolls were made, some sweetened and stuffed with fruit. Sauces, seasonings, and other gourmet touches are only a matter of surmise. Along with their other thoughtless omissions, the ancient Egyptians have not provided us with a cookbook.

The Egyptians ate not only for nourishment but for conviviality. Some of the tomb reliefs which show people eating together may have been designed to insure the dead a perpetual banquet in the afterlife, but they probably also reflect the pleasant custom of dinner parties. People ate with their fingers, and when the meal was over a servant, or a daughter of the household, came around with water which was poured over the hands. Judging from some reliefs, such as the ones from Amarna which show the royal family dining on rolled roasts and whole roast ducks, à la Henry VIII, some substitute for napkins was certainly necessary.

But the important part of the banquet, one imagines, was not so much the eating as the drinking. Quiet family parties did not end in orgies, of course, but big celebrations, given, no doubt, like modern cocktail parties, to get rid of one's social obligations or impress one's friends, often ended in unhappy spectacles of undue merriment. One banquet scene graphically shows a lady guest ridding herself of her dinner, and other diners look as if they need help to stand erect. We need not conclude that everybody got roaring drunk at these parties, but the euphoric effects of wine and beer were certainly enjoyed.

At banquets like these there was a floor show. Singing and musical instruments accompanied the feasting. A basic orchestral instrument was the harp; several different types are shown in the reliefs, from small portable instruments to big floor models, taller than the harpist. Percussion instruments, small drums, and tambourines beat out the rhythm and were augmented by the hand clapping and finger snapping of the dancers. Other instruments appear later, after the beginning of the Eighteenth Dynasty; they may be Asiatic in origin—the lyre, the oboe, and the lute.

Unfortunately we cannot provide the music to any ancient Egyptian songs. The tunes were passed on from master to apprentice, so a notational system never developed. But we do know some lyrics. This is one of the "Harpers' Songs":

> Spend the day merrily; put unguent and fine oil to your nostrils, and lotus flowers on the body of your beloved. Place singing and music before your face. Cast all evil behind you and think of joy, until that day comes when harbor is reached in the land that loves silence. Spend the day merrily, and weary not therein; lo, none can take his goods with him; lo, none that has departed can come again.

Not a very cheerful song—but perhaps it all depends on the point of view. However, songs like this one—and there are a number of different versions of the same theme—are known to us from the tombs, where the singer is performing for his dead master. Maybe they were not sung at real parties. However, there is no reason to suppose that they would have seemed morbid to the Egyptians. The advice is practical, really—"eat, drink, and be merry" because "you can't take it with you."

A stock figure in the orchestra was a bent, elderly male harper, often blind. The rest of the musicians were girls, and if they were as young and pretty as the paintings suggest, their appearance provided additional pleasure for the feasters. Their costumes, like those of the dancers who appeared with them, were quite flimsy; sometimes they wore only a string of beads and a girdle.

Dancing seems to have been a spectator sport or a religious exercise; I know of no representations of boys and girls dancing together for fun. The slim little girl dancers were professionals, and some were trained to do acrobatic tricks. Music also seems to have been reserved for professionals. However, one relief shows a vizier's lady playing a harp, so it is possible that people of leisure enjoyed performing music as well as listening to it.

Thus the wealthy entertained their friends. The middle classes probably tried to imitate their betters on a smaller scale; and for people who enjoyed drinking for its own sake there was always the local tavern. Egyptian towns had such establishments, and they may also have had their town drunkards. Although mild inebriation was tolerated, public drunkenness was regarded as disgusting. One of the sages warns his audience of the dangers of the corner pub:

"Don't take to drinking," says Ani, "because if you speak, something else [other than what you meant] will come out of your mouth; you won't know what you are saying. You will fall down and break your limbs. Nobody will take you by the hand; your drinking companions will stand apart and say: Look at that sot! If someone comes to look for you, to ask your advice, he will find you lying on the floor like a little baby."

Another popular spectator sport was wrestling. Our illustration (see page 113) shows only a few of the dozens of wrestling holds illustrated in a Middle Kingdom tomb. They look quite expert, and I am told by those who know that some are like modern holds. Incidentally, the match was not necessarily waged by a Nubian and an Egyptian. The

Harpist and dancers

Wrestlers

contrasting colors of the men's bodies is a device of the artist, to make clear what would otherwise be a confusing tangle of arms and legs.

While we are on the subject of amusements, we must mention storytelling. It may seem like quite a jump from wrestling to literature; but the latter word is misleading. The reader will note, if he examines the table of contents, that there is no chapter on "Egyptian Literature." Instead, I have tried to look at the subject as the Egyptians might have looked at it, under a number of different categories—love songs under love and marriage, hymns and prayers under religion, the maxims of the sages under the subjects to which they pertain. A student of comparative literature is justified in lumping all these compositions together into a single category, but the unity is artificial because it is a modern, not an ancient, viewpoint. By the time we are through we will have examined the major subdivisions of Egyptian literature, with one exception—the epic, which did not exist. The compositions praising the valor of a king are hymns rather than epics, and the only other possible contender for the position of an epic hero is Osiris, who must be counted out, if for no other reason than on the grounds that he is dead during most of the story.

Egyptian prose fiction includes tales of several different types.

Some are more sophisticated, more "literary," than others; they were meant for audiences who could appreciate puns, an elegant flow of rhetoric, and a refined style. Other stories rely on plot rather than style for their interest, and a few are as melodramatic, as bloodthirsty, and as implausible as any bad modern thriller.

The question of humor in Egyptian stories is not so easy; it is always hard to tell what may strike someone else as funny. The Egyptians' sense of humor shows up in other media, particularly in painting and relief. There are several late drawings, on papyri and ostraca, which are obviously meant to be satirical; they show animals busily engaged in a number of human activities. A mouse lady, seated at a dressing table, is being attended by a number of cat servants, while a cat nurse carries a mouse baby; a mouse king, mounted in a chariot, attacks a fortress manned by cats; a lion plays a board game with a gazelle. One devastating little model from Tell el Amarna shows a group of monkeys driving in a chariot; the charioteer monkey has, upon close examination, a terrible resemblance to the king, Akhenaton, who is often seen in his own chariot. Other humorous touches are less satirical and broader—a very fat woman and her very small donkey. We can be reasonably sure that these satirical pictures appealed to the Egyptians' sense of humor. As for the stories, there is only one which was almost certainly regarded as a comic tale—"The Contendings of Horus and Set," which we will consider in detail in another chapter. It is a broad, bawdy story which pays scant respect to the immortal gods, and much of its humor is of a visual nature. The divine assembly of the gods brawls and bickers like a group of spoiled children, Isis bustles about playing tricks on her enemies, and Astarte gets the supreme god Re out of a fit of the sulks by exposing herself to him. These touches are not especially subtle, and they are certainly meant to be funny. Some of the other tales are not so easy to diagnose. Take the story of Wenamon, for instance.

Wenamon was an Egyptian official who was sent to Byblos to get cedar at a time when Egyptian prestige abroad was pretty low. He had a perfectly terrible time, being robbed, insulted, threatened, and sneered at. After he got to Byblos he sat around for a month without being allowed even to see the prince, and as he remarks, "[The prince] sent to me every day, saying, 'Get out of my harbor.'"

I think this is funny; in fact, all of Wenamon's tribulations amuse me tremendously. Did they amuse the Egyptian readers of the story? Probably not. The Egyptians didn't admit, much less enjoy, national or personal humiliation. I don't know many people who do.

Since most Egyptians were illiterate, and since they lacked those blessings of the illiterate, movies and TV, they probably relied on professional storytellers. These itinerant figures are known from other nonliterate cultures, although I must admit I know of no specific reference to them in Egypt. Still, there was a place for such a wandering minstrel; gathered around the water jar in the village square, in the cool of the evening, the villagers may have listened to just such a story as I am about to relate to you.

Once upon a time there were two brothers. Anubis was the name of the older, and Bata the name of the younger. Anubis had a house, he had a wife, and his younger brother lived with him like a son. It was the younger brother who took care of all the elder's needs. Indeed, the younger brother was a fine lad. There was no one like him in the whole country; the power of a god was in him.

Now one day when he was walking behind the cows, they said to him: "The grass is good over in that place." Bata took them there, and they became very beautiful, and multiplied.

One day when the two brothers were working in the field they ran out of grain, and the elder brother sent Bata home to get more. He found his brother's wife fixing her hair, and when he asked for grain she told him to go and get it himself. He came out of the granary with a sack so huge that the wife realized he was very strong; and she wanted to know him with the knowledge of a man. But when she said, "Come, let us spend an hour sleeping together," Bata became angry. "What is this great abomination which you have said to me?"

Bata went back to the field and worked with his brother, saying nothing. But when the older brother returned to his house in the evening he found the house dark, and his wife lying down very sick, like one who has been beaten. She told him that Bata had made evil suggestions to her, and that, when she recoiled in horror, he beat her and threatened her. So Anubis took his spear and ran out to find his younger brother, who had not yet returned from the field. He hid himself behind the stable door and waited. But when Bata came to the stable with the herd of cows the head cow said, "Watch out! Your brother is there, waiting with his spear to kill you. Run away from him!" The next cow said the same thing, and so did the one after that. At last convinced, Bata looked down and saw his brother's feet under the door. Dropping his burdens, he ran as fast as he could, with his brother after him.

As he ran, Bata prayed to Re to help him, saying: "Thou art he who judges the wicked from the just!" Re heard, and caused a body of water filled with crocodiles to appear between Bata and his older brother. And his older brother beat his hands together, in a rage at not being able to kill him. Then Bata argued with his brother, telling him what had really happened. And he took a knife and cut off his penis, and threw it into the water.

This dramatic gesture convinced the older brother (as well it might); seeing the boy fainting and in pain, he wept and groaned aloud.

Now up to this point the story is fairly simple, and effective; the Egyptian audience was probably groaning in sympathy and yearning to see the virtuous and misused young brother rewarded. The complications begin with the story Bata proceeds to tell his remorseful brother as they stand one on either side of the river. He says he is going to the Valley of the Cedar, where he will put his heart in the top of a tree. If his tree is ever cut down, so that his heart falls to the ground, he will be in trouble, and then Anubis must come to his help. He tells Anubis how he will know when the fatality occurs, and then he departs, leaving his brother to return home and deal with his treacherous wife. He kills her and throws her to the dogs. Then he sits down and weeps for his younger brother.

Now we switch to Bata in the Valley of the Cedar. He manages well enough until the gods decide he needs a wife. They make one for him—a girl more beautiful than any in the land, and Bata falls in love with her. Bata's self-mutilation in the first part of the story is blandly ignored by the storyteller; perhaps it is assumed that the gods took care of that little matter too.

Appreciating the desirability of his bride, Bata warns her not to go out for fear of the Sea God. Naturally the girl ignores this unreasonable warning; naturally the Sea God rolls up in pursuit as soon as she goes out. She makes good her escape, but leaves a lock of her hair, which the god takes to Egypt. So wonderfully fragrant is this beautiful hair that when the washermen of Pharaoh come down to wash his royal clothes, the perfume from the hair impregnates them. Vexed, the chief washerman goes down to the bank to find out where the perfume is coming from. He finds the lock of hair and takes it to the king, who consults his magicians about it. They tell him where the girl is living and advise him to send for her.

But the messengers sent by Pharaoh are killed by Bata, all but one—whom he sends back to tell the king what has happened. Next time the king sends soldiers in great number—and, more cannily, a lady chaperone, "whose hands were filled with all sorts of beautiful women's adornments." That does the trick. The girl goes back to Egypt with the escort (we must assume that Bata was out hunting that day), and, preferring the position of royal favorite to a dull life in the Valley of the Cedar, she betrays the secret of Bata's heart to the king. Down goes the tree, down goes Bata's heart; and one day Anubis (I hope you have not forgotten the remorseful older brother) sees that his pot of beer has gone bad. Knowing this for the sign, he snatches stick and sandals, clothes and weapons, and sets off for the Valley of the Cedar. After a long and arduous search he finds Bata's heart and gets it back inside Bata, whom he has discovered lying dead on his bed.

Bata is himself again, but he must revenge himself on his wife. Turning himself into a magnificent bull, he has Anubis take him to Egypt, where the king welcomes him as a sacred animal; but the worthless girl tricks the monarch into killing the beast. Next Bata becomes a pair of trees. The girl again works his destruction, but before the trees are cut down a seed from one of them falls into the girl's mouth. She becomes pregnant—with Bata himself, who, as the king's supposed son, eventually succeeds him to the throne. Bata's first act as pharaoh is to drag his wife-mother before the magistrates, who unanimously condemn her to death. He then appoints his elder brother Anubis as heir to the throne, and they live happily ever after.

I like this story, despite its misogynist attitude. I like its sublime indifference to motivation, its easily identified heroes and villainesses, and the rich inventiveness of episodes which defy logical sequence. As in the case of "The Doomed Prince," the "Tale of Two Brothers" has several familiar motifs—the hero's transformations, the talking animals, the wonderful lock of hair, and the stock hero figure of the "younger son" who overcomes numerous tribulations to become king. The first part of the story has been compared to the tale of Joseph and Potiphar's wife, while Bata's temporary death and self-castration are as harmless as the poisoning of Snow White and the Sleeping Beauty, since they can be cured by magic.

Not all Egyptian amusements were as indolent as the ones we have described. Hunting was a popular activity and, as practiced by noblemen and kings, its purpose was pleasure, not the production of food. Fowling expeditions, as we have seen, had some of the aspects of a family Sunday in the country. In the reliefs this sport was pursued in marshy regions, where the reeds grew higher than the hunter's head. He poled his light boat (made of papyrus stalks bound together) through the shallow water until he reached a spot where the birds might be hiding. If he used bow and arrow to bring them down, the arrows were blunt, designed to stun rather than kill. The throw sticks and boomerangs used in this sport were equally nonlethal; since they could be wielded by one hand, the hunter might hold a decoy in the other—a live duck which obligingly flapped and squawked to alert its wild fellows as the hunter clutched it by the feet.

Obviously it took some skill to hunt successfully with these missile weapons. It was their archery, however, in which the Egyptians took the greatest pride. The bow was used in warfare, but also in hunting, and boys practiced assiduously to gain skill in this art. They were perhaps the first of the great bowmen of history, and if we can believe the boasts they recorded, Robin Hood might never have won the golden arrow had Amenhotep II been present at the match in Nottingham Town. The Egyptian records suggest, however, that force in shooting was as important as accuracy. Amenhotep's chief pride was that he could shoot an arrow through a metal target three inches thick. "There is no one who could draw his bow," says one inscription, "not among his own army, among the rulers of foreign countries, or among the princes of Retenu, because his strength is so much greater than [that of] any king who ever lived."

The Egyptians hunted wild cattle, ibex, gazelle, and the like, but the royal prey was the lion. It took courage to hunt a lion with bow and arrow, even mounted, as the king was, in a chariot. The flimsy vehicles could easily be overturned by an enraged beast, and although the king was accompanied by attendants, there was always the chance that the lion might catch the king instead of vice versa. Thutmose III almost lost his life on one hunt, not to a lion, but an elephant; he was saved by one of his soldiers, who stepped in under the "nose" of the charging beast and drove a spear into it. Thutmose encountered his elephant on one of his Asiatic expeditions; they were not to be found in Egypt.

When he got home, exhausted and perspiring after his hunt, an Egyptian gentleman might relax with a quiet game of senet. Several board games of this type were played, and they look so intriguing that I regret that I am unable to tell the reader how to play them. You can see game boards in many museums; some Egyptians were so addicted to them that they took the games along with them into their tombs, and a few have been carefully mended, after being worn out by frequent use. The handiest

Hounds and jackals board game

of the boards were made in the shape of flat rectangular boxes, with the layout for senet on one side and another game on the other; a drawer in the box held the pieces.

The senet board had thirty squares, in three rows of ten; the pieces were little cone-shaped affairs, six to each player, and the moves were determined by the fall of a set of carved wands, thrown like pickup sticks. Senet was more like parcheesi than chess; the aim was not to take the opponent's pieces, but to progress through them back to the starting point, or to the opposite end of the board. Versions of this game can be purchased from various museum shops, but although the form is ancient, the rules are modern; it's anybody's guess as to how the fall of the sticks determined the moves. No treatise on "How to Win at Senet" has ever been found, and it is not likely that it ever will be, because the Egyptians seldom wrote textbooks.

Some scholars believe that games such as senet, like almost every other aspect of Egyptian culture, had a religious meaning; passing the hazards on the board guaranteed the player success in surviving the perils of the journey through the underworld. I offer this for what it is worth.

There is one other Egyptian habit, possibly to be classed as an amuse-ment, which I cannot resist describing, because it seems, offhand, so improbable. They went sightseeing. Not abroad, however; not if they could avoid it. A good many Egyptians did get to see the world, as royal envoys or soldiers or couriers, but the literary evidence suggests that they hated every minute of it. Wenamon, who went through a series of hu-miliating adventures when he sailed to Byblos in search of cedar, had good reason to dislike Dor, where he was robbed, and Byblos, where the prince insulted him and his country, and Cyprus, where the inhabitants tried to kill him. But an earlier story, that of Sinuhe, who won fame and fortune among the Bedouin, has the same attitude; riches and reputation notwithstanding, Sinuhe continued to long for home, and as soon as he received a summons from Pharaoh he dropped his Bedouin wife, chil-dren, and noble rank to hurry back to Egypt.

Although they were home-loving people who enjoyed the quiet of their walled gardens, some Egyptians traveled a good deal within Egypt. Clerks, officials, merchants, farmers taking produce to market—all made use of that cheap and convenient road, the Nile. And when their business in Memphis or Thebes was concluded, they did what many another weary businessman has done—they went sightseeing.

It is not surprising that the Egyptians should have been interested in their own antiquities. To an Egyptian of the Middle Kingdom the pyramids of Giza and Dahshur were as far removed in time as the oldest medieval castles are for us. And by Saite times, in the seventh century B.C., the Egyptian tourists were viewing relics that had stood for two millennia—relics that were as old, for them, as the Colosseum and the Roman Forum are for us.

There are inscriptions—we call them graffiti—scribbled all over the walls of the pyramid temples of the Fourth Dynasty by the sightseers of later periods. The pyramid at Medum was a popular spot; Eighteenth Dynasty visitors left their names and the date, and one added the comment that he found the temple "as though heaven were within it, and the sun rising in it." The private tombs were also visited, and some Saite tourists found the paintings and reliefs so admirable that they had them copied, down to the last detail, in their own tombs. But the case that intrigues me most is that of a tomb found at Deir el Bahri and excavated in 1925 by a Metropolitan Museum expedition under Herbert Winlock.

I have quoted extensively from Mr. Winlock, here and elsewhere, because he wrote a book which is, for me, one of the most delightful works on archaeology ever composed. It has the forbidding title *Excavations at Deir el Bahri*, and it is the season-by-season report of the Metropolitan Museum's excavations at that site. It was written for a "lay" audience; most of it is drawn from the reports written for the museum's bulletin. (It's not on the reading list because it is long out of print and difficult to find.)

The big monuments at Deir el Bahri are the temples of Hatshepsut and of the Eleventh Dynasty king Mentuhotep II Nebhepetre. In the 1924–25 season (expeditions in Egypt work from the fall of one year to the spring of the next, since the summer climate is frightful), the Egyptian government decided to restore the facade of Hatshepsut's temple. It had been known since the days of Mariette that there was a tomb under the temple, the tomb of a queen named Neferu, but it had never been cleared, and to visit it, it was necessary to crawl "like one of the snakes one feared to meet" (Winlock) over nasty heaps of rubbish through pitch-black underground passages. Another factor that might have deterred modern visitors was the heap of dismembered, half-burned Roman mummies that filled the tomb chapel from floor to ceiling.

When the front of the temple was cleared, the excavators found the brick facade of the queen's tomb, with the corridor leading down to the chapel. They carried out the unpleasant job of cleaning chapel and corridor, but found nothing there to reward them for their labors. Hundreds of years after the queen had been buried, the chapel had become a factory for limestone dishes, made out of the blocks that lined the walls. Only tiny fragments of the original reliefs were discovered.

From the chapel another corridor led down to the tomb chamber. This had been walled up in ancient times—fruitlessly, since robbers had penetrated the burial chamber and taken everything in it. The excavators were intrigued, not by the all-too-common evidences of theft, but by indications that the chapel had been a popular ancient tourist spot. On the small scraps of stone littering the floor, the remnants of the once-beautiful reliefs, were the names of visitors, whose admiration for the sculptures evidently did not inhibit them from scribbling all over them.

Queen Neferu lived during the Eleventh Dynasty, somewhere around 2150 B.C. Since Hatshepsut built her temple over and across the original entrance, blocking the tomb, it was assumed that the visitors who left their names must have come during the period between the Eleventh and Eighteenth Dynasties, before the temple was built. But the excavations of 1925 brought out a surprise—a narrow tunnel, built at the same time as the Eighteenth Dynasty temple, which led north from the upper temple court to the door of the tomb. There is only one plausible reason for the construction of this tunnel— to allow access to the tomb after its old entrance had been closed by the temple terrace of a later and greater queen than Neferu. Someone wanted the masterpieces of ancient relief to remain accessible, and frankly, I can't think of any religious reason why this particular monument should have rated such extraordinary effort. Was that someone Senenmut, the supposed architect of Deir el Bahri, or the queen herself, moved by some antiquarian bent? Or was it simply the demands of the "tourist trade"—despised by modern intellectuals, but prompted, in ancient Egypt as today, by the love of beauty and the sense of wonder?

Seven

"BE A SCRIBE, PUT IT IN
THY HEART"

EDUCATION

L et us return to the little Egyptian boy whom we left, some pages
back, just entering into manhood. Candor compels me to admit,
against my feminist inclinations, that Egyptian culture as we
know it was primarily the product of these grown-up boys—artists,
sculptors, administrators, kings, scribes, carpenters, goldsmiths.

We have already discussed some of the trades, and others will fall
into place as we proceed. Now it is time we took a look at the professions. If a boy wanted professional status and prestige higher than that
of a mere craftsman, his career might end in a number of different
ways, but it almost had to begin in one place—the scribal school.

Sometimes we talk about scribes as if they constituted a separate
profession, but they were really the raw materials out of which most of

the professions were formed. At the top of the ladder were administrators, courtiers, high-ranking priests, and soldiers. On the lower rungs were army scribes, court scribes, temple scribes—the secretaries and clerks and white-collar workers who kept the machinery of the state running smoothly. John A. Wilson has coined the term "white kilt" workers for this group; it is a very neat and apposite expression, which would have made sense to the Egyptians. The scribe's clean white clothes were prestige symbols, like the long fingernails of Chinese nobles; they meant that he did not have to do manual labor.

The boy whose father came of this "white kilt" class, and the boy whose ambitious father wanted to raise him into it, attended a school of some sort where he was taught to read and write. We know very little about such schools. Were they run by the temples, or by the state, or by private teachers? At what age did the boys start school? Did girls ever attend? How long did the course take? Were there postgraduate courses in foreign languages or accounting? We can guess at some of the answers, but we don't really know.

There were no little mud-brick schoolhouses in Egypt—at least none have ever been found. Some of the boys may have been taught in the nearby temple. Others might have gone to a school run by a local scribe in one room of his house. Wealthy and noble youths, one may reasonably surmise, would have had private tutors. A few privileged youths were educated in the palace itself. Some of them were the children of foreign princes, sent (willingly or under pressure) to be brought up in Egypt. Others were Egyptians of various ranks and social status. How boys were selected for this honor is unknown, but it must have smoothed the path of advancement. An ancient "old boys' network"!

The equipment for a schoolroom was simple; there were no little desks or blackboards to survive to gladden the eye of a future archaeologist. There were no schoolbooks either. Basic exercises consisted of dictation. The boys only needed writing equipment: the equivalent of pen and ink, plus a pile of ostraca—smooth fragments of broken pottery or stone which they used as slates. Beginning students didn't use papyrus; it was too expensive.

The scribe's outfit is well known, from actual examples and from drawings. The so-called palette was a narrow, rectangular piece of wood with a slot down the center to hold the pens, and depressions for cakes of ink. The pens were slender rushes pounded or chewed at one end to form a fine brush; when not in use they were kept in a pen case, which was often made in the shape of a pretty, rounded column with a flower capital. The ink came in solid form; the black was usually some kind of soot, and the red, made of red ochre, was used for rubrics, or headings. The scribe needed water to moisten his ink cakes; it was kept in a small shell or pot. One of the common hieroglyphic signs shows the scribe's outfit—the little water pot between the long palette, with its two rounded ink cakes, and the pen holder. To complete his equipment a scribe might have a burnisher for smoothing out rough spots in the papyrus, a grinder for preparing his ink, a ball of linen thread to tie around the papyrus roll when it was finished, and a rag for rubbing out mistakes. The most convenient eraser, however, was a quick swipe of the tongue.

The scribe wrote sitting on the ground, with his legs crossed; the front of his kilt, pulled taut across his knees, provided a sort of writing desk on which he could unroll his papyrus. The pot of water was on the ground at his right, the palette in his left hand; he dipped his pen into the water, rubbed it on the cake of ink, and he was ready to take dictation.

Papyrus used to grow lavishly in the swampy parts of Egypt. It is not to be found there today except in specially cultivated plots—which is a pity, because it is a pretty plant, with tall slender stalks and a feathery green tuft on top. The art of making papyrus is not lost; it is still being produced and can be purchased at souvenir shops in Egypt and museum shops elswhere. The papyrus plant must be fresh. It is cut low down, just above water level; the lower part of the stem makes the best writing material. It is cut into lengths, and the outer rind removed. The inner pith can then be cut or separated into strips one-eighth to one-fourth of an inch thick. The strips are placed on some absorbent material, parallel to one another and slightly overlapping; another lot of strips goes on top, also overlapping, and at right angles to the bottom layer. The papyrus maker then pounds the whole business with a wooden mallet. It takes an hour or more of steady pounding, in case any reader is considering the experiment. The material can be put in a press later, but the initial pounding is essential. The result is a sheet of thin "paper" whose surface can be burnished with a stone. The juices of the papyrus weld the strips together without the need of any other adhesive, but glue was used to fasten separate sheets together into the rolls the Egyptians used instead of books.

Though papyrus was comparatively cheap, it was not cheap enough to be used for the first bumbling efforts of little schoolboys, and anyone who has supplied a first-grader with notebooks can understand why Egyptian parents refused to buy papyrus for their beginners. Hence the ostraca, an ample supply of which was available in any town, free for the taking. The sweating children had to learn at least two types of writing, the pretty picture hieroglyphs and the cursive hieratic script. (Later a third form of writing, demotic, came into use.) Considering that there are hundreds of different hieroglyphic signs, the task of the budding scribe was not easy, but at least he wrote essentially the same language in all three scripts.

Once the boys had learned the signs and had acquired some vocabulary, they wrote texts from the teacher's dictation, and then the teacher corrected them. Some of the texts were fun—stories and tales—but others were less entertaining. Like most human beings, the Egyptian schoolteachers were unable to resist inculcating a moral when they had the chance. The most popular moral was the superiority of the scribal profession over all others. One text points out the spiritual advantages:

A man is perished, his corpse is dust, all his contemporaries have gone to dust; but it is writing which causes him to be remembered in the mouth of him who utters [the prayers for the dead]. More beneficial is writing than the house of a builder, or tombs in the West. It is better than an established castle, or a stela in the temple.

The text goes on, in a similarly lofty tone, to mention the names of great scribes of the past, whose tombs have been forgotten and whose houses have crumbled into dust, but whose names are remembered because of their writings. It must be emphasized that the Egyptians did not want to have their names remembered for sentimental reasons; the survival of the name, even in someone's memory, implied the survival of the personality after death.

Other texts with a related theme are less exalted. They describe, with ghoulish relish, the horrors of other occupations. The metalworker has fingers like a crocodile's hide and stinks worse than fish roe. The craftsman is so tired at night that he can hardly move, and the barber is still shaving when night falls. The contractor is dirtier than a pig from carrying mud, and the weaver has to sit in his shop all day, breathing stale air, with his knees jammed up against his belly. And so it goes, through embalmers, cobblers, bird-catchers, and every conceivable activity. But the scribe! He never goes hungry; he reaches the halls of the magistrates. Most important of all, "there is no profession free of a boss, except for that of the scribe—he is the boss!"

The boys copied all sorts of things—hoary advice from antique sages, stories, long tedious lists of nouns, poems, business letters. They did not always copy them correctly, and since some of our only copies of important literary texts come from these schoolboy exercises, we have good reason to deplore the students' lack of skill. Egyptian is not the easiest language in the world to read, particularly when it is being elegant and literary; if we have to correct the grammar and spelling of the ancient schoolboys as well, we do not have an easy time of it.

BIRDS, BEES, AND FLOWERS

The hieroglyphic Egyptian script is the most beautiful system of writing ever devised. I'll stick to that, without even a "probably." Each small sign, bird, animal, plant, could be and often was a work of art in itself. One might say, as some scholars have, that Egyptian art in general was a kind of writing—that every image has a symbolic (that word again) or specific meaning which carries a message as explicit as a written text. They can say this if they want to. I am going to confine myself in this discussion to the practical aspects of Egyptian writing.

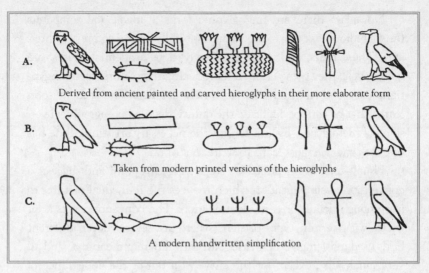

A. Derived from ancient painted and carved hieroglyphs in their more elaborate form

B. Taken from modern printed versions of the hieroglyphs

C. A modern handwritten simplification

Types of hieroglyphic scripts

Incidentally, the correct noun form for the little images is "hieroglyphs." Popular writers occasionally call them "hieroglyphics," and this small error scratches at the sensitivities of Egyptologists like a fingernail on a blackboard. The hieroglyphic (adjective) script is, of course, quite distinct from the Egyptian language. A particular script may be used to write a number of languages, and a given language may be written in more than one script. The hieroglyphs were never used to write any language other than Egyptian, but Egyptian was written in several scripts.

When I first began my study of Egyptian I was, like many students, primarily fascinated by the hieroglyphic script. This was back in the days before copying machines, and it was sometimes necessary for the advanced student to copy texts by hand, since some of the material he wanted (or was ordered) to translate occurred only in books which were out of print or hideously expensive. The little birds and flowers and people were such fun to copy that there was a deplorable tendency to spend one's study hours reproducing yards of small pictures instead of memorizing tedious grammatical rules.

Nowadays there are hieroglyphic fonts available for computers (and a tedious task it is to use them, especially for the computer illiterate). These fonts, and those used by various academic presses, are quite lovely; they come close to reproducing the pictures as the Egyptians carved them, and they are finely detailed. The student soon learns that he cannot duplicate the dainty, detailed typographical versions of hieroglyphs. Even if he has the necessary artistic skill he has not the time. He must learn to write, not draw.

Usually one of his professors steps in at this point and suggests a convention of simplification which reduces the individual pictures to just enough detail for easy identification. The convention gets a bit tricky with certain types of signs; there are several dozen different birds used in hieroglyphic writing, all with different meanings, and all very much alike except for the curve of a tail or the appearance of crests and tufts at strategic spots. One interesting fact which emerges from the simplification techniques is that the hieroglyphic handwriting of two different people is as distinctive as their English hands. We students could usually tell who had copied a particular text even when it was not signed.

Once the student has conquered his initial preoccupation with the pretty pictures and learned to write a few hundred signs, he comes up against a rather awful fact—namely, that he is learning not only a script, but a language. This comes home to him, if it has not already done so, when he begins to use the standard textbook, Sir Alan Gardiner's *Egyptian Grammar*. This book, which has over six hundred pages, is now in its third edition. Although arranged like a typical grammar, with exercises and vocabulary after each lesson, it is also a standard reference work.

The student sails along bravely through the beginning chapters of the monumental *Grammar*. Egyptian lacks declension endings and has only two genders, which facts make the noun and adjective in Egyptian fairly simple. But then the student gets to the second semester and hits the Egyptian verb, and the casualties begin. I do not intend to discuss the Egyptian verb. The proper study of the phenomenon requires a lifetime. Suffice it to say there are a lot of different verb forms

Bird hieroglyphs in a modern handwritten convention

in the language, written almost identically and differing widely in meaning.

However, let us assume that the student has survived the first year of Egyptian. What he has learned—not too well—is only one form of the language, and not the earliest form. The "classical" dialect of Egyptian is what we call Middle Egyptian, although its use was not restricted to the Middle Kingdom, and it is this which the student tackles first. During the earlier Old Kingdom another form of the language was written, and Old Egyptian was not exactly identical with the dialect which we have in the Pyramid Texts. In the late Eighteenth Dynasty the form known as Late Egyptian begins to be used for written texts. Probably it had been a spoken language earlier than that time; it is not unusual for the written language to be slow in reflecting the changes which have taken place in spoken idiom.

So far, we have been talking about various forms of the Egyptian language, all of which are written in hieroglyphic script. They were written in another script as well—the "shorthand" form known as hieratic. The hieroglyphs looked handsome on the walls of tombs and temples, but they were as unwieldy for a busy Egyptian scribe as they are for us. Just as we simplify the hieroglyphic pictures in order to write them more quickly, the ancient scribes began to use cursive forms. Over the years—and the process began very early, almost as soon as writing itself appeared—the forms became more and more cursive, until eventually the hieratic signs bore only a distant resemblance to their hieroglyphic ancestors. The hieratic was written with a brush, on papyrus or potsherds, but even this script was too tedious for the overworked scribes of the later bureaucracy. About 700 B.C. they developed another script, called demotic. Hieratic writing is child's play compared to demotic; at its worst demotic consists of row upon row of agitated commas, each of which represents a totally different sign. It is perfectly dreadful stuff to read. Take a look at the right-hand column of the box and picture yourself trying to decipher a page of

Examples of hieroglyphic, hieratic, and demotic signs

that—not on clean white paper, but on yellowed, faded, crumbling, rotten papyrus.

Stoop-shouldered and myopic, suffering from headaches and pains in the lumbar region, our hypothetical modern student has now, we may assume, mastered all the forms of the Egyptian language and script mentioned so far. But he is not finished. The last form of Egyptian, Coptic, was not written in hieroglyphs or demotic or hieratic, but in the Greek alphabet, eked out with a few signs derived from demotic to express sounds which did not occur in Greek. Coptic was replaced by Arabic as the national language of Egypt after the Moslem Conquest, but it survived in the liturgy of the Coptic (Egyptian Christian) church. There are no longer men in Egypt who speak the tongue of Thutmose III, but there were small Coptic-speaking groups in remote regions of the country as late as the 1930s.

Coptic employs the Greek script, but it is an Egyptian language, although there are numerous Greek words added to the vocabulary. The literature is not too exciting to an Egyptologist, who usually closes his book at the Persian Conquest; the monks who wrote the texts were concerned with abstruse theological doctrines, not history. But it is one of the subjects in which a candidate for the doctorate is supposed to show proficiency—laughable word—along with demotic, hieratic, Middle and Late and Old Egyptian, archaeology, art, history, and the archaeology and history and languages of related areas which he has also studied.

Since it used the Greek alphabet, Coptic reproduced the vowels. Thus, we know how this form of the language was pronounced, which is not true of any other form of Egyptian. Hieroglyphic writing expresses only the consonants, and since hieratic and demotic are derived from hieroglyphs, the same is true of them. Therefore, when Egyptologists transliterate Egyptian into English script, they write a word with only the consonants: "nfr" or "bn." When students read the texts aloud in class they follow a convention which inserts an "e" between consonants to facilitate articulation: "nefer," "ben." Some of the so-called semiconsonants are vocalized as vowels: the reed leaf as a long "i," the chick as "oo" or "w," and the akh bird as "a." But if you listen to someone reading Egyptian aloud, following this convention, you will not be hearing Egyptian "as she was spoke" in 750 B.C. The convention is allowed only because the true vocalization is still in doubt. Indeed, it is wonderful that we have attained a state of doubt, rather than one of pure ignorance, in view of the fact that we have only the consonants. We have the Coptic, yes; but it was not written down until almost three thousand years after the first texts in Old Egyptian were composed. A language can change quite a lot in three thousand years. Another useful but limited clue comes from the examples of Egyptian words written in other ancient languages; the names of the kings and queens mentioned in the Amarna letters are rendered in cuneiform script, whose syllabic signs consisted of a consonant plus a vowel.

When we come to the problem of rendering Egyptian names in English, we run into another field of controversy. Among themselves Egyptologists transliterate, reproducing only the consonants which are given by the hieroglyphic signs. But you cannot call Thutmose the Great "Djhwty-ms" and expect anybody but an Egyptologist to recognize him. The name "Thutmose" is one of the more deplorable conventions. The element "Thut" comes from "Thoth," the Greek word for the god of wisdom, whose Egyptian name was Djhuty. "Mose" means "born" in Egyptian. So we have a bastardized form, half-Greek and half-Egyptian, which is unaesthetic and inaccurate, but so well known that it is inexpedient to attempt to change it. I have taken the easy way out in this book by using the versions which come most readily to me, even when more learned persons disagree. The word for the little servant statues which the Egyptians put in their tombs has been read as "ushebti," "shawabti," and "shabti." I learned the first rendering, so that's the one I use. I have tried to avoid such "dated" forms as Ikhnaton, which is what James Henry Breasted called the Great Heretic; the initial sound was probably pronounced "akh" rather than "ikh." (The "kh" is a guttural, like German or Scotch "ch.") But when it comes to Amon versus Amen versus Amun, the reader can take his choice. (Whichever one he uses, he will probably be scolded by some Egyptologist.)

The said reader being intelligent and well educated, I will not insult him by mentioning that hieroglyphs are not an alphabetic script. The first steps in the process of writing were probably based on whole words. The picture of a bee meant "bee," and the picture of an arrowhead meant "arrowhead." But the utility of writing could be readily expanded by the application of what we call the rebus principle. The word for "brother" had the same consonants as the word for "arrowhead"—"s" and "n." The Egyptians could then use an arrowhead to write the word "brother." But there was an ambiguity in writing which did not occur in speech. The two words may have been pronounced differently, but since the vowels were not written, they looked exactly alike in script. The Egyptian solution to this problem was typically ingenious and typically complex. When they wanted to write "brother," they added a second sign to the arrowhead—a seated man, which designated the class "human." By the use of the class signs, or determinatives, the Egyptians could distinguish many words which, in their consonants, were otherwise identical.

The consonantal signs, as opposed to the determinatives, represented sounds—one or two or more consonants. A single consonantal sign might represent an entire word, or it might be combined with other signs to make up a word. Let's look at a few examples.

The sign which is transliterated "nfr" and pronounced "nefer" depicts the heart and windpipe of an animal, but for some reason it means "good," or "beautiful." Nefer is a triliteral sign, expressing three consonants all by itself, without any help from anybody (a). But when the Egyptians wrote the word "beautiful," they usually added the signs for "f" and "r" (b). The word was not read "neferefer" but "nefer"; the additional signs merely firmed up the reading. However, the nefer sign could be used alone, in a compound word such as "nefer-hat" (c), "diadem." The second sign in this group is the forequarters of a lion, and it means, as you might expect, "front." Now when "nefer" was used as a noun, a determinative was added to the sign—a papyrus roll tied with a bow, which indicated the class of abstractions (d). "Neferet" could also be a woman's name—the additional "t" is the feminine ending—and in this case the determinative for the class "woman" is

Various uses of the hieroglyphic signs

added (e). Logically enough, this determinative is the tiny figure of a seated woman. As this example shows, the hieroglyphs were not the mysterious, esoteric signs that earlier scholars believed them to be. At times they are almost too concrete for refined tastes. The determinative for the verb "to give birth" (f) is self-explanatory.

Incidentally, the plural in Egyptian is indicated by three strokes or by a threefold repetition of the word sign, and it adds a "w" to the reading of the singular. "Neferew," "beauties," is written with three windpipes (g)—a particularly unfelicitous choice, I admit. Some years ago a novel on ancient Egypt contained a heroine with the melodious name "nefer-nefer-nefer." After reading the preceding paragraphs, you can see that no Egyptian lady, even a courtesan, would have had such a name, and you can also understand the misinterpretation which led the author into his little error.

You have no doubt noted another point worth pursuing, though I slid over it very slyly. If "nefer" can be written with separate signs for "f" and "r," did the Egyptians have an alphabet after all?

Curiously enough, they had the makings of one. There are about two dozen signs which represent single sounds. With a certain amount of ingenuity, these could have been used to write the entire Egyptian vocabulary. You can use them to inscribe your name, or any other English word, in hieroglyphs, if you ever feel an urgent need to do so. The Egyptians never took the seemingly simple but tremendous step of eliminating all but single-sound signs. Don't ask me why, because I don't know. Yet the birds and bees of the ancient Egyptian script may have a more direct relationship to our own alphabet than we realize.

Back in the first decade of the twentieth century, the ubiquitous Flinders Petrie was working in the wilds of the Sinai Peninsula, disregarding its hellish climate with his usual equanimity. There were plenty of Egyptian inscriptions to copy, for the Egyptians had mined the beautiful blue-green turquoise of Sinai since earliest times. But among the material Petrie found were tablets carved in a curious script, some of whose signs were clearly derived from hieroglyphs, while others were of unknown origin. Petrie copied the texts, although he could not read them, in the same spirit which had led him to preserve his tattered scraps of linen. A decade later, the material came to the attention of Professors T. E. Peet and Alan H. Gardiner, who were working over the entire body of Sinai inscriptions. Gardiner took up the copies of the strange unknown script reluctantly, for he had little hope of eliciting anything useful from them. The first sign he noticed was an ox-head, and he remembered an old theory that the letters of the Hebrew alphabet had been based on the acrophonic principle. Let not the reader be dismayed by this word; he has been acquainted with the principle from a tender age, unless he is young enough to have been subjected to a "progressive" education; the old first-grade readers used acrophony in their "A is for apple, B is for ball" routines. In regard to the Hebrew alphabet, the original simple picture sign came to stand for the initial letter of the word depicted, and the name of the letter was the same as the object. "Aleph," which in Hebrew corresponds to our "A" as the first letter of the alphabet, meant "ox-head."

Could the strange script be an alphabetic one, Gardiner asked himself, with the ox-head standing for "aleph"? The examples from Sinai have been dated to the Eighteenth Dynasty, which seems too early for such a development; yet there were Semitic-speaking people in Egypt and in Sinai at that time. When Gardiner looked further he found other correspondences. His moment of triumph came when he was able to read the word "Baalat" by using the Semitic meanings he had assigned to various signs. This is the name of the feminine counterpart of the Baal of the Old Testament and would logically appear on tablets dedicated by Semitic workers to a goddess whose Egyptian form was Hathor, goddess of love and beauty—and Hathor was the protective divinity of this mining community, where she was known as "Lady of the Turquoise."

The process by which these unsung geniuses derived a system of alphabetic writing might have been as follows: they knew the shapes of the hieroglyphic signs, which covered the rocky cliffs where they worked, although they could not give them their Egyptian names. So they took the water sign, which is Egyptian for "n," and read it as their word for water—"mem," or something of the sort. Application of the acrophonic principle gave them the meaning "m" for the sign. Using Egyptian signs, and their own words for the objects they represented, the Semitic miners worked out a genuinely alphabetic script which spread to Phoenicia and heaven knows where else, and eventually became the ancestor of our own alphabet.

"Baalat" was Gardiner's high point; other attempts to apply the principle to additional groups of signs did not work so well.

However, in the past few years John and Deborah Darnell, a pair of Egyptologists working in the desert areas west of Thebes, have turned up new inscriptions that indicate the beginning of an alphabetic system several hundred years earlier than the Sinai inscriptions. The graffiti, relatively crude and short, were presumably left on the limestone cliffs of the Wadi el Hol by men who patrolled the tracks leading to and from Thebes, and like the Sinai inscriptions they are thought to be the work of Semitic-speaking people—possibly mercenaries from Asia, who developed a crude but easy-to-use system of writing from the pictograms of Egyptian hieroglyphs. Clever chaps, these Semites! (It should be added that Semitic is a linguistic, not a racial, term. Arabic and Hebrew, among others, are Semitic languages.)

The Egyptian schoolboys had no easy-to-use system. They had to memorize hundreds of different signs. Since there are no textbooks, we assume that most of the instruction was oral. How far this instruction went we cannot know. Egyptian grammar has been analyzed according to modern rules, derived, in part, from the model of Latin grammar, so our Egyptian textbooks take up nouns and verbs and adjectives and tell the student what forms of a verb express futurity, participial action, and so on; but this is a modern convention that would have made little sense to an Egyptian scribe.

It is unlikely that Egyptian schoolchildren were treated to lectures on grammar and syntax. They learned the correct forms as children learn to speak their native tongue correctly—by example and practice. I have always suspected, without being able to prove it, that Egyptian scribes may have been aware of the functions of such things as determinatives, and that they might have had a few simple verbal rules for their use. For example, the word "sesh," written with the hieroglyph of the scribe's palette, could be a verb, "write," or a noun, "scribe." (It could mean other things too, but let's not confuse the issue.) If the word in question was supposed to be "write," the determinative indicating the class of abstractions was added to the palette sign. If it was "writer, scribe," the man determinative was used instead. In its most obvious form, the determinative principle is one a harassed schoolboy might have worked out for himself. Suppose he encounters the word "scribe" in dictation for the first time. He knows how to spell the verb "write," and with other examples in mind, and the cold eye of the teacher upon him, he might extrapolate and write "scribe" as "write," minus the abstract determinative and plus the man determinative. He was stimulated to do his best by a principle succinctly expressed by the Egyptians: "A boy's ears are on his back, and he listens best when he is beaten."

Reading and writing were the main subjects, but some scribes had to acquire other specializations. Arithmetic must have been a basic course, for whether he ended up as an army scribe calculating rations, or a temple scribe in charge of the god's property, or a court scribe concerned with architecture and construction work, the scribe usually had to be able to do simple arithmetic. The subject was certainly taught, but how, and by whom, we don't know.

Another specialty which became important after the beginning of the New Kingdom was foreign languages. Even if we had no evidence we would suspect that at a wealthy cosmopolitan court there would have to be some men who knew enough foreign tongues to deal with traders, envoys, and messengers from other countries. The Amarna tablets, found at that site, show that Egyptian kings of this period carried on constant correspondence with their representatives in the conquered cities of Syria-Palestine, and also with brother kings in the great empires of Mitanni, Hatti, and Babylonia. The "Foreign Ministry" scribes did not need to learn all the languages of these areas, for the diplomatic lingua franca of the period was Akkadian, just as Latin was an international language in the Middle Ages. There must have been a group of scribes at the royal court who could read Akkadian and press the little wedge-shaped characters onto the clay tablets on which they were commonly written.

The boys would absorb some history (or the Egyptian equivalent) and some literature, rhetoric, and ethics through the texts they copied. We will probably never know what other subjects, if any, were imparted straight from the mouth of the teacher into the heads of the boys. They had a formidable task just with reading and writing; the happiest moment of the day must have been lunchtime, when their mothers appeared with their bread and beer. But when they graduated from the schoolroom they had, in their knowledge of the "writings," the key to advancement. It could lead to high office or, more commonly, to a comfortable, respectable post in the entourage of king, god, or noble.

THE HEKANAKHTE LETTERS

On the veranda of his house, a youngish man named Mersu relaxed after the noonday meal. It was a day in July or August, somewhere in the neighborhood of 2000 B.C. The sun beat down on the dusty earth of the courtyard; from the women's quarters at the rear of the house came the shrill voice of Mersu's wife, trying to collect the children for their afternoon rest. The noise did not disturb Mersu; he was used to it.

He was just about to close his eyes and drift off into slumber when the sight of a man—a newcomer—passing through the gates brought him upright in his chair. The man was a messenger; in one hand he carried a roll of papyrus. Mersu clasped both hands over his belly; there it was again, that odd little pain that had bothered him lately, especially after eating. Then he stood up to receive the letter from his father.

Mersu's father, Hekanakhte, was ka-priest of a vizier named Ipi, who lived and died during the First Intermediate Period. When this great man was buried in his tomb near Thebes, he left estates in that area whose produce was to be spent on the upkeep of his tomb and the ceremonies necessary to keep his spirit alive and well nourished. Hekanakhte was the man in charge of the funerary arrangements on behalf of the vizier; his own salary came out of the produce of the estates. He lived in a little village called Nebsyt, a few miles from Thebes and the tomb he tended. His sizable family included his five sons—Mersu the eldest, Senebnut and Sihathor, both grown men, and the younger boys Anubis and Snefru. The older sons were married, and their families lived with Hekanakhte. In addition, there were various unattached women: Hekanakhte's old mother, a poor relation called Hetepet, and a woman who may have been a widowed daughter. An important member of the group, though not a member of the family, was Hekanakhte's assistant, Heti. It was a big family and, as one might suspect, not always a harmonious one.

From time to time Hekanakhte had to leave home in order to visit the other properties for which he was responsible. He stayed away on these trips for many months, leaving Mersu in charge of things; but though he was gone he was not forgotten. He bombarded Mersu with letters, and Mersu, who was trying to manage his father's obstreperous household as well as carry out his priestly duties, used to take these lengthy epistles up to an empty tomb near the bigger tomb of Ipi, where he could ponder their words of wisdom in peace. When the empty tomb was ready to be occupied, the workers swept the accumulated debris, including the letters—which Mersu evidently discarded after reading them—into a hole in the floor and covered them up. There they stayed until they were discovered by archaeologists in

1922. They form one of the most fascinating pictures of family life from any ancient culture. One of the people intrigued by them was Agatha Christie, who used the characters, though not under the same names, as the basis for her story of murder in ancient Egypt, *Death Comes as the End*.

I always picture Hekanakhte as a skinny little old man, somewhat flabby around the middle, but active as a cricket. In my mental image he has no hair on top of his head, only a fringe of gray over his ears. When he remembers to do so he slaps a dusty black wig on his head. He carries a long staff, which he uses like a vaulter's pole to turn his shuffling walk into a series of quick hops. His face is wrinkled and his nose is beaky, but his black eyes are bright and alert, peering suspiciously out at the world from under lowering brows.

The letter Mersu received that summer afternoon asked him to send his father five bushels of wheat and as much barley as he could scrape together, plus any food that was not needed for the family. The inundation was about to begin, and Hekanakhte's letter includes the following ominous remarks: "As for any flooding on our land, it is you who are cultivating it, and I shall hold you responsible. Be very active in cultivating, and be very careful. Guard the produce of my grain! Guard everything of mine; for I shall hold you responsible for it. And if my land floods—too bad for you!"

Several other letters followed this one, but Mersu did not save any until the next summer, during which time Hekanakhte remained away. Conditions in Egypt were bad; the inundation had been low, and crop failures had caused near-famine in many areas. Hekanakhte's letter says that he has managed to find some food and plans to send it to the family. Evidently it was not an abundant supply, for the old man meticulously lists the shares due each member of the family. "Now you must not be angry about this," he insists. "See, the whole household, as well as the children, are dependent on me, and everything is mine." Then he quotes a pair of hoary proverbs—"The hungry must hunger" and "Half life is better than dying altogether"—and proceeds, working himself up into quite a passion: "Why, here they have begun to eat men and women! There are none anywhere else to whom such food is

given. You must give this food to my people only while they are working. Mind this! Make the most of my land, strive to the uttermost, dig
the ground with your noses. See, if you are industrious, men will praise
God for you. Lucky that I can support you! And if any one of the men
or women spurn the food, let him come here to me, and stay with me,
and live as I live! Not," he concludes self-pityingly, "that there is anyone who will come here to me."

Between lectures on general behavior, Hekanakhte gave explicit
directions for the management of the property in Thebes—what field
to sow with what seed, the names of men to whom land was to be
rented, and so on. Hekanakhte was worried for fear someone would
get more than his due, and he warned his harassed son that if anyone
was overpaid, the excess would be deducted from Mersu's own share. It
seems that Mersu had everything to lose and nothing to win; when
there were losses he had to make them good, but Hekanakhte never
offered to reward him for gains made by his good management. One of
the letters found in the cache had never been opened until the modern excavators broke its seal; it was full of helpful hints on business,
and one cannot resist the suspicion that Mersu, driven to distraction,
dropped it unread into the handy hole in the floor and went on to do
his work in his own way.

One surprising factor about life at this period is the amount of
letter-writing which must have been carried on. We have only Hekanakhte's letters to Mersu, but from what he says it is evident that he was
getting letters, not only from Mersu, but from other relatives, all complaining, tattling on one another, and going behind Mersu's back to
report their animosities to the absent father of the family. Hekanakhte
threw himself into all the quarrels with relish. The poor relation Hetepet was evidently unpopular; in one letter Hekanakhte says irritably,
"I have already told you, do not keep a woman friend of Hetepet's away
from her. Take great care of her, although of course you don't want her
with you." The two youngest boys were also a trial to their elder brother.
Anubis wrote to the old father complaining that Mersu had taken
some of his things, and Hekanakhte shot right back with "Give back to
him any article of Anubis's that you have, and whatever is missing, pay

him back for it. Don't make me write to you about it again! I have already written to you twice about it!" The youngest boy, Snefru, was his father's spoiled darling, and Hekanakhte constantly nagged Mersu to be sure the brat was kept happy. "I have been told that [Snefru] is unhappy. Take great care of him, and give him food, and salute him from [me] a thousand times, a million times! Take great care of him and send him off to me directly after you have cultivated." But Snefru refused his father's invitation, and the following year Hekanakhte wrote feebly, "And if Snefru wants to look after the bulls, then put him to looking after them. He doesn't want to be running up and down cultivating with you, nor does he wish to come here with me. Indeed, whatever he wants, you must let him enjoy it."

One would think that Hekanakhte had troubles enough with his quarrelsome brood of children and dependents, but he did not know when to leave well enough alone. He never mentions a wife, so presumably he was a widower. In a burst of elderly vigor he decided to take a concubine or second wife (the word used indicates a status above that of a mistress), and this damsel destroyed what little peace was left in the house. She had not been there long before Hekanakhte was writing: "What am I supporting you for, you five boys, and what can my concubine do to you? As to doing any harm to my concubine, take warning! You aren't associated with me as my partner! If you would shut up, it would be a very good thing," he concludes vulgarly.

The concubine, Iutenheb, managed to irritate everybody. Hekanakhte ordered his son to fire one maid who had threatened or offended the girl; he warned Mersu against the third son, Sihathor, too. There was also trouble with a tenant named Ip. In despair the old man finally instructed Mersu to send the charming bone of contention to him; this letter is full of sententious complaints like "How can I ever live with you in one establishment, if you will not respect a concubine for my sake?"

It is no wonder that Miss Christie, the expert on murder, saw violent potentialities in the Hekanakhte household. But perhaps they were no worse than they are in a lot of families, particularly those which are complicated by poor relations, grandmothers, and the equivalent of a stepmother living with grown sons. (Just what was Sihathor doing to the concubine, one wonders?) It is certainly an amusing and nearly unique picture of daily life—the daily activities, quarrels, and resentments of an average "white kilt" family of the second millennium B.C. We do not get such periscopes into the past very often, and it is amazing how effective this one is, and what a clear picture we are given of the personalities involved. Hekanakhte is more than a personality; he is a "character" in the full slang sense of the word, with his fussy "now mind this" and "pay attention to what I say" larding every letter and his constant prickling reminders that the whole family is dependent on him. Some of the relationships I have described have been questioned; it has been suggested that Mersu was a younger brother, not a son, of Hekanakhte, but that doesn't alter my image of him as prematurely balding and suffering from an incipient ulcer. Let us hope that when the crotchety old man died he left the property to the man who had been charged with its maintenance, and that Mersu was able to get his contentious relatives in order.

THE SCRIBE AND THE BUREAUCRACY

One of the significant aspects of Egyptian life which is brought out by the Hekanakhte letters is the combination in one man of functions which we would consider incompatible, or at least divergent. Hekanakhte's "job" was that of ka-priest to the deceased vizier, which meant that he was supposed to make the offerings to the dead man's soul at such times as the mortuary contract stated. We would define this as a priestly function. However, Hekanakhte's letters show that he spent a lot of time administering the lands left by the vizier to supply his tomb offerings. He was more of a bailiff than a priest.

The higher the position in the bureaucracy, the greater the variety of the official's responsibilities. There was considerable division of labor in the Egyptian economy, and craftsmen were real specialists in their own lines. We know of sandal-makers, bakers, carpenters, bird-catchers, beekeepers, janitors, mat-makers, incense molders, goldsmiths and coppersmiths, fishermen, and dozens of others. But when we get to the upper echelons of high officials, we find that they could turn their hands to just about anything.

The career of Senenmut, Hatshepsut's favorite, is a good example. He was a prophet of Montu (priesthood); chief steward of Amon and overseer of the god's storehouses, orchards, and other property (temple administration); chief steward of the king (civil administration); overseer of works (construction, engineering, architecture); tutor of the queen's daughter and steward of her estates, prince and count, sole companion, wearer of the royal seal; and at one point in his active life he may also have been a soldier. It is true that many of these offices could have been rewards for a particular talent for administration. The president of a big modern corporation may have under him artists, machinists, truck drivers, engineers, and so on; in the Egyptian sense he could be described as overseer of truck drivers, chief artist, and supervisor of engineers. Perhaps some of the talents which we ascribe to these Egyptian jacks-of-all-trades may have been supervisory only. Even so, it is evident that some of our modern categories are not applicable. The president of the corporation would not preach sermons from the pulpit on alternate Sundays, nor be sent as a field officer to lead an army on a campaign, as one Fourth Dynasty official was.

An Egyptian official would have been baffled by the suggestion that he render unto Caesar those things which were Caesar's and unto God those things which were His. Caesar was God—or at least god—and there was no functional difference between church and state. At some periods a single man might hold both the vizierate and the high priesthood of Amon, the supreme civil and sacerdotal positions. This concept explains, to some extent, the apparent overlapping of functions which we find in so many official careers.

However, we must also take into account the attitude of the ancients toward aptitude and talent and professional training. Parents did not worry about selecting a career for their boy which would employ his highest abilities or suit his fancy. Undoubtedly there were men of genius who followed their proper bent, and boys of ambition and talent who raised themselves out of obscure backgrounds to the rank of "prince and count." Except for the scribal schools, however, training must have been by the apprentice system, and a boy's best teacher was his father, who could not only teach him the tricks of the trade but could bequeath to him the tools and the goodwill which he had acquired. Even the high administrative offices, though theoretically bestowed by the king, tended to run in certain families. When the king's faithful old vizier died, his logical successor was the son who had so long profited from his father's wisdom and experience.

At the top of the ladder, of course, was the king. Actually, he was not really on the ladder; he sat suspended in air several feet above it. The notion of the divinity of the king has been questioned, but not seriously shaken; by dogma he certainly was a god, and if his subjects, singly or en masse, ever regarded him as less than sacred such a viewpoint never got into an official publication. He owned the land and its people; he bestowed all offices, heard all complaints, led all armies, and was high priest of every god. Obviously there was a gap between dogma and practice; the king could not be in a hundred places at once. His religious functions were delegated, and his executive activities were supported by the vizier and by a whole cabinet of officials.

The vizier was the highest of all officials, the deputy of the king in all the affairs of state. In the Old Kingdom the office was usually held by a prince of the royal blood, as were other important positions. Later, commoners could aspire to the job.

The vizier's responsibilities were awesome. He was in charge of just about everything. Though many of his duties were delegated, the office apparently got too complicated for a single occupant, and by the Eighteenth Dynasty there were two viziers, one for Upper and one for Lower Egypt. This was Egypt's imperial age, and as one might expect, the bureaucracy expanded with the empire. It isn't always easy for us to understand the table of organization, since the Egyptians didn't use the same categories we do. The Ministry of Works, for example, involved viziers, treasurers, and priests. However, from the inscriptions of the period it is possible to get a general idea of how the system worked.

Under each vizier was an Overseer of the Treasury, who kept track of taxes and tribute. The Overseers of the Granaries and of Cattle worked closely with the Treasurer, since much of the national wealth consisted of produce rather than cash. The king's personal officials included the Steward, who administered the vast royal estates, the Chamberlain, in charge of the domestic details of the palace, and the First Herald, who supervised the palace guard and did a lot of other things we wouldn't consider consistent with that semimilitary post. The army had its own organization, as did the temples, but these categories were not mutually exclusive; a man might hold the supreme priestly office at the same time he occupied a high administrative position. The highest office was not always the one that wielded the greatest power; Senenmut, Steward of Amon under Hatshepsut, was certainly one of her most influential officials, though he was technically subordinate to several other men. This phenomenon is not entirely unknown in modern times.

There were literally dozens of other titles—Fanbearer on the Right of the King, Overseer of the Harem, Pages and Scribes of this and that, Overseers, Accountants, and Herdsmen. The title of Judge is known, but justice was apparently one of those categories which the Egyptians didn't consider a separate department, as we do. The king was supreme judge, of course; the vizier was instructed, when he assumed office, that the administration of justice was in his hands, but actual courts of law, that of the vizier as well as local courts, varied in composition from case to case and were presided over by priests and soldiers as well as by different officials.

There are no written law codes as such from ancient Egypt. However, the judge, whoever he might be, was expected to follow certain standards—conformity with maat, the divine order, which, as various references make clear, implied justice and impartiality. In theory even the humblest citizen could demand his rights from high officials.

The so-called "Tale of the Eloquent Peasant" (all such titles are modern) embodies this ideal. It's one of the most intriguing texts from ancient Egypt and must have been extremely popular, since several copies have survived. It starts as a simple narrative. The peasant, Khun-Anup, heads for Egypt from his home in the Wadi Natrun, in order to barter grain and other commodities. As he nears the house of a minor official named Nemtynakht, the official covets his goods and concocts a scheme whereby he can get possession of them. The path at that point is narrow, with a field of barley on one side and water on the other side; Nemtynakht spreads a sheet across the path and warns the peasant not to let his donkeys step on it. "Okay," says the peasant. (I translate freely.) "I'll just go around." The only way he can go is along the very edge of the barley field. Nemtynakht complains again, and while they are arguing one of the donkeys takes a mouthful of barley. That gives the corrupt official his chance; he confiscates the peasant's property, donkeys and all, in compensation for a "wisp" of barley, and beats the victim until he flees, weeping. The peasant then appeals to the High Steward, Nemtynakht's boss. His protest, which is given in full, is so beautifully expressed that the steward tells the king about it, and the intrigued monarch orders Khun-Anup detained, so that he will go on making elegant speeches. "Have a scribe write down everything he says and have it brought to me."

There are nine petitions in all, and they are indeed eloquent, embodying sophisticated literary techniques that would certainly be remarkable if they came from the mouth of an illiterate peasant. At the end the peasant prevails and is given all the property of the crooked official.

The story is fiction, of course, and the peasant's eventual triumph is due not so much to the rights and wrongs of the case as to the fact that he is an orator of superb caliber. Still, his venturing to approach the High Steward in the first place, and his stubborn persistence, are indicative of an ideal of fair play. One nice little touch is that at the beginning of the poor fellow's ordeal the king orders that food be given to him every day, adding, "Provide for his wife and children too. A peasant like that doesn't come here until his house is almost empty."

Peasants were at the bottom of the heap, the base of the social pyramid—so, the text implies, if one of them can sue for justice, anybody can!

Slavery, as a widely practiced institution, cannot be definitely proved in Egypt before the Eighteenth Dynasty, but it certainly existed then. Slaves were prisoners of war or criminals, working out their sentences by toiling in the mines or on public works. Not on the pyramids of Giza, though. The men who built these astonishing structures and others like them were Egyptians and free men. Recent excavations at Giza have found not only the nice little tombs they built for themselves in their spare time, but the kitchens and bakeries that supplied them with the food that was part of their pay. The privilege of building a tomb in that favored location was certainly a valued perk, and though the bones of the workmen show the results of hard physical labor, they also show that medical services were available.

In later periods most slaves were owned by the state—which included the temples—but private persons, some of them pretty low in the social scale themselves, might also have a slave or two. Although these unfortunates could be bought and sold or rented out like any other piece of property, they were in some ways better off than the ordinary peasant. They were entitled to food and lodging, clothes and ointment, and those who worked in great households might rise to positions of considerable importance. We know that some were emancipated, and others even married into the families of their owners.

The poor farmer on his little plot of land might well envy the well-dressed, plump slaves of the great noble. Technically he was a free man, but in actual fact he was not much more than a serf. He was harassed by numerous obligations to the state and to his immediate superiors, and he spent most of his waking hours at work in his fields—when he was not hauling stones for pyramids and other buildings or "chastising" various enemies of Egypt. We know very little about them, these men and women who made up the great majority of "the Egyptians." It seems unfair that we should have less information on the long generations of "common folk" than on any of the better-known pharaohs. Yet not one of the mighty rulers of Egypt—not even Akhenaton—seems quite as real as a fussbudget named Hekanakhte, who was only an insignificant ka-priest of an unimportant vizier named Ipi.

Eight

"I FOUGHT INCREDIBLY"

THE ARMY

A t some point in his life almost every little boy wants to be a
soldier. These days he can be a Roman soldier, complete with
plastic greaves and breastplate, an intergalactic trooper, or a
knight in armor, but these are merely variations on the basic theme—
a love for legitimized mayhem, which is a congenital characteristic of
most human males (and, admittedly, some females). The little Egyptian boy was probably no different. Since there were no toy manufac-
turers to influence his tastes, his choice was obvious: he wanted to be
an Egyptian soldier.

Among the texts which schoolboys had to copy were several which
might be subtitled "Why Not to Choose a Military Career." Here is
one of them:

Come, let me tell you of the woes of the soldier! He is awakened at any hour, and he is driven like a donkey. He works till the sun sets. He is hungry, his body is exhausted, he is dead while yet alive.

He is called up for Syria. His marches are high in the mountains. He drinks water every three days and it is foul with the taste of salt. His body is broken with dysentery. The enemy comes and surrounds him with arrows, and life fades from him. They say, "Hasten on, brave soldier—win a good name for yourself!"—but he is barely conscious and his legs are weak.

When victory comes, His Majesty hands over the captives to be taken down into Egypt. The foreign woman is faint with marching, so she hangs on to the neck of the soldier. His knapsack falls and others take it while he is loaded down with the Syrian woman. His wife and children are in their village, but he dies and never reaches it.

Frightful, isn't it? I have had to prune this text considerably, for it goes on at length. We might suspect that the glamour of the military life was great, since the schoolmaster had to conjure up such horrific pictures to combat it. We may also wonder whether budding scribes had any choice in the matter. There was a form of military conscription; was there also such a thing as student exemptions from the draft? Not very likely.

The text I have quoted dates from a period when soldiering could be a profession. In the Old Kingdom, under the pyramid builders, there was probably no large standing army. When trouble arose with the Libyans or the Nubians, the king ordered his local governors, or nomarchs, to levy troops. This may have resulted in a situation resembling the press gangs of eighteenth-century England, with the nomarch's men dragging reluctant heroes out of pretended sickbeds or caves in the hills or local taverns. One gets the impression that the Egyptians were never keen on fighting. "The army," if one can give that name to a big disorganized militia, was not only called up for military campaigns. Under regular military commanders it was also employed for state work projects—quarrying, digging canals, and perhaps helping to build pyramids.

Some scholars believe that there must have been some sort of professional standing army even in the Old Kingdom. They assume that the king had sense enough to realize the danger of relying on troops who owed their immediate loyalty to the local prince who had called them up. This is a reasonable assumption, but there is no evidence that it was the case, except for the royal bodyguard, whose members could officer an amateur army in case of war. Although there is mention of a rank called "army commander," possibly the equivalent of "general," one of the most famous of the Old Kingdom campaigns was led by a man who held no military rank. His name was Uni, and he served under the kings of the Sixth Dynasty. When it was necessary to chastise the Sand-Dwellers, Uni, a mere Overseer of the Tenants of the Palace, was placed at the head of the army, although there were many men of higher rank available. He was chosen, he says, because he could manage the men better than anyone else.

Uni's military career is an example, not of royal favoritism, but of the "Lord High Everything Else" tendencies of Egyptian officials, which we discussed in the preceding chapter. Once again it is a question of administrative ability; and, really, what other talent would be needed to manage an army? For the Egyptians, there was no such thing as military science. You just got your men out to where the enemy soldiers were standing, and then they shot arrows at one another and whacked one another with clubs and axes until one side got tired of it all and ran away. Some famous battles of the later period, when standing armies were the rule and kings prided themselves on their role as warriors, indicate a degree of ineptness and lack of common sense—let alone military strategy—that is astounding. So there was no reason why a judge and overseer like Uni couldn't have been sent to chastise an enemy—and done it, as he claims, successfully. Even in modern wars the best soldiers are not always graduates of military academies.

After the Sixth Dynasty the local rulers used their local troops for their own purposes, set themselves up as independent princelings, and dared the king to do something about it. One nobleman bragged that he had resisted the Royal House when it attacked him. Nobody claims that the downfall of the united monarchy was caused by feudalistic military organization. It may have been the other way around—the nomarchs took advantage of a situation which they would never have dared to exploit when the monarchy was strong.

When forceful centralized government was restored in the Middle Kingdom the powerful nobles still maintained their own armies. Probably they didn't get away with it for long. Senusert III, the great warrior king of the Twelfth Dynasty, seems to have subdued his proud nobles just as he subdued the Nubians. By this time the army had become a more regularized institution. It was recruited (perhaps this is a polite word for "conscripted") by the army scribes, who got quotas from various districts. We assume that most of the conscripts—the "young men," as they are called—served for a specified time and then went home, but other troops, whose name we translate as "warriors," seem to have been real professionals. Another possibility is that "young men" was the designation of the raw recruits, and "warrior" a rank equivalent to the private first class. Then there were the "shock troops," who may have been seasoned veterans.

An elite corps was formed by the "retainers," who seem to have been young men of rank chosen to go into battle with the king. They were not the same as the royal bodyguard, though some of them seem to have been selected from it. In any case, it was an honor to be a retainer.

At the head of the whole business was the "great overseer of troops," or the commander-in-chief. He had generals under him; some of them were no more than overseers in charge of quarrying operations, some actually led troops in the field, and others commanded the forts of Nubia. There was a host of army scribes, responsible for everything from recruiting to supply. One title has always fascinated me: "Master of the Secrets of the King in the Army." If the Egyptians did not use secret agents, the people they fought may have done so; there is a wonderful story of the great Ramses being deluded, on the eve of battle, by two men who pretended to be deserters from the opposing army in order to assure the king that most of the enemy forces were far away from the town. They were actually creeping up on Ramses at that very moment, and his credulity lost him the battle and almost lost him his life. However, reluctant as I am to do so, I don't believe the Master of Secrets was in charge of military intelligence—or, for that matter, any variety of intelligence.

We do not know how much actual training, if any, a young recruit had before he was marched out to fight. However, young Egyptian boys probably learned to use the throw stick and the bow in hunting. Weapons were very simple during this period; bows were just lengths of springy wood, and war arrows might be made of hardened wood, without even stone points. Archery was a skill in which the Egyptians took some pride, and they probably started practicing when they were still young.

The bowmen made up one group among the soldiers. Others carried axes. The actual weapons which have been found include slings, spears, daggers, and clubs. We are still in the Bronze Age here; except for rare items like Tutankhamon's iron dagger, that metal was not widely used until much later. Presumably a battle began with the archers and slingers softening up the enemy from a distance, but it ended in hand-to-hand combat with axes and clubs. I have always had the feeling that there would not be many wounded after these battles— that if a man went down everybody jumped on him. However, one of the medical treatises deals with wounds, particularly with fractures of the skull, and this last would no doubt be a common casualty in a battle fought with clubs. Nobody wore armor, although soldiers did carry big shields covered with hide.

The Hyksos, that mysterious people from Asia who took control of part of Egypt after the fall of the Middle Kingdom, seem to have been responsible for a host of innovations in the art of war—if it can be called an art. We are constantly being forced to modify the statements we make about the Hyksos; the name itself may be incorrect, as applied to the whole mass of invaders, and some of the artifacts ascribed to them have been seriously questioned. It is undeniable, however, that there was a drastic change in the Egyptian arsenal and in the Egyptian attitude toward war after the Hyksos.

The Hyksos are usually given the credit for introducing the horse and chariot to Egypt. Apparently it never occurred to any of the early Near Eastern civilizations to mount soldiers on horses and turn them into cavalry. Perhaps the animals were too rare and too valuable. Most Egyptologists think the ancient Egyptians didn't actually ride them. I think they did, upon occasion, though there are few representations of men on horseback. It's an undignified pose, when you come to think about it, and the well-established canon of Egyptian art was not receptive to innovation. But surely the utility of horsemen as scouts and messengers is too obvious to be overlooked. A horse can move faster than a man on foot, over terrain that would be impossible for a chariot.

Horses were primarily used to draw chariots, though. We have several Egyptian chariots, from the tomb of Tutankhamon and from the tomb of his presumed ancestor Yuya, whom we mentioned back in the first chapter. Yuya was a captain of chariotry, so naturally he would want to take a chariot with him—though his appears to be too small for an adult. A model, perhaps? Or did he have a sentimental attachment to his first chariot?

At first glance, these vehicles seem to be mostly wheels—two big ones, with four spokes per wheel and leather tires around the wooden rims. Between the wheels was the body of the chariot, floored with woven leather strips and partially surrounded by a curved railing. The back was usually left open. They look like light, flimsy vehicles, with a tendency to tip. To make them as stable as possible the chariot-makers put the axle at the very back of the carriage body; the pole went under the floor and then bent up at an angle to join the collar which went around the horse's neck. The chariots had to be light if they were to be pulled by the little horses then in use. In warfare two horses might be used to each chariot, but they had to pull two men, the driver and the warrior. In some of the reliefs the valiant king is shown all alone in the chariot, with the reins tied behind his waist so that he can wield his bow. It's a good trick if you can do it.

Egyptian weapons changed significantly at this same period. Copper arrowheads became common; and a new variety of dagger appeared, cast all in one piece to lessen the strain between hilt and blade. Perhaps these were used for overhand, stabbing blows, wherein the dagger was held at right angles to the length of the arm. The older daggers may have been held in such a way as to continue the line of the forearm and used to slash upward; the strain on the joint of the hilt would not be so great as it was in stabbing. Sometimes the dagger was strapped to the upper left arm; otherwise it was stuck through the warrior's belt. Swords were used, and there are a few with a long grip which may have been used two-handed; they are sharp on both sides but relatively dull at the point, which means they must have been used like a saber rather than a rapier. There was no art of fencing, which is not surprising when we consider that even in the Middle Ages sword fights simply consisted of hitting the other fellow as hard and as often as you could. One curious and romantic-looking Egyptian sword was a sort of scimitar with a curved blade. The old clubs and axes still continued in use along with the new weapons. So did the bow, but it had undergone a considerable change. Instead of being a single piece of flexible wood, the new compound bow was built up of several layers of tough springy wood, or alternate layers of wood and horn, glued together and covered with bark. It was curved in the reverse direction from that in which it was to be shot, to give it greater power. These bows were harder to make, though, and they were susceptible to warping, so the good old long bow continued in use.

By the middle of the Eighteenth Dynasty body armor was beginning to be used by some. Even foot soldiers had protective wrappings of linen or leather over vulnerable spots, and a kind of helmet to protect the head. More elaborate armor consisted of a linen or leather shirt covered with overlapping metal scales. It must have been horribly heavy and cumbersome (though not as bad as medieval armor). The king's Blue Battle Crown, of leather sewed with metal discs, probably began its career as a head protector in battle, although it soon became one of the ceremonial crowns. Charioteers carried big shields to protect themselves and the warrior they drove, and even the horses wore heavy blankets that covered most of their backs. The little mare that may have been owned by Senenmut, Queen Hatshepsut's henchman, had such a blanket of quilted leather lined with linen to prevent chafing.

Above: compound (top) and regular
(bottom) bows, with arrow

Left to right: khepesh scimitar, post-Hyksos dagger, long-sword,
pre-Hyksos-type dagger, axes (Scale is 4:1 except for the bows, which are 6:1.)

Weapons

The army that carried this arsenal into battle was a different thing
altogether from the conscript armies of the Old Kingdom. We can
give some of the credit for this—if credit it is—to the Hyksos again,
since it was the effort of driving these foreigners out of Egypt that began the habit of campaigning which ended in imperial conquest.

Beginning with Ahmose, who pushed the Hyksos out of Egypt into Palestine, and culminating in Thutmose III, who brought Syria-Palestine under Egyptian control and defeated the powerful kingdom of Mitanni, the kings of the Eighteenth Dynasty were seasoned campaigners. Under Thutmose III the army went out to fight in Asia every year for almost twenty years; it must have been an annual occurrence as predictable as the inundation. The men who survived these campaigns were no longer amateur soldiers.

The army of the Eighteenth to Twentieth Dynasties was divided into groups of about five thousand men, each division being named after the god whose standard it bore. These standards are fascinating objects—images of gold or gilded wood, carried on high poles so that they could be seen above the dust of battle and, presumably, spur their defenders on to greater valor. Each division consisted of twenty-five companies of two hundred men each, and these companies also had their standards. Some were simple painted squares of wood, others bore designs like the one that showed two men wrestling. The royal marines carried standards shaped like ships. The literature of war contains no noble, high-sounding references to these standards or to the soldier's honor which was attached to similar devices in Roman times; but it is not far-fetched to suppose that the standards came to have some such significance to the men who marched under them.

Chariotry was the elite branch of the service; it led the charge, to clear the way for the foot soldiers behind. The infantry was made up of several types of soldiery called by different names, the meaning of which is not always clear to us. There seems to have been a distinction between veterans and new recruits, and perhaps also between volunteers (career army types) and conscripts. The "Braves of the King" sounds like a select group, and in at least one case their commander led the attack on the besieged city. Then there were military specialists: the heralds, who may have acted as dispatch runners, carrying the general's orders to various parts of the field; the scouts, mounted on horseback (there was still no cavalry as such); and a whole battery of scribes. Thutmose III had an officer who was responsible for the royal quarters at night when the army was on the march, and presumably transport, supplies, communications, and other support groups were also organized.

We have some references to and depictions of naval battles. In the twelfth century Egypt was attacked from the north by a loose confederation of tribes we know as the Sea Peoples, and Ramses III met them on land and on water. Even here, hand-to-hand combat, ship-to-ship, was the rule, and the weapons were the same.

Some of the male slaves captured in the Asiatic and Nubian wars were allowed to serve as soldiers, thus earning their freedom, and as time went on such mercenaries became an important part of the military forces. Another originally foreign group of soldiers were never slaves; they became not only thoroughly Egyptianized but an elite corps. These men were Nubians, perhaps related to the warlike C people who gave the Middle Kingdom pharaohs such a hard time during their conquest of Cush. A delightful group of model soldiers found in an Eleventh Dynasty tomb shows that by that period they were already an integral part of the armed forces; the black men are as well armed and bear themselves as proudly as their brown-skinned counterparts from the same tomb.

During the Second Intermediate Period a large group of this warlike people moved into Upper Egypt. They were allied with the hated Hyksos, who occupied much of northern Egypt; this put a nasty squeeze on the princes of Thebes, who were, if we can believe the propaganda texts that have survived, chafing under Hyksos arrogance. Eventually the Thebans drove the Asiatics out and pursued them all the way to the Euphrates—with, it is now believed, the active assistance of Nubian troops. However, it was not long before the Nubians ceased to be a separate ethnic entity. Their distinctive graves, some so shallow that they have given the name "pan-grave people" to this group, disappear at the beginning of the Eighteenth Dynasty—not because the Nubians left the country, but because they adopted the customs of their new nation. The round Nubian huts became Egyptian houses, the graves turned into tombs, and the "pan-grave people" became the famous Medjay, skilled bowmen and soldiers who served Egypt for centuries as scouts, policemen, and guards. After a few generations they might be assimilated physically as well as culturally, for the Egyptians, whatever their other sins, were never stupid enough to discriminate against people on the basis of skin color. The Medjay were first-rate fighting men, and that was what counted with Egypt's warlike pharaohs of Dynasty XVIII.

We have fairly detailed descriptions of two ancient battles, and as I said, neither indicates much foresight on the part of the Egyptian general, who was, in theory, the king. The cities attacked were in the contested territory of Syria-Palestine, which was sometimes controlled by Egypt and sometimes by the Hittites of Anatolia or the Mitannian kingdom of north Syria. In both cases the assault was to be made on a walled town, and in both cases the enemy did not wait to be assaulted, but sallied forth to meet the Egyptians. Thutmose III, who was attacking Megiddo, had the nerve to lead his army along the most direct path to the city, which happened to be a narrow mountain road over a pass. The obvious idea of an ambush does not seem to have occurred to the enemy; or possibly the road was not as dangerous as Thutmose's official report makes out, since its aim is to show the king's daring contrasted with the cautious timidity of his staff. And, of course, a rash act that succeeds is daring, while one that fails is just stupid.

Ramses II, at the battle of Kadesh, did something equally rash, but in his case it turned out to be stupid. Kadesh, on the Orontes River, was then allied with the Hittites. In the first place Ramses took the unsupported word of two casual passersby that the main enemy force was a long way off, which wasn't the case. In his manly zeal Ramses had outstripped two of the four divisions of his army, so that half his troops were too far behind to be of any use to him in case of trouble—which he promptly found. The activities of the enemy commander—who is referred to, in the engaging Egyptian fashion, as "the Fallen One of Khatti"—suggest that elementary notions of strategy (or is it tactics?) were not unknown. If he did send out the enterprising liars who told Ramses the fairy tale about his whereabouts—Egyptian texts say he did—he was a better strategist than Ramses. He followed it up by leading his troops out behind the opposite side of the city, hidden from the approaching Egyptians; he swung them around in a circle and hit, not the first division, which was closest to the city, but the second. This division, that of Re, was caught completely unawares, and the enemy commander scattered it. He then attacked the first division, that of Amon, which had set up camp with its king.

From that point on the story becomes a trifle misty. One version explains that immediately before the attack the Egyptians had captured two more enemy scouts (were they always sent out in pairs, or is this just for symmetry?), who admitted, after some strong persuasion, that the Hittites were close at hand. This bit of information, which would have been useful at an early stage, came too late. Ramses was still trying to decide what to do about it when the enemy struck. Egyptian versions attribute the survival of the king to his own valor in holding off, single-handedly, the whole enemy army until reinforcements arrived. Ramses II has never inspired much confidence in me, so I have serious doubts about this version. However, reinforcements did arrive in time to save the king's skin—not the belated regiments of Ptah and Set, but another group referred to as the Na'arn, who seem to have been high-ranking Egyptian troops sent to Phoenicia by sea, and who came overland to Kadesh by another route.

It is possible to make a coherent, consistent narrative of these events, but I prefer not to do so since I don't believe the Egyptian version. The arrival of the Na'arn, whoever they were, literally in the nick of time, seems a little too fortuitous considering the distances that were traveled and the difficulty of communication between them and Ramses. Then there are those two sets of spies. . . .

On the other hand, if Amon was watching over his "chosen people," that explains everything.

Thutmose III had less difficulty than Ramses, perhaps because his opponent was not so good a strategist as the Fallen One of Khatti. Thutmose got his army out of the pass without incident and thus was able to conduct his battle in approved style. The enemy was waiting, and both armies proceeded to arrange themselves in battle order, on a wide plain which gave everybody room to spread out. The trumpeters then sounded the charge. . . .

I cannot resist a digression here. There are war trumpets in several museums, but the most famous are those of Tutankhamon. One was of silver, the other of copper alloy. The funnel-shaped bell was attached to a slender tube almost two feet long. They were in such good condition that the temptation to play them was irresistible. In a 1939 BBC broadcast a bandsman blew several blasts on the silver trumpet before it unexpectedly shattered. One can only imagine the poor man's consternation—especially since, as some critics have suggested, it was the insertion of a modern mouthpiece that caused the disaster. What did it sound like? Raucous, according to some; but I've listened to the recording, and the very idea that I was hearing an instrument that had been silent for over three thousand years made chills run up my spine.

To resume: the trumpets sounded, and off went the chariotry, led by Thutmose, at a mad gallop, kicking up stones and dust and making a considerable racket—springs crackling, wheels rattling, and everybody yelling. The mounted archers began to shoot, though how they could have expected to hit anything I don't know; I suppose if the enemy was thickly massed they were bound to hit something. The enemy front line also consisted of chariotry, at least in the Asiatic territories; the two sets of chariots engaged, or one swept the other away; at any rate, the field was now cleared for the infantry, who came running up waving their axes, clubs, swords, and daggers. Eventually, in the Egyptian narratives, the enemy broke and fled—to their city, if they had one close at hand. A siege usually followed, and it was sometimes maintained until the enemy was starved out. Thutmose III, who was a busy man and had a lot of cities to conquer, took some of them by storm, using siege ladders and sappers to undermine the walls. Judging from his accounts, clemency was the order of the day, not a brutal sack of the conquered city. Since it now belonged to Pharaoh, with all its people and their possessions, the common soldiers could not be allowed to loot it. Perhaps this is why the poor soldier in our quotation had to carry the Syrian woman instead of leaving her to die by the wayside, but it would be nice to think that compassion had something to do with it.

Some of the conquered peoples chose or were chosen to serve the conquerors as soldiers rather than slaves. They could earn freedom and promotion thereby. No doubt the Egyptians were glad to have mercenaries doing their fighting for them. The armies of the Late Period came to be made up more and more of foreign mercenaries. Such men, like the famous Medjay, had served Pharaoh at an earlier time, but not until the later New Kingdom was a majority, perhaps, of the army made up of men whose only loyalty to Egypt came through their pay. What, if anything, this had to do with Egypt's later failures on the field of battle no one can say for sure, but it may have had its effect.

The army coup d'état is a familiar occurrence in some areas of the world; as far back as the Year of Four Emperors, when the Roman legions nominated their own Caesars, the army has been an entity capable of wielding political power. It is only natural that we should look for the same thing in Egypt after the rise of the professional army, and since we are looking for it, naturally we find it. At the end of the Eighteenth Dynasty, after the fall of the royal house of Amarna, the throne of Egypt was held successively by two men who had, among other titles, that of "general." Harmhab served under Tutankhamon and perhaps under Akhenaton as well. By the time he assumed the Double Crown there was probably no man alive who had a legitimate claim, by birth and blood, to the kingship, but this does not explain why it was Harmhab, and not some other commoner, who won it. Harmhab had no surviving sons, and his successor was probably another army man, perhaps an old buddy of Harmhab's. It's all very confusing, but confusion is compounded by the fact that both Harmhab and Ramses were other things besides generals.

A similar case occurred at the end of the Twentieth Dynasty, when a man named Herihor turned up in Thebes with the resounding titles of Vizier of Upper Egypt and High Priest of Amon and removed— rather politely—the reins of power from the last of the feeble Ramesside kings. So for a long time the history books reported that the increasing power of the priesthood of Amon culminated in a theocracy which ruled at least part of Egypt. Then somebody noticed that before Herihor got to be high priest he was Viceroy of Nubia and Commander of the Army. The religious coup became a military coup, and once again, as in the case of Harmhab, the army got the credit for controlling the state.

With all deference to the distinguished scholars who have supported this interpretation, I cannot help but feel that it oversimplifies the ancient Egyptian scene and forces modern viewpoints on a culture to which they were not applicable. The army, the bureaucracy, the church, and the state—these categories were not as clear-cut in Egypt as they are today. We do not know how Harmhab and Herihor seized power, or which of their many titles conceals the real source of a strength great enough to enable them to mount the throne of the Two Lands. Their success may have been due to their control of the army, or to their high rank—or, for all we know, to their beautiful brown eyes.

FORTS AND FORTIFICATIONS

Egypt had strong natural frontiers—the deserts on the east and west, the Sinai and the sea on the north, the unnavigable rocks of the First Cataract on the south. There were ways around or through all these obstacles, however, and various enemies took advantage of them. By the time of the Middle Kingdom the open borders of the Delta were defended by fortresses. Once Egypt expanded southward into what is now the Sudan, some very fancy forts were built to establish control over the region. Alas, the best of them are gone now, fathoms deep under the waters of Lake Nasser. Knowing that the building of the Aswan Dam would create a vast body of water, which would mean the destruction of innumerable archaeological sites, the international community of scholars united in a magnificent effort to preserve or at least record as many of these as was possible. Some temples were moved, but the majority of the ancient remains could not be saved. Among the lost were the ruined but still impressive fortresses built by the Egyptians during the Middle Kingdom above the Second Cataract in Nubia. This area of tumbled stone and rushing water formed a natural frontier which was virtually impassable to ships. The forts allowed Egypt to control trade and military passage.

Fortunately we have fairly detailed excavation reports about several of the major forts. Perhaps the most impressive of the ruins were those at Semna, where the Nile passes, narrowly constricted, through a region of hard rock. Two forts, one on either side of the river, controlled traffic north and south. Semna West was the bigger of the two; Semna East, also called Kummeh, was opposite. These two have been excavated, but a third fort, Semna South, turned out to be impracticable for the expedition, under George Reisner, which worked on the other two forts. It seems that once a herdsman brought his two camels into the ruins of the fort to graze. He decided to take a nap, and when he awoke, groggy with sleep, he saw a white gazelle bounding along in front of him. He snatched his rifle and fired; and then discovered that the gazelle was really one of his own camels. This was not a small financial loss, it was a catastrophe, and the herdsman decided he must have offended some powerful spirit to be so afflicted. The ruined fort thus acquired a taboo, and none of the natives would work there. At least that was the story they told Reisner.

The three forts of Semna, plus another one three miles away, formed an administrative unit under the commander of Semna West, the biggest of the group. The excavator calculated that the four forts could have held at least three hundred men, and perhaps twice that number, in view of the ability of the ancients to live in spaces we would consider impossibly cramped. Thus, the commander could send out a force of from one hundred fifty to two hundred men against local raiding parties, which would be the usual problem he had to contend with. In case of a serious widespread revolt, the Egyptians sat tight inside their walls and waited for reinforcements from home.

The forts were built to command the river, which was the main artery of traffic, military and commercial. The north-south road ran through the west fort at Semna, so that the commander could keep an eye on land traffic as well. There were magazines and storehouses inside the fort, and it had a covered stair, protected by thick walls, leading down to the river, so that water was obtainable even under siege. Semna would have been a hard place to take; the brick walls, six to eight meters thick and perhaps ten meters high, were bonded with heavy timbers to make them stronger. Square bastions projected at intervals, with towers on each corner; the reconstructions of such forts look amazingly like medieval castles. The tops of the walls have not survived, but we assume there was a walkway on top. Around the fort, except on the river side, where it perched on top of the Nile cliffs, ran a wide ditch, the outer face revetted with dry masonry.

Inside the fort was a small town, complete with a temple and a house for the commander. Assignment to one of these forts must have been received with hearty groans; at best it was dull duty in an arid, unfriendly region, and there was always the chance that a patrol sent out to investigate rumors of unrest might discover, in a direct and unpleasant way, that the rumors were true.

There were compensations. The towns in some of these forts were as comfortable as most Egyptian towns, with markets and temples and probably a tavern or two. Some of the men brought their families with them, and others married local women.

All the same, perhaps the teachers of the scribal schools were right. The chances of booty and promotion were slight, and the "woes of the soldier" were great.

Nine

"I KNOW THE MOVEMENT OF A FIGURE, THE STRIDE OF A WOMAN"

PAINTING AND SCULPTURE

My grandmother, who was of Pennsylvania Dutch stock, used to say, "Oh, it's just for pretty," about some of her possessions or the ornamentation on them—a flower painted on the side of a bowl, for instance. It has taken me a long time to realize that this seemingly naive statement is actually a pretty good description of "fine art" as opposed to crafts. *Ars gratia artis*—art for the sake of art, not for utility. If you read books about Egyptian art you will come across sentences like these. "Egyptian art was solely utilitarian, designed for magical (religious, protective, symbolic, philosophical) purposes. Aesthetic qualities were irrelevant. Beauty was not a factor."

All very true, no doubt, but statements like these bother me. Perhaps it's because they sound—quite unintentionally, I am sure— somewhat patronizing. It does seem to me that they make unnecessary and meaningless distinctions. A great deal of what we call "art" is utilitarian, and the "fine art" of the Western world, enshrined in museums and drooled over by critics, includes innumerable paintings and pieces of sculpture that had religious (magical, philosophical) functions. A Gothic cathedral was constructed for the glory of God, and its elements, architectural and decorative, are full of symbolism. The great Renaissance painters specialized in saints and martyrs, and they were subsidized by wealthy patrons who often insisted on being included in the painting, kneeling in prayer and looking pious. The motive of these noble patrons was as "utilitarian" as that of an Egyptian who had himself portrayed offering to the god or the king. Both hoped it would help them get into heaven.

Now that I've got that out of my system, I will try to talk about Egyptian art. Before describing what they did and how they did it and offering a few informed guesses as to why they did it, one must first consider various approaches to the subject.

Over the years Egyptology has become a full-time job for a scholar. To an outsider it may seem very narrow, yet it is so complex that no living Egyptologist would claim to be a universal expert. New discoveries are constantly being made, new theories published; the language itself, like the ability to play the piano, requires daily practice in order to maintain proficiency. The result is specialization within specialization; if you approach one Egyptologist to ask his opinion on a scarab you bought in Egypt, he may pass you on to a colleague with the remark that "my field is plant ornament; so-and-so, at the Boston Museum, is the man for scarabs."

This being the case within Egyptology itself, you may imagine how wary Egyptologists are of venturing into other fields such as anthropology or comparative religion—or art criticism. Most Egyptologists would agree that it must be done. No field of history is isolated, and the broader one's background the more easily one may be able to interpret specific meanings. Some attempts have been made to solve the dilemma of specialization versus generalization through symposia or conferences where historians and scholars from different fields sit around a table sipping water and giving talks to one another. Despite the fact that the people who participate in these conferences are often brilliant scholars, I have yet to see one which in my opinion produced a genuine synthesis of ideas. Even in a symposium scholars tend to talk in narrow terms about their own fields (which is natural enough, with a battery of experts waiting to pounce on the first mistake), and the scholars who listen to them can usually think of too many exceptions, in terms of their specialities, to allow of generalization.

Many art historians and art critics, not to mention critics of literature and music, hold that no work of art is comprehensible out of context; a corollary is the biographical method, in which it is maintained that the artist's work cannot be apprehended without a knowledge of his life. Another critical school, however, argues that the artist's motives, his childhood experiences, and his cultural background are extraneous to a study of the work of art. Its form can have sufficient meaning in itself.

Let's get down to cases. Take a look at the illustration (opposite) which shows the Egyptian style of drawing a walled garden with a pool. Above the Egyptian pool we have a modern perspective drawing of the same object, which should make clear to the reader, more conveniently than words could do, how the Egyptian style of representation differed from our own. The reality of the Egyptian drawing is not visual reality, yet no one would deny that it is reality of a kind. All the parts of the garden are there: pool, trees, doors in the wall, duck in the pool. Not all these elements are visible in the perspective drawing, which is thus inferior to the Egyptian version with regard to the complete and accurate rendering of an object in all its parts. The same principle holds with the depiction of the offering table (page 172), which looks as if the offerings of fruit and flowers and bits of meat are piled in a two-dimensional tower. They were, of course, laid out on the surface of the table, which is shown from the side; but the artist had to

The Sheikh El Beled. Cairo Museum. (Photograph by D. Forbes)

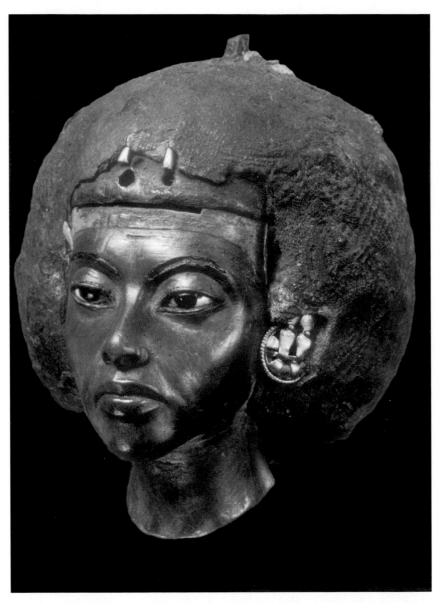

Queen Tiye. Ebony head. Berlin Museum. (Photograph by D. Forbes)

Sarcophagus of
Prince Thutmose's
cat Tamiut.
Cairo Museum.
(Photograph by
D. Forbes)

Mummy of dog from Valley of the Kings' tomb.
Cairo Museum, Animal Mummy Room. (Photograph by S. Ikram)

Crowns of Princess Khnumit. Cairo Museum. (Photograph by A. Dodson)

Toilet chest with mirror.
Cairo Museum.
(Photograph by S. Ikram)

ABOVE:
Deir El Medina.
New Kingdom
tomb builders'
village (*foreground*)
and necropolis.
(Photograph by
D. Forbes)

RIGHT:
Deir El Medina.
Private tomb.
(Photograph by
D. Forbes)

Model of an Amarna villa. Overall view (*above*); interior (*below*).
(Garth Denning illustrations, courtesy of KMT Communications, D. Forbes)

Senet board and pieces. Cairo Museum. (Photograph by S. Ikram)

Chariot from tomb of Yuya. Painting by Howard Carter. (Photograph by D. Forbes)

Two groups of model soldiers. Egyptian spearmen (*above*);
Nubian bowmen (*below*). Cairo Museum.
(Photographs by S. Ikram)

Akhenaton. Detail of colossal statue. Cairo Museum. (Photograph by D. Forbes)

Akhenaton. Detail of small limestone statue. Cairo Museum.

(Photograph by D. Forbes)

Step pyramid complex, Sakkara. (Photograph by D. Forbes)

"Astronomical" ceiling of tomb of Senenmut, Thebes. (Photograph by D. Forbes)

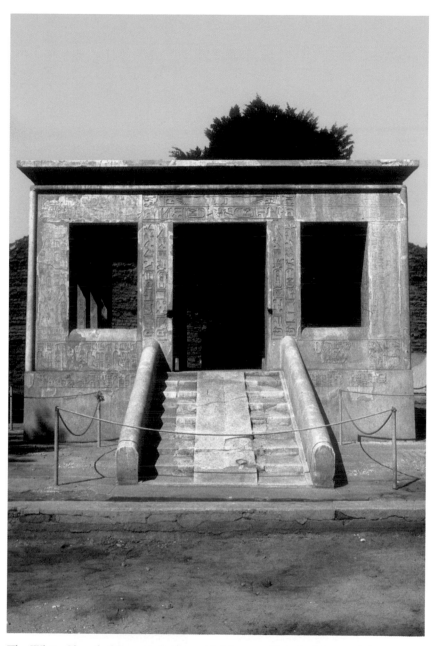

The White Chapel of Senusert I. Open Air Museum, Karnak. (Photograph by D. Forbes)

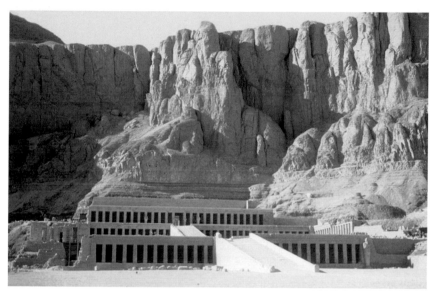

Hatshepsut temple, Deir El Bahri, Thebes. (Photograph by D. Forbes)

FACING PAGE: Coffins.
Herakleopolitan (*above*), coffin of Akhhotep,
Metropolitan Museum of Art, New York; Anthropoid (*below left*),
coffin of Khnumhotep, Royal Museum of Scotland; Rishi (*below right*),
Museum of Fine Arts, Boston. (Photographs by A. Dodson)

Portrait head of one of the canopic jars from tomb no. 55, Valley of
the Kings, Metropolitan Museum of Art. (Photograph by D. Forbes)

Modern perspective drawing

Egyptian version

Walled garden with pool

use a different technique for the offerings themselves, or we (and the recipient of the goodies) wouldn't know they were there.

One obvious characteristic of Egyptian two-dimensional art, which can be seen in our examples, is the absence of foreshortening. This is demonstrated by the Egyptian way of drawing the human figure. Suppose you—and by "you" I mean an untrained, untalented artist, like myself—suppose you want to draw a man. If you show him in front view you will run into several problems of foreshortening. Unless you are satisfied with a sort of blob, you, the untrained artist, cannot draw a nose that looks like a nose. Feet are even worse; they will look like wooden blocks. So you decide to draw your man in profile. Now

Offering table

the nose looks like a nose, and the feet have a certain resemblance to feet. But what are you going to do with the shoulders?

What the Egyptians did was to combine two points of view—profile and front view. The face was drawn in profile with the eye in front view; the shoulders were again in front view and the feet in profile, but in between the body was gradually turned so that there was no abrupt change in point of view. The drawing of the garden combines the two points of view less ingeniously. It is really a combination of what we would call plan and elevation.

We may tend to be a little patronizing about the Egyptian style of drawing, considering it inferior to a style which understands and uses perspective. Yet perspective in drawing is actually uncommon. We do not find it in two-dimensional art in any of the ancient cultures of the Near East. This does not mean that they were unaware of its more obvious effects. Anybody can see that the farther an object is from the beholder the smaller it appears, and obviously an object may be concealed by one in front of it. And although the vanishing point would not be defined and understood for a long time, the Egyptians were surely aware of the subtle distortion that was its effect. So why didn't they draw things that way?

Perhaps because it was easier to draw things their way, without perspective? I find it easier; I can produce an acceptable Egyptian painting much more easily than I can produce a copy of da Vinci or Dürer. But this is a ridiculous explanation, particularly for a civilization which built the pyramids without mechanical power or iron tools.

It is at this point that the formal approach fails us. We can describe what we see in Egyptian paintings; but what we see is really meaningless unless we know why the particular forms were chosen. There are aesthetes who rhapsodize over Egyptian painting because of its purely formal qualities; and certainly it has many appeals. The colors are pretty, the drawing has the crisp assurance of long-established and accepted technique, and some details appeal to the eye or to the emotions. But there is, I think, a touch of that condescension I mentioned earlier in these evaluations, a suggestion of "how quaint these primitives were!" Egyptian painting was not quaint, and it was not primitive. The rules of style, the "canon," were established by the middle of the third millennium B.C., and they were not greatly altered until after the end of Egypt's existence as a distinct cultural entity. We may speak glibly about the static quality of Egyptian culture to explain this remarkable continuity, but the fact remains that these rules would not have been followed for so long unless they had satisfied the demands of the society. What those demands were we must now try to investigate.

Though I don't believe that the utilitarian approach says all that can be said about Egyptian art, there is no denying it was important. The tomb paintings were not meant to make the place look pretty. They insured that the dead man would be provided with all the objects and all the pleasures which the paintings depicted. Ancient art in general is thought to have had its origin in magic. The wonderful cave paintings of European prehistory, like those at Lascaux, were not made by a Neanderthal Pinturicchio, commissioned by Ug the chief to adorn his mansion. Many of them are stuck away in dark, unfrequented corners. By depicting the animals desired for food the prehistoric artists were invoking magical laws which promised them a successful hunt.

Now if magic is at the basis of art, including Egyptian art, it is important that the object be shown as complete and whole, so that nothing vital is missing when the spiritual similacrum is given to the soul of the deceased. As we saw in the drawings of the garden, the Egyptian version shows the whole garden, with the pool. The perspective drawing cannot show the pool, and so the spiritual garden of the dead man, in the Land of the West, might lack this desirable feature.

This is the conventional explanation for the "why" of Egyptian painting. There are two objections to it: one is the old quibble that we can never be sure that our analyses of the motives of dead and dust foreigners are correct; the other is that the magical thesis does not explain all the eccentricities of Egyptian two-dimensional art. If you want to draw a "whole" man, and make sure that no essential part of him will be missing when he is reborn into eternal life, you do not show his head in profile. The Egyptian version gives a man two shoulders, two arms, two legs, and a body, but it deprives him of one eye and one ear. The Egyptians could draw heads in front view; one of the common hieroglyphs takes this form, and the little god Bes is always depicted from the front, face and all. So perhaps the theory of magical utility is only a partial answer to our "why." However, it does explain some of what we would consider the peculiarities of Egyptian painting and bas-relief.

Relative size is one of these peculiarities. It often indicated importance and rank, not actual dimensions or distance from the observer. So in some periods the king towers over his tiny wife, and the nobleman looms above the bodies of his workers. Showing two people seated side by side, as they actually appeared to the observer, would mean that one person was partially or entirely concealed by the body of the other. The Egyptians ignored this effect of perspective because it didn't suit their purpose. The tomb scenes showing husband and wife, where it appears that she is sitting or standing behind him, actually depicted two people next to each other, side by side.

The magical approach can be applied to the study of sculpture as well as of painting. Some of the statues of gods and kings in our museums come from temples, but the others, particularly statues of private persons, were meant for the tombs. The utility of a tomb statue is easy to explain in magical terms; in a culture which put so much stress on the preservation of the body, we may reasonably assume that some sort of physical representation of the dead man was a prerequisite for eternal life. If the mummy were damaged or destroyed, a handsome statue could be an acceptable substitute. Statues of gods and kings in temples established their presence and formed foci of worship.

Whether they were primarily magical or not, Egyptian works of art were more than just utilitarian; they were also beautiful. Many people find the sculpture of ancient Egypt easier to enjoy than the painting, since it was not affected by the absence of perspective, which distorts—for our eyes—the two-dimensional art. There was a canon for sculpture as well as for painting; both were set early in Egyptian history, and both were followed for over two thousand years. The essential quality of Egyptian sculpture, which strikes most beholders at once, is its squareness. When you look at a statue you can almost see the block it was cut out of. The Law of Frontality applies, since most statues were set up against a wall and were meant to be seen—if they were seen at all—from the front; but a statue may be subject to this law and still not be "square." In Egyptian statues almost all the lines are right angles or parallels. A seated statue—one of the most popular poses—was particularly "square." Right angles at hips and knees, straight legs, rigid back, and stiff neck—there is never any twisting of the torso or turning of the head. It is all straight up and down.

Another general remark which applies to Egyptian sculpture in the round of all periods is that the body is not treated in detail. Musculature is barely indicated; the torso is a series of smooth planes, the legs and arms are shaped columns. Even when, in the Late Period, an attempt was made to show musculature, it was as formalized and lifeless as the Assyrian sculpture of approximately the same period. It is hard to find the right word for this phenomenon, because the terms we might be tempted to use have misleading connotations. Some scholars say Egyptian sculpture is abstract; this always makes me think of the blocks of concrete filled with holes, called "Woman Nursing Child" or "Aspiration," which may be found in modern art museums. Egyptian sculpture is too close to reality to be called abstract. We can't call this treatment "sketchy" either; it is too complete and too finished. It is better to avoid such labels altogether.

Though one is entitled to generalize about Egyptian art, there were variations over time. Not all of them are obvious to the untrained observer, but they are very important to Egyptologists who want to date uninscribed objects—most objects, that is.

Sculpture and bas-relief of the predynastic and early dynastic period is restricted to small objects such as the famous Narmer palette.
Slate palettes were used for grinding cosmetics, but the large, decorated versions were made to commemorate noteworthy occasions. In
this case the occasion seems to have been the unification of Egypt
under King Narmer. The symbolism is fairly obvious—the falcon, representing the god Horus of Upper Egypt, leading prisoners to the king,
fallen bodies of the foe, and so on. It's a battle or a war we see here,
with the ruler of Upper Egypt triumphing over his foe. Even at this
early age the conventions of depicting the human form had been established. There are a few small statues from the earliest dynasties, but
monumental sculpture did not develop until the Old Kingdom. However, the Egyptian artist caught on fast. Some people consider this the
high point of Egyptian art. The heads of Old Kingdom monarchs suggest the divinity of kingship: calm, assured, inhumanly regal, the
finely cut features might be those of a god. Private statues like that of
the Sheikh el Beled and Hemiun, to mention only two, are equally
impressive.

The Old Kingdom royal heads are quite unlike the careworn, stern
faces of the Twelfth Dynasty Amenemhats and Senuserts. This period
followed a time of anarchy, when local rulers asserted their independence and decorated handsome tombs in their provincial capitals, so
maybe Senusert III and his son had some reason to look worried. The
fact is that nobody knows for sure what lay behind this change. It is
very distinctive, however, and makes it easy to distinguish Middle
Kingdom from Old Kingdom royal statues.

Another period of social and political breakdown followed the
Twelfth Dynasty, before the local dynasts of Thebes reunited the
country. Thus begins the New Kingdom, which is considered by other
experts to be the high point of Egyptian art. By the time of Amenhotep III, whom you may know as "Amenhotep the Magnificent," or
"the Sun King," huge building projects were under way at Luxor and
Karnak temples and up and down the Nile, featuring enormous
statues of the king. The biggest surviving are the so-called Colossi of
Memnon, which once flanked the entrance to Amenhotep's mortuary

temple, but they are so sadly battered that the features are indistinguishable. Never mind; there are a lot of other statues of Amenhotep. It isn't difficult to distinguish sculpture of this period from that of the Old and Middle Kingdoms. Though the bodies of kings remain young and strong, the faces show a softening of contour and of expression; Hatshepsut and Thutmose III smile enigmatically, and Amenhotep III develops chubby cheeks. (This is an oversimplification, of course; a detailed description would take volumes.)

Although details varied from century to century and sometimes from year to year, the basic rules did not change. These rules, or canons, fixed not only the form of sculpture and painting, but the poses and postures as well. The canon applied most rigidly to persons of rank. The lower the individual in the social scale, the more freely he could be portrayed; children and animals were just about at the bottom of the scale, and that is one reason why Egyptian animals and birds are particularly charming. They could fly and prance and crawl and flutter without injuring a dignity they did not possess. Servants were fairly undignified, so they could be shown indulging in activities which were not proper for the nobility. The small tomb models of the

Deviations from the canon

First Intermediate Period show bakers and butchers and weavers ani-matedly engaged in various aspects of their work, and tomb paintings include quite a variety of poses, including wrestling, dancing, and ac-robatics. Our illustration shows a few such deviations from the canonical rules; some are really delightful, and they indicate that Egyptian artists were not as limited as one might think. Other at-tempts were not so successful.

While the servants work and cavort, the nobleman and his wife sit or stand in stiff aloofness, removed from the reality of the scene. The seated and standing postures were the most popular for persons of dignity, but distinguished persons were also allowed to kneel before the gods or the king. The king, being more dignified than anyone else, only knelt to the gods. Another favorite pose during certain periods was that of the "seated scribe"—a man sitting cross-legged with his kilt drawn taut across his knees and his shoulders slightly bowed. There are few recumbent Egyp-tians in our artistic representations, except dead ones. The mummy, of course, lies flat, and the anthropoid coffin itself might be regarded as a sculptured, supine figure. Limited as they are, these poses are eminently satisfactory—dignified, stately, and sometimes graceful.

If the canon applied rigidly to the pose of the kings, it was equally inflexible about the royal physique. Trim and muscular, shapely as the body of an Apollo—this is the form of the king's statues—almost al-ways.

AMARNA ART

If we stroll through the halls of the Cairo Museum contemplating kings—Menkaure, the Senuserts, the Thutmoses—we see them all as similar in shape: broad-shouldered, slim of waist and hip, straight and strong. Then we come upon Akhenaton, with his potbelly, his sagging breasts, his elongated skull, and spindly shanks! Carrying tact to an unnecessary extreme, his wife and the nobility of his court were rep-resented in the same way, so the tomb reliefs of the period teem with oddly shaped people. Postures too are radically different in Amarna art. Tutankhamon is shown leaning on his staff or slouching—in the royal throne! Akhenaton kisses his wife and bounces his children on his knee.

Here we must pause for a brief historical digression in order to set the scene. Akhenaton was the heir of a perfectly respectable, conventionally pious royal family whose members built temples to various gods, particularly Amon-Re of Thebes, and divided their time between Thebes and Memphis, the northern capital. Shortly after he came to the throne, Amenhotep IV, as he was then named, went off the rails. He changed his name to Akhenaton, honoring a fairly obscure sun god, Aton, and built a new city in a new site, several hundred miles north of Thebes. It is known today as Tell el Amarna, hence the designation of this period and its characteristics. Among the characteristics was a rejection of the extensive Egyptian pantheon. Akhenaton worshiped only his "sole god" Aton and sent emissaries around the country to excise the names and images of the gods, with special emphasis on Amon of Thebes. His "revolution" died with him. His successor, young Tutankhaton, changed his name to one that honored Amon and moved the court back to Thebes. We don't know what happened to Akhenaton's remains, or those of his beautiful wife Nefertiti, or those of their six daughters. We all know what happened to Tutankhamon.

The art of the Amarna Period is as distinctive as the new religious attitudes. It's not only the drastic changes in the depiction of the human figure. There is an overall relaxation of the older rigidity, a greater use of curved lines, one might even say a loosening of rules, which may be interpreted as charming freedom or dreadful decadence, depending on one's general attitude toward Akhenaton and his new ideas. Scholars have been arguing for decades about what prompted the change. According to some, the clue may lie in the word "maat," often translated as "truth," which was the leitmotif of Akhenaton's reign. He wasn't the only pharaoh who honored maat, but he emphasized it more than many other kings, adding the epithet "living in truth" to his titulary.

Unfortunately, maat, like our own "truth," means a lot of different things. That it involved a code of ethical conduct seems undeniable. A judge is expected to render "maat"; a virtuous man speaks "maat." "Justice" and "truth" are the obvious translations, and I believe they meant the same to the Egyptians as they do to us.

"True" has another meaning, that of accuracy. One does see in Amarna art an increased emotional content, an expressiveness—not, please, expressionism—of genuine feeling. This may be viewed as the logical consequence of maat, "candor," or an effect in itself.

However, Amarna art never really challenged the basic canons. Grotesque as the forms may be, unusual as the postures may appear, they are distortions, not violations, of the old forms and the old poses. Sculpture is softer and more rounded, but it is still frontal and still, despite the deceptive suggestion of curves, essentially straight up and down. Painting and relief give the human body in the familiar combination of profile and front view, depictions of houses and palaces are the same confusing blend of plan and elevation. Of course, the court artists were used to working in this style, and most of them would have found it utterly impossible to break away from it, but I cannot help suspecting, particularly in view of earlier successful, if spasmodic, attempts at deviation from the canon, that a talented young painter could have made a closer approximation to visual reality if that had been what the king was demanding. Akhenaton wanted something different from the old formal style, assuredly; but what he wanted and why he wanted it we may never know.

In some cases early Amarna art may strike a modern viewer as less pleasing than the canonical style. The plant and animal forms attract us because of their increased freedom; but the human figure still has the disadvantages of the unfamiliar perspective (or lack of it), plus the new distortions which rob the body, male or female, of its grace. The two little Amarna princesses, who are often reproduced and admired, are really rather horrid. Their bodies are boneless, their arms and legs have a rubbery flaccidity, and their long, naked skulls suggest a pair of extraterrestrials out of H. G. Wells. These elongated skulls are characteristic of the Amarna princesses—there were six of them, as I have said—but it usually isn't possible to tell one from another. Naturally, the reasons for the distortion are still being debated. The old theory, that the girls must have had their heads deliberately flattened, as was done in some other cultures, has now been abandoned, and since most of the sculptured skulls have been carefully carved, they can't have been covered by crowns or wigs. Surely this was not a literal rendering of reality. It meant something, and you will find various theories mentioned in various books on Amarna art, but since nobody knows for certain, I will not trouble you with them.

In both painting and sculpture Amarna art went through several distinct stages of development even in its brief lifetime. In the first years of Akhenaton's reign, this "candor," if we want to call it that, could almost be termed caricature. The most striking examples are a group of colossal statues which Akhenaton had made for a temple at Thebes. His face is impossibly elongated, with a hanging chin and a disturbing smile; his body shows what seems to be a pathological condition, in extreme form. Perhaps the reason why they strike some Egyptologists as grotesque is that they are in Osirid form, and the contrast between the classic, sacred image of the god and the brutal violation of his traditional shape is almost painful to the trained eye. Yet there is a strange fascination about these statues; the more you look at them the more they "get" to you. Some scholars believe that these statues and the reliefs that show similar peculiarities depict a pathological condition from which the king suffered. I don't. I can't prove I'm right, any more than they can, since Akhenaton's mummy is missing, but it seems more than likely that these representations are expressions of religious or philosophical concepts.

After the move to Amarna the exaggerated forms become modified and more realistic, and some of the statues of this later period are among the most famous known from Egypt. Tell el Amarna has been excavated by several groups, but it was Ludwig Borchardt, working under the auspices of the Deutsche Orient-Gesellschaft, who turned up the most exciting object found in the ruins of Akhenaton's short-lived capital. He found it in the debris of what had been the workshop of a sculptor named Thutmose.

Thutmose lived and worked in the same house. It was one of the

large, handsome Amarna villas, for he was a successful man, Chief of
Works and master sculptor, with several apprentices. Within a few
years after Akhenaton's death, the exodus from the doomed city began. At first the inhabitants thought the removal back to Thebes was
only temporary. They followed the court, locking up their houses and
taking with them only personal possessions. Later it became evident
that the city which had enshrined Akhenaton's jealous god would
never be tolerated by the followers of Amon-Re. Some of the house-
owners returned to Amarna and cleared away all their possessions,
even carrying off door frames and columns to use in the new houses
they were building in Thebes. Scavengers may have finished the
clearance; very little in the way of furniture, jewelry, or personal possessions has been found at the site. But for some reason or other Thutmose's workshop was not completely cleared. The German excavators
surmised that the sculptor gathered together all the unwanted or unfinished pieces he had on hand, walled up the door to the storage
room, and then left.

One can't help wondering how Thutmose felt about this. He must
have known that the abandoned pieces included masterpieces of sculpture. He may have worked on some of them himself. He had been
personally acquainted with the royal family, who had honored and
encouraged him. There's something suggestive and sad about that
blocked doorway. Did Thutmose hope he could one day retrieve his
unfinished work, or was he only trying to protect something he cared
about because of its beauty or its personal meaning?

Among these abandoned pieces of sculpture was an extraordinary
collection of faces—plaster casts, death or life masks, or, more likely,
casts made from works of sculpture in process—that show a degree of
realism greater than is commonly found in Egypt, but the chef d'oeuvre
was undoubtedly the bust of Queen Nefertiti, which has been reproduced in every medium from postcards to dress material. She really is
beautiful, with her long, arched throat and faintly smiling face, tinted
with the colors of life. When she made her first appearance in the
Berlin Museum a loud shout of admiration arose from all the world.
One voice in the general clamor, however, did not express admiration.

It came from the Egyptian government, and it said, in essence: "How did she get there?"

Ever since Mariette's time there have been laws in Egypt regarding the export of antiquities. Mariette and his successor Maspero were fairly lenient about sharing objects with excavators, but foreign archaeological expeditions were supposed to spread out their finds at the end of the working season for the inspection of an official from the Department of Antiquities. He made his selection for the Cairo Museum, and the expeditions got only what he chose to give them, unless other arrangements were made in advance. The general rule was that the Egyptian government kept the unique objects and shared the rest.

In the case of Nefertiti, the Egyptian government maintained that it never would, never could, let such a unique treasure out of the country. This is probably true. I have heard several stories about the escape (or kidnapping) of Nefertiti, and it is hard to make out precisely what did happen. The archaeologists of the Deutsche Orient-Gesselschaft insisted that the whole thing had been open and aboveboard. By the terms of their agreement with the Antiquities Department they were entitled to all artworks recognized as models or pattern pieces. Nefertiti was there, on the table with all the rest of the objects; her unique beauty was obviously not recognized by the inspector, and she was passed on to the excavators with the other models.

Seeing Nefertiti as she is today, it is hard to believe that an inspector could have failed to recognize her as unique unless he was drunk, blind in both eyes, or—but we will not mention a word which might be actionable. However, we must bear in mind that she did not have all her elegant beauty when she was dredged out of the wreckage of Thutmose's studio. Possibly—to be charitable about it—the government inspector was just not very alert. If he really did miss Nefertiti, one could hardly expect the excavators to take him aside and carefully point out that he had overlooked one of the masterpieces of Egyptian sculpture.

Or maybe one should expect that. The rights and wrongs of the case of Nefertiti are involved with the larger and rather touchy question of the division of antiquities. In most Near Eastern countries the host country claims the right of decision, and if it chooses to keep all the objects found, nobody can argue with it. The claims of the host country are indisputable; it owns the land. But what about the claims of the excavator, who contributes time, money, expertise, and elbow grease? *Scientia gratia scientia* is all very well, but the museums which sponsor archaeological expeditions want some return for their money. Another consideration is the availability of the material. For scholars there are certain advantages in a single great collection; they do not have to travel all over the world to see what they want to see. But not everyone can visit the Near East, and there are a lot of people who are interested in Near Eastern archaeology. Dispersal in one sense is a service, since it makes it possible for greater numbers of people to see and enjoy the masterpieces of ancient cultures. Oh, well, we could go on debating this issue forever. Let's get back to Egyptian art.

A number of the objects found in Tutankhamon's tomb were made at Amarna or influenced by its artistic canon. After the Amarna heresies were obliterated by the orthodox successors of Tutankhamon, art returned to its conventional forms. Many of the works from this period, especially sculpture and relief, continue the finest traditions of New Kingdom work; like their Eighteenth Dynasty predecessors, the nobles of the Nineteenth Dynasty commissioned statues of themselves for their tombs, and those that have survived are absolutely stunning, including several pair statues of husband and wife. Maybe the originals weren't that handsome, but the sculptures themselves exemplify male and female beauty and aristocratic dignity.

However, to many of us the sculpture of the Ramesside Period is more notable for size and ubiquity than for beauty. The colossi of Ramses II at his rock-cut temple of Abu Simbel strike many observers as chunky and graceless.

Under the vigorous Cushite kings of the Twenty-Fifth Dynasty a new sculptural technique appears alongside the older one. A few heads of this period combine a smooth, polished surface with hard, precisely defined facial planes. The bodies are in the classic style, youthful and firm, but some of the faces are hard, almost grim. The following Saite dynasty produced some striking pieces of sculpture, but Saite art is, for the most part, a deliberate imitation of the great periods of the past. Entire tombs were reproduced, so accurately that it is sometimes difficult to tell the original from the copy.

Foreign contacts had little effect on art, except in decorative motifs, and the splendid Greek art, even after the conquest of Alexander, produced in Egypt only second-rate provincial Greek imitations or peculiar amalgamations of the two techniques. The decorative work of the Greco-Roman periods in Egypt becomes ornate and extravagant. The only new development of merit (i.e., the only one I like) was the so-called mummy portraits, sometimes referred to as the Fayum portraits, since the majority of them come from that area. These paintings, in wax on flat boards, replaced the mummy masks of earlier periods, covering the bandaged head of the mummy, after, perhaps, being displayed in the house during the lifetime of the subject. The best of them—all by anonymous artists—are as beautiful and evocative as anything in Renaissance Western art. Not even I would deny that these are true portraits; they look you straight in the eye and demand acknowledgment of their humanity. But the style is Greek, not Egyptian.

Which brings us back to the subject of portraiture. I believe it is safe to say that portraiture in the modern sense, an exact likeness of the subject, is not found in ancient Egypt before the Greek period. To some extent that interpretation is subjective; but I cannot resist the opportunity of reproducing, for the reaction of the reader, two so-called portrait heads from two different cultures. The Egyptian head shown is that of a Middle Kingdom ruler, unidentified by inscriptional material. The other photograph is a bust of the Roman emperor Caracalla. To my eye there is a great deal of difference between these two "portraits"; I have the feeling that if I met Caracalla's bust attached to a body and strolling down the street I would recognize the fellow at once (and run fast in the opposite direction). Even the

Middle Kingdom royal head

Caracalla

trunkless stone heads have unique identities as they balance on their necks on the shelves of Roman museums; the merest amateur soon learns to recognize the chill beauty of Augustus, the wide-eyed glare of Caracalla, and the pudgy, narrow-lipped face of Vespasian.

The Egyptians? Perhaps we might know some of them. I think I would recognize Akhenaton; for one thing, he doesn't look like any other pharaoh. But what did he really look like? In the flesh? Like the strange Karnak colossus, with its elongated face and diabolic mouth, or like the sensitive, grave little statue in the Cairo Museum?

An exact likeness wasn't what the Egyptian artist was after. The magical efficacy of the name identified a statue or a painting. A man's name was more than a handy label; it was an integral part of himself, carrying a spark of his own essence. Inscribing a statue with this magic spell, the name, gave the stone form not only identity but a sort of animation. If a king wanted to "borrow" the statue of one of his predecessors he often didn't bother remodeling the features, he simply cut his name over that of the original owner.

And yet, says the informed reader, there are genuine portrait sculptures from ancient Egypt. They look like portraits. Some, though uninscribed, have been identified beyond any reasonable doubt—Nefertiti, Queen Tiye, Amenemhat III. . . .

It would be ridiculous to claim that Egypt never produced a single portrait statue; whatever the canon and its requirements, the talents and tastes of individual artists varied widely. From time to time a skillful sculptor did produce a work of art which suggests portraiture in the strictest sense of the word. The trouble is, we don't always know whom the heads are portraits of. In the case of Queen Tiye, to take only one example, we can be fairly sure of the general period to which the wonderful wooden head should be dated. However, a few scholars think the lady in question is not Tiye, but her daughter, Sitamon. The features do bear a resemblance to other so-called portraits of Tiye which are identified by name; but then, Sitamon may have looked like her mother.

I think the reader would be surprised to learn how shaky many of the accepted identifications of sculptured heads really are. Unless they are inscribed, the ones that are "certain" ought to be labeled with a question mark, and the ones that have question marks probably should not have names at all. The question mark seems to be regarded as a magic sign which legitimizes a guess and turns it into a scholarly theory. The same magic sign is applied to many of the Amarna heads which were found in Thutmose's abandoned workshop. Not a single piece bears a name or an inscription, yet some scholars believe they can recognize all the members of the royal family and many of the high officials. I admire their enthusiasm and respect their expertise; experience gives an expert a feeling for relationships and resemblances which may be valid even though it cannot always be made explicit. Yet this sort of scholarship can be treacherous; postulated resemblances have been used as the basis for elaborate theories of chronology and genealogy for which there is little or no textual evidence. The eye is easily misled by the unfortunate tendency to see, not what is actually there, but what it wishes or expects to see. Any parent of a newborn infant knows, for instance, that the poor child may be identified as the "spitting image" of half a dozen different, doting relatives. Even the experts often fail to agree on the identity of a particular head unless it is inscribed. No one could possibly mistake a bust of Tiberius for a portrait of Augustus; but the same head has been identified by different scholars as a portrait of Akhenaton, his successor Smenkhkare, and his wife Nefertiti.

I am willing to admit that the famous bust is Nefertiti, even though her name is not on it. Why? For one thing, there's that long, elegant throat. Primarily, however, it's the crown. She is the only queen known to have worn it. This is called an iconographical feature, and although "iconography" is a word I detest and a subject I had sworn to avoid, some reference to it is necessary if I am to be fair to the scholars who are specialists in Egyptian art and who identify works of art on that basis. I refuse to define it, however. Examples get the point across better. Nefertiti's distinctive crown is such an example. Most other iconographical features are not so unique. Crowns, ornaments, elements of costume, the shape of a wig, the size of an earring, have been analyzed, classified, and attributed. Some of the arguments are very persuasive, but I still feel that identifications based solely on iconography are worrisome.

THE ARTIST

We have been talking about painting and sculpture in the round exclusively, so that it may seem that we have neglected the elegant Egyptian relief sculpture. However, most of the general remarks we have made about painting apply equally well to relief, since it was also two-dimensional. Most Egyptian relief sculpture is low relief, and it was usually painted as well. When we admire the wall reliefs in the Old Kingdom tombs, with their delicate rendering of forms, we tend to forget that in many cases the relief sculptor's skill was covered over by that of the artist painter.

Before the sculptor began carving a scene on the wall of a tomb or temple, the surface to be decorated was carefully smoothed, and any cracks or holes were filled with plaster. If the stone being used was of poor quality, the whole wall might be covered with a thin coating of plaster. When the plaster was dry, the outline draftsman—as we translate his title—made his appearance. His task was to draw the outlines of the scene upon the plastered wall. To insure accuracy, and to follow the canon of correct proportions, he used a grid, which was applied directly upon the wall surface before the actual drawing was begun. The intervals between the lines of the grid were measured by means of an instrument similar to a ruler or straight-edge, but the lines themselves were made by a string dipped in red ochre, held taut, and then

plucked like a bowstring. With the same red ochre the artist then
drew his figures, using the squares of the grid to guide him. Some of
the grids have been found. They differ slightly in their relative proportions, but according to one, a human being was nineteen squares high
from soles to crown. Specific parts of the body, such as the foot, forearm, and torso, also had their proper size in terms of grid squares. This
was a practical and ingenious technique, for it could be used to draw
figures of any magnitude; the artist merely decreased the size of the
squares for small figures and enlarged them when an immense king or
god was required. The faded lines of these grids can still be seen, by
sharp-eyed tourists, on a few Egyptian monuments.

The outline draftsman's sketches were corrected, presumably by
his boss. On some wall surfaces the surer, darker lines are still visible.

When the draftsmen had packed up and gone home, the relief
sculptor took over. His usual method was to cut away the background,
leaving the figures raised, but in some cases the figures and hieroglyphs
were sunk into the surface. Obviously this latter technique saved a lot
of time and effort; one can only wonder
why it wasn't done more often. One explanation that has been proposed is that
raised relief worked better on exterior
walls, where sunlight could sharpen its
outlines. Makes sense, I suppose.

After he had cut out the forms, the
sculptor finished the interior surfaces,
indicating details of clothing and musculature, but the real finishing detail was
left to the third and last technician, the
painter, who may or may not have been
the same as the outline draftsman. His
palette varied from age to age, but it was
always relatively simple, and it was restricted by certain conventions. Clothing was painted white, hair black, human
skin reddish brown for men or yellow for

Human figure and grid

women. A few people were shown with black skin, and so was Osiris, Lord of the Dead, except when he was green. Both colors must indicate some special status, since other deified persons show the same feature, but I prefer not to be dogmatic about what they mean. Green for the new crops, rebirth? Black for the fertile soil that nurtures vegetation?

With the humble animals the artist was allowed a wider scope, and there his talents showed up best. The brilliant birds are among the most delightful characters in Egyptian reliefs; they have been so accurately drawn that the species can be identified, but the colors applied to them were not always those of nature. Attempts to indicate the texture of feathers or fur, and even the rounding of the body, have been discovered in certain animal paintings.

The painter's brush was made out of a length of fibrous wood pounded at one end to separate the fibers into bristles. He used different brushes for different colors; these were almost always mineral-based pigments, which is one reason why so much ancient painting has survived so well. The black color was usually carbon; the other popular tints derived from green malachite and red and yellow ochre. The ground minerals were mixed with a vehicle, which was not an oil but an adhesive; Egyptian painting was tempera, not oil painting. The precise adhesive used is uncertain, not because of the mysterious lost art of the Egyptian painter, but because it is hard to analyze a minute proportion of a substance in a minute chunk of paint. One of the adhesives used was certainly beeswax, either mixed with the pigment as a binder or applied over the finished painting as a protective coating. Sometimes varnish was used for the latter purpose; it must have seemed like a good idea at the time, but it has usually turned yellow or brown, obscuring the original brilliant colors.

All sorts of things were painted—boxes, chairs, columns, floors of palaces, walls of temples—but the majority of great Egyptian paintings come from the tombs. So do many of the great works of sculpture.

Most Egyptian statues are made of stone, a material which admirably suits the stiff angularity of the style. Unfinished pieces show that the outline of the statue was drawn on all four sides of the block, and the whole figure was roughed out before final details were done. The sculptor's tools were of copper; he used chisels and drills and saws. After the statue was finished it was polished with an abrasive stone or sand, and then painted. Limestone and other soft-stone statues were painted all over, with the usual white for clothing and red or yellow for skin. Statues of hard stone such as granite or basalt, which were prized for the beauty of the texture, were only picked out in paint—eyebrows might be painted black, or the details of a headdress or crown indicated. Sometimes details were added by insets of other materials. The eyes were often inlaid, so well that a certain number of Egyptian statues have quite an unnerving stare.

Composite statues, with different parts of the body made of different materials, were especially popular during the Amarna Period. They have survived only as bits and pieces, but some of the splendid Amarna heads were meant to be used in such composite statues—the face and hands carved of a polished stone such as quartzite, the clothed body of fine white limestone, the ornaments and crowns of gold and semiprecious stones or glass. None has survived intact, but a number of sculptured heads were intended to be a part of such composite statues. They have long protrusions, or tenons, on the top of the head, which would have been inserted into cavities in a crown or wig. Another tenon at the base of the neck fit into a hole in the torso of the statue.

There is one fragment of yellow jasper, polished to a mirror sheen, which depicts the lower part of a face—the face of a woman, because of the color. The material was so valuable and hard to work that the lady must have been a queen, and an Amarna queen at that; the provenance is unknown, but the style is distinctive. She's been identified as Tiye, Nefertiti, and a secondary wife of Akhenaton's. Never mind who she was, the completed statue must have been stunning, if somewhat baroque: the shimmering surface of her golden yellow face, the alabasterlike white of her linen robe, with perhaps a wig of carved lapis lazuli curls and a crown of gold, gold earrings, a broad collar of genuine gemstones set in gold.

Other materials were also used for sculpture. Some of the hand-somest statues we have from Egypt are of wood; the head of Queen Tiye (?) and the Sheikh el Beled are outstanding examples. The metal statues are perhaps less well known than those of wood or stone, and they deserve mention because they show impressive craftmanship. As early as the Sixth Dynasty, Egyptian metalworkers produced a greater-than-life-size statue of Pepi I in copper. It was not cast, but hammered over a wooden core. By the Late Period statues of bronze, and even gold, are found, and these were certainly cast by the well-known ciré perdue method, in which a wax model is covered with a mold and heated. The wax melts and runs out through a hole left for that pur-pose, and the metal is poured into the resultant vacant space. Hollow or solid statues can be cast by this method, the former employing a core of some material under the wax; hollow statues, naturally, were cheaper than solid ones. One of the best of the Egyptian bronze stat-ues is that of the lady Takushet of the Twenty-Fifth Dynasty; the de-signs with which she appears to be tattooed represent the decorations of her elegant robe, and they are inlaid in silver into the copper.

Having discussed the works of art, we ought to say a few words about the artists. The praise that is their due must be given them as a group citation and anonymously, for few names of individual painters and sculptors have come down to us, and even those few can rarely be connected with a given painting or statue. There is not a single signed work of art from ancient Egypt, unless we view the rough figures of Senenmut, hidden behind the sanctuary doors of the temple he is thought to have designed, as equivalents of "Senenmut fecit." Tradi-tion, or the circumstances of discovery, sometimes allow us to ascribe names to particular pieces; perhaps Thutmose of el Amarna can claim the beautiful head of Nefertiti as his chef-d'oeuvre, but we cannot be sure. Names of other artists have survived, though not in connection with specific objects. Bak, the sculptor of Akhenaton, "whom His Maj-esty himself taught," gives us a tantalizing hint about the heretic king; was Akhenaton a dilettante sculptor as well as a religious fanatic? Then there was Iritsen, who lived during the Middle Kingdom and who was, if we can believe his own words, a sculptor of no mean talent:

I am a craftsman successful in his craft, one who comes out on top through that which he knows. . . . I know the movement of a figure, the stride of a woman . . . the cringing of the solitary captive, how one eye looks at another, how to make frightened the face of the outlaw, the pose of the arm of him who harpoons the hippopotamus, the pace of the runner.

The word "craftsman," which Iritsen uses, is important because it describes the status of sculptors and painters. Their trade lacked the semimystical sanctity of the "fine arts"; it was not even a profession, but a craft, on a level with carpentry and jewelrymaking. Within the general category of art there were specializations: the painter, the outline draftsman, the relief sculptor, and the sculptor in the round. In the workshops connected with the palace and the temples these craftsmen worked together under the supervision of the chief sculptor and the overseer of craftsmen. There was division of labor; one man might carve a statue and another man paint it. But perhaps there was no strict "union" separation of jobs. A single individual might learn all the aspects of his craft and be outline draftsman, painter, and sculptor in turn, with the hope of working up at last to the supervisory position of overseer of craftsmen. There are several indications that sculptors were regarded as superior to painters; for one thing, the tombs, stelae, and other monuments left by successful sculptors far outnumber those left by painters, which implies that they were richer and more prominent.

Most artists, and certainly the best of them, worked for the state. Sometimes the king might order a statue or even a whole tomb to be made for a friend or good servant, as a mark of favor, but there were also artists whose services could be obtained by the private citizen. Were these the state artists "moonlighting," or was there a class of privately employed artists? We don't know. The same mystery surrounds the training of artists. Since workshops existed, it is not unreasonable to suppose that "likely" boys were sent to them for training. I imagine that the boys were chosen because of family connections rather than special talent. In many cases known to us, son followed father in the trade, as he did in other trades and professions. It is the apprentice system in operation once again, with the father as the master. Yet some artists obviously took pride in their trade and enjoyed using their talents. Although the canon of art was limiting, there was room for the exercise of both skill and imagination; the great works of art surviving from Egypt show that although genius may not have been recognized as such, some ancient Michelangelos did find their way into the trade which was, for them, a genuine calling.

THE ARCHITECTS

The monumental achievements of Egyptian architects are still dramatically visible along the Nile; of all the aspects of Egyptian culture, the temples and tombs make the greatest impression, and live longest in the memories of visiting tourists.

Evidently building temples was considered a more respectable occupation than carving statues. At any rate, the men who built them mentioned these achievements in their tomb biographies. We can thus attach names to specific structures, which is not the case with statues. The tomb of Thutmose I was constructed by a man named Ineni; the Karnak obelisks of Thutmose III were erected by his official Puemre. Of all the names that have survived, three stand out above the rest; no account of Egyptian architecture would be complete without them.

The first, and perhaps the foremost, was Imhotep, Vizier and Overseer of Works for King Djoser of the remote Third Dynasty. To this man probably belongs the credit for the Step Pyramid, Djoser's massive tomb, which still dominates the site of Sakkara. Not only was the Step Pyramid a major engineering work, it was, so far as we know, a creative original—the first pyramid, and the first attempt to build on a grandiose scale in stone. Imhotep's talents were not limited to architecture. Later generations of Egyptians honored him as a sage and master physician, and eventually he was worshiped, in this latter capacity, as a veritable god.

So fabulous were Imhotep's achievements, and so remote the time in which he lived, that some scholars used to doubt his existence. A few years ago a statue base with Imhotep's name, found in the Step Pyramid enclosure, not only solidified him historically but tied him specifically to the great monument which tradition had long ascribed to him. And for a while it was hoped we were on the brink of a discovery which would give the long-dead genius real identity as a historical personage.

The story begins over fifty years ago, when Walter B. Emery, the excavator of the early dynastic tombs of Sakkara, had a little time left over at the end of his digging season. He had long been interested in a particular part of the site, the westernmost section of the archaic cemetery of North Sakkara. This cemetery contains tombs of the very ancient First to Third Dynasties, and yet, in one place, the surface of the ground was covered with broken bits of pottery which dated from the Greco-Roman period. As we know, the worship of Imhotep was very popular in Greco-Roman times; and scholars have long believed that if a tomb of Imhotep existed, it would be in this archaic cemetery, where the other nobles of his period were buried. So, just before closing down his dig in 1956, Emery sunk two test pits in the area. The pits showed Third Dynasty brickwork. They also held the remains of sacrificed bulls, and ibis mummies.

The ibis, the long-legged bird sacred to Thoth, was one of the attributes of this god taken over by Imhotep when he attained divine rank. The evidence, then, looked promising. But it was not until 1964 that Professor Emery was able to pursue his investigations. What he found was both unexpected and significant.

The whole area was covered with tombs dating from the Archaic Period and the Old Kingdom. In Ptolemaic times their walls had been leveled, and the spaces between the tombs filled in, to form a huge flat surface. Why was this done? A reasonable explanation is that the leveled site was the platform for a big building, perhaps a temple. The sacrificed bulls, although they could have been tomb offerings, might have been foundation deposits for such a building.

The excavators proceeded to clear some of the tombs. In the burial shaft of one, thirty-five feet below the ground, they literally fell through into a fantastic underground structure—a vast stonecut labyrinth, like the Serapeum of Sakkara where the mummies of the sacred bulls were buried. The chambers of Emery's structure also contained mummies—thousands upon thousands of ibis birds, embalmed and placed in pottery jars.

A later season of excavation uncovered galleries of mummified baboons—like the ibis, sacred to Thoth and his godson Imhotep. The baboon burials were those of sacred temple animals; the chests containing the mummies bore short demotic inscriptions giving the animal's name and the date of its burial. Also found were plaster casts of parts of the human body—feet, hands, heads, and so on—which remind us of the votive thank-offerings left by pilgrims who had been cured at shrines of healing—a practice which has continued into the present century.

Regrettably, Emery did not live to complete the Sakkara excavations, but other archaeologists uncovered still more catacombs containing animal mummies, including the burials of the sacred cows who were the mothers of the holy Apis bulls buried in the Serapeum. The restrained scholarly prose of the preliminary excavation reports still manages to convey an astonishing image of a honeycomb of dark, convoluted galleries riddling the subterrane of this much-excavated area. In Ptolemaic times there was not one but a large complex of temples here, and one of the gods worshiped was certainly Imhotep, whose name has been found on dedicatory stelae. The excavations yielded rich finds of archaeological material, including fragments of the temple archives, which were written in Aramaic and Greek as well as Egyptian.

Yet the burning question remains unanswered. Was one of the battered, vandalized Third Dynasty tombs that of the master architect? Among the largest was a mastaba designated only as number 3517, since no name or other identification was found. The superstructure had been leveled to a height of about a meter, and the burial shafts and chambers had been filled with sand. At the head of each shaft Emery found the remains of sacrificed bulls. Were they foundation deposits for a temple built over the tomb, or offerings to the unknown occupant of the tomb? Another mastaba, number 3518, has been dated to the reign of Djoser by means of a jar sealing found nearby. Unlike other tombs in the vicinity, it has precisely the same orientation as the Step Pyramid, and anatomical models—votive offerings—were found outside its entrance.

We will probably never know the answer. Even if the tomb had been found, it is unlikely that it would have given us any useful information. Tombs of this period are poor in inscriptional material, and it is unlikely that Imhotep's tomb would have escaped the depredations of tomb robbers and other vandals. It would have been a thrilling discovery, though, surpassing, in certain ways, the gold of Tutankhamon. Monuments to the triumph of the human intellect are rare.

The second great architect, who, like Imhotep, was worshiped as a god long after his death, was born a thousand years or more after his predecessor. He was Amenhotep, son of Hapu, and he served the king whose namesake he was—Amenhotep III of the Eighteenth Dynasty. He was the son of unimportant parents in the Delta town of Athribis, and he started his career as a humble military scribe in charge of recruiting. It was evidently his superior talents which led to the recognition he eventually achieved from the king; not only were statues of him erected in the temple of Karnak, but he had the unprecedented honor of a mortuary temple on the west bank of Thebes near that of the king who thought so highly of him. His titles have the "Lord High Everything Else" quality of many officials, including King's Scribe and Overseer of Recruits—and Overseer of the Works of the King. But was he actually an architect? Some scholars credit him with the design for the Temple of Luxor, which is one of the most harmonious structures in Egypt. His own inscriptions claim that he was responsible for the two most prominent surviving remains of Amenhotep III's mortuary temple, the Colossi of Memnon.

The career of the third member of our trio contrasts ironically with the honor and respect, culminating in actual divinity, which was granted the other two. Senenmut, the friend of Queen Hatshepsut, is usually supposed to have constructed her beautiful funerary temple at Deir el Bahri. He was not a popular man. After his royal mistress died, enemies attacked certain of his monuments and left his sarcophagus in fragments. Within a few generations of his death, probably his very name was forgotten. William Stevenson Smith has pointed out the most ironic touch of all—in later times a shrine with the names of the deified Amenhotep and the deified Imhotep was erected at the site of Deir el Bahri. There the two were worshiped, while against the very same cliffs stood the building which many people consider the most beautiful temple in all Egypt, with the desecrated, empty tomb of its builder beneath. Senenmut built two tombs, one on the hillside where nobles of the period were buried, and the other under the temple of the queen. His mummy has never been found, but in remote corners of the temple small, hastily cut figures of him survived the revengeful destruction of his enemies.

Now that we have waxed poetical over the names of Imhotep, Amenhotep, and Senenmut, it is only fair to state that we don't know whether they were architects at all, in our sense of the word. We do not consider the head of the firm of Jones, Smith, and Brown the architect of a skyscraper if he orders Jones Junior to draw up the actual plans. We cannot be sure that the Egyptians made the same distinction. There is no Egyptian word for "architecture"; there is not even a title which can be read "architect" with any certainty. Some Egyptologists have used the word to translate a title which means "overseer of works," and we still describe men as architects if they say, in their biographical inscriptions, that they erected an obelisk or built a shrine.

Unlike the artist or the sculptor, the overseer of works was not a craftsman. He was a high official, and he usually had other important titles which gave him noble rank. He must have been the equivalent of the head of the ministry of public works, and he was responsible for building operations, from the quarrying of the stone up to the dedication of the finished building. Obviously his subordinates did most of the actual work. Scribes calculated the amount of stone necessary and the loaves of bread per day which would be eaten by the workmen. Foremen managed the gangs of stoneworkers in the quarry, and ships' captains were in charge of the barges on which the stones were loaded. Painters and sculptors did the decorative work, and masons fitted the stones. But who drew up the plans?

I wish I knew. I would also like to know how they drew up the plans, and whether they did. There are a few tattered drawings now in museums which may be architects' sketches. None of them are detailed enough to rank as blueprints, or even as reliable plans. Most are drawings of small elements—a doorway, a courtyard planted with trees. One such plan, more comprehensive than the majority, is reproduced in our illustration, together with the plan drawn by a modern scholar, S. P. K. Glanville, on the basis of the measurements given by the Egyptian scribe in the short inscriptions written on his drawing. Obviously the Egyptian version was not a scale drawing; the proportions are all wrong.

Another sketch gives the plan of a tomb. The drawing is accurate enough to enable us to identify the tomb as that of Ramses IV. However, either the architect changed his mind while the work was under way or the plan does not attempt to be precise, since there are several important discrepancies in the measurements. In any case, a rock-cut tomb is a fairly simple structure compared with a temple. It is no more

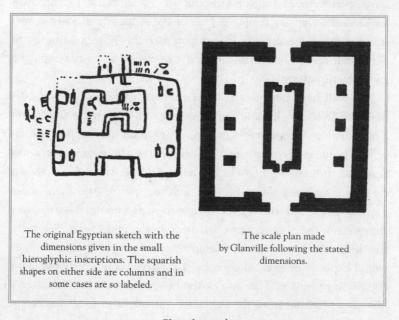

The original Egyptian sketch with the dimensions given in the small hieroglyphic inscriptions. The squarish shapes on either side are columns and in some cases are so labeled.

The scale plan made by Glanville following the stated dimensions.

Plan of a temple

than a series of regularly shaped holes in the rock, the sort of thing an amateur could design without straining his mental equipment: "All right, men, make that room a little longer so the sarcophagus can fit in, and cut a door over there so we can have a storeroom."

Obviously this lighthearted technique would not work with a temple like that of Deir el Bahri, or with any other temple. Deir el Bahri is so lovely, so perfectly proportioned, so harmonious, that it almost demands the existence of a model. Although the Egyptians made model buildings for funerary purposes, no architect's aid has ever been found, with the possible exception of one miniature building. It is an uninspired, rather crude structure, though, and certainly no model, or plan, of any known temple has been discovered.

There are references to an archive of master plans, kept by certain temples. This is not solid proof, but it does support the assumption which the very existence of the architectural masterpieces forces us to make—that either plans or models or both were used to build them. Of course, there were full-size models all over Egypt, the temples of earlier kings. Senenmut had such an inspiration close at hand, for there was an Eleventh Dynasty temple at Deir el Bahri itself, and Hatshepsut's structure has some elements in common with the older building. But if Senenmut started out by imitating the Eleventh Dynasty temple, he ended by surpassing it.

We still have not answered the essential question: who actually designed Deir el Bahri and the other gems of Egyptian architecture? There are two tenuous types of argument which may support the assumption, made by many archaeologists, that the overseer of works designed the temples himself. In the first place, there is no known candidate for the position of royal architect per se—no man whose name is connected with a given temple in such a manner as to suggest that he, not the overseer of works, drew up the plans for it. Secondly, the design and appearance of a temple were of major importance; they would logically be decided upon by the man who was responsible for the whole operation. That's about the best we can do; it is admittedly unsatisfactory. But until the Egyptian equivalent of Jones Junior appears, claiming to have planned the "beautiful temple of Djeser Dje-seru," I am content to give Senenmut the credit.

In conclusion, perhaps the best advice I can give anyone who wants to learn to enjoy Egyptian art is to go out and look at it. The best place to go is Egypt, of course; the second-best is a museum. The bookstores and libraries teem these days with picture books on Egypt. Increased photographic skill and new reproductive techniques make some of these books joys to behold. However, there is absolutely no substitute for viewing the real thing.

Ten

SORCERER, SCIENTIST, AND PRIEST

MAGIC, SCIENCE, AND RELIGION

The antiseptic whiteness of a scientist's laboratory; glowing stained glass under the dim arches of a Gothic cathedral; a shabby back room where a man in a preposterous turban bends over a crystal ball. Three different environments and three different systems of thought, as distinct from each other, surely, as the three angles of a triangle.

Up to this point we have been talking about life in ancient Egypt in its more concrete aspects—activities, occupations, objects. This is fine so far as it goes. But beneath the practical everyday world of food and furniture, funny stories and love songs, lies another stratum—the level of attitudes and ideas. In a culture like that of ancient Egypt these abstractions are seldom explicitly stated; yet they are, rather than the shape of pots or the canon of art, the really significant and definitive aspects of the culture. Although the Egyptians sat on chairs and liked to drink beer, their view of the universe was not the same as ours, and one of the basic differences lies in the way they thought about the three categories we are now discussing: magic, science, and religion.

Magic: The use of means that are believed to have supernatural power . . . to produce or prevent a particular result believed not obtainable by natural means.

Science: Accumulated and accepted knowledge that has been systematized and formulated with reference to the discovery of general truths or the operation of general laws.

Religion: A personal awareness or conviction of the existence of a supreme being or of supernatural powers controlling one's destiny.

Normally, definitions are a good way of beginning a discussion. They nail down the terms to be discussed and prevent ambiguities. But let us suppose that we are conversing with a Theban priest of the Eighteenth Dynasty. We want him to tell us about Egyptian science; and in order to explain what we mean, we give him Mr. Webster's definitions.

The priest would not disagree with the definitions; he simply would not know what we were talking about. We would have some difficulty in translation, to begin with, since the ancient Egyptians had no word for "science." They had no word for "religion" either. Magic? There is a word which we translate by that term, but our priest would not apply it to the same things we do. He would scratch his shaven head as we tried to explain the difference between "natural" and "supernatural," and if we finally succeeded in getting across "an organized body of knowledge, systematized . . . and arranged in accord with certain laws," he might very well give us a lecture on the systematized Egyptian calendar of religious festivals and the rituals appropriate to them.

The point is one which cannot be made too often or too emphatically. To the Egyptians, as to many other peoples, the categories which we have distinguished were not mutually exclusive. They were not even separate. If a man came to an Egyptian doctor with a broken leg, the physician might apply a splint, rub the leg with a mixture of honey and herbs, pronounce a magical incantation, and hang an amulet, like a religious medal, around the sufferer's neck. We would say that he had employed several different methods of healing, only one of which could be considered effective. But the Egyptian patient would have been highly indignant if his medical adviser had only used the splint.

It would be an oversimplification to say that the difference between an Egyptian doctor and a modern M.D. is that the former believed in magic. We have two problem words: "magic" and "believe." What does magic suggest to us? A series of kaleidoscopic images— Swami Hassan with his turban and crystal ball, a cute little Merlin out of Walt Disney, damned Faustus and the pale shade of Helen. Magic . . . one of the most evocative words in the language, ranging from glamour to horror, from the glimmer of Titania's wings in the moonlight to the old women screaming in the fires of the Inquisition. Magic to primitive man was something altogether different.

I am going to try very hard to avoid the word "primitive" here, though I may not succeed. It's an old anthropological term, with implications of inferiority and wrongheadedness. And no, I am not being politically correct when I reject it; the word itself exemplifies the attitude I've been complaining about: the notion that all other systems of belief are less valid in all cases than our own. They are not invalid in the context of their own cultures, and who is to say that we have attained the ultimate heights of knowledge? Not me.

First let's tackle the word "believe." The Egyptians and a lot of other people believed in magic. The sophisticated reader may find this statement obvious to the point of tedium. He already knows that.

The sophisticated reader may think he accepts man's faith in magic. He probably does not. This is one of the great problems facing historians, archaeologists, and ethnologists—the difficulty of really accepting a theorem which is, we like to think, so alien to our own point of view. Of course, it is impossible to get inside another man or woman's skin and think the way they do. When we interpret a culture as different from our own as that of ancient Egypt, we are translating. We cannot even break down the facets of culture into chapters suitable for a book without violating the essential unity of the lives of these other people; and everything we say about them is said in our words, each of which has a backlog of associations and meanings which are not those of the culture in question. We cannot solve this problem, we can only remember, constantly, that we are translating, and that something is always lost in translation.

I have accused my sophisticated reader of not really believing that which he thinks he does believe. I will prove my point by citing an example.

There once appeared, in a learned Egyptological journal, an article by a learned Egyptologist on the harem conspiracy under Ramses III of the Nineteenth Dynasty. The plot itself was the sort of thing one expects from an irregular institution like a harem: one of the ladies had decided that her son ought to be the next king instead of the legitimate heir. In order to insure this desirable goal it was necessary for the old king, Ramses III, to be sent to join his father the Sun somewhat ahead of schedule. The lady succeeded in interesting a number of important officials in her project, but it failed in at least one of its aims. Owing to the ambiguity of the official record, we do not know whether Ramses III actually was murdered by the conspirators or not; but the legitimate crown prince, later Ramses IV, discovered the plot in time to save his throne and his own neck. The plotters were tried and executed, except for a few who were only deprived of their ears and noses, and a few others—perhaps the most highly placed—who were "allowed" to commit suicide.

One passage in the text is particularly interesting. In order to seize power and reach the inner precincts of the palace, the conspirators had made writings "for enchanting and for confusing . . . and [they] began to make people of wax so that they could be taken inside" (the palace or the harem itself).

The most reasonable interpretation of this passage is that the plotters used magic. The waxen images are magicians' props, known from all over the world. The written spells controlled the will of the loyal guards and courtiers who protected the king.

This is the accepted explanation. However, the author of the article I mentioned does not believe that the plotters used magic at all. His counterarguments deal with the passage I have quoted, and necessitate new and hitherto unknown translations of such words as "enchanting" and "gods." Egyptian is a good language for this sort of argument, because its vocabulary is still not completely fixed; new meanings do turn up, now and then, for known words. As for the significant phrase "made out of wax," the author wants to make it a figure of speech, not a figure of magic. Anyone who has ever studied a foreign language has probably noticed the infuriating propensity of prepositions in other tongues to mean almost anything. The preposition we translate "out of" can, by some stretching, be made to mean "into"! Things which are made "into wax" are made malleable, susceptible to influence.

These arguments are plausible, although the figure of speech is an English idiom rather than one the Egyptians would have used. But the philologist who tampers with established vocabulary must have motives purer than Caesar's wife. He cannot invent new meanings in order to support a preconceived theory. The author of the article states his theory quite candidly: "The conspirators were in too risky a situation to entrust the outcome of their plot to magical procedures."

The reader can see, I am sure, the point of this discussion. The author of the article on the harem conspiracy does not "believe" that the Egyptians believed in magic. He "knows" that they did; Egyptian culture is full of examples. But when he comes right down to a specific case, one in which he would certainly not have trusted to magic, he wants to give his friends the Egyptians credit for an equally practical (another loaded word) approach.

I have gone into this at some length, not to pick the bones of Scholar X, but to show that if he can commit such a basic blunder, the rest of us had better beware of complacency. Of course, it was in just such a risky situation that the Egyptians would have used magic.

Magic was not a game, or the last resort of the incompetent. It was a tool—possibly the most important tool of all.

In terms of Mr. Webster's definitions, pyramidology and psychic research can be called "sciences." In case the reader is unfamiliar with pyramidology, let me beg, in the names of Breasted, Petrie, Erman, and Champollion, that he will never, ever, confuse it with Egyptology. Pyramidology is the study of the mystic and prophetic import of the Egyptian pyramids. No one who has read the volumes published by pyramidologists (or pyramidalists) can deny that the subject is organized, accumulated (only too much so), accepted (by many people), systematized, and based on what its followers claim are general truths. Possibly some of them *are* general truths. But it is certainly not a science. Nor would I include psychic research in that category, although its tenets have been formulated, and a formidable mass of documentation has been collected by its numerous adherents.

Obviously there is something wrong with our definitions. They do not really distinguish between the three categories we are discussing, even in our terms, and they certainly have given us no insight into Egyptian magic. Let us tackle the problem in another way; let us take our categories in pairs and try to distinguish the essential differences between them.

Magic and science have much more in common than one might suppose. Like science, magic was an attempt to formulate principles through which the forces affecting man could be understood and manipulated. These principles had to be based on assumptions about the world. When the assumptions were false, man got magical principles; when they were correct, he had science. In this sense magic might be called a bastard, or pseudo, science, for primitive man had no way of telling false assumptions from true assumptions.

This interpretation of magic as a pseudo-science has been challenged, naturally; what scholarly theory has not? The challengers maintain that people knew quite well the difference between magic and the rational techniques which may be called primitive science. When a Trobriand Islander plants a garden he is careful to weed and water and protect his plants. He uses magic too; but, says Dr. Bronislaw

Malinowski, he would smile if you suggested he grow crops by magic alone, without water or weeding or seeds.

Much as I admire Dr. Malinowski, I am not sure that he is making a significant point. His Trobriand Islander might smile if it were suggested that he grew crops by rational methods alone, without magic. To the people who believe in it, magic is just as important as the water or the seed.

It might be claimed that primitive (sorry) men used practical techniques, primitive science, whenever they could and only resorted to magic to cover areas in which unpredictable factors—luck or chance—might affect the results. But garden magic was not used only to ward off destructive storms or kill pests; often the spell covered the whole process: "Make this corn grow!" Furthermore, this distinction assumes the impossible: that primitive man's definitions of the predictable and the unpredictable were the same as ours, and that he made our distinction between the natural and the supernatural. In one sense all of his life was supernatural, shaped by powerful forces which acted directly on his fragile body and his few possessions. He did the best he could, with his seeds and his watering can, and then he plastered the whole process over with a thick, protective coating of magic. To assume that he recognized a qualitative difference between his rational and nonrational techniques is to make an assumption which the evidence does not justify.

One of the differences between magic and science, then, lies in the validity of the assumptions which underlie their structures. However, it is not always easy to distinguish between false and true assumptions. The best way of recognizing a true assumption is to see whether it actually works out, in practice. It is an ironic fact that when magic works, it is no longer magic, but science. Hypnotism, once an adjunct of the black art, is now semirespectable and unglamorous; the beginnings of the physician's craft are to be found in the hex bag of the tribal witch doctor.

Let us consider a theoretical case in order to see how plausible such false assumptions may appear. Imagine that you are a Neanderthaler whose mate has been taken away by a bigger, fiercer Neanderthaler.

Even a caveman had sense enough to avoid combat with someone who could tear him limb from limb; still, our caveman resents the theft. Now he has no one to gather firewood, and toast his chunk of mammoth over the coals, and carry his baggage when the tribe shifts hunting grounds. He has to do all these menial chores himself. It upsets him. Standing well out of his rival's sight, so that his behavior will not be interpreted as a challenge, he has a temper tantrum. He stamps up and down; he bellows; he waves his pointed stick and pretends to thrust it into the body of his enemy; if he knows any bad words, he swears. After he has exhausted himself and his store of invective he collapses onto the ground and wipes his perspiring brow. And then, of course, he feels much better. Who wouldn't, after such an enjoyable release?

The performance in which our Neanderthal man imaginatively thrashes an opponent who is too big to be thrashed otherwise has an immediate, practical result. It relieves him. Suppose something else happens. Suppose next time the hated rival goes hunting, the mammoth catches him, instead of vice versa, and rams a horn into him. One need not rely too heavily upon coincidence to assume that this happened now and then; life was hard in those far-off days. Now what is our hero to think? A rudimentary sense of sequence, reinforced by hatred and a desire for revenge, may enable him to connect his fit of rage, which was followed by a strong emotional reaction, with the subsequent accident. He has killed his enemy! He knew at the time that something important had happened; he felt so good!

Now this is one of the places at which magic and science part company. Sequence is not causality, although it is easily mistaken for it. One morning about 4:00 A.M. I may put on a flowing yellow robe and do a dance on the balcony. An hour or two later the sun rises. Here we have not only sequence but intent, and a contrived similarity between the "cause" and the "effect"—the yellow robe and the graceful bounding leaps with which I will, no doubt, imitate the rising of the solar orb. Did I make the sun rise? You may laugh, intelligent reader, but if I went about it properly I could probably collect a few people, even in our day and age, who would believe it. We talk very glibly, many of us, about cause and effect, but in the complex, everyday world the causes of particular phenomena are not easy to isolate. What causes two people to fall in love? What causes a plant to grow, a bird to fly, a child to catch measles? What is the cause of war or of a Mozart symphony? What makes my geraniums die while my neighbors' plants flourish? Even when we can pick out a single "cause" it has to be qualified. I suppose a child catches measles because he picks up a measles germ; but he may wallow in germs without contracting the disease if he has natural immunity, or if he has had measles before—or for other reasons which as yet elude us. Let us make allowances for our ancestors. It is not surprising that they could not tell good causes from bad causes, when some modern logicians wonder whether they exist at all.

But back to our Neanderthal hero, flushed with success and triumph. If he has enough imagination to make the connection between his tantrum and his enemy's death, he will also see the implications. This is a great discovery! Perhaps he is noble and altruistic; if so, he will rush home after the hunt and explain his new invention to all the neighbors, so that they too can influence men and mammoths. Chances are, though, that he will not. Chances are that he will tell them about it, and then explain that he is the only one clever enough to do the job. So he becomes a witch doctor, or shaman, or warlock— the first of a long line of workers in magic who lived for countless ages on the credulity of their fellows.

We have already established the fact that it is not easy to distinguish a true "cause" from something which is not a cause at all. Still, a genuine cause should consistently produce the same result. Would not the patrons of a magician notice that he could not always get results from his spells?

No, they wouldn't. People don't see the things they don't want to see; they have selective imaginations. A success is remembered, a failure forgotten, just as pleasure remains longer and more vividly in the memory than does pain. Furthermore, the magicians were men of superior intelligence and craft; if they were not, they probably didn't last long. This is another of the symptoms of magic that distinguishes it from science—that much of its effectiveness depends on the personality of the magician. The scientist who eventually discovers the cause of cancer may be an unpleasant fellow personally, but his character will have no effect on the cancer virus, or whatever it turns out to be. A good magician, however, must have a lot of personality, or that quality called "charisma"—the ability to move men.

There is no profession in which charisma is more useful than in magic (except, of course, for politics). Take the field of medicine, which was, until relatively recent times, riddled with magical techniques. The "psychosomatic" ailments, which may include everything from backache to blindness, are not affected by modern surgery or medicine; but imagine the effect upon them of a powerful assertive personality, reinforced by the patient's belief in magic. Certainly the sufferer would be relieved. Even the pain of physical ailments would be alleviated. "Yes, Doc, I do feel better!" Today the doctor's bedside manner may help or hinder his patients, and the importance of "mind over matter" in some illnesses is being recognized. In magical medicine the bedside manner was 90 percent of the battle.

A really clever shaman could also experiment with herbs and drugs, the proper use of which would increase his percentage of cures. The practical application of the magician's intelligence could thus bring under control certain aspects of a given magical problem, which would make him much more effective. Take hate-magic—spells designed to defeat or cripple or kill an enemy—one of the most important subfields of the black art. The use of poison as an aid to witchcraft is well known, even in comparatively recent European history. The man who pays the magician his fee is satisfied with results; he doesn't know or care whether it was incantations or arsenic that laid his enemy low.

An experienced poisoner, then, could set up a respectable practice in "spelling" people to death. In love-magic some practical auxiliaries might also help—anything from bribery and blackmail to advice to the lovelorn: "Comb your hair once a week and file your teeth to sharper points." Even in weather-magic, where charisma is admittedly limited in effect, the shaman could employ his superior intelligence to observe phenomena which his duller-witted contemporaries might miss. If he could not produce rain on call, he might be able to predict it ahead of time, from cloud formations or recollections of seasonal variations. If he were called upon to stop an eclipse, all he needed to do was to keep on waving his arms and chanting until the shadow over the sun passed away. And in the last extremity, if all his efforts resulted in crashing failure—he could talk his way out of it. Adverse magic from some rival sorcerer, failure of a supporter in observing the necessary rituals—any such argument, if emphatically pressed, might convince his hearers. Being a cynic, I am inclined to agree with those anthropologists who believe that the most successful magicians may have been men who didn't believe in magic. An honest man, overcome by failure, might admit that he didn't know what had happened to thwart his spells. In some cultures he would not survive such an admission very long.

Another reason why magic seemed to work was because it did work; it worked because people believed in it, and they believed in it because it seemed to work. This is not as paradoxical as it sounds. Expressed hostility and malevolent intent can certainly cause anxiety and fear, nervous indigestion, and illness. A curse can kill—if the victim believes in it. Conversely, a potent protective charm may act as a psychological prop, increasing a person's self-confidence and, consequently, his effectiveness. No, it is no wonder people used to believe in magic. The real wonder is that we no longer do so. Do we?

How many of us really understand the principles of such a common household device as the ordinary land-line telephone? We know it works by scientific laws, not by magic, because various authorities, from our teachers to *Popular Science* magazine, assure us that this is so. But if, starting next week, the teachers and *Popular Science* said that the messages are carried by little fairies who run along the wires from town to town, a lot of us would be just as happy to accept that explanation. And if the right people told us that human blood makes the corn grow taller, some of us would go right out and sprinkle the corn. Not believe in magic? Who, us? We have our faith healers and our demagogues and magicians who sell us spells entitled "positive thinking" and "how to win friends and influence people." Surely, there is a sound psychological basis to such spells; so was there to much magic. We are science-minded, modern people, but there are those among us who refuse to have children inoculated and who deny themselves blood transfusions, on the ground that such acts are contrary to the will of God—although I do not recall that He has ever expressed Himself on either of these subjects. Some of us still march around in funny costumes carrying signs proclaiming our superiority to other races and religious groups, and others think it's okay to blow up children in order to make a point. Most of us are not science-minded; we are not even rational. We live in an intellectual climate which accepts "science" as a vague general principle, but we "believe" in science just as uncritically as the Egyptians believed in magic, and most of us can't tell a theory from an unsupported premise. It is not because we are more rational than our remote ancestors that we find it hard to understand their system of thought. It is only because our kind of magic is different.

If there is some science in magic, there is also a lot of magic in some religions. Conventionally, magic and religion are distinguished by the means employed to affect the supernatural beings with whom both fields deal. Magicians command and threaten demons; priests adore and beseech gods. Once again, the standard definitions fail. The priests of some ancient religions seem to have adopted a blackmailing tone more suitable to a shaman than to a humble worshiper: "Either you bring the rain, Great Spirit, or no offerings!" Sometimes magicians invoked the assistance of supernatural beings, gods or demons, but they could, and did, use spells which required no outside aid—spells which, it was believed, worked directly upon the object to be affected, as our caveman's ritual gestures and curses "killed" his enemy. The supernatural beings invoked by ancient magicians were normally divine rather than diabolic, so that the professions of priest and magician often overlapped. Indeed, the notion of magic as a "black art" did not gain real strength until after the spread of the monotheistic religions. Their Gods were jealous gods, and their priests regarded themselves as the only legitimate intermediaries between man and the supernatural. The Egyptians were not so narrow-minded; there was a goddess of magic, and as we shall see, the Egyptians sought immortality not only through moral rectitude, "which the god desires," but through the crudest of magical trickery—spells which would deceive or control the divine tribunal which judged the soul.

In Egypt religion and science had their areas of overlap too. The gods were the first scientists—Thoth, who invented numbers, Khnum, the divine potter, Osiris, who taught men the science of agriculture. And some scientists, such as Imhotep, became gods. Church and·state were never separated in ancient Egypt, and a learned man served the temple and the king without feeling that he was serving in two different capacities. Architects and physicians were often priests as well. The famous "House of Life" attached to some temples was probably not a university but a scriptorium, where scholarly books were written and stored. Medical lore was part of this heritage, and doctors were included among the staff.

Sorcerer, scientist, and priest—the three categories were not so far apart after all. If we recognize this, and accept the sincere belief of man in the phenomena we call magic, we will have acquired a key to many of the otherwise baffling beliefs of the ancient Egyptians.

EGYPTIAN MAGIC

Since we have just demonstrated, at some length, that we ought to try to look at the world as the Egyptians looked at it, we will have to talk about magic, so far as is possible, in their terms. It is "no fair" to construct an artificial subject called "Egyptian magic" and dump into it all the activities we would call by that name.

What are these activities? They would certainly include the following: cursing (including killing); curing; erotic magic; agricultural (including weather); divination; resurrection. Since magic and medicine are hard to untangle, and since the Egyptians did not, as a rule, try to untangle them, we will discuss curative magic under medicine. Resurrective magic, designed to reanimate the dead and insure them a happy existence in the hereafter, is perhaps the area about which we have the most information. We would call it magic since, by our system of belief, any attempts to win immortality except the ones set forth in our own creeds are nothing but pagan superstition. This is a little hard on the Egyptians, who undoubtedly thought they were being properly religious. So we are going to talk about resurrective magic under mortuary beliefs.

This still leaves us with a respectable body of material. However, not all our categories are represented in ancient Egypt, or else they are represented only by hints or casual allusions. We know very little about weather and agricultural magic, and most of what we do know would have been called religious by the Egyptians—if they had possessed a word for religion. The prosperity and productivity of the country did not depend on rain but on the annual rise of the Nile, whose inundation watered and fertilized the soil. The river itself was a god, named Hapi, and the great mortuary god Osiris was connected not only with the resurrection of the dead but with the rebirth of the new grain. Great state rituals, conducted by the king or his representatives, honored these gods and assured the yearly inundation on which the crops depended. I suspect, from what we know of other societies, that the ancient fellahin (peasants) of Egypt may have had their own magical ceremonies to make sure the crops were abundant. But nothing is known of this, if it was done.

Spells designed to curse and kill an enemy conform more closely to our definition of magic, in that they are normally free of invocations to a god. Egyptian cursing texts were written on rough pottery bowls or on figurines, which were then flung down and smashed to bits. The inscriptions name the enemies whose lives are to be broken as the bowls are smashed. Many examples name rulers of cities in Syria or Nubia, so they must have been official state curses. Others name Egyptians: "Ameni shall die, the tutor of Sit-Bastet." These may have been private grudges. With the meticulous thoroughness which I like to consider typically Egyptian, another text curses: "Every evil word, every evil speech, every evil thought, every evil plot, every evil thing, every evil dream," and so on, through a long list of evils. In the cursing ritual, the efficacious elements are two in number: first, the ritual act, which is an application of the principle of imitation (as the bowl is "killed," the enemy is killed); second, the power of the word, which is also twofold. The identity of the enemy with the object to be broken is assured by the writing of his name upon it; the phrase "he shall die" is a homicidal attack, magically speaking.

Some of the "magico-medical" texts also give spells for destroying an enemy; they are more complicated than the quick and easy smashing of an image, but they include the all-important verbal element. The medical texts are full of love charms too; several, which I find rather sad, are designed to make a man's wife love him. Some of these spells would only work with a wife or concubine, for their successful application depends on the man being on fairly intimate terms with the lady he wishes to encharm. Love charms may be considered a legitimate part of the physician's art; they often involve a prescription to be applied externally or taken internally. Others, surely related to love charms, are designed to "make an old man into a young man," or just to make the old man look young—hair restorers, wrinkle removers, and the like.

It has been argued that divination—attempts to predict the future—and related fields such as astrology are not really magic, because magic involves a conscious act, an attempt to control what is going to happen. This is quibbling, I think; nobody wants to know the future unless he hopes to guide his behavior by that knowledge, if only in a negative way. June is an unlucky month? We abstain from doubtful activities, or even stay home in bed. The tarot cards inform us that a tall dark man will bring trouble and sorrow? We confine ourselves to short blond men. The fatalism which resigns itself to misery, bad luck, or illness without trying to avoid such predictions would not bother resorting to divination in the first place.

Contrary to popular belief, the Egyptians were not astrologers; they did not have the concept of the zodiac on which, if I understand the problem correctly, modern astrology is based. But they did have charts of lucky and unlucky days, which remind us of the paragraphs that appear regularly in many newspapers, purporting to tell us how to regulate our conduct according to our horoscopes.

In the Egyptian charts, each day is divided into three parts and marked with signs meaning "good" or signs meaning "bad." Thus, for the fourth day of the month, Paophi, we get this: "Bad, good, bad. Under no circumstances go forth from your house this day. He who is born on this day will die of the plague." The next day, the fifth, is consistently dangerous: "Bad, bad, bad. Under no circumstances approach a woman. On this day men shall make offerings to the gods. . . . He who is born on this day shall die of lovemaking." Perhaps some people might not consider this such a bad way to go. Even better is the prediction for the man born on the sixth, which is "good, good, good." He will die drunken.

Another method of foretelling the future was by dream analysis. One papyrus gives over two hundred interpretations of dreams. Here are a few:

If a man sees himself in a dream:

—seeing a large cat: good; it means a big harvest
—plunging into the river: good; it means cleansing from all evils
—seeing his face in a mirror: bad; it means another wife (!)
—looking into a deep well: bad; it means taking away his property

These interpretations do not follow the theories of Professor Freud. However, it is possible that the Egyptians did not consider the dream papyrus to be true magic; the symbolic images which kept popping up in their dreams may have had as much rational validity for them as the modern interpretations of other dream images have for us. If we want to be certain about what the Egyptians regarded as genuine sorcery, we must refer to their own descriptions. And there is one ancient papyrus which, in my opinion, gives us some pertinent examples.

The protagonist of the tale is no less a personage than the great King Khufu of the Fourth Dynasty. One day he called his sons to him and asked them to amuse him with tales of wonderful events. Thereupon the first son related how a magician punished his unfaithful wife. He made a waxen image of a crocodile. When it was thrown into the river it came to life, growing to normal crocodile size, and when the wife's lover came to the water to bathe, the crocodile seized him. The adulterous wife was burned.

The second story told by the princes described an equally talented magician who folded up a lake, leaving the bottom dry so that one of the royal ladies could retrieve an ornament she had dropped into the water. The greatest magician of all, however, was one who lived during Khufu's reign; when his younger son told the king about this man, Khufu ordered that he be summoned to court to display his spells. The old man, whose name was Djedi, had the best trick of all. He could put back a head which had been cut off. Khufu asked him to do it and offered a criminal, condemned to death, for the experiment. But the wise man replied, "Not a man, O sovereign, my lord!" and used a goose instead. I have always liked this story because its spirit is so un-like that of many later Oriental fairy tales. Even a condemned crimi-nal is rejected by the old magician; for to work magic on men, the "cattle of the gods," that is forbidden.

These tricks, then, are real magic, regarded by the Egyptians them-selves as marvels. Other examples can be found in other stories, such as the ones we have quoted earlier in this book. The crocodile image is particularly interesting because it is a very ancient example of a type of sorcery which has flourished until modern times in many parts of the world. It also confirms our belief that such waxen images were used by the conspirators in the plot against Ramses III.

The talented wonder-workers in the tales related to King Khufu were not called magicians; in the text they have the title "lector priest." This title designated one of the classes of priests who served the temples and who specialized in a knowledge of the sacred writings; they were, perhaps, the scholars of the hierarchy, and they were often skilled in magic. Doctors were part-time magicians too; as everyone knew, illness could be caused by demons or by the spirits of the dead, and a physician had to know how to deal with them. But the greatest of all the practitioners of magic, old Djedi, was neither a priest nor a physician. Not only could he restore the dead to life; he knew the numbers of the secret chambers of the sanctuary of Thoth, the key to powerful magic, and he could foretell the future. Knowledge of the magic art was not restricted to priests; there was a title of "magician," and another title which has been translated as "amuletman." The amulet-men sometimes formed part of the staff of royal expeditions sent into the deserts for copper or stone, and we suppose that they supplied the workers with the little charms which could protect them against some of the dangers of the barren, waterless waste. But it is likely that all of them had had priestly training and priestly affiliations.

No, magic was not a toy or a parlor game. The wrinkled, balding official who paid a doctor for a prescription to make himself young—in order, perhaps, to win the heart of a foolish girl who preferred good looks to wealth—was not playing games. Magicians were on the royal payroll; and magic could be, as in the case of the cursing texts, a tool of international relations—we can hardly call it "diplomacy." But let us not call it superstition. It was inextricably interwoven with the practices of a religion that suited its worshipers well enough to endure for almost four thousand years—a pretty impressive record.

Eleven

"THE USEFUL THINGS THAT ARE ESTABLISHED FOREVER"

Having demonstrated that the terms "magic," "science," and "religion" have no real meaning, we will begin our study of Egyptian science in the same negative manner, by stating that there was no such thing. The Egyptians were skilled at a number of practical crafts, many of which involved the application of scientific laws. But these laws were seldom if ever explicitly stated. We can have, as we had in Egypt, technology without science: knowing how to do something without necessarily knowing why it works.

MATHEMATICS

Perhaps the nearest thing in Egypt to a pure science was mathematics. The Egyptians used a decimal system in which a single stroke repre-

Egyptian numerals

sented one. Two strokes stood for two, and so on, up through nine. Ten rated a separate sign, like a croquet hoop. From eleven to nineteen the figures were formed by adding the requisite number of strokes to the ten symbol. Twenty was two croquet hoops, twenty-one was two hoops and a stroke. Besides ten and one, the only other numerals that had separate signs were one hundred, one thousand, ten thousand, one hundred thousand, and one million. There was no zero.

This system is even more cumbersome than Roman numerals. The Romans could write "1965" with only six signs. The Egyptians needed twenty-one separate symbols to express the same figure. Just on the basis of the Egyptian numerals we might reasonably suspect that Egyptian arithmetic was a tedious process. It was.

Egyptologists seem to take a grisly delight in disillusioning people who believe the Egyptians were masters of sciences lost to the modern world. If they were, they were masters of sciences so obscure that we have no evidence of them. In all the known sciences they were not remarkably advanced; they are admirable, not because of their wisdom, but because of what they were able to accomplish with the knowledge they did have. Egyptian mathematics was no more advanced than any of the other sciences. Indeed, the Egyptian method may not even deserve to be called mathematics; it was hardly more than simple arithmetic.

Their arithmetic was essentially additive. Even multiplication and division were done by an additive process. To take an example, let us multiply eight by sixteen as the Egyptians would have done it.

1	8
2	16
4	32
8	64
16	128

What we have done is to double each side of the table until we reach the desired answer. If our problem is one that does not work out evenly by such a process, we simply add the two factors necessary for the required sum. Ten times eight, using the above table, is the sum of eight times eight and two times eight—sixty-four plus sixteen, or eighty.

Division was done by the same method, only backwards. To divide ninety-six by eight, we would double eight (the right-hand column of the above table) until we obtain two figures which can be added to make ninety-six. Thirty-two and sixty-four meet this requirement. The corresponding numbers on the left-hand side of the table, which we have, of course, doubled as we doubled the right-hand column, are eight and four. Eight plus four equals twelve—the answer.

Sometimes the doubling method did not give the exact answer. Thirteen divided by three ends up as four threes with one left over. How did the Egyptians deal with the leftovers?

Egyptian fractions are lovely objects. They were expressed by the word "r," "part," written over a number. "R" over five was one-fifth, "r" over a croquet hoop and four strokes was one-fourteenth, and so on. There are separate signs in hieroglyphs and in hieratic for one-half, one-fourth, two-thirds, and, rarely, three-fourths. But in ordinary computation, the only kinds of fractions the Egyptians could express were unit fractions, in which the numerator is one.

But, says the reader, with such a limitation one cannot do arithmetic! As soon as you add or multiply a fraction—almost any old fraction—you get an answer in which the numerator is more than one. The Egyptian method of doubling would work with fractions in which the denominator was an even number; twice one-fourth equals two-fourths, which can immediately be reduced to the unit fraction one-half. Twice one-third equals two-thirds, and the Egyptians had a sign for that fraction. But twice one-fifth, or twice one-seventh, gives a result which the Egyptians could not express at all.

They did express it; but not as two-fifths or two-sevenths. Instead of two-fifths, they wrote one-third plus one-fifteenth—which is the same thing expressed in the necessary unit fractions.

Admittedly this is not a simple procedure, and it would have taken a scribe some time to work out the necessary unit fractions for every fractional computation. Hence, the Egyptians developed tables of such problems, presumably for reference, so that when a scribe had to double one-ninth, he merely looked at his table and found that the answer was one-sixth plus one-eighteenth. Our illustration gives excerpts from such a table which presents solutions to problems of addition of fractions.

We are told by a specialist in pre-Greek science, Otto Neugebauer, that "experience teaches one very soon to operate quite rapidly within this framework." I am sure it taught him to do so, but it would take more than experience to let most of us "operate" easily with fractions like these! However, we are handicapped by the knowledge of our own framework. If we had been taught arithmetic by the Egyptian method from the beginning, presumably we would find it easy too.

We don't know for sure how the Egyptians worked out these tables. They had no algebra. They did have geometry; they could calculate areas of triangles, trapezoids, rectangles, and circles, and there were problems for similar elementary volumes, including a correct computation of the volume of a truncated pyramid. This last was the most impressive achievement of Egyptian mathematics; equally admirable, perhaps, was their value 3.16 for pi, which is reasonably accurate. It has been claimed that the Moscow mathematical papyrus gives a solution for calculating the area of a hemisphere, but Neugebauer thought a simpler interpretation of the problem is more likely.

Not only was mathematics, the basic tool of the sciences, fairly simple, it was also completely pragmatic. The mathematical texts from which we derive our knowledge contain tables and sample problems of the type a working temple or court scribe would have had to be able to do—finding the area of a field, or the number of bricks needed to build a ramp of a given size. The Greeks had nothing much to learn from the wisdom of the Egyptians in mathematics; in many ways the Babylonians were far ahead of their contemporaries down south.

ASTRONOMY

The Egyptians have a certain reputation as astronomers; this may derive from their invention of a good calendar, since they have no other claim to fame in that field. Their calendar is the distant ancestor of our own, with its twelve months of thirty days each, plus an extra five days, to make the total of 365. The year is longer than 365 days, of course, but it was a long time before anyone figured out how to work in the extra one-fourth (and a fraction) day per year. The Egyptian calendar did not take the extra into account, and as a result it soon got out of step with the real solar year. Still, it was a decided improvement over the flexible lunar calendars used by other peoples.

Our twelvefold division of day and night is also Egyptian in origin. The sixty-minute and sixty-second divisions are not; in fact, hours of fixed length probably did not appear until the invention of mechanical clocks. Egyptian hours varied in length depending on the season of the year. An hour was the twelfth part of the time from sunrise to sunset for day, and from sunset to sunrise for night. In winter the night hours would be longer than the day hours, and in summer the reverse would be true.

The hour divisions can hardly be called astronomical, however, and it is doubtful whether the Egyptian calendar owed anything to astronomy. It may have come from observations of the annual Nile rise, which culminated in the vital inundation. This phenomenon, in turn, was at some point connected with the reappearance on the horizon, after a period of invisibility, of the star Sirius. But it is yet to be proved that we owe our calendar to the astronomical talents of the ancient Egyptians.

What, then, did they accomplish in this field? Surprisingly little. Not until Hellenistic times, when Egyptian thought was influenced by ideas from Greece and Babylonia, do we find any texts involving mathematical calculations of astronomical phenomena. The only things which could possibly be called astronomical from pharaonic Egypt are the decan charts.

The decans are constellations whose risings, or transits, fall ten days apart (hence "decans") and which may be used to tell time during the night. On coffin lids of the Middle Kingdom and on ceilings of later tombs we find representations of the night sky with the decanal constellations inscribed thereon. The most elaborate of these are the ceilings of the tomb of Senenmut, the architect of Queen Hatshepsut, and of the cenotaph of King Seti I at Abydos. At first glance, Senenmut's ceiling looks as if it ought to mean something. There are circles subdivided into pie-shaped wedges, stars, mysterious deities, and short identifying inscriptions.

Unfortunately, with a few exceptions, it has thus far proved impossible to identify Senenmut's stars with known constellations. Part of the difficulty may lie in the Egyptians' willingness to subjugate accuracy to neatness, and reality to an artificial order. There are indications in Senenmut's ceiling that the original sketch was redrawn, possibly to make it look more artistic. Obviously we cannot hope for accurate drawings under those circumstances. Another consideration which may have affected accuracy was the mechanical copying of older texts, which were no longer accurate for the later period, and which may not have been copied correctly. Religious requirements—each hour was under the guidance of a particular god—may have caused further deviations. In this last consideration we see the working of the now-familiar principle—the impossibility of separating science from the other categories which we call religion and magic. The so-called astronomical texts are usually found in tombs or in coffins; their function was not scientific, but religious, and they were probably altered, as necessary, to best serve that function. The decans had some effect on astrology, but they never had an influence on the development of astronomy.

HOW TO BUILD A PYRAMID

The Egyptians could not calculate the volume of a hemisphere or predict an eclipse, but they do not seem to have been disturbed about this. They got along; and they did some surprising things with the knowledge they did possess.

We have already mentioned a few of the technological processes at which the Egyptians excelled, such as metalwork, papyrus-making, weaving, beer- and wine-making, faience, glass, and pottery. Eventually we will discuss mummification, which, in Egypt, can be viewed as a technical skill. Perhaps the best way of studying Egyptian technology is to take a specific example and see how it was done. I have chosen to examine the Great Pyramid for several reasons; in the first place, the construction of a pyramid involved a number of different technical problems, and in the second place, Khufu's pyramid has been analyzed, measured, described, and discussed at greater length than has any other structure in Egypt.

The Great Pyramid is the largest of the three pyramids of Giza, and the tomb of King Khufu (Cheops in Greek) of the Fourth Dynasty—around 2600 B.C. I have already been taken to task by several friendly pyramidologists for refusing to admit that Khufu's tomb is the Master Plan of the Universe and a monumental prophecy in stone;

but at the risk of incurring further correspondence I must cling to my narrow-minded opinion. The Great Pyramid was a tomb, and that is all it was.

The Great Pyramid is impressive. It is impressive to look at, and quite overwhelming when you consider the statistics. The more than two million blocks of which it is composed average about two tons apiece in weight; the biggest blocks weigh fifteen tons. The four sides measure approximately 755 feet each. No two are exactly the same length, although the difference between the longest and shortest sides is only 7.9 inches. The structure was, when completed, 481.4 feet high. The area covered by the base is 13.1 acres.

Even more amazing than the size of the pyramid is the accuracy with which it was put together. The sides are oriented almost exactly in line with true north, south, east, and west, the greatest error being on the east side, which is only 5'30" west of north. The angles are almost perfect right angles: 90, 3, 2; 89, 59, 58; 89, 56, 27; 90, 0, 33. The casing blocks which cover the exterior were fitted together with joints of one-fiftieth of an inch—so small that you can hardly get a pin into them. And the whole massive building rests on a dressed-rock platform which has a deviation from true level of only 0.004 percent.

It is no wonder that generations of travelers have been moved to extravagant speculations about this pyramid. All sorts of wild theories, from djinns to "unknown lost sciences," have been invented to account for its existence. But there is no need for such fantasies. The Great Pyramid and its smaller relations could have been built with the simplest of tools and technology.

Before the actual hauling of stones began, the Egyptian architect had to meet two separate problems. The first was the leveling of the plateau; the second, the plotting of the angles and the orientation of the building.

Once the sand and gravel had been removed down to bedrock, the area to be leveled was surrounded with low walls of brick and then flooded. By measuring down from a number of points on the surface of the water, a network of trenches of equal depth could be cut. The water was then released, and the areas between the trenches leveled to the same depth. The Egyptians had a long history of experience with flooded fields, irrigation trenches, and the like; this method would have come naturally to them. That it was actually used, as most authorities believe, is suggested by a curious fact—when the prevalent north wind of the Cairo area is blowing it would cause precisely the error from true level, on the water surface, that is actually found on the Great Pyramid plateau.

This is one theory. Other scholars, including Mark Lehner, who went so far as to build a small pyramid of his own—no, not to be buried in, just to see how it was done—have raised practical objections. For one thing, it would require an awful lot of water. The areas on which the pyramids of Khufu and Khafre were built was not level, and they were never completely flattened out—a large chunk of rock was left in the middle. Lehner has suggested that holes around the pyramids in question may have contained stakes cut to equal lengths or carrying reference lines tied from stake to stake to establish the pyramid baseline.

For some reason or other a pyramid had to be made so that its sides faced the four cardinal points. We know, from later reliefs, that temples were oriented by "looking at the sky, observing the stars, and turning [one's] gaze toward the Great Bear." However, simple observation of even so prominent a star as the North Star, would not give results commensurate with the remarkably accurate orientation of the pyramids. So it has been suggested that the Egyptians might have found true north by sighting on a star in the northern sky and then bisecting the angle formed by its rising and setting positions and by the position of the observer. In order to do this accurately it is necessary to have an artificial horizon—a wall, in other words, which is perfectly level and which is high enough to cut off everything but sky from the view of the observer. Said observer stations himself behind his wall and waits for the chosen star to appear. Following his directions, an assistant marks the spot on the "horizon" wall where the star is first visible. A second mark is made at the point on the wall where the star sets, or disappears from the sight of the observer. Plumb lines are then dropped down from the top of the wall and marks made on the ground immediately below the marks on the wall. Lines drawn from the observer's position to the two marks on the ground form an angle whose middle line gives true north. The other compass points are found by constructing right angles to the line of true north. Then there's the sun-and-shadow method—bisecting the angle of a vertical pole cast at different times of day. I refuse to go into detail about this procedure; you can read about it in various books, including Dr. Lehner's, if you are interested. The point is that the Egyptians could have used such simple methods to attain the desired result.

While the pyramid plateau was being cleared and leveled, stoneworkers were already busy in the quarries, cutting out the first of those two million blocks of stone. The material used for the bulk of the Great Pyramid was a kind of limestone, the same stone of which the pyramid plateau itself is composed, and it was cut right on the spot. The casing stones, which gave a smooth covering to the structure, were of a different, finer-grained limestone. They must have been brought from the well-known Tura quarries just across the river from Giza, in the Arabian hills near modern Cairo. Limestone counts as a soft stone—soft as stones go—and it can be cut with copper tools, like the ones the Egyptians had. With copper chisels the workers cut the desired block free on all sides except the bottom; it was detached from its base by wedges.

Not all the stone used in the Great Pyramid was soft stone. The pavements of the mortuary temple next to the pyramid were of basalt, a decidedly hard stone. The great sarcophagus in which the king was buried was made of granite; so were the walls of the King's Chamber, or Burial Chamber, and the plugs which were meant to block the passage leading to the royal mummy. Granite was used for casing parts of the Second and Third Pyramids at Giza; in the Third Pyramid probably the greater part of the casing was of this hard-to-work stone.

Granite and basalt cannot be cut with copper chisels. One of the happiest of the claims made for the ancient Egyptians is that they must have had steel—two thousand years before they had iron in any quantity—in order to cut such difficult materials. An alternative theory is that they had some method of tempering copper to make it fantastically hard. So far, there is no evidence for either of these no-tions, except for the undeniable fact that these hard stones were cut. But there are simpler, if not easier, ways of accomplishing this feat.

One method of quarrying granite, which was certainly used later in Egypt, was to pound it out with heavy dolerite balls—a tedious, heartbreaking job, certainly, but so is building a pyramid. Another possibility is the use of copper saws and/or drills. Saw marks have been found on the granite sarcophagus from the Great Pyramid and on the basalt pavement blocks from the temple of that pyramid, and drills were certainly used for hard stone statues and vases. It is true that cut-ting basalt with a plain copper saw would be somewhat difficult. Now-adays we sometimes cut hard stones by using points of even harder stones which are set into a drill or saw. The use of diamond points in industry is well known. Diamond ranks 10 on a measure known as the Mohs scale; it can cut just about anything, including quartzite, the hardest stone the Egyptians ever quarried (7 on the Mohs scale). But, sad to say, the Egyptians did not have diamonds. Neither did they have topaz (8) or rubies and sapphires (9) or even beryl (8) before the Greek period. We must conclude, then, that the Egyptians did not use hard-stone points, or teeth, to cut their granite and quartz.

There is another method of cutting hard stone: with an abrasive powder. Diamond dust is used to cut diamonds. Having no diamonds, the Egyptians had no diamond dust either, nor, so far as we can tell, did they use pumice or emery powder. They did have quartz sand. If diamond dust can cut diamonds, quartz sand can cut quartz. The re-mains of such sand, perhaps mixed with water, have been found at the bottom of drill holes and cuts in various types of stone. So that's prob-ably how it was done, using copper drills and saws.

Once the blocks were cut, they had to be transported to the pyra-mid plateau. The limestone used was either from Giza or from quarries across the river. The dolerite probably came from the Fayum, not too far away, but the granite was cut at Aswan, six hundred miles south of Giza. All the stones were transported as far as possible by water, being floated across the river from Tura to Giza in the case of the limestone, and car-ried by boat downstream from Aswan in the case of the granite. Probably the transport was done during the period of high water, when much of the valley lay under the inundation and the stones could be floated right up to the base of the plateau. The hardest part of the job was the distance from the bottom of the plateau up to the pyramid site.

Although we have no description or drawing of stones being dragged up to a pyramid site, there is an interesting scene in a Twelfth Dynasty tomb which depicts the transport of a colossal statue. The colossus rests on a sledge without wheels, which is pulled by 172 men. Perched precariously on the knee of the statue, the overseer claps his hands to set the rhythm for the "heave-ho" chant which still accompanies heavy labor in the Near East. Another man, on the front part of the sledge, pours water onto the ground to lubricate the track. This colossus must have weighed fifty or sixty tons. The blocks for the pyramid ranged from a mere two tons to a possible, staggering, two hundred tons (in the temple of the Third Pyramid). But there is no doubt that they were pulled, just as the statue was, without assistance from wheels or engines.

Now we have the stone and the site all prepared. It remains only to build the pyramid.

Archaeologists are still debating the details of pyramid building, just as they disagree about a number of other things relating to ancient Egypt. There is little disagreement, though, about the main point: that these mammoth structures, and all the other colossal building works of Egypt, were constructed without motive power other than that of human muscle, and with the simplest of tools. The Egyptians had plumb bobs and set squares and a few other simple gadgets; you can see them in museum cases. It has been claimed that they had pulleys, but you won't see any of them in museum cases, which is a pretty strong indication that they didn't exist. The conventional view is that the stones of the pyramids must have been dragged into place, just as they were dragged across the land between the river and the pyramid site. Ramps are the only possible method, and ramps must have been used. The remains of several have, in fact, been found.

If you put two Egyptologists into a room together and mention a subject—any subject—connected with ancient Egypt, you will probably get two different theories. A ramp is a simple affair, and most Egyptologists agree that ramps must have been used. Nevertheless, there are two different ramp theories. According to one, a main ramp was built straight out at right angles to the face of the pyramid, with subsidiary ramps or scaffolds on the other three sides. An alternative theory suggests that one or more ramps wrapped around the pyramid as it rose. There are several variants of both theories, of course. The subject is too complex to go into here. The important thing is: no pulleys, no hoists, only muscle power and ramps.

Naturally no ramps were needed for the first layer of stones; they were hauled up to the leveled site and shoved into their designated places. Wooden rollers may have been used for precise placement. Then the ramp was begun. It would have been raised for each new level, and the next layer of stones would have been dragged up and positioned.

The process was not that casual, of course. You can build a pyramid by piling blocks on top of other blocks, but if you want to build a really BIG pyramid you have to align those blocks with absolute precision. The angles of the slopes and the diagonals of the four sides must match and meet. Again, accurate measurements could have been (and obviously were) made with the simple instruments available. In many pyramids additional stability was given by internal casings, or accretion faces. The blocks of these inner casings, made of the finer Tura limestone, were built into the core of the pyramid as it went up.

Something else was built in—the "substructure." In the case of Khufu's pyramid, it was located not under the structure but in its very heart—mortuary chambers, ramps, and passages. One of the pyramid mystics' favorite arguments has been the fact that the sarcophagus is too big to go through the passage leading up to the burial chamber. I don't know what this could possibly prove (djinns?) except the obvious—that the sarcophagus was put in from up above before the chamber was roofed over.

The interior of the pyramid presents us with several mysteries (though not the kind of mysteries pyramidologists love). There is an entrance in the north face, some fifty feet above the ground and about twenty-five feet east of the center of that side. From here a corridor leads down at an angle of approximately twenty-five degrees, through the pyramid and down into the rock of the plateau. The entrance was probably masked by casing blocks which looked like all the other casing blocks, and the passage itself is less than four feet high; it was not designed for the convenience of inquisitive tourists. The descending passage goes along for 345 feet and levels off, ending in a small, uncompleted chamber. On the far side of this chamber the passage continues for a little way before ending abruptly.

According to the conventional theory, this chamber and passage were part of the original interior plan, which called for a burial chamber under, rather than in, the pyramid. Subterranean burial chambers are found in other pyramids, including both the other Giza tombs. But later on, this theory maintains, Khufu changed his mind. By that time the pyramid itself was partly built, so the workers had to cut a passage up through the roof of the descending corridor at a point about sixty feet from the entrance. The new, ascending passage runs up through the blocks of the pyramid core, going up at the same angle as the older corridor went down. It is about 130 feet long. Then it levels off, and at the end of the level stretch, right in the middle of the pyramid, a chamber was built. It is the so-called Queen's Chamber, although it was not meant for a queen, but was the king's burial chamber in this second stage of design. The corridor leading to it is so low that present-day tourists have a choice of two equally awkward positions: hands and knees, or an angle, at the waist, of ninety degrees.

Before the Queen's Chamber was finished, Khufu changed his mind again, or so it is claimed. He went back to the top of the ascending corridor and built the Grand Gallery. It goes on up at the same angle as the ascending corridor, but instead of being only a few feet high its ceiling is 28 feet above the floor. The walls are only seven and a half feet high, and above them there is a corbel vault of astounding size, some 153 feet long. It is still one of the most imposing sights in Egypt, in spite of the naked lightbulbs and the crude stairs which have been constructed to aid weak tourists in reaching the Burial Chamber.

You didn't think it would be that simple, did you? More recent re-search claims that Khufu didn't change his mind, that all three cham-bers were built at the same time, and that they have specific cultic meanings. The Queen's Chamber may have served the same purpose as the later serdab, the closed-in room where the statue of the deceased was placed. The so-called Subterranean Chamber and the cramped, unfinished tunnel leading away from it could represent the Under-world. So there you have it, for whatever it's worth. I have no opinion on the subject.

The King's Chamber was the final burial chamber. It is lined with granite blocks and is rectangular in size, measuring about 34 by 17 feet, and 19 feet in height. It does not open directly off the Grand Gallery but is reached through a low passage and an antechamber. The King's Chamber is perfectly plain—no paintings, no inscriptions, no reliefs. The walls are smooth except for two curious breaks—shafts, which start from the north and south walls and go through the pyra-mid at angles of thirty-one and forty-five degrees, respectively. We don't know why these shafts were built; they are too small for anything bigger than a mouse. The most obvious suggestion is that they were for ventilation—not so absurd as it sounds, since the king was not really dead. However, it is doubtful that the Egyptians realized the healthful value of fresh air, and anyhow the shafts don't reach all the way to the surface. They provided no such shafts in later tombs. Presumably there was a religious reason—orienting the king's spirit toward the eternal stars, for instance. The Queen's Chamber has similar shafts, but they were never finished. In recent years one of these shafts has been pen-etrated by a little machine—a robot camera—which reached a dead end blocked by a cut stone with a couple of copper objects in it. What this means nobody knows. But I am going to go on record as predict-ing that if investigators ever get past the blocking stone they will not find the Key to the Secrets of the Universe or even a cache of uncut emeralds.

Although the King's Chamber has a flat ceiling, this is only the base of a remarkable architectural element. Above the ceiling there are five small rooms or compartments, one above the other. The lower four have flat roofs, and the highest has a pointed roof. All these little chambers were invaded by modern searchers looking for hidden treasure, but it is unlikely that anything was ever concealed in them. They were meant to relieve some of the strain on the ceiling of the burial chamber; and it was quite some strain, we must admit. Modern calculations suggest that there was, in fact, no necessity for such elaborate safeguards. The Egyptian engineer may have overcompensated for a pressure which certainly was present, but no one can deny that overcompensation is better than not enough.

Among the objects which were inserted into the heart of the pyramid while it was being built were several huge granite stones. Their function was to plug up the ascending passage after the funeral and keep out (Khufu hoped) ambitious tomb robbers. Three of them were actually found at the bottom of the passage.

Several minor but intriguing points are raised by these stone plugs. In the first place, they really are plugs, being less than half an inch narrower than the width of the corridor, and only about an inch less in height. Maneuvering these huge blocks into position up a sloping passage would have been a tricky job even for the Egyptians. How, for instance, could they keep the first block from sliding back down and braining them while they pushed numbers two and three in behind number one?

The answer is that they didn't. The entrance to the ascending passage is an inch narrower than the plugs; they couldn't have been shoved into it from below, via the descending passage. Therefore they must have been put into the pyramid from above and stored in some spot above the ascending passage until it was time to use them. Measurements show that the only space big enough for them was the Grand Gallery. After Khufu's coffin had been deposited in the huge granite sarcophagus, amid the lamentations of his women and the solemn prayers of the priests, the funeral cortege departed, leaving a crew of workmen in the Grand Gallery. These men levered up the stones which had been stored there and slid them down into the ascending passage, one after the other; they continued to slide until they reached the lower end, whose mouth was too small to let them pass. There they piled up, forming a very effective barricade between the dead king and the outside world.

But what about the workers? Their situation looks bad; they are barricaded from the outside world too. Have we another example of barbaric sacrifice for the benefit of the dead?

Look at the plan of the pyramid (opposite). At point N you will see a long well, or shaft, leading down from the Grand Gallery to the lower part of the descending corridor, near the abandoned burial chamber of the first stage. After the entombed workers had lowered themselves down the shaft, all they had to do was walk up the descending corridor, bypassing the plugs in the ascending corridor, and go out. The entrance (A) was the last part to be blocked. It has been suggested, somewhat absurdly, that the workmen put in some strenuous overtime on this escape shaft, without official permission. There is no reason to suppose that Khufu planned to share his tomb with a group of motley workers; this sort of thing was not done during the Fourth Dynasty. Nor is it likely that a work of such magnitude could have been carried out unbeknownst to the official powers.

By the time the interior of the pyramid was finished, the exterior resembled a high flat platform whose sides were hidden by ramps and embankments. Up the main ramp a sweating, chanting gang of workers pulled the stones for the next course of masonry. These stones had already been flattened on the bottom—the bedding joint—and the masons had smoothed the top of the previously laid course to receive the new stones. When the fill, or core, stones had been positioned, the casing blocks of fine Tura limestone were hauled up. Masons had prepared them while they were still on the ground, cutting the jointing sides and the bottom level and marking the outer surface to indicate the correct angle. Before the stones were slid into place a thin layer of mortar was spread over the bedding joint and the other faces. This was done not so much for adhesion, since the weight of the huge stones made them stable enough, but to facilitate movement and make final adjustments easier. The casing stones were then levered or shoved into position, using the bosses left in place for that purpose; and then, while the masons smoothed the tops of the stones

(A) entrance; (B) descending passage; (C) incomplete burial chamber of first stage;
(D) entrance to ascending passage; (E) ascending passage; (F) Queen's Chamber;
(G) grand gallery; (H) burial chamber; (I) antechamber; (J) air passages (?) from King's
Chamber; (K) same from Queen's Chamber; (L) relieving chambers;
(M) plugs blocking ascending passage; (N) entrance to well; (O) well;
(P) connection of well with descending passage

Plan of the Great Pyramid of Giza

in the new course, the ramp was raised in preparation for the next course of stone. The very top of the pyramid, 481 feet off the ground, was finished off with a pointed pyramidion, a miniature pyramid of hard stone, sometimes plated with gold.

Then the workers started to demolish the ramp. As it went down, masons swarmed over the face of the structure, smoothing the face of the casing stones so that each block matched neatly with its neighbors. The Egyptians used scaffolding in later periods, so presumably they would have employed it for this purpose. As the ramp descended, the masons worked down, finishing their work by smoothing the lowest course of stones, and the pyramid stood in all its glory, smooth and shining, tipped with gold.

How long would it take to build something this size? Herodotus, the energetic Greek traveler, gawked at the mass of the Great Pyramid as thousands of later tourists have done, and like them, he asked his guides for statistics. He reports that it took twenty years to finish the work, employing one hundred thousand men "for periods of three months" on the transport of the stone. Presumably this meant four gangs of twenty-five thousand each. Petrie calculated that one hundred thousand men might have been employed in a given year. This is almost certainly too large. Calculations of the numbers needed for separate operations admit a workforce of twenty thousand, and that includes the support groups—the men who sharpened the copper chisels, for example. (They took a lot of sharpening.) Khufu reigned for forty-three years, possibly longer, so he had a lot more than twenty years to get the job done.

Herodotus describes how a pyramid was built, but there is no point in quoting him since he did not know as much about it as we do. One sentence, however, is worth repeating: "The upper part of the pyramid was finished first, then the middle, and finally the part which was lowest and nearest to the ground." Obviously Herodotus is—correctly—describing the final polishing and finishing of the casing blocks, but I will never forget the first, wonderful image that popped into my mind when I read this sentence: the top third of the pyramid hanging unsupported in the middle of the air, while the workers shove the middle part under it, and then put the bottom under the middle.

Often when I think about pyramids and the workers straining to drag the monumental blocks, I remember a scene from a film, one of those day-long, wide-screen, Technicolor extravaganzas about the Hebrews. The Hebrews were, in this scene, dragging stones for a temple. Watching the work was Moses, dressed in kilt and collar, which costume showed off his admirable physique. As the sweating slaves groaned and staggered along, one old lady got the hem of her flowing robe (an admirable uniform for stone dragging) caught under the block she was helping to haul. Moses did not know that the old lady was really his mother. Being the hero of the film, however, he tried to get the overseer to stop the block and let the old lady disentangle herself. The cruel overseer refused. The next ten minutes of the film were very exciting. First we saw Moses, rushing frantically around the plateau trying to find someone with enough authority to stop the wicked overseer. Then we flashed to the stone, grinding remorselessly onward, and the elderly female tugging weakly at her skirt—which must have been woven of iron. Back to Moses; back to the old lady. Nobody in the theater laughed—except me—so apparently it did not strike the audience as incongruous that the Egyptians would employ feeble old ladies for such heavy labor, or that the old lady would prefer a messy death to the immodesty of taking off her dress, or that nobody in the vicinity thought of whacking off the tail of her robe with a knife, or that the overseer would rather run her down than get on with his work. True, a modern automobile is not much deflected when it hits a human being, but a monolithic stone on wooden rollers would probably come to a grinding halt. None of the reliefs show women engaged in work of this sort; masons, stonecutters, laborers, are all men. An old lady wouldn't be worth her bread and onions. I suppose no one enjoys films about ancient Egypt more than Egyptologists; it gives them the generally popular opportunity, rare in their specialized profession, of sneering at someone else's ignorance.

We are also inclined to sneer, I am afraid, at the pyramidologists who, in defiance of all the evidence, persist in believing in the occult properties of the Great Pyramid. It was built, they say, by supermen of ancient times (Anglo-Saxons, usually), and if you know how to read its message, it mentions all the important events of world history—most of which were future events for the pyramid builders, who were thus not only supermen but prophets.

It is easy to understand why people are driven into such beliefs. The pyramid itself promotes extravagant theories; it really is hard to believe that it could have been built by people as poorly equipped as the Egyptians. Another motive which probably prompts the pyramid mystics is the rather pathetic desire to find answers to questions which never can and never will be answerable in terms of feet and inches. I can understand these people, but they irritate me nonetheless, because their views cheapen a rather impressive accomplishment. We need not ask whether the Great Pyramid was worth the effort. The Egyptians, or some of them, thought it was, and their opinion carries more weight than ours. Whatever the reasons and whatever their moral value, the fact remains that a structure like the Great Pyramid shows what people can do if they want to badly enough. Without iron, without machines, with only human muscle power and human will, they quarried these monumental stones and put them into place. There is more wonder in this than in any marvels of magical lore.

BOATS

We could describe a number of other examples of Egyptian technology, but for lack of space, we will have to restrict ourselves to only one more. I want to talk about boats.

There are few other countries in which boats have been as important as they were in ancient Egypt. Not only was the river the most convenient form of transportation, flowing straight and navigable for almost six hundred miles, but it split all of Upper Egypt into two halves. Constant communication between the east and west banks was necessary, particularly when a city was built on the east side and its cemetery, as dogma preferred, on the west. Without boats, it would have been a long walk around. The Delta, with its many small streams and canals, found water transportation equally convenient. Some places could only be reached by water, and boats were a lot more comfortable than donkey back or shank's mare. Perhaps the pyramids and the massive temples could never have been built without the river; blocks of stone which were transported six hundred miles by water could never have been hauled the same distance.

The earliest boats in Egypt were bundles of papyrus tied together. Little skiffs of this type, propelled by poles or paddled, were used far into dynastic times by sportsmen fowling in the marshes, and all through Egyptian history by the peasants, who could afford no more elaborate craft. Before the beginning of the First Dynasty, however, fancier boats had been built. We can see rough outline drawings of

Reed float

Predynastic boat

Funerary boat

Seagoing ship of Eighteenth Dynasty

Some Egyptian boats

them on pots of the late predynastic period. I don't know how accurate these drawings are; I would think a boat so sharply curved would sink like a stone. However, we can assume that such boats had twin cabins and were propelled by banks of oars.

These oared predynastic boats must have been made of wood, as were later boats. The Egyptians had a serious problem with regard to wood, since none of their native trees produced good long planks. The boats of the king and the gods were sometimes fashioned of cedar, imported all the way from the Lebanon, but the great majority of craft were patchwork affairs, made of many small pieces of wood fitted together with the matchless skill early displayed by Egyptian carpenters.

Modern boats have a keel, with closely set ribs. Egyptian boats had no keel, only a shell or framework of planks with light ribs at intervals. The deck beams, or thwarts, did not interlock on the frame to give added strength, but were fastened directly to the hull planking.

In calm waters, boats like these would do well enough. But heavy seas, such as might be encountered on voyages to Punt or Asia, could break the back of such a frail structure. Some sort of additional strengthening, to compensate for the absence of a keel, was desirable. The Egyptians did not use nails. Their boats were pegged together or laced with rope, and they used rope to give added strength to the hull. Some of our examples show heavy cables wrapped around the hull at bow and stern; attached to these was another stout cable which passed fore and aft, over crutches, along the length of the ship.

Oars or paddles like the ones on the predynastic ships were used throughout Egyptian history. When boats sailed downstream with the current, against the prevailing north wind, or when bends in the river made the wind ineffective, the oarsmen got to work. When boats went upstream, with the wind, the sails were raised. Since sails were only useful part of the time, masts were built so that they could be unstepped or, as I would say, taken down. They were then laid on high crutches so as to be out of the way of the steering gear and the rowers. The sails were made of linen and were square. The earliest sails had only a single yard; they were "loose-footed" and flapped. Later sails had two yards, so that the sail could be used to maximum advantage. Sails also got bigger as time went on, until some were enormous affairs, wider than they were high.

The steering apparatus was simple at first—two or three large paddles, without tiller or rudder post. At the end of the Old Kingdom there was a technological breakthrough in steering; rudder post and tiller were added, and the steering oars were reduced to one. The helmsman followed the directions of an officer who stood in the bow with his eyes wide open and his sounding pole ready. In certain stretches of the river, such as the narrows we referred to in the first chapter, he had to be on his toes.

The Middle Kingdom is the period of models—houses, workers, shops—and boats. We have a number of model craft, all of them quite charming with their little crews and ornaments, including the owner, lounging in a chair and sniffing a flower. Wealthy noblemen of this period may have owned a whole fleet of boats. One lucky fellow had twelve models of various types placed in his tomb.

Models and drawings are all very well, but Egyptologists have something better—the boats themselves. Khufu's so-called solar boat, which was buried alongside his pyramid, is one of the most marvelous sights at Giza. But it isn't the earliest boat ever found. An American expedition working at Abydos, the holy city of Osiris in Middle Egypt, discovered an entire fleet, fourteen or more vessels, which are believed to be associated with the burial of a First Dynasty king. That's around 3000 B.C., three hundred years before Khufu. According to the experts, they were not models but viable ships which could have been used. One of them is about seventy-five feet long and between seven and ten feet wide (in the middle). The thick wooden planks were lashed together with ropes and caulked with bundles of reeds. Boats and boat pits have been found near several pyramids, and there are certainly more to be found. They were apparently essential equipment for the dead king.

The standard riverboat might be thirty to forty feet long. Some traveling boats belonging to nobles were extremely elegant, with big cabins made of leather over a wooden framework. The busy official could carry his luggage, his servants, and even a minstrel to sing to him while he sat in the shade, under a canopy, and watched his crew of eighteen ply the oars. When he got hungry he headed for the banks and had the mooring stake pounded in; up bustled his kitchen boat, which had been following at a respectful distance. From the small utility cabin of this boat, joints of meat and jars of wine were fetched, and the women servants brought out the bread they had prepared during the day's travel.

Other boats were designed for the dead rather than the living. The funeral bark proper, which carried the dead pilgrim to the holy city of Abydos, was of a characteristic shape; the curved bows, ending in stylized papyrus flowers, recall very ancient boats made of papyrus or reeds. Other boats placed in the tomb were solar barks, like the ones used by the sun-god, or regular craft which the dead man might need in the hereafter—which was bound to be, the Egyptians argued, as full of water as this present world.

The height of Egyptian boatbuilding was reached during the New Kingdom. Models were dying out, but we have some lovely drawings of boats from tombs and from places such as Hatshepsut's mortuary temple. The great queen dispatched a fleet to the mysterious southern land of Punt in order to bring back exotic trees for the temple she was having built for herself and her father, the god Amon. Punt was probably somewhere along the Somali coast, and since there was no canal between the Nile and the Red Sea in ancient times, boats sailing south to Africa had to be built on the seacoast. There was an ancient port on the Red Sea, not far from the end of the Wadi Hammamat, which led east from the Nile in the vicinity of Coptos. Hatshepsut's great vessels must have been built there: they were true seagoing ships.

Ships sailing north to Asia had no such problem; they simply went down the Nile and out into the sea. There have been a number of wild claims as to the Egyptians' seafaring exploits, but so far there is no evidence from reliable sources that they circumnavigated Africa or passed the Pillars of Hercules to carry civilization to the wild lands of the Western Hemisphere. Very little is known about their methods of navigation; but we suppose that, like most ancient sailors, they preferred to keep land in sight. This would have been possible during the voyages to Punt, or north to Syria-Palestine, but the Egyptians had commercial and diplomatic contacts with the Aegean Islands and Crete and, later, with Mycenaean cities on the mainland of Greece. They must have lost a lot of ships out there in the Great Green, but they were probably as skilled as any of their contemporaries. Indeed, it is now generally believed that instead of borrowing from their neighbors, the islanders of Crete or the famed seafarers of Phoenicia, the Egyptians actually originated certain types of ships used by the latter. The "Byblos" and "Cretan" vessels were built by the Egyptians for voyages to those places.

But back to the boats themselves. One authority has compared the lines of Eighteenth Dynasty boats to those of modern racing craft. The hull was deeper than that of older boats; the deck beams now passed through the hull and were fastened outside, for added strength. The sails had two yards, the lower of which was stationary. The deck was boarded across. The oars went through loops of rope which served as oarlocks and, perhaps, as a means of holding the oars when the boat was moored. Ships of this type are extremely attractive in appearance, and the size of the sail suggests that they were capable of considerable speed.

In addition to sailing ships, there were barges and freighters. Barges towed by regular boats were used for massive pieces of stone such as obelisks. Hatshepsut depicts two of her obelisks lying end to end on such a barge, which was pulled by thirty boats with almost a thousand rowers. The towing boats had to be rowed, since they were traveling downstream from Aswan to Thebes, against the wind.

Boats were also used in war. Most of them would probably be considered troop transports rather than warships, but some of the texts do mention battles on sea as well as on land. In the Twentieth Dynasty, Ramses III had to fight off a threatened invasion of the Sea Peoples, who came at him from every direction except the air. His warships had long low hulls with raised bulwarks to protect the rowers. They must have been fairly efficient; Ramses won the battle.

MEDICINE

The next time a scorpion bites you, you might try this. Recite:

> I am the King's son, the eldest and first, Anubis; my mother
> Sekhmet-Isis came after me forth to the land of Syria, to the

hill of the land of Heh, to the nome of those cannibals, saying, "Haste, haste, my child, king's son, eldest and first, Anubis. . . ." And you lick [the bite] with your tongue, while it is bleeding, immediately; then you recite to some oil, you recite to it seven times, you put it on the bite daily; you soak a strip of linen, you put it on it.

There is no field of ancient Egyptian knowledge in which the mixture of magic, science, and religion is seen so clearly as in medicine. Most of Egyptian medical lore is, in spirit as well as in form, like the prescription quoted. The only part we would consider efficacious is the licking of the wound, which may imply sucking out the venom. But perhaps the incantation, which invoked the divine names of Isis and Anubis, had some value if it strengthened the patient's will to live.

Egyptian physicians had an excellent reputation in Greek times. Herodotus mentions that there was specialization, some doctors tending to the feet, some to the teeth, some to the eyes. We have evidence of this specialization even in the Pyramid Age, with doctors of the belly, the head, and the teeth, among others. Physicians were men of some social standing. They owned handsome tombs and equipped them well.

The diseases treated by these men included ophthalmia, bowel trouble, running ears, rheumatism, and parasites. That's only a partial list, and there were frequent accidents resulting in fractures and dislocations (and maybe a missing leg if the accident took the form of a crocodile). Some of these ailments can be found in mummies, but diseases which affected only the soft organs of the body are, as a rule, undiagnosable by modern mummy investigators. One poor old lady had been an invalid for so long that she developed a bad case of bedsores, but we do not know what her trouble was.

Since dentists keep telling us that cavities are a result of soft food and too many sweets, we expect people who do not enjoy these dangerous luxuries to have excellent teeth. Not many Egyptians suffered from dental caries. But they had other troubles. Inevitably, grain got mixed with sand and bits of gravel from the grinding stones. The result was attrition of the hard parts of the teeth, with resultant exposure of the pulp, and alveolar abscesses.

Now we come to the pertinent question: what did the Egyptian physician do to alleviate all these woes, and others which have left no traces on the physical remains of the long-dead sufferers? For this information we must rely, for the most part, on the medical texts.

In this field the Egyptians were—for them—surprisingly communicative. Considering the vast areas of knowledge and activity for which we have no written documentation, we are pleasantly surprised to find approximately a dozen papyri dealing with medical problems. Several are specialized; the Kahun papyrus deals with veterinary medicine and gynecology (an interesting juxtaposition), and the Edwin Smith with the surgical treatment of wounds and fractures. Others are collections of miscellaneous material.

The information we derive from the medical texts is certainly useful, but not consistently so. The texts tell us something about medicine and drugs, yet we are still a long way from complete knowledge on this subject. Medicine was given internally in various liquids; water, milk, honey, wine, and beer are mentioned. Other medicaments were applied externally, and these were usually mixed with fat to form a salve. The burning question for us is, what ingredients were mixed with the liquid or the fat? What, in other words, was the effective pharmacopoeia of the ancient Egyptian doctor?

Some ingredients came from animals, and these are fairly easy for us to identify. Blood, fat, bones, and organs of various mammals, reptiles, and insects were used, as well as entire bodies if they were small enough to be macerated or taken intact. One remedy used for children's diseases was a skinned mouse, swallowed whole; evidently this nasty object was a last resort, for the remains of the mouse have been found in the alimentary canals of several little bodies. Warren Dawson points out that the use of mice as a children's medicine has continued up to modern times, in Europe as well as in the Near East. However, an ordinary M.D. would not be apt to write you a prescription for it.

The plant and mineral ingredients in prescriptions are still giving archaeologists trouble. Perhaps an example will show why. Suppose that you find, in your medical papyrus, a word "abet." You know it is a vegetable substance because it has the determinative that signifies the category of "plants." But you have never met it in any but a medical context, and it is not related to any word you do know. You look at the prescriptions in which it occurs, and you find that it is used to prevent baldness and to cure excessive menstruation, eye infections, and warts. What is it?

Thanks to the really brilliant analyses of some specialized scholars, we can now identify a certain number of these vegetable substances. Often plants seem to have been selected for magical values, as was also true in medieval leechcraft. Thus, a red fruit might restore a patient's healthy color, or a plant leaf shaped like the organ affected might be selected to cure an injury to or deficiency in that organ.

Were any of them, animal, vegetable, or mineral, actually effective?

Not many. I understand that the green malachite has some mild antibacterial properties, and the salt natron would help to dry out an infected wound. The most useful was probably honey, which the Egyptians employed widely, taken internally or applied to open wounds. Some strains of bacteria won't grow in honey, so it may sometimes have accelerated healing. But don't try this at home.

We have a lot of other things that work better. As for analgesics—pain relievers—the best the Egyptians could do was get the sufferer drunk. (Don't try this at home either.) There is no conclusive evidence that the analgesic (or euphoric) effects of opium and cannabis were known to the ancient Egyptian doctor.

Given the early development of medical specialization, as indicated by the titles of doctors, we might anticipate a high degree of anatomical and physiological knowledge. And considering the dreadful condition of ancient teeth, we would expect the doctors of the teeth to be especially active.

One of the surprising facts brought out by the study of human remains from Egypt is the paucity of surgical treatment. Some operations certainly were performed. A very ancient scene shows the act of circumcision, which was commonly practiced in Egypt. In this picture the "doctor" squats on the ground in front of the patient, who is standing. Sometimes an attendant holds the victim's wrists, but one valiant lad is unconfined; he places one hand lightly on the operator's head and has the other resting on his hip. (According to Egyptologist Ann Macy Roth, his nonchalance may be owing to the fact that the instrument in alarmingly close proximity to his penis is not a knife, but a razor. Shaving body hair was done for reasons of ritual purity. Even so. . . .)

Although other ancient cultures certainly did practice trepanning, the evidence for it in Egypt is questionable. Splints were used, and so were bandages and pads of various sorts, and in these cases the art of the embalmer and that of the physician may have overlapped. Splints were employed to hold damaged mummies together, and of course mummy bandaging was an old skill; but we cannot tell whether splints for the living preceded splints for the dead, or vice versa. One medical text describes how to treat a dislocated jaw; the procedure sounds effective, if painful.

Particularly noteworthy is the apparent absence of any sort of dentistry. I cannot imagine what the doctors of the teeth were doing! Great claims have been made for Egyptian dentistry on the basis of one hole in one jawbone from the Fourth Dynasty which, according to enthusiasts, was drilled in order to drain an abscess under a tooth. But if that was the purpose of the hole, it is very strange indeed to find no other evidence of the activity of the doctors of the teeth. If any man merited their attentions, it would have been the king; and yet one mummy—tentatively identified as that of Amenhotep III—had teeth so badly abscessed that they must have reduced the poor man to a state of screaming misery and semi-invalidism.

Up to this point we have done nothing but criticize the ancient Egyptian physicians; now we must look at their accomplishments. In some areas these accomplishments were quite impressive. So let us abandon our mummies in favor of the medical papyri, and investigate these texts in greater detail. We are going to concentrate on one papyrus—the so-called Edwin Smith. It is named after its first (modern) owner, an American who worked in Egypt in the 1860s.

Edwin Smith was a member of a class which has been—politely—called "adventurers." Many of the pioneers of Egyptology, such as the flamboyant ex-circus performer Giovanni Belzoni, belong to the same category. Smith's avowed professions were those of moneylender and antiquities dealer. Both professions give, on occasion, ample scope for skulduggery. Few of the antiquities dealers of that era were overly scrupulous about the sources of the objects they bought, and Smith has been accused, among other things, of forging some of his stock.

In January of 1862 a group of Egyptians appeared in Smith's office with a papyrus roll for sale. It was incomplete and looked as if someone had trimmed its edges to make them neater, but Smith recognized it as a valuable acquisition. He bought it. To this day no one knows where the thieves found it—but that they were thieves no one can deny, since the previous owner had never officially bequeathed it to them. It may have come from the tomb of that owner, a physician of ancient Egypt.

Two months after the first sale, the Egyptians turned up with another medical roll. Smith looked it over and realized that it was a fake, made up of odds and ends and covered, to lend it verisimilitude, with scraps which had been cut off the first papyrus! Nevertheless, he bought this roll too; and among the fragments so rescued was one containing a particularly important section of the original scroll—a passage on the action of the heart.

Smith never disposed of the papyrus which is still called by his name. He left it to his daughter, who gave it and his papers to the New-York Historical Society. The Society called in James Henry Breasted to translate and publish the text, which he did in 1930. To his surprise, Breasted found that Smith had left extensive notes on the text, which he had tried to translate. Like many of his fellow "adventurers," Smith was no simpleminded crook. His notes display a surprising understanding of the Egyptian language, considering that during his lifetime the modern knowledge of the hieroglyphs was less than fifty years old. The text is written in the cursive hieratic script, which was at that time even less well understood than hieroglyphic writing.

By a strange coincidence, Edwin Smith was also at one time in possession of another extremely important medical text—the papyrus later bought by the German Egyptologist Georg Ebers, and named after him. The Ebers and the Edwin Smith papyri are the most useful and interesting of all the texts; the others are either fragmentary or so hopelessly mixed with magic as to give little information on medical knowledge.

Ebers is the longer of the two—the longest, in fact, of all the medical texts. It is twenty meters long; rather an unwieldy size, we might think, but the Egyptians were accustomed to handle such rolls. This text is really a mixture, much less homogeneous than Edwin Smith. It contains: recitals of incantations before treatment; internal diseases; diseases of the eye, skin, extremities, head, and sense organs, diseases of women, and housekeeping matters; general medical notes; surgical cases.

Much of this, particularly the earlier sections, belongs to the category which has been called "magico-medical," as opposed to true medicine. We cannot avoid the suspicion that what we have in Ebers is a one-volume reference library for a practicing physician who copied down, perhaps from other volumes, all the remedies and reminders and prescriptions that he found useful in his daily profession. Yet there are sections in the Ebers papyrus which indicate an approach quite alien to the magico-medical parts. This approach can best be seen and described, however, in the shorter Edwin Smith papyrus.

The Edwin Smith text was probably written during the New Kingdom, but it contains material copied from a much older source—a source that may go back as far as the thirtieth century B.C., before the pyramids were raised at Giza. The text, in its original form, is so old that four or five hundred years after it was first composed a copyist decided that it would be a good idea to explain some of the then-archaic terminology. He added a section of explanations—archaeologists call them "glosses"—after each case, a sort of commentary on confusing phrases and words.

Considering that we are living four thousand years after this first commentator felt it necessary to emend his "archaic" text, Breasted's accomplishment in translating the papyrus becomes quite impressive.

Some minor modifications have been suggested, but they don't change the basic accuracy of his version.

Edwin Smith deals with the surgical treatment of wounds and fractures. As it now stands, it contains forty-eight cases, starting with the top of the head and moving down; but unfortunately our copy stops just below the shoulders. Was the scribe interrupted, or is the remainder lost? The order is interesting; it is a logical way of organizing cases dealing with the human body, and it was, in fact, the standard order through the Middle Ages.

All the cases in Edwin Smith are arranged in the same manner. First comes the title: "Instructions concerning" the injury. Then follows a description of the symptoms. The third element is the physician's diagnosis, beginning with "you should say concerning him," and ending with a prognosis, which may take one of three forms: (1) an ailment which I will treat; (2) an ailment with which I will contend; (3) an ailment not to be treated. The meaning is obvious, isn't it? Pity the poor devil whose ailment was "not to be treated."

Following the prognosis comes the suggested treatment. At the end of the case we find the glosses which explain difficult words and phrases. I am fascinated by this papyrus, so I'm going to quote a specific case, amending Breasted's translation as it suits me.

Instructions: a gaping wound in his head, penetrating to the bone, perforating the suture [?] of his skull.

(Description of symptoms) You should palpate his wound, [though] he shudders greatly. You should cause him to lift his face. [If] it is difficult for him to open his mouth, and his heart is weary to speak; if you observe his spit upon his lips, not falling to the ground, while he gives blood from his nostrils and ears, and he suffers a stiffness in his neck and is not able to look at his shoulders and breast; then you say concerning him:

(Diagnosis) "One having a gaping wound in his head, reaching to the bone, perforating the sutures [?] of his skull; the cord of his mandible is contracted; he gives blood from his nostrils and ears; he suffers a stiffness in his neck."

(Prognosis) An ailment with which I will contend.

(Treatment) Now if you find the cord of that man's mandible is contracted, you should have made for him something hot, until he is comfortable, so that his mouth opens. You should bind it with fat, honey, and lint, until you know that he has reached a decisive point.

If then you find that man has developed fever from that wound which is in the sutures [?] of his skull, while that man has developed severe pain [?] from that wound: you should lay your hand upon him. Should you find his face is wet with sweat, the ligaments of his neck are tense, his face is ruddy, his teeth [and] his back . . . the odor of the box of his head is like the urine of goats, his mouth is bound, his eyebrows are drawn, while his face is as if he wept, you should say concerning him:

"One having a gaping wound in his head, reaching to the bone, perforating the sutures [?] of his skull; he has developed acute pain [?], his mouth is bound, he suffers a stiffness in his neck;

"An ailment not to be treated."

If, however, you find that that man has become pale and has already shown exhaustion, you should have made for him a wooden brace, padded with linen, and put it in his mouth. You should have made for him a draught of w'h fruit. His treatment is sitting, placed between two supports of brick, until you know he has reached a decisive point.

(Commentary)

As for "perforating the sutures [?] of his skull," it means: what is between shell and shell of his skull, and that the sutures [?] are of leather.

As for "the cord of his mandible is contracted," it means: a stiffening on the part of his ligaments at the end of his ramus, which are fastened to his cheekbone, that is, at the end of his jaw, without moving to and fro, so that it is not easy for him to open his mouth because of his pain.

As for "the cord of his mandible," it means: the ligaments

which bind the end of his jaw, as one says "the cord" of a thing, as a splint.

As for "his countenance wet with sweat," it means that his head is a little sweaty, like "a thing is wet."

As for "the ligaments of his neck are tense," it means: that the ligaments of his neck are stiff because of his injury.

As for "his face is ruddy," it means: that the color of his face is red, like the color of the tmst-fruit.

As for "the box of his head is like the urine of goats," it means: that the odor of his crown is like the urine of goats.

As for "the box of his head," it means: the middle of his crown next to his brain; the likening of it is to a box.

As for "his mouth is bound, both his eyebrows are drawn, while his face is as if he wept," it means: that he does not open his mouth that he may speak, both his eyebrows are distorted, one drawing upward, the other drooping downward, like one who winks while his face weeps.

As for "he has become pale and has already shown exhaustion," it means: becoming pale, because he is a [case of] "Undertake him, do not abandon him, in view of the exhaustion."

At first glance this excerpt may seem long and confusing, but one cannot help but be struck by the difference in approach between Edwin Smith and texts like the one quoted at the beginning of this section. In the description of the skull fracture and in the other cases discussed in Edwin Smith, the approach is rigorously matter-of-fact. There are no appeals to divinities, no dubious prescriptions, no incantations, and no mention of demons. In fact, another case explicitly states that the illness is not caused by something entering from without, like a malicious ghost; it is "a thing which [the patient's] own flesh has made."

The Edwin Smith papyrus is also noteworthy for the detail and accuracy of the physician's observations, which are meticulously recorded. The doctor recognizes the significance of various symptoms and changes his treatment accordingly. His anatomical knowledge is very detailed. The texts give words for skull, for brainpan or braincase, and for the brain itself. The jawbone and temporal bone (Breasted's "cheekbone") are distinguished; it is observed that the end of the jawbone joins to the temporal bone. The ramus of the mandible—or, in nonmedical terminology, the end of the jawbone—is described, in Egyptian, as a "claw"-shaped object. In the commentary to another case it is further explained as resembling the claw of a certain bird, which has two opposing members. Thus, the bone, whose location is precisely named, ends in a double-headed connecting part; so the translation "ramus" is obvious.

The "cord" of the mandible is, equally obviously, the muscle that connects the jawbone to the temporal bone and allows it to move. If it is "bound," or locked, the man cannot open and close his mouth. Here again the physician's knowledge is extremely accurate.

The word used for muscles, tendons, and ligaments was the same word, and it could also mean "vessel"—a hollow tube which carried the bodily fluids. It is strange to find one word covering such disparate entities, particularly when, as seems probable, the Egyptians knew quite well the difference between the functions of a ligament and those of a blood vessel.

The section of the Edwin Smith medical papyrus which deals with the heart and the vessels—a section also found in Ebers—is one of the most interesting and significant aspects of Egyptian medical lore. These vessels run to various parts of the body—to the eye, the anus, the arms, and so on. Yet it seems that vessels can carry not only blood but other bodily fluids. It was well known that blood sometimes flowed from the nose, not only in an ordinary nosebleed but as the result of a hard blow on the head. Therefore, some of the vessels leading to the nose must carry blood. But the nose also secretes mucus. Then, argued the Egyptians, two of the vessels must carry this mucus to the nose from somewhere inside the body. Vessels also carried urine, semen, and water.

Where did the vessels originate? They were connected with the heart; yet we cannot say that the Egyptians recognized the heart's function as a pump for passing blood around the body. The heart was a vital organ, perhaps the most vital of all. Other, nonmedical texts make it clear that the heart was thought to hold not only the emotions but also the functions we know to be connected with the brain.

One of the great achievements of Egyptian medicine was the discovery of the pulse. It was called the "voice of the heart," and in one section, found in both Ebers and Edwin Smith, the physician is told where in the body this voice "speaks." Remarkable as this is, it is not enough to let us claim that the Egyptians anticipated Harvey in the discovery of the circulatory system. Yet they knew not only that the pulse was connected in some way with the heart, but that it was a factor the physician had to note. They did not count the pulse; they could not have done so, since they could not measure small units of time accurately. But its usefulness as a general symptom was certainly known.

The functions of the brain were never really recognized. Yet the surgical papyrus shows that the medical writer of the text recognized that injury to the brain could affect motor activities. One case gives a beautiful description of a case of partial paralysis of one side of the body resulting from a blow on the head.

The physician took full advantage of skull injuries to observe the brain. One case refers to something inside the skull which resembles copper slag; it is generally agreed that this must be the gray brain matter itself, with its convolutions. There is mention of a membrane enveloping the brain and of a liquid which can only be the cerebrospinal fluid.

The word "tepau," which Breasted translated as "sutures," is somewhat difficult. Perhaps the ancient commentator found it difficult too, but it cannot be said that his explanation helps us a great deal. He says it is between two "shells" of the skull. These "shells" must be bones of the head, and the only things which can be said to be "between" them are the sutures, the lines of union. Yet the commentator adds that these "sutures," or whatever they are, resemble leather. This does not sound like a good description of the texture of the suture.

The Egyptian physician's extensive knowledge of the anatomy of the brain and skull must have been derived from his observation of head injuries; he could not have learned it from his friend the embalmer. The contributions of the craft of mummification to anatomy were limited; the only area of the body in which the embalmer did any extensive excavating was the abdominal cavity. The brain was left in situ or removed piecemeal and discarded.

I began this chapter on science by remarking that there was almost no such thing in Egypt. "Almost" is not "altogether"; and if any production of ancient man can be called scientific, the Edwin Smith surgical papyrus deserves that description. It is indeed one of the high points, not only of Egyptian empirical knowledge, but of thought and reasoning. In its sober, rational approach, its careful organization and meticulous documentation, and, above all, in its attempt to reason from observed data, without demons, Edwin Smith is a work of science in the strictest sense of that word. Yet how are we to interpret it? As a separate, distinct current of speculative thought which existed side by side with the leech-magician's lore? As the work of a single great man or school whose results were copied for countless generations, not because the copyists recognized the greatness of its implicit content, but because they found it useful? Or as one aspect of the Egyptian "multiplicity of approaches," which excluded no idea simply because it was inconsistent with another, so long as it had limited value?

Being a romantic, I have been fired by the suggestion that Edwin Smith, Ebers, and a few of the other texts derive their surgical lore from a single, very old source. And my imagination inevitably reacts to the fact that this postulated source book may come from a period roughly contemporaneous with Imhotep, the Old Kingdom sage. Imhotep's reputation as a physician outshone even his fame as an architect; it was as a medical man that he was deified. We would be going far beyond the evidence if we suggested seriously that the surgical papyrus owes its existence to Imhotep. Still, if I were a physician today, I would join the movement—already begun, I believe, by some historically minded doctors—to give to Imhotep the honored position, now accorded Hippocrates, as the father of medicine. As George Sarton has pointed out, "Hippocrates comes about halfway between Imhotep and us." He also comes about halfway between us and the lost original of the Edwin Smith surgical papyrus, which is thus the oldest scientific document in the world; and its author, whether it was Imhotep or another unknown genius, ought to rate, at the very least, a plaque in some medical institution.

Twelve

"THE GOD IS SATISFIED WITH HIS OFFERINGS"

THE OFFICIAL RELIGION

There will come a time when it will be seen that in vain have the Egyptians honored the deity with heartfelt piety and assiduous service, and all our holy worship will be found bootless and ineffectual. . . . Oh Egypt, Egypt, of thy religion nothing will remain but an empty tale, which thine own children in time to come will not believe; nothing will be left but graven words, and only the stones will tell of thy piety. And so the gods will depart from mankind.

Yes, the gods are gone—Amon and Isis, jackal-headed Anubis, even Osiris, lordly judge of the dead. In a way, it seems a pity. For if man does make gods in his own image, the

Egyptian gods testify to the tolerance of their creators. They lacked the nasty habits of some other deities, who thrived on incinerated babies and dripping human hearts or required the complete annihilation of people who held differing opinions on religious matters. Except for one brief period, Egyptian religion was the most broad-minded of faiths. If a foreigner could not find some Egyptian god or other to worship, he was very hard to please; but even in that case the amiable Egyptians allowed him to worship his own god, or adopted it themselves.

The Egyptians were just about the most polytheistic people who ever lived. No one knows exactly how many gods they had; one list gives over eighty, and I suspect it is incomplete. Before we get into the mainstream of the symposium, we had better start with the Cast of Characters—a list, not of all eighty, but of the principal gods, and their attributes, to whom we will be referring. The list itself is an oversimplification. There is still debate on who the gods were, how they got to be that way, and what they stood for:

GODS

Amon—One of the eight gods of chaos; god of wind or air. In the New Kingdom, as Amon-Re, he became King of the Gods. Wife: Mut. Son: Khonsu. City: Thebes. Sacred animals: ram, goose; but always shown in human form.

Anubis—God of cemeteries, embalming. Son of Osiris and Nephthys. Animal: jackal or other doglike beast.

Aton—Solar god, adopted by Akhenaton as his sole object of worship. Early representations show him as a hawk-headed human; under Akhenaton he was always depicted as the sun disc with rays ending in human hands.

Atum—Creator god, later identified with Re. The setting sun. Gave birth to Shu and Tefnut.

Some of the principal gods

Left to right: Thoth, Anubis, Ptah, Osiris

Left to right: Sobek, Khnum, Bes, Set

Left to right: Horus, Amon, Aton

Bes—Dwarfish, bandy-legged god of the bedchamber and toilet table; wears leopard skin and ostrich headdress.

Geb—Earth god. Son of Shu and Tefnut, husband of Nut, father of Osiris, Isis, Nephthys, Set. Animal: goose.

Hapi—The Nile; more specifically, the Inundation. Shown as a plump man with pendulous female breasts.

Horus—Originally sky god, hawk-headed, whose eyes were sun and moon; identified with king. In his form of Horus of the Horizon, Harakhte, merged with Re to become Re-Harakhte. Became identified with Horus the son of Isis and Osiris, the great antagonist of Set.

Khephri—Morning sun, creator god. Identified with Re. Animal: beetle.

Khnum—The "Molder," creator god, who made mankind out of clay. City: Elephantine. Animal: ram.

Khonsu—Moon god. Son of Amon and Mut. Shown as handsome boy with sidelock. City: Thebes.

Min—Ithyphallic, fertility god. City: Coptos.

Montu—God of war. City: Hermonthis (Thebes). Animals: bull, falcon.

Nefertum—Son of Ptah and Sekhmet. Human form. Insignia: lotus.

Osiris—God of the dead, judge of spirits. Shown in mummiform human shape. City: first Busiris, then Abydos. Wife: Isis.

Ptah—God of artisans, craftsmen; always in mummiform human shape. Husband of Sekhmet, father of Nefertum. Animal: Apis bull. City: Memphis.

Re—*The* sun-god. City: Heliopolis. Animals: falcon, Mnevis bull.

Set—God of oases, desert, foreigners, storm. Brother and murderer of Osiris. Animal: doglike, composite beast. City: Ombos, later Tanis.

Shu—God of atmosphere, who separates Geb, earth, from Nut, sky. Son of Atum, husband of Tefnut.

Left to right: Bastet, Hathor, Maat, Nephthys

Taweret and Isis nursing Horus

Some of the principal goddesses

Sobek—Crocodile god. Centers of worship: Fayum, Kom
   Ombo.

Thoth—Divine scribe, inventor of numbers. Associated with
   moon. Animals: ibis, baboon. City: Hermopolis.

Wepwawet—Mortuary god. City: Assiut. Animal: wolf and/or
   dog.

GODDESSES

Bastet—Goddess of pleasure, dancing, music. Animal: cat. City: Bubastis.

Hathor—Goddess of love, beauty, joy; mother goddess. Animal: cow. City: Denderah.

Hekat—Frog goddess. Midwife who assisted birth of sun.

Isis—Symbol of devoted wife (of Osiris) and mother (of Horus). Animal: cow. Insignia: throne.

Maat—Goddess of truth, law, order. Daughter of Re. Symbol: feather. Shown as human-headed, with a feather on her head.

Meskhenet—Goddess of childbirth. Shown as woman with two long curved shoots on head.

Mut (pronounced "moot")—Mother goddess. Wife of Amon, mother of Khonsu. Animal: vulture. City: Thebes.

Neith (pronounced like "night")—Goddess of hunting and war. Symbol: crossed arrows. City: Sais.

Nekhbet—One of the Two Ladies who protected the king; tutulary goddess of Upper Egypt. Animal: vulture. City: Nekheb.

Nephthys—Sister of Isis and Osiris, wife of Set, but sympathetic to Osiris; hence, one of the goddesses who guarded the dead.

Nut (pronounced "noot")—Sky goddess. Wife of Geb. Animal: cow.

Sekhmet—Goddess of battle. Wife of Ptah. Associated with medical profession. Animal: lion. City: Memphis.

Selket—Daughter of Re; presides over embalmed entrails; protectress of the dead. Animal: scorpion.

Seshat—Goddess of learning. Symbol: star on a pole with inverted horns.

Taweret—Hippopotamus goddess of childbirth.

Tefnut—Goddess of moisture. Mother of Geb and Nut, wife of Shu.

Wadjet—Second of the Two Ladies; goddess of Lower Egypt. Animal: cobra. City: Buto.

One of the things that makes a discussion of Egyptian religion so confusing is not so much the number of gods, but the fact that they refuse to stay in the neat little slots we construct for them. Through the process called syncretism, one god might assume the name and attributes of two or three others, as Amon of Thebes became Amon-Re Harakhte. Instead of sharing names, he might usurp some other god's titles, or insignia, or job. So Osiris took first the insignia of an ancient Delta god named Andjti, and then the title and position of a mortuary god of Abydos. The animal-headed gods overlap frightfully— a falcon may represent Re, Horus, Montu, or any one of a number of others. All these factors are relatively unimportant, however, compared with a really serious problem of overlap which has annoyed most students of Egyptian religion. We will see it best through an example. So let us go back to the beginning of all things and see how, according to Egyptian dogma, the world was created.

In the beginning there was the primeval abyss—chaos—formlessness. Out of the waters of chaos there gradually emerged a small hillock of wet ground, just as, after the annual inundation begins to subside, little mounds of earth come into view above the falling waters. On this primeval mound appeared Atum, the Creator.

Atum was a male god. Despite this handicap, he produced the first couple, the god Shu and the goddess Tefnut, air and moisture. In a relatively refined version of the story he accomplished this by spitting. A more pragmatic version makes the hand and phallus of the god the agents of creation. Whatever his method, once the first pair of male and female deities appeared, reproduction proceeded normally thereafter. Shu and Tefnut bore Geb (earth, male) and Nut (sky, female), who bore Isis and Osiris, Set and Nephthys. This group of nine deities constituted the Ennead of Heliopolis; Atum had adopted the sun god Re of that city and was called Re-Atum.

Even this one creation story gives alternative explanations of the method of creation—a third version provides Atum with a female consort. But Atum was not the only creator. Khnum, the potter, who made mankind out of clay, was another. The most provocative of the creation stories is the one called the "Memphite Theology."

Geb, Nut, and Shu

According to this text, the real creator was Ptah, chief god of Memphis:

> The sight of the eyes, the hearing of the ears, the smelling of
> air of the nose, they report to the heart. This it is which causes
> every completed conception to come forth, and it is the tongue
> which proclaims that which the heart thinks. . . . Indeed, every
> command of the god came into being through that which the
> heart thought and the tongue commanded.

Here we have creation viewed, not as a physical act, but as the
result of divine will and divine utterance. For "heart" read "brain" or
"mind"; the Egyptians thought of the heart as the seat of the intelligence. The Memphite Theology is one of the Egyptians' finest
achievements in philosophic thought. It is more abstract than the
other creation stories; its resemblance to the doctrine of the Logos
has been pointed out by many scholars. Yet—and this is the point of
our example—neither the Memphite version nor any other creation
story ever superseded all the others. For each cosmological phenom-

enon there was, not one explanation, but many; and all were equally valid.

For a more concrete example, let us look at the sun. Re was a sun god, and so was Harakhte—Horus of the Horizon. Horus being originally a sky god, the sun was regarded as one of his eyes. But it was also a boat in which Re sailed across the sky, and a hawk which flew on outspread wings.

The most fetching of all the sun myths is the one which identifies the solar orb with Khephri, the beetle-headed god—that same beetle whose form is commemorated in scarabs. How did an earthbound insect get to be a sun god? Well, the dung beetle of Egypt may be seen pushing a little round ball of clay ahead of him as he plods through the sand. From this ball, the ancients believed, the beetle's young emerged, just as the new sun was reborn each morning. Modern science, always disillusioning, says that the ball does not, in fact, contain the grub of the beetle, but the Egyptians didn't know that. (And if they had known, they probably wouldn't have cared.)

A similar "multiplicity of approaches" can be found in almost every object or phenomenon the Egyptians thought seriously about—death, immortality, the rise of the Nile, the stars, and so on, ad infinitum. Some scholars find this lack of logical consistency infuriating, and there have been many attempts to pummel the big, floppy system into some sort of solid shape. It will not work. Egyptian religion was not consistent, in our terms. It may have had a consistency of its own, but it is so different from ours that we refuse to call it by the same name. We might reasonably ask how many theological systems are logical to nonbelievers; the subject matter is not particularly suitable to principles of reason. Furthermore, what we see in Egyptian religion is not an artificially constructed theology, formalized by arbitrary pronouncements from a single source of authority, but a hodgepodge from dozens of different temples, covering a period of more than three millennia! Certainly we can construct a system to explain everything if we are determined to do so, but we may find ourselves in the awkward position immortalized by an old song:

Last night I saw upon the stair
A little man who wasn't there.

My tolerance of Egyptian inconsistency is perhaps, in part, personal; like the Egyptians, I have no trouble believing several contradictory things at once, and I find the universe too complex to be comprehended through a single system of thought. For this reason, or for others which are more defensible, I like the term "multiplicity of approaches." It is a description of what the Egyptians did, rather than a pseudo-psychological explanation of why they did it; and it neatly, and correctly, describes the underlying assumption of Egyptian religion:

There are a dozen different ways of explaining anything that really matters; and all of them are right.

Our modern approaches to Egyptian religion are not necessarily inconsistent, but they are certainly numerous. No longer can a book on this subject restrict itself to a catalog of deities. Some studies attempt to synthesize the theology and explain the symbolism—neither of which the Egyptians ever bothered to do; others investigate details of dogma or ritual. One school stresses the historical aspect. A fairly factual history of Egyptian religion can be written, on the basis of the texts and reliefs of dynastic Egypt, but some scholars have tried to penetrate far back into the misty, unknown years of prehistory to describe the very beginnings of religion in Egypt.

In the beginning, then, instead of Atum squatting on his primeval hill, we see Egypt as made up of dozens of little villages, each with its own local chieftain and village god. Many of the local gods took animal forms, and they may have been the totems of the primitive communities. As time went on, two things happened. One was an amalgamation—under duress, usually—of the little villages into larger units. The other was a series of invasions of people from outside the valley. As the villages joined together, so did the gods join forces to form a pantheon; and they were accompanied by foreign gods imported by the invader, or invaders, or traders, or whatever they were. Among the invading gods, according to some scholars, was the well-known mortuary god Osiris, whose murder and resurrection form the Egyptian Passion. Settling first in the northern Delta, Osiris became god of the north, and eventually, when the two kingdoms of north and south came to blows, the conflict was viewed as a struggle between Osiris and the indigenous southern god, the redheaded warrior Set. The Great Antagonists, however, are not Osiris and Set, but Set and his nephew, Osiris's son Horus, who was also a northern god. The eventual defeat of Set by Horus commemorates, in mythological form, an ancient conquest of the south by the north.

Another powerful god whose fame goes back to prehistoric times was Re, the sun god. His city was Heliopolis, but some scholars see him as another foreign god, from a northern region where the sun's life-giving warmth would have been more valued than in Egypt. Unlike Osiris, who owed his popularity to the appeal of his resurrection, Re rose to power through the machinations of a clever, well-organized priesthood.

The reader can find one or more of these interpretations cited, as a fact, in many books about Egypt. I will now proceed to tell you what's wrong with them. First and foremost, polytheism is not an additive process. It is unlikely that each little village worshiped only one god, distinct from all the other gods of all the other villages, and it is still more unlikely that the swarming pantheon of historic times was obtained by adding up all the monotheistic gods of all the villages. Totemism is another of those seemingly happy thoughts which cannot be supported. The distinctive traits of the totemic system, such as exogamy and the identification of the members of the tribe with the animal of the totem, are not found in Egypt.

As for Egypt's famous animal gods, they cannot be described so simply. Some gods were never shown in animal form. Ptah was associated with a sacred bull, the Apis, but he never has a bull's head, nor are bulls, as such, sacred to Ptah. Amon did not borrow even the head of his sacred animal, the goose. Other divinities sometimes have animal forms and sometimes human forms; Hathor may be shown as a shapely woman, or as a woman with a cow's head, or as a shapely cow. The gods were not conceived of as animals, nor were animals worshiped as gods. The gods were beings who could be, at times, interpreted as, or symbolized by, an animal or part-animal form.

Egypt may have derived some of her gods from abroad, but as yet we cannot prove that Osiris or Re were immigrants. As for the conquest of the "Followers of Set" by the "Followers of Horus," the only conquest we know of was the historic event which marks the beginning of dynastic history, and that was vice versa—south conquered north. The only evidence for the predynastic conquest, which is often mentioned, is this very myth. Myth may be a poetic description of political or historical events, but this approach can be overworked. Some interpreters see every new, powerful god as the patron of a new, powerful invading army or political party. In these terms the spread of Christianity must have been owing to the ferocity of that conquering sect from Palestine, which first overran the Roman Empire and then defeated the rest of the Western nations.

Even after the beginning of historic times—that is, the First Dynasty—we are exceedingly short on evidence with which to construct a legitimate history of Egyptian religion. The uncertainty and the debate over questions relating to prehistoric religion extend into the Archaic Period. We know that many of the gods prominent during later periods were being worshiped then, and that Horus was already identified with the king. Strangely enough, the name of Set, Horus's implacable foe, also crops up in royal titles during the early dynasties. The quarrelsome redheaded god's significance, from the political and religious aspects, is still the subject of considerable academic discussion. Some authorities believe that Re of Heliopolis was already a powerful god; others argue that Osiris had established himself as Lord of Abydos by this time. The actual evidence for both these last statements is, at best, vague.

By the Old Kingdom we are in slightly better case; for one thing, the inscriptional material has increased. The belief in immortality goes back to the earliest periods in Egypt; prehistoric graves include such pathetic but significant vanities as cosmetic palettes, beads, and pots which once contained food and drink. But it is not until the Fifth and Sixth Dynasties that we know much more about mortuary religion. The Pyramid Texts of this age tell us that Re and Osiris had both acquired status as gods of the dead. During the same era we see an increased importance for Re, the sun god, in court dogma as well as in the mortuary cult. However, despite the convincing, carefully documented arguments of several distinguished scholars, it is as yet impossible to explain why Re became so important.

During the Middle Kingdom Re continued to hold his own as divine father of the king, who was at the same time Horus, son of Osiris. The cult of Osiris also spread during this period; the blessing of the resurrected god was now available to commoners, if it had not been so earlier. The rulers of the Middle Kingdom came originally from Thebes, and in the Twelfth Dynasty a hitherto minor god of that city, named Amon, becomes a major divinity. Amon's real nature is somewhat obscure. His name means something like "the Hidden One," and he may have represented the wind or the air. Early in the proceedings Amon associated himself with Re and other sun gods and took the name of Amon-Re-Harakhte. Whether this was a sound political move, or merely sound theology, we do not know.

Amon's real rise to power did not begin until the Eighteenth Dynasty, when, after a second period of political breakdown, Egypt was reunited under a king of Thebes. Unlike the unifiers of the Twelfth Dynasty, the new Theban kings did not leave home after their conquest. When they set up the national capital in their native town, a temple to Amon was already there; and as the little villages on the Theban plain grew into "Thebes of the Hundred Gates," so the humble temple of Amon mushroomed into the spectacular structure of Karnak, still, even in its ruins, one of the greatest sights coming down to us from the ancient world. Amon-Re was the divine father of the king and the patron of the warrior pharaohs of the early Eighteenth Dynasty. As Egypt spread out across the Near East, the spoils of empire poured into Thebes, and a goodly share of the booty fell to the temple of Amon-Re.

By the middle of the Eighteenth Dynasty the once-obscure local god of Thebes had become King of the Gods, and "the sole one, who made everything which is." Here Amon is not only a creator, but he is the only creator—the only god, if we are to take the text literally. This cannot be done, however. The worship of the other gods continued, and some of them also claimed the epithet "sole god." It is only another example of that pleasant inconsistency which is so characteristic of Egyptian religion.

During the period of Amon's aggrandizement we begin to find occasional references to a god called Aton. Like Amon-Re, he was a sun god, but he was a very small fish. Then, somewhere around the year 1390 B.C., a son and heir was born to King Amenhotep III and his chief wife, Tiye. The young prince was named Amenhotep, in honor of Amon; he was raised in the royal palace in Thebes, where he surely was trained to pay homage to the gods, chief among them the patron of his house and his city. When the youthful Amenhotep IV came to the throne, he was crowned at Thebes. He worshiped Amon. He also built a temple to the obscure godling Aton, who was shown in the form of a hawk-headed human figure, like Re-Harakhte.

Then—almost overnight, or so it seems to us across the gulf of the centuries—came the revolution. Amenhotep IV cast off his official name and chose a new one which incorporated the name of the god Aton—Akhenaton. He moved his court from Thebes to a brand-new city, also named after the Aton, and ordered his tomb to be built within its precincts. In the temples raised to his honor in the new city, Aton was shown, not as a man or an animal-headed man, but as a featureless disc whose only anthropomorphic feature was the row of rays ending in human hands, which extended the sign of life to the king and queen. Some time after the move the king sent emissaries throughout the country, ordering them to chisel out the names of the ancient gods from the walls of tombs and temples. Amon was especially persecuted; not even the name of Akhenaton's father Amenhotep was spared, because it incorporated the hated element. In some cases the plural word "gods" was excised from the inscriptions.

So much is—we are fairly sure—fact. From this point on we enter into a realm of speculation and theory which is so permeated with unscholarly prejudices that it is almost impossible to separate people from their passions. I am certainly not free of prejudice myself; perhaps I still am affected by the glamour of my first meeting with Akhenaton in the pages of James Henry Breasted, who viewed the heretic king as "the first monotheist" and "the first individual in history." Breasted admired Akhenaton; his masterful prose and his scholarly prestige created an unforgettable picture of a pale dreamer, frail in body but great of soul, who stood up unflinchingly against the forces of reaction to create a god who was—almost—God.

Who could resist an image like that one? It still clouds the surface of my intellect when I try to talk rationally about Akhenaton; and I suspect that the violent antagonism of some scholars is in direct ratio to the effort they must make to obliterate that same glamorous picture. The reaction has been violent indeed. Some modern interpreters see the whole Amarna experiment as the degenerate product of a sick, autocratic brain, and Akhenaton as deformed in body and perverted in soul.

It is impossible to talk about "Amarna religion" without talking about Akhenaton himself; here, surely, is one time when the individual as a force in history cannot be denied. The difficulty is that we know almost nothing about Akhenaton except what we can infer from his activities; and the interpretations of those activities are almost always colored in some way by the personality of the interpreter.

Just as we must view statements about Akhenaton the man with extreme caution, so we must be equally suspicious of interpretations of Akhenaton's new religion. The Amarna "revolution" involved several new ways of doing things. We have already mentioned the art forms of the time. It is possible to emphasize the new developments and stress the iconoclastic nature of the reforms; it is equally possible to point out antecedents and insist that Akhenaton really did not change so much. Although there are precedents for some of the elements in the Aton faith, such as the claim "sole god," which was also applied to Amon, I think it would be quibbling to deny that something strange, something radically different, was happening to Egyptian religion.

The first, vital question is: what did Akhenaton actually worship?

The Aton was depicted as the rounded disc of the sun. Thus, to some scholars, it is the most physical, the least abstract, of all the gods of Egypt. The curious half-animal, half-human forms of other gods may have been—they had to be!—symbolic; but the sun is there, up in the sky. Other scholars say that the sun disc was a symbol too, and as such it was the most abstract of all the forms of the godhead.

I have my own prejudices about what Akhenaton worshiped; but I think it is almost impossible to know what *he* thought he was worshiping. The great Aton hymn, which has been compared with the 104th Psalm, is not much help. It is full of beautiful but vague compliments to the god, and it gives a charming picture of the dependence of all creation, animal as well as human, on the light and heat of the sun— or on the joy and love of the creator, depending on how you want to interpret the words.

Another important question is whether the Aton faith was monotheism or something else. Breasted thought it was monotheism. Most modern scholars are more cautious. The Aton had a set of titles, a regular royal titulary, in which he was equated with Shu and Atum and other gods. This, say the skeptics, is not monotheism. The cautious scholars also point out that Aton was not worshiped directly by anyone except members of the royal family; he was approached through Akhenaton, who was his son, the "only one who knew him."

Since nothing can be written on the subject of the Aton monotheism that is fact—it is only one man's theory against another's—I may as well tell the reader what I think. Pure monotheism, of the type implied by the reservations mentioned above, is just about nonexistent. The idea of a divine son as an intermediary between god and man can be found in modern times in a faith which would certainly take affront if it were called polytheistic; it also admits a multiple godhead and worships the deity under many names and epithets. The king of Egypt was at all times the primary adorer of the god; his towering figure makes offerings on behalf of the land and the people. Private citizens could also be shown in postures of worship. It is not strictly accurate to say that prayers were never directed to the Aton by those outside the royal family. There are a number of such texts.

To me the conclusive evidence of Akhenaton's faith being, so far as he was concerned, monotheistic can be found in the persecution of the other gods. Such bigotry is a sure sign of monotheism. It is true that Amon is particularly often defaced, but the other gods were not spared, and there are the rare, but extremely significant examples of the obliteration of the plural word "gods." At the city of Amarna itself no temples to other gods have ever been found. In the workmen's village the old gods lived on, for official proscription does not destroy a divinity in the hearts of his worshipers. The question is not whether the Aton faith "caught on," but what its true nature was. And the answer, it seems to me, is a fairly good version of monotheism.

Perhaps one of the reasons for the reservations about this conclusion is the fact that Atonism, as we know it, seems to be lacking any ethical system. The "higher religions" have codes of conduct regulating the relations between god and man, and between man and other men. A similar moral code can be found in such Egyptian texts as the "Declaration of Innocence." There is very little sign of moral values in the Aton hymn, which is the only statement of the faith surviving to us.

The Aton hymn is about the length of one of the longer Psalms; it is, like the Psalms, a hymn of praise. To assume, because we cannot find in it the Ten Commandments or the Sermon on the Mount, that equivalent statements did not exist is unfair argument. We have so little material, really, and we are accustomed to working over each little scrap so thoroughly, that we tend to forget that what we have is only a small percentage of the total picture. Akhenaton reigned for seventeen years, and the religion he created died with him. It is not surprising that we lack documentary statements of belief from a period so short, when we have so few from the whole three-thousand-year span of pharaonic history. I cannot make any exalted claims for Akhenaton as a moralist; but neither can his adversaries dogmatically state that the Aton faith lacked this element. There is that continued emphasis on maat, not unique to Akhenaton, but surely implying the same values of truth, justice, and order.

We do not know the motives that impelled the soi-disant Amenhotep IV to take a step so alien to his heritage. Various theories have

been suggested—naturally. There is the idea that the religious reformer
was not Akhenaton but his wife or mother, and that this philosophi-
cally inclined female, whoever she was, came from one of the northern
kingdoms—Mitanni is a favorite candidate—where a sun god was worshiped. Others suggest that the court party (a strictly modern concept)
had become alarmed at the growing temporal power of Amon's priesthood and sought to restrain it by setting up a new god. Neither theory
makes sense. The "evidence" of Tiye's foreign ancestry is extremely tenuous, as we pointed out in the first chapter; Nefertiti's claim to Mitannian
blood is now discounted. As for the idea that someone other than
Akhenaton was responsible for the Aton faith, there is nothing to support or even suggest it.

The political interpretation gives Akhenaton credit for acumen so
great as to amount to clairvoyance. We can see now, from where we
stand, the development of a process which was to end four hundred
years after Akhenaton with the high priests of Amon as rulers of
Thebes; but there is no reason to suppose that the king, or anyone else
at court, could see it.

Both these theories, like all the others, break down on the really
essential point: that the Aton faith, if not true monotheism, was so
different from true polytheism as to be quite alien to the thought of
the time, in Egypt or Mitanni or anyplace else. The most obvious way
of explaining the phenomenon of Amarna is to resort to the unpopular but almost inescapable theory that Akhenaton himself was one of
those rare, spiritually inspired individuals who occasionally emerge
from the placid masses of mankind and, for better or worse, work their
will on the course of history. No matter what we think of Breasted's
fondness for Akhenaton, we must admit that there is a grain of truth
in that sweeping characterization, "the first individual in history." Deformed, inspired, depraved, or what you will, Akhenaton is the only
one of the pharaohs who has come down to us as more than a handsome hard-stone statue. The very magnitude of the controversy that
rages around his vanished figure testifies to his uniqueness.

Whatever its character, it is probable that the religious revolution
was the work of one man. When he died—how, we do not know—the

new faith also died. Akhenaton's successors were boys, married to two of his daughters; one of them, Smenkhkare, probably did not survive his father-in-law, and young Tutankhaton was only nine years old when he ascended the throne. A few years later he had abandoned the city of Aton, changed his name to Tutankhamon, and restored the worship of Amon, repaying the god fourfold for all that he had lost under the persecution. Tutankhamon was the last of the house of Amarna; he was succeeded by a man of unknown antecedents who reigned for only a few years. The next king, Harmhab, who had been—we think—a follower of Akhenaton's, completed the return to orthodoxy with a vengeance. Harmhab denied the existence of all the rulers between Amenhotep III and himself, claiming their years of kingship under his reign. Eventually Akhenaton's very name was wiped off the pages of history. The heretic king was referred to only as "that criminal." The victory of Amon was complete.

The new family of kings who made up the Nineteenth Dynasty were thoroughly orthodox except for one slightly peculiar factor—the prominence they gave to Set, the old enemy of Osiris. Osiris was not neglected. One of the most beautiful temples in Egypt was built in his honor, at Abydos, by two of the kings of this dynasty. Since one of them, Seti I, had a name which was singularly inappropriate at Abydos, incorporating as it did the name of Osiris's murderer, the little figure of Set in the king's cartouche was replaced throughout the temple by the Osiris figure. Even I find this inconsistency mildly startling; if the king's name was so offensive, he should never have selected it in the first place. The solution, of course, lies in the familiar "multiplicity of approaches." At Abydos, Set was his brother's murderer and anathema; some place else he was something else, and perfectly all right. Set's position is an unusual one, and it is still imperfectly understood. Whether or not it is understandable in our terms is another matter.

The Nineteenth Dynasty kings tried with some success to reestablish the old Egyptian Asiatic empire, which had been threatened during the reigns of Akhenaton and his father. One result of foreign contacts was the introduction of alien gods into the Egyptian pantheon; Astarte,

Baal, and others were worshiped in Egypt, though none of them ever became outstandingly popular.

Above all the others, supreme in the pantheon, Amon-Re continued his triumphant progress. By the end of the Twentieth Dynasty his priests were in control of a vast amount of property; one estimate makes it as high as 15 percent of the people and 30 percent of the land. The end of the dynasty saw what some scholars have viewed as the inevitable conclusion. The High Priest of Amon took over the functions, if not the titles, of the king. It does not matter whether he seized power by virtue of his priestly power or his control of the army; he ruled as spokesman of the god. At this time Egypt was again divided, the north being ruled by men who claimed the title of king, the south by the high priests. A reunification made no difference to Amon. A benevolent monarch, allowing many lesser suns to shine in his heavens, he continued to rule the pantheon until Greek times, and after; Alexander the Great found it expedient to make the hard journey out to the Oasis of Siwa in order to be acknowledged King of Egypt by Amon of that place. The Greek and Roman rulers of Egypt, polytheists all, had no difficulty in worshiping the Egyptian pantheon and in adapting it to their needs. Isis was particularly popular; her worship spread throughout the Roman territories. Amon and his cohorts were not supplanted until Jehovah pushed Amon from his throne, and His Son replaced Osiris as a pledge of eternal life. Then, and not until then, could it be said that the gods of ancient Egypt were dead.

TEMPLES AND RITUALS

Anyone who has visited Egypt on one of those whirlwind five-day tours probably comes back with jumbled memories of Egyptian temples—heavy towering gateways, forests of columns, headless statues, and walls of austere pale stone covered with unintelligible pictures. Many of the existing "tourist" temples are Ptolemaic in date. Edfu, Denderah, Kom Ombo, Philae—all were built during the Greek or Roman occupation of Egypt, after 300 B.C. Their plans are much the same as those of the dynastic temples, but the decoration and the overall impression are different.

Of the dynastic temples still surviving, the most famous are in Upper Egypt—Karnak, Luxor, Abu Simbel (in Nubia), and Abydos are the main ones. Some of the other conspicuous temples of the Theban area, such as the Ramesseum, Deir el Bahri, and Medinet Habu, were dedicated to the mortuary cult of the king—though not exclusively. The distinction between mortuary and divine temples is useful, but, as is often the case in Egypt, the two categories overlapped.

The earliest temples in Egypt were little one-room affairs made of reeds, wood, or brick. Naturally, none of them have survived, but archaeologists can guess at their appearance from pictures, especially the hieroglyphic signs. The extremely scanty remains of one such temple, whose appearance has been brilliantly reconstructed from clues that would baffle Sherlock Holmes, was found at Hierakonpolis, once the capital of Upper Egypt. Few of the pre–Eighteenth Dynasty temples have survived. Perhaps the most interesting is the little temple of Senusert I, which dates from the beginning of the Twelfth Dynasty, but it was not found intact. Its stones were disinterred from the inside of one of the pylons at Karnak and put together by archaeologists. The Egyptian kings were fond of claiming pious respect for the works of their ancestors, but like so many virtues, it was more honored in the breach than in the observance. The royal builder of the third pylon, looking around for material, took the temple stones to prop up his pylon, and there they remained until they were found in modern times. I should add that some scholars feel this was not an impious act; the pieces of the dismembered shrine remained in the temple, after all. Frankly, this argument strikes me as somewhat disingenuous.

Senusert's temple is a very simple one—a plain rectangular building with a flat roof and open windows all around. It stands on a platform, reached by ramps on opposite sides; and it is, for all its simplicity, a handsome, dignified little structure. This type is called a peripteral temple, and others of the same type were built during the Eighteenth Dynasty.

The standard temple plan of the New Kingdom, which is found in

*Perspective of a New Kingdom temple: Reconstruction of the temple
of Amon-Re at Karnak*

most surviving temples, is not so simple as that of the peripteral temple, but it is not as complicated as it appears to be. Basically it consisted of four elements: a pylon or gateway; a court with rows of
columns along one or more sides; a wide, columned (hypostyle) hall;
and the sanctuary room (or rooms). The whole thing was surrounded
by a wall, usually of mud brick, with an open space in front of the
gateway.

The pylon gateway was made of two towers with sloping sides and
flat tops. It is believed to represent the mountains between which the
sun rose each morning, and it does resemble the hieroglyph for "horizon." The gate was between the towers. Beyond was the colonnaded
court, usually unroofed except for the part over the colonnades. Beyond this came the hypostyle hall. The biggest and most impressive of
these halls is the one at Karnak; it is a jungle of columns so crowded
together that it is hard to realize how big the place is. If you stand at
one end and look down to the other end and see a minuscule guide
squatting at the base of one of the mammoth pillars, you begin to
grasp the size. Some of the columns in this hall are forty-two and a
half feet high, and twenty-seven and a half feet around. The hall was

Reconstruction of a pylon gateway, with obelisks, statues, and standards
(temple of Amon-Re at Luxor)

dimly lit by a clerestory raised on the two central rows of columns; the giants in these rows are sixty-nine feet high, and it has been calculated that one hundred men could stand on each of the enormous capitals—although I would not care to be one of the ones who stood along the edges.

Behind the hypostyle hall the favored priests might enter the shrine itself—the dwelling place of the god. This was a simple, windowless room; at the far end stood a statue of the god. Some temples were dedicated to more than one god, or to a god and his family. Triads were popular—father, mother, son—so often a temple will have three shrines. Surrounding the shrine were storerooms, offices, and the like.

The progression through these stages is from light to less light to utter darkness, and, as some scholars believe, from the chaos of ordinary life to that divine order (maat) with which the creation began, and which must be continually reconstituted through ritual. Or, to put it another way, the temple itself was the threshold between man and the divine. The rock-cut temples such as Abu Simbel were essentially a transfer of the standard style into solid stone. The facade of Abu Simbel represents the pylon, with gigantic statues like the ones often found in front of the regular temples; inside the cliff are the usual pillared halls and the shrine.

The casual visitor finds it hard to trace this plan in the Egyptian temples of today. This is because the basic elements could be multiplied, not only by the original builder but by succeeding rulers. When a king wanted to improve a temple, the usual procedure was to build another court and/or pylon in front of the ones already there. Karnak demonstrates this procedure very well. As it stands today it represents the pious royal efforts of over a millennium, and that figure does not include the Middle Kingdom temple, which is now lost. Karnak has eight pylons, not counting the ones which belong to the other nearby temples.

Prominent among the minor decorative elements of a temple were obelisks, and these also might be added by later kings, willy-nilly, to honor the god. Hatshepsut tore down part of her own father's hall at Karnak in order to insert, quite inappropriately, two fine obelisks. These tall, slim square pillars, tapering to a pyramid point on top, often stood in front of the pylon gateway; their surfaces were covered with inscriptions praising, in no modest terms, the ruler who had erected them. The obelisks, some of which are almost a hundred feet high, are not what one would call easily transportable; and yet there are probably more standing obelisks today in Rome than there are in Egypt, and others are scattered all over the world, from New York to

Istanbul. I don't know what there is about obelisks that makes people want to steal them, but the form seems to have its appeal. The Washington Monument is the same shape, and from Roman times onward rulers of other countries went to considerable effort to carry them off from Egypt.

Personally I'd rather have a statue. Statues were an important architectural element too, and in keeping with the massiveness of the temple, they were large. They stood in rows against the walls or between the columns of the courtyard. Massive figures of the king might adorn the gateway as well. Like sculpture, reliefs and paintings played an important part in the decorative effect. Most of the flat wall surfaces were covered with carvings; the subject matter concerned the king and the gods.

Columns played an important part in Egyptian architecture. They were used in houses and palaces, but naturally we see them to their best advantage in temples, since these have survived better than has domestic architecture.

There were several distinct types of columns, characterized by their capitals. Most, archaeologists think, were derived from plant forms, even, in some cases, from bundles of reeds used to support the

Column types

Left to right: papyrus cluster, lotus, palm, papyrus flower, multiple flower, Hathor

light roofs of early huts. The first column in our illustration was probably a bunch of papyrus stems, whose bound stiff tops form the capital.
Another column derived from the ubiquitous and useful papyrus was
number four, whose capital was a single papyrus top bent back, as would
be natural, by the weight of the roof it supported. The second column
looks, in actuality, so much like the papyrus cluster that it is hard to
tell them apart. It is derived from the lily (lotus). Its stems are rounded
in section, while the papyrus stems are triangular, but the easiest way
of distinguishing them is that the column base tapers in the papyrus
type and is straight in the lotus.

The palm column, number three, is not so common, nor is the open
papyrus type. Our last example is a curious one; the squared capital has
heads in bas relief and full face of the goddess Hathor, with her cow
ears. These columns were used in shrines dedicated to the goddess, and
similar ones, with figures of the little pygmy god Bes, also appear now
and then. In Ptolemaic times several complicated composite plant capitals appeared; dozens of them can be seen at Denderah, Edfu, and other
late temples. We must not forget to mention the simplest and, in some
ways, the most effective of all Egyptian columns, which require no
illustration—the beautiful fluted cylinder, which reminds us of Greek
types. Archaeologists and art historians seem to agree that there is no
connection between the Greek and Egyptian columns, although to an
untrained eye they certainly look a lot alike. The Egyptian variety is
probably seen to the best advantage at Hatshepsut's mortuary temple at
Deir el Bahri, but the type goes back a long way in Egypt.

One other type of temple ought to be mentioned, although it survives today only in plans. The temples Akhenaton erected in honor of
his sun god Aton are quite different from the standard type. The glowing orb was not worshiped in a dark sanctuary but in an open court,
approached by a series of colonnades and courtyards with great gateways. It was surrounded by offices and storerooms, and in the center,
under the open sky, was the altar of the god, on a platform approached
by steps. Akhenaton's temples may not be so heretical as they first appear; sun temples of the Fifth Dynasty also had an altar, surmounted
by an obelisk, in an open court as the center of worship.

It is no wonder that the tourist (and I use this word in an honorable sense, referring to a group of which I am often one) comes away confused about temple plans. The real pity is that he gets a totally misleading impression of what these temples looked like. They seem austere and dignified, almost ponderously so, and they add to the impression many people have of Egyptian culture as being equally ponderous and dignified. In their pristine state these temples were, of course, very big. But they blazed and glittered and shone as brilliantly as a sunlit baroque church.

As the visitor approached the pylon, his first impression was not so much one of size as of color, bright enough to hurt the eyes under the golden Egyptian sun. The flat surfaces of the towers which formed the pylon were painted with enormous figures of men and gods—orange and blue and green and red, they stood out against the clean white background as brilliantly as a billboard, and much more attractively. The obelisks before the gate might be tipped with gold or even completely covered with that gorgeous material. The tall flagstaffs in front of the portal also had golden tips and floated scarlet pennants. Going in through the gate, the visitor found himself in a court whose pillars were painted in the same bright colors and were covered with the elegant little pictures of hieroglyphic inscriptions. The massive statues, in serried ranks, looked very handsome with their heads and arms and noses all in place and their surfaces polished to a gleaming sheen. The limestone statues were painted—dazzling white clothing, red-brown skin, inlays of semiprecious stones, and gold on crowns and collars.

By the time the visitor passed from the sunlight of the court into the hypostyle hall, where shafts of clear light from the clerestory pierced the shadows, some of the brilliance of the first part of the temple was dimmed. But still the rich ornamentation continued. The doors might be of beautifully grained cedar or of copper plated with gold. The best picture comes from the words of the Egyptians themselves:

> . . . a very great portal . . . wrought with gold throughout. The
> Divine Shadow, in the shape of a ram, is inlaid with real lapis

lazuli wrought with gold and many precious stones. . . . Its floor
is adorned with silver, towers are over against it. Stelae of lapis
lazuli are set up, one on each side. Its pylons reach heaven like
the four pillars of heaven, its flagstaffs shine more than the
heavens, wrought with electrum.

Unlike churches, the temples were never filled with crowds of lay
worshipers. Only the highest priests could enter the holy of holies and
approach the god. By official dogma the king was the celebrant of the
divine rites and high priest of all the gods; but, since he could not be
in a dozen places at once, he had to delegate his duties.

In the morning, as the sun rose over the cliffs, the priest in charge
of that day's ritual entered the sanctuary, breaking the seals on the
shrine. Within was the god's statue, very possibly of solid gold. (Naturally, none of these have survived except in fiction.) With the slow
care of religious ritual, the god was washed and anointed, clothed in
new garments, and decked with jewels. The morning offerings of food
and drink were made. Hymns of praise were chanted; the "Singers of
the God" performed for his entertainment. At sundown the shrine
was closed and sealed; the high priest, or priest in charge, backed out
of the sanctuary, sweeping away the traces of his footprints in order to
leave the sacred place ritually clean.

The priesthoods were organized into several groups, or phyles,
the precise number varying from period to period and shrine to shrine.
The head of the establishment was the high priest, or "Chief of the
Servants of the God"; you may find him called "First Prophet" in some
books. The high priests of certain gods had special titles; the head of
Re's temple at Heliopolis was the "Greatest of Seers." The word we
translate "prophet" is somewhat misleading, for it does not imply prediction of future events but was simply the designation of certain
high-ranking ecclesiastics, perhaps the ones who were allowed to meet
the god face to face. Other orders were the lector priests, the scholars
in charge of the ritual and the sacred writings, and the wab or lustra-
tion priests. Women served the god as dancers and singers and sometimes, particularly in the case of female divinities, as priestesses.

In all this elaborate activity the common people had little or no part. The only time they saw the god, or his gorgeous golden shrine, was when he went traveling on the occasion of some festival. Luckily for the Egyptian laboring man there were many festivals; at some periods almost one-third of the days were holy days. Evidently the gods became bored sitting all day in their shrines. Sometimes they visited one another, as when Hathor went from Denderah to call on Horus at Edfu.

One of the biggest festivals of the year was Amon's Feast of Opet, at Thebes, when he went down from Karnak to his Luxor temple to see what was going on there. The festival took place during the Inundation, when the river was overflowing and many of the peasants were unable to work their land; they undoubtedly enjoyed the celebration very much. Amon was carried from his Karnak sanctuary to the divine boat at the river. This was a gorgeous affair built of cedar from Lebanon, gilded and adorned with carvings, rich hangings, and flowers. On the deck was a dais for the shrine of the god. The barge was towed by a royal flagship manned by high-ranking officials, who fought for the honor of transporting the god, and by gangs of workmen on towropes along the bank. The river must have been crowded with other boats—private vessels of well-to-do people dressed in their best, munching sweetmeats and singing songs; hired craft jammed with sightseers of the lower classes. Other spectators followed along the bank, dancing, buying trinkets and tidbits from the booths erected along the route, being robbed by pickpockets and solicited by prostitutes and whined at by legless beggars. When, amid shouts of rejoicing, the divine boat reached the Luxor temple, the god was carried in procession, led by the king, into his Luxor shrine. The crowd of followers stopped at the gates to the courtyard. There they could jostle and gape and point out important personages in the procession, like the crowds at the first-night performances of plays and films. Sooner or later free food would be distributed, with plenty of bread and beer.

Perhaps the humble worshipers of the god actually did get to see a theatrical performance, of a sort. There is no evidence in ancient Egypt of secular drama, but several papyri mention dramatic performances in connection with the king's coronation and certain religious rites. The written dialogue is sometimes accompanied by specific stage directions. One Twelfth Dynasty official boasted of having been selected to play Horus in the mystery play of Osiris. This was probably the most famous of all Egyptian dramas, representing the god's death and triumphant resurrection.

The full story does not come down to us from pharaonic Egypt but from the Greek writer Plutarch, who apparently found it remarkable enough to preserve. It was new to him, of course; to the Egyptians it was so well known that they never bothered to write it out in full, though frequent references make it clear that Plutarch got the plot more or less right. In an earlier chapter I described Osiris's death and resurrection, the burial of his body by his devoted wife Isis, and the birth of his (extremely) posthumous son Horus. A number of cities claimed to have pieces of the god (it's rather suggestive of medieval saints' relics, isn't it?), but his chief center was Abydos, where the head—or, according to some versions, the entire body—was buried. Thus, Abydos became the holy city of Osiris, the goal of devout pilgrims, and the scene of the famous drama.

The devout Egyptian audience may have wept and cheered and hissed the villain at appropriate moments, just as medieval pilgrims did during the representation of the Christian Passion. And when the resurrected god arose, it was the symbol and the promise of eternal life for them. Eventually the god's name became a common title, referring to the dead man or woman: "The Osiris so-and-so."

On a more frivolous note, one cannot help but speculate as to why Ikhernofret was chosen for the part of Horus—a starring role if ever there was one. Dramatic talent? Good looks? I jest, of course. Ikhernofret was Chief Treasurer, among a lot of other important titles, and his selection was probably a mark of royal favor.

THE CONTENDINGS OF HORUS AND SET

And now the story continues. This "sequel" to the life and death and rebirth of Osiris does survive from an Egyptian text, and it is quite unlike the solemn ritual we have described. It shows, more vividly than my own words could do, that the Egyptians didn't always take their religion too seriously.

The story opens in the supreme tribunal of the gods, who are here referred to as the Ennead; the word no longer means "nine gods," just a lot of them. Chief of the court is Re-Atum, and the case under consideration is that of Horus and Set, the contenders for the throne of Osiris. Horus is now grown up and ready to take up the role of avenger of his father.

In the beginning, everyone except the president of the court seems to agree that Horus ought to inherit his father's throne. Re-Atum is in favor of Set—perhaps because that god helps him repel his snaky enemies during the trip through the underworld—and while his authority is not enough to overrule the rest of the council, it is strong enough to create a deadlock.

The gods then request Thoth, the scribe, to write asking the advice of Neith, the ancient goddess of Sais; perhaps, as an old lady, she is supposed to be wiser than the rest. Neith replies: "Give the office of Osiris to his son Horus!" On hearing these words, the council shouts with one voice: "This goddess is right!"

Re, the lofty god of the sun, then loses his temper. He sneers at Horus: "The office is too much for you—you boy, still smelling of sour milk!" A general slanging match ensues; the petty god Baba, drawing himself up, shrieks at Re: "Your shrine is empty!"

That is too much—telling Re that he is not a god. The scandalized Ennead scolds Baba for lèse-majesté, and Re goes off to his tent to sulk. There he sits until Hathor, goddess of love, sidles in and exposes herself to him. This indelicate act restores the supreme god's good humor; he returns to the tribunal and tells the contestants to present their cases.

Set's plea is more notable for rhetoric than for reason. "As for me, I am Set, great of strength among the Ennead. Daily I slay the enemies of Re, I am in front of the Bark of Millions; no other god can do this. I should receive the office of Osiris!"

The fickle Ennead immediately bellows: "Set is right!" Thoth is almost the only consistent one. He speaks up for his candidate, Horus, but his reasoned arguments are submerged in an exchange of insults, which ends with Isis getting up and cursing the whole tribunal. Her threats terrify the immortals; they assure her that everything will be fine, everyone will get what is due him. Set promises to kill one god per day unless judgment is given in his favor, and he refuses to discuss the matter any further unless Isis is thrown out of court. In desperation Re suggests that they all move to an island where they can debate in peace. Strict orders are given to the ferrymen not to take any woman across the water.

Anti, the ferryman, is just as irresponsible as his betters. When Isis appears, disguised as an old woman, he lets himself be bribed into taking her to the island. Sneaking up, Isis sees the Ennead at dinner. She changes her form into that of a beautiful girl and strolls back and forth outside the window until Set catches a glimpse of her. It is love at first sight; he rushes out. "Beautiful maiden, I am here with you!" he announces rapturously.

Isis slyly presents him with a fictitious case. She is the widow, she says, of a poor herdsman, and a foreigner has come and stolen all the cattle from her son, the heir. Set, inflamed by love or basically stupid, exclaims indignantly, "Shall the cattle be given to the foreigner while the son of the man is alive?" Isis turns herself into a bird and flies up into a tree, cawing triumphantly, "It is your own mouth which has said it; it is your own cleverness which has judged you!"

Set bursts into tears. Weeping copiously, he returns to the tribunal and tells them the whole story. "Well," says Re, in effect, "now you've done it." Even the supreme god has no choice now but to decide in favor of Horus.

Stubborn Set refuses to accept the verdict; he demands a trial by combat. Changing themselves into hippopotami, the two gods plunge into the river to see who can stay down the longest. Isis, pacing up and down in an agony of concern for her son, finally can stand the suspense no longer. She heaves a harpoon into the water—like the heroines of modern thriller fiction who try to bat the villain on the head while he is wrestling with the hero. Naturally, her weapon misses Set and hits Horus; he has to come out of the water and tell her to take her magic weapon out of his hide. Next time Isis manages to hit Set, but when he emerges, appealing to her as his sister, the inconsistent woman frees him too. This annoys Horus, who cuts off his mother's head to teach her a little lesson.

After a time, Isis's unpleasant condition dawns on Re. "Who is this woman who has no head?" he inquires. Thoth, who knows all, tells him, and Re decides that Horus shall be punished. In the meantime Set finds the boy asleep and gouges out his eyes. Horus is cured by Hathor's magic, and once again the Ennead goes into executive session to try to settle the case.

The story goes on and on. There is one bawdy episode in which Set tries to play a sexual trick upon his nephew, but it is turned back on him by the wiles of Isis. There are battles, and more hippopotami, and endless ranting in the tribunal. The issue is finally decided by a threatening letter from no less a personage than Osiris; Set concedes to Horus, Horus is crowned, and Set is consoled by Re's promise that he shall "thunder in the sky and be feared."

Obviously this story is not official dogma. It is rude, insulting, and frivolous, and I think there is no doubt but that the Egyptians regarded it as a humorous tale. It is a far cry from the solemn ritual which casual students think of as the only manifestation of the religious attitude in ancient Egypt. Yet frivolity was not the sole alternative to ritual, nor does the Horus and Set story represent the secret cynicism of the people as opposed to the official piety of the court. We know relatively little about popular religion in its day-by-day manifestations. But the few sources we do have give a third, and very significant, picture of religious attitudes.

THE RELIGION OF THE PEOPLE

Though they were not admitted to the inner precincts of the great temples, the people had their centers of worship. They made pilgrimages to certain shrines, and they also worshiped at home. Poorer houses had a small shrine in one room of the house; nobles might possess a special pavilion set in the beauty of the garden. The gods worshiped in the household shrines could be the great gods of the pantheon, and perhaps a craftsman might prefer to offer to Ptah, and a scribe might choose Thoth, the inventor of numbers and the patron of writing. Hathor was a favorite; her small shrine at Deir el Bahri yielded hundreds of pieces of broken faience objects which had been offered to her by pilgrims.

Two of the most popular household gods, whose worship was almost entirely restricted to small shrines, were very peculiar-looking. If we did not know that Taweret was a good-natured goddess, we would certainly take her for a monster. She was a hippopotamus goddess and the protectress of women in childbirth. One would think that the sight of her would frighten a pregnant woman into fits, but beauty is in the eye of the beholder. Another favored household god was Bes, whose grotesque figure often decorated the bedchamber. He is unusual in that he was the only Egyptian god to be painted, consistently, in direct front view. He does not look very Egyptian, really; his round bearded face and dwarfish body suggest something from inner Africa, as does his costume. Perhaps he was imported. But although he was not handsome, Bes was a jolly godling, in charge of fun and games generally.

The most important documents relating to popular religion come from little memorial stones found at Deir el Medina, the village of the necropolis workers of Thebes. One of these prayers is dedicated to a goddess named Meretseger, "She Who Loves Silence," who was also called "The Peak of the West" after a prominent mountain near the Valley of the Kings. It was written by a necropolis worker named Neferabet, who calls himself "an ignorant and witless man." "I knew not good or evil," he says. "When I did the deed of transgression against the Peak, she punished me, and I was in her hand by night as well as day. . . . I called out to the wind, but it did not come to me. . . . But when I called to my mistress, I found her coming to me with sweet breezes. She showed mercy unto me, after she had let me see her hand. She turned about to me in mercy."

This is really an extraordinary text to have been written by one of the cheerful, bumptious Egyptians, who bought magic spells to keep their consciences from testifying against them on the day of judgment. It is not unique, however. Another prayer, in much the same tone, addresses itself to no less a divinity than Amon-Re, king of the gods. The petitioner, an artist named Nebre, appealed to the god when his son fell ill, "in a state of death." Amon, who is given the astonishing epithet "he who comes at the voice of the poor man," responded to the father's plea. He rescued the son from death. Nebre, filled with thanksgiving, praised the god in these words: "Though the servant is inclined to do wrong, yet the Lord is inclined to be merciful." In this prayer we see a consciousness of sin, a humility, and an awareness of divine mercy which, it has been claimed, does not occur in ancient times outside of the religious literature of the Hebrews. Yet it is surely a factor in Egyptian religion of the Late Period.

In a sense these prayers are the essence of ancient Egyptian religion. Long lists of bizarre deities and philosophic interpretations of what we think the Egyptians thought are less significant than the actual words of a man to his god. The gods are dead, but once they lived—not as cold golden statues in a darkened shrine, but as forces which could command the awe and devotion of living men.

Thirteen

SO WHO WANTS TO BE
AN ANCIENT EGYPTIAN?

Quite a number of people claim that they were, and they can prove it. One technique is called, among other things, "past-life regression"; what happens is that the subject is put into a trance and sent back in time, following the hints of the hypnotist, to childhood and infancy—and if the claims of the persons involved are to be believed, back into the womb and further back still, until he or she recalls events that happened during a previous incarnation.

Ancient Egypt has always been popular with those who believe they have lived before. Most of them believe they were royalty. Nefertiti's ka must have cloned itself a thousand times in order to accommodate all the ladies who claim to have been she. I don't know of anyone who thinks he was privy-cleaner for Ramses III.

One of the most intriguing cases is that of a woman named Dorothy Eady, who was born in England in 1904. Fascinated since childhood by ancient Egypt, she believed she had been the lover of King Seti I. (His is unquestionably the best-looking mummy to have survived.) Miss Eady finally got to Egypt by marrying an Egyptian (they were later divorced) and worked as a draftsman and clerk for the Antiquities Department and for various Egyptologists. Not until seventeen years later did she reach Abydos, the home of her dreams, where Seti's magnificent funerary monuments still stand. Known in the village as Omm Seti, Mother of Seti—she had named her son after her dream lover—she lived in great happiness and considerable squalor until she died at the age of seventy-seven. She is still fondly remembered by many Egyptologists who enjoyed her caustic wit and respected her knowledge of the Abydos complex.

Omm Seti had worked out the details of her former life as the daughter of humble parents who left her at the temple of Isis to be raised by the priests. However, if she—or you, or I—had lived in the Nineteenth Dynasty, it is extremely unlikely that we would have caught the eye of Seti or been raised as a priestess of Isis. The temples didn't serve as orphan asylums or demand eternal celibacy. Miss Eady was sufficiently dedicated to her dream to live like a Nineteenth Dynasty peasant in a mud-brick shack without modern amenities except for the gifts she accepted from her friends. Give her credit for consistency at least. I wouldn't have done it, and I doubt you could have stuck it out all those years either.

If we had lived in ancient Egypt our father would probably not have been a priest or an official—much less a pharaoh—but a farmer. It cannot be emphasized too strongly that practically everything we have discussed so far relates to the upper classes of society—kings, nobles, scribes, craftsmen, skilled artisans. Even the workmen's villages connected with tombs and pyramids were inhabited by people several cuts above the ordinary peasant. The peasants didn't build tombs or prepare elaborate funerary equipment, and it is from these sources that we derive much of our information about "daily life." In other words, this is going to be a short chapter. However, we can make a few generalizations.

We would have lived in a one-room hut built of sun-dried mud brick roofed with reeds and shared it with the domestic animals, if Dad was lucky enough to own any. It doesn't rain often in Upper Egypt, but when it does rain it can rain hard. A heavy downpour would reduce a peasant's house to a pile of mud. On the positive side, such domiciles were easy to build.

On the face of it, farming in ancient Egypt sounds like a pretty good deal. Every year, regular as clockwork, the Nile overflowed onto the strips of cultivated land bordering the river, depositing the rich silt picked up during its long journey from the highlands of Africa, fertilizing and irrigating at one and the same time.

It wasn't as easy as that. In times of low Nile, there was not enough water. Excessively high Niles destroyed villages and flooded the fields. Even in good years, irrigation ditches and dikes were necessary to regulate the flow of water and increase the land available for cultivation. To be effective, these activities had to be communal and cooperative. Sooner or later, probably sooner, they were organized and run by the local governor. Eventually the system of land and water control came under state management, and a percentage of the crops went to the king, the local officials, and the temples. The biblical story of Joseph suggests that a strong, benevolent government could store grain in good years and and distribute it when times were bad. State socialism in ancient Egypt?

The three seasons of the Egyptian year were based on agriculture: "inundation" (akhet), when the Nile overflowed; "emergence" (peret), when the water receded and the crops were planted; and "drought," or "summer" (shemu), the dry season, the season of harvest. Most of the land came to be owned by the king or the temples or the local princes. All of the work was done by the peasants—digging canals, sowing seeds, harvesting the crop. The main crops were barley and emmer wheat, used for the staples of the Egyptian diet, bread and beer, and flax, for the vast quantities of linen needed in life and in death. Even the poorest wore linen, though theirs was more coarsely woven than the delicate fabrics worn by the elite.

The agricultural processes are shown in a number of tomb scenes, since the noble owner of the tomb expected they would continue in the hereafter, supplying him with the good things of this world. A common scene in later funerary papyri shows him and his wife, doggedly hacking away at stalks of grain that extend a depressingly long distance. It is a safe assumption that the noble gentleman hoped he would never have to do this. In the earlier tomb scenes the nobleman isn't doing anything except looking on. There he sits, several sizes larger than the toiling workmen while they hoe and plow and harvest, and by depicting them doing these chores he probably expected they would go on doing them in the next world. If all else failed, the dead were supplied with little servant statues that could be animated with a magic spell and forced to work for their owner.

After the water had subsided and the soil was dry it had to be prepared for planting. Farming is hard work, even with mechanized tools. It was a lot harder when a plow had to be dragged by men or oxen through the resistant earth, and then hoed—by hand—to prepare it for sowing. It may be necessary to remind those who have never done it that the plowman's job was not just to stroll along behind the oxen. He had to keep pushing down so that the point of the plow wouldn't pop up out of the ground. It was a great way to develop the pecs. Hoes were unlike ours; the handle was set at an acute angle to the part that went into the ground. It was a great way to develop backaches. (It's amazing how long it took people to figure out that long-handled implements were more effective and a lot easier on the back.) By the New Kingdom another device made the peasant's labor somewhat easier. The shaduf was used to raise water from a lower to a higher level. A pot was attached to one end of a long pole and a weight to the other; the weight lessened the strain of lifting the filled pot. These devices were used up till modern times.

If it was a good year, the season of "drying out" or "summer" brought a bountiful crop. Reaping was done with wooden sickles set with flint chips, and only the heads of the grain were whacked off—a considerable saving of time and back strain—leaving the straw to be harvested later. The reapers were followed by women who picked up the grain that had fallen. This seems to have been a "perk" which was jealously guarded; one tomb scene shows a pair of women fighting over their shares.

The grain was then taken to the thrashing floor and trodden by oxen to remove the husks, then winnowed by men who tossed it into the air so that the wind would blow the chaff away.

All these activities are shown in several Eighteenth Dynasty tombs—not those of the men and women who did the dirty work, but those of the nobles for whom they worked. Often these scenes are enlivened by snatches of dialogue, written above the workers like cartoon balloons. "Let's work," one man exclaims enthusiastically, and another declares that he will do even more than is expected of him "for the noble." One is entitled to harbor a certain amount of skepticism about these admirable sentiments.

We don't know what percentage of the land was "privately owned," if that word has any meaning in ancient Egypt. Part of the land belonged to the nobleman and part to the king or, particularly in later periods, to the temples of the gods. Even when the farmer kept part of the results of his labor, he had to pay taxes. "Nothing is certain except death and taxes" is a saying that might have originated in ancient Egypt.

The amount of tax due was estimated by the scribe who worked for the temple or the government. It was paid in kind, and woe betide the unhappy laborer who could not come up with the right number of bushels. "He is beaten hard. He is tied up and thrown into a pool. He is ducked and thoroughly soaked, and his wife is tied up in his presence."

It could be worse, I suppose. One would like to believe that harsher penalties would have violated some code of justice or morality, but there was probably a practical reason; death or mutilation would have deprived the state of a worker.

The peasant also had to contribute a certain percentage of his time to communal activities such as digging ditches and maintaining dikes. One document lists the punishment for men who deserted or "ran away"—seized, one must suppose, by a fit of temporary insanity, since the penalty for the last misdemeanor is less grave than the one for a deserter.

There was a certain amount of free enterprise, however. Some people were paid, not in money—there was no coinage in ancient Egypt before the Persian period—but in goods. The well-off workers of Deir el Medina were supplied by the state not only with living quarters and food, but with other necessities and even luxuries, including laundresses. Not so the peasant, but it was possible for industrious (and lucky) individuals to accrue wealth in the form of produce or manufactured goods. They could trade linen or grain or pots for other things they needed, as the "Eloquent Peasant" we met in chapter 7 hoped to do. A few papyri give relative values—a piece of linen was worth so many measures of wheat or so many weights of copper—but these varied from period to period and obviously depended on scarcity and need. In other words, an object was worth whatever you could get for it. (The same thing is true today in flea markets and auction houses.) There are references to a unit of value called a deben—a certain weight of copper—but it is unlikely that the metal itself often changed hands.

Many of the markets were set up near the docks, where incoming ships brought exotic goods from abroad and men long at sea (or Nile) made good customers. One such scene shows the boat being unloaded, and three small booths where private merchants offer sandals, cloth, and other commodities. An even more intriguing scene (from a tomb, of course) shows a lively open-air market with stalls offering all sorts of things, from fish to fabric. This one is fun because it provides dialogue. "Give [me] your property" is one stallkeeper's introductory "pitch" to a prospective customer. He goes on to tell what he will give in exchange—figs or fish or excellent vegetables.

Even these scenes, which surely represent a common activity, may show only the more prosperous members of the working class. The ordinary farmer didn't have time to accumulate much beyond bare subsistence. However, there must have been small village markets, as there are even today.

Skilled workers had a number of perks, including days off and possibly medical care. Not the peasant. His working day began at sunrise and ended at sundown. Artificial means of lighting in the humble quarters of the peasant consisted, at most, of a rag floating in a vessel of oil, and oil was expensive. The means of entertainment were limited, but storytelling and gossip and the pleasures (and aggravations) of family life were available to all. The national religious festivals, of which there were a great many, gave the peasant a little holiday and a little excitement and perhaps free beer.

It's no wonder the life span of these toilers was approximately thirty-five years. Studies of Egyptian mummies show that these people suffered from a number of diseases, most of which went untreated. Poor nutrition and inability to cope with infection contributed to high infant mortality. The flour ground on stone querns contained large quantities of grit that wore away tooth surfaces. Cavities were fairly infrequent, since the Egyptians didn't have refined sugar, but a number of mummies have hideous gum abscesses. In at least one case the bursting of the abscess caused blood poisoning, which brought to an end a life that must have been agonizingly painful. The skeletons of the stone workers at Giza show the effect of long years of heavy labor, including fractures.

Recent studies of mummies have turned up a variety of other diseases, including malaria, tuberculosis, and smallpox. Black lung disease resulted from the smoke-filled, poorly ventilated houses, and desert lung disease from the constantly blowing sand. Perhaps the worst and most common illness was parasitic infection, which still occurs in Egypt today. The most pervasive parasite goes by two names, bilharzias or schistosomiasis. I won't go into the details, since they are really revolting, but if not treated the infection produces calcification of the bladder, fibrosis of the intestine, scarring of the liver, serious anemia, chronic fatigue, and possibly heart disease. It isn't fatal except in rare cases, but the sufferer probably wishes it were. Can you imagine hoeing the fields and hauling stones for pyramids when you are suffering from something like this? Some mummies suffered from not one but several potentially fatal diseases or infections.

So who wants to be an ancient Egyptian? Any ancient Egyptian? Even the mighty pharaohs had to do without many of the comforts we take for granted—antibiotics, plumbing, air conditioning, dentists, television. . . . Well, maybe the absence of television wouldn't have been all that bad.

Before we start feeling superior to our "primitive" predecessors, we should bear in mind that a good many people in today's "civilized" world live under conditions that are as bad or worse as those the ordinary ancient Egyptian endured. No, like most of us I am too spoiled to live that way, even for a short time, even as Nefertiti. But if I could pick my time and place . . . a conference with Hatshepsut and her chief advisers just before she announced her kingship . . . a private chat with Akhenaton about his reasons for elevating a new god (and the real meaning of those egg-shaped heads) . . . a safe vantage point at the battle of Kadesh to see what Ramses II really did. . . .

It will never happen, and that's probably just as well. Nobody would believe me anyhow.

PART II

THE WORLD
OF THE DEAD

Fourteen

"AN EXCELLENT, EQUIPPED SPIRIT"

ATTITUDES TOWARD THE DEAD

The subject of undertaking (and I wonder how that euphemism ever originated?) seems to have a macabre fascination for many people—witness the success of such books as Jessica Mitford's classic *The American Way of Death*. Ms. Mitford was not the first commentator to criticize that earnest craftsman, the American undertaker, or to wonder at the position he has come to hold as arbiter of a mortuary etiquette which often contradicts traditional religious dogma. Mark Twain, who missed few of the follies of which men are capable, was roused to sardonic comment on the same subject over a century ago. In *Life on the Mississippi*, he created a mortician—who, we devoutly hope, was purely fictitious—and had this personage make the following remarks:

"Why, just look at it. A rich man won't have anything but your very best; and you can just pile it on, too—pile it on and sock it to him—he won't ever holler. And you take a poor man, and if you work him right, he'll bust himself on a single lay-out. Or especially a woman." He goes on to explain how he got Mrs. O'Flaherty, widow of a poor workman, to "bust herself" on her husband's funeral.

The morality of this sort of thing is beyond the scope of our present discussion; it hardly requires comment in any case. What interests us as students of ancient Egypt is the ironic fact that we seem to see, today, the survival of a concept which was once believed to be limited to primitive heathens back in the dawn of civilization— the idea that the dead body, the corpse, must be: (a) preserved, and (b) treated as if it retains the individuality of the deceased. The parallelism of our cult with those of some ancient cultures is embarrassingly close—the painting of the dead person's face, the burial of jewelry and trinkets in the coffin, the ornate and expensive coffin itself.

Modern embalmers would claim, no doubt, that the motivation underlying their activities destroys the apparent parallels. They are not assisting the dead by means of magic, they are comforting the survivors by "psychology." We may reasonably doubt whether the embalmer's psychology is any more valid than the sympathetic magic of the witch doctors. But most suggestive of all is the fact that, beneath all the psychological claptrap, we can discern an extremely ancient, dichotomous attitude toward death and the dead—an ambivalence which may be found even in the graves of the wandering hunters of Paleolithic Europe.

Throughout the inhabited world, and far back beyond written history, there runs the unifying thread of agreement on one idea— survival after death. It is as old as man, older than *Homo sapiens*; it existed among Australian aborigines and African bushmen. We may find it hard to believe that the brutish Neanderthal hunters shared this same faith, and yet there is no other reasonable explanation for the skeletons carefully buried in the caves in which they had lived, laid to rest with their weapons beside them and their ornaments still resting on their crumbling bones. In these humble graves we see the beginning not only of a belief in some sort of life after death but of the careful tending of the physical remains.

Now any savage with two eyes in his unkempt head knows that the body is corruptible. After passing through changes which are perturbing to contemplate, the corpse is reduced, within the span of one observer's lifetime, to a state which bears little resemblance to the human form. We will not be crediting primitive man with too much insight if we assume that he knew the body itself did not survive. Whence, then, did he derive the immense concept of immortality?

At first the visible signs of death resemble those of other phenomena, such as coma or sleep. "Sleep is a little death," and Thanatos and Hypnos, to many men, are brothers. But the sleeper awakes. And sometimes, in his waking state, he remembers adventures he had while his physical body lay unresponsive and inert on his bed. In his unconscious travels the sleeper is not limited by physical time or space; he may even see friends who no longer exist in the waking world. From such experiences there might arise the concept of a Dweller within the House of the Flesh who can leave the sleeping body to venture abroad and who, at the time of death, abandons its former dwelling forever.

This is not an answer to the question of how the notion of immortality began; it is only a suggestion of a possibility. But most people who have left us any statements of belief imagine a dweller within the body—one or more. They call it by various names; we call it the soul.

The soul outside its body is, of course, invisible, and it is only seen by the living under special conditions. Unseen, it may linger near its old home or it may join other spirits in another place—a place which can be visited by the living in dreams. The views of the dreamland where the dead live vary considerably; sometimes they go down below, sometimes up above. The hereafter may be visualized as a Paradise where the soul enjoys all the pleasures it cherished on earth, only more so, and experiences none of the pain. Sometimes the regions of the dead are sad and gloomy; sometimes they are etherealized and utterly removed from the gross activities of the body.

Blissful Paradise or melancholy Hades, in no culture do the living really look forward to the time when they will go there. The attitude of the living toward death is not ambivalent; they are most heartily against it. But there is an ambivalence to be observed in the attitude of the living toward the dead.

When Mark Twain's unpleasant undertaker described his exploitation of his customers, he ascribed his success to the application of an unworthy old principle—"keeping up with the Joneses." But this is only the superficial explanation of why people will beggar themselves to buy equipment which is not only superfluous but slightly obscene. What the undertaker is really exploiting is the ancient ambivalence of the living toward the dead.

On the one hand, there is grief and love which cries out for expression. But mingled with grief and love is a complex of contradictory emotions which people do not so readily admit. Reactions to the corpse itself range from mild distaste to superstitious horror; and since the dead flesh was once the habitation of the beloved soul, the living relatives feel guilty about their repugnance. Another reaction of the living—though few of them will own it—is relief. "Whoever is dead, it is not I. Thank God!" Or, to paraphrase St. Augustine: "Lord, let me join my dear one in Paradise—but not just yet!" This sense of guilty relief has to be paid for—nowadays, apparently, with copper-sheathed, satin-lined coffins.

In *The Golden Bough,* James Frazer has said—very cogently, I think—that the fear of the dead arises out of the fear of death. If the living rejoice in the fact that they still breathe and eat and love and walk abroad under the sun, they can assume the corollary: that the dead hate not being alive. The malignancy of the dead is a logical next step—a blind malignancy, directed against all the living.

We do not have to leave our own supposedly rational culture to find evidence of the fear of the dead. Few of us would care to spend the night with a dead body as sole company, and we still shun graveyards after dark. I don't believe in ghosts, but I prefer not to read Poe or Lovecraft when I am alone in the house at night. The ghost story itself specializes, not in kindly spirits, but in malignant specters; its wide appeal testifies to its probing of a deep-seated human emotion. And the principles of the modern ghost story, now relegated to folklore, were part of the tenets of the church not many centuries ago. Indeed, I believe there is still a formula for exorcism in some rituals.

We can jump back over ten thousand years and find the same belief. Among the oldest of all surviving burials, those of prehistoric man, there are a few unusual graves. The skeletons found in them had been laid in painfully cramped positions, knees drawn up against the chest and legs tightly flexed. Such a position could only have been maintained by binding the limbs of the corpse with cords, and it has been suggested that this was done in order to keep the dead man from wandering around and annoying the living.

There is a theory that burial itself did not originate from love or sanitary motives, but from fear. The very notion of inhumation, pinning the body down under earth and stones, may have arisen out of a desire to keep it confined. A more drastic method of restraint is dismemberment, and this too is found occasionally in prehistoric graves. Perhaps cremation was the most effective defense of all; there is no more thorough way of rendering a man powerless than by reducing him to ashes. If cremation and dispersal of the ashes was practiced by prehistoric man, we would naturally have no evidence of it; the partially burned bodies in some ancient graves were not cremated, and in these cases the fires may have been accidental. We cannot recognize cremation burials as such until the ashes are preserved in pots or urns, and by this time the fear of the dead has been superseded, consciously at least, by other motives.

Another method of defense against the dead is propitiation: if you keep them happy and well tended they will not harm, and may even help, you. They will be more favorably inclined, perhaps, if you keep your hands off their property. So, to be on the safe side, you bury it with them, including their women, horses, and slaves. This would explain the "grave goods" which, from earliest times, were buried with the dead. An alternative explanation is that such objects as jewelry, weapons, and wives were sent along with the dead man to be of use to him wherever he was going.

Propitiation has one advantage over violence and destruction as a method of rendering the dead harmless to the living: it does not offend the often simultaneous emotion of grief. The old argument as to whether burial of the dead was first motivated by fear or by affection is pointless; there is no reason why both should not have operated. They are contradictory emotions, perhaps, but they are not mutually exclusive.

One howling inconsistency still stands out. Whether we love them or whether we fear them, we all agree that the dead are dead—that the body is corruptible. Repugnance for the corpse and terror of the bodiless ghost are not the same, and attempts to control the ghost by binding the corpse seem senseless. So does the opposite technique: furnishing the unresponsive, insensible body with elegant tombs and dead slaves.

Yet there is a good deal of sense in the attentions paid to the dead body if we believe in sympathetic magic. Since the soul was once part of the body or intimately associated with it, then the soul can be affected by that which is done to the flesh. This principle is at the basis of many sorceries, those practiced for the benefit of the living as well as the dead. Many of the rituals in honor of the dead are explicable in these terms, including the effort to preserve the corpse and give it, at least temporarily, the appearance of life.

While the principle of sympathetic magic may account for dismemberment or mummification with equal facility, it does not have any bearing on the American way of death. We do not believe in magic. There must be some other reason for our desire to preserve the dead clay and to surround it with comforts which it cannot sense.

Some Christian sects include among the articles of their creeds the phrase: "I believe in the resurrection of the body." If these words are taken literally, they would account for embalming—indeed, they would justify far greater efforts than the ones we put forth. However, ministers and priests of all sects have been vehement in opposing the ostentation of American funeral customs, and the problems involved in the literal resurrection of the physical body are rationally insoluble. Some of these problems seem rather funny to us, but they were not at all amusing to the medieval theologians who propounded them so earnestly. Take the classic case of the cannibal who is converted to Christianity. He is assured of a resurrection in the flesh if he joins the right church; but whose flesh is it? What about the Christian missionaries whom he absorbed, in his unregenerate days, into that now-hallowed flesh of his? They are entitled to a resurrection in the body too, but someone is going to be missing a part when the Day of Judgment comes around.

When I put the problem of the cannibal to a Jesuit friend, he gave me an answer suited to my simple mind: "But it is not the same body." The God who made man out of the dust of the earth, and woman out of one of his least important bones can, if He wills it, restore to the blessed any body He wants them to have—"the same body," if necessary—the cannibal's body and those of the missionaries, all complete and original. The somber words of Ecclesiastes, "Then shall the dust return to the earth as it was," are resolved by the magnificent paradox of Job: "And though worms destroy this body, yet in my flesh shall I see God."

In these terms the preservation of the body is irrelevant, and the American mortuary cult is inexplicable by the words of the very creed which is read over the coffins of the painted and embalmed dead.

I sometimes amuse myself by wondering whether archaeologists of a future day would be able to find our credo in the coffins of our dead. Suppose that by the year A.D. 5000 all written records of our culture are destroyed (not necessarily such a fantastic assumption), but that some of our frail bones do survive. Jones's guaranteed, lead-lined, moisture-proof coffins may, by pure accident, live up to their claims, and a few bodies may be found in all the bravery of tuxedos, toupees, and plastic surgery. How will the learned scholars of the intergalactic empire of A.D. 5000 interpret the mortuary beliefs of the primitive earthmen of our era? Sympathetic magic is the obvious answer; and perhaps, fantastically, the intergalactic experts may be right. How many of the people who submit to the witch doctors of the modern American mortuary cult do it because they still harbor, deep down in their livers and bowels, some seed of their primitive ancestors' faith in magic? Is it in the undying superstition of the human race that we must ultimately seek the reason for the American way of death, rather than in the overt appeals to pride, or misapplied piety, or love?

Let us turn now, with some relief, to a simpler cult—that of the ancient Egyptians. It, at least, makes sense in terms of its own expressed premises. Complex and bizarre as it seems, the Egyptian way of death is comprehensible on the basis of a few simple assumptions. The first assumption is that a man, or one aspect of him, can survive physical death. The second is that his postmortem existence is affected by what is done with, and to, his body. Neither of these assumptions is peculiar to Egypt; both form part of a very ancient and very widespread system of belief. In the light of this general background, we will begin with the first premise and ask how, where, and in what form the ancient Egyptian expected to live on after death.

HEAVEN AND THE SOUL

The road which led from Memphis and Thebes to Paradise was beset with perils, and the dead man could not even set foot upon it until he had fulfilled a number of ritual obligations. The fact of death did not make man immortal. A soul was made, not born.

Strictly speaking, there is no concept in ancient Egypt which corresponds to our idea of the soul: an invisible, nonmaterial dweller within the flesh which animates the body during life and leaves it after death to seek whatever fate its owner's deeds and beliefs have destined it for. The Egyptian texts refer to many nonmaterial aspects of a man as having some sort of existence apart from his body, including his shadow and his name. But there are only three entities which have a consistent application to life after death.

The ba is the easiest of these to describe; it took the form of a bird with a human head, sometimes preceded by a small lighted lamp. Its normal environment was the tomb or its vicinity. We see it perching solicitously on the breast of the mummy or flying down the tomb shaft to rejoin the mummy after a short trip outside. The word "ba" is often translated as "soul"; but as a rule it did not come into existence until after death, and even then only as a result of special ceremonies which were designed to "make a man into a ba."

Another candidate for the word "soul" is the ka. When the creator god Khnum shaped the body of a new child on his potter's wheel, he also made the child's ka in its exact image; in relief and in painting the ka is the double of the man to whom it belongs. But the ka is not quite the same as the soul, since it did not necessarily dwell within the body. When a man died, he joined his ka in the hereafter. The ka needed to be nourished; offerings were made to it, and it seems to have been a helper in insuring postmortem existence. It had roles to play in life too, exerting a generally beneficent and protective influence. The concept of the ka is extremely difficult; the variety of ways in which it has been translated shows the lack of agreement as to its precise nature: "double," "guardian spirit," "personality," "vital essence," "will or power."

The god Khnum shaping the child and its ka

However we translate it—and Egyptologists usually prefer not to trans-late it at all—it was, among other things, one aspect of a man before and after death.

The third of the trio, the akh, is the most abstract of all. It had no pictorial form. The word is written, in the texts, with the crested ibis, just as "ba" was written with another long-legged bird and "ka" was written with the two upraised arms. But unlike the ba and ka, the akh was never shown in relief or painting. The word can, like ka, mean a number of things, from "effective" and "beneficial" to "glorious." Some-times it is rendered as "spirit," or "transfigured spirit." Often the word is used in the plural, as we use "the dead" or "the blessed" to refer to an impersonalized group. It is at once the vaguest and the most spiritual-ized of all the Egyptian words for the dead.

There is no point in trying to distinguish between these three forms of the spiritual man in logical terms. We cannot say that under condition A he might become a ba, while conditions B and C neces-sitated his appearance as ka and akh, respectively. There is considera-ble overlap in the way the words are used.

We will not be surprised to discover that the Egyptians were no more consistent in their views of the hereafter than they were about the soul. We find almost the complete range, from a subterranean to a heavenly paradise; and the god of the dead may be celestial or chthonic.

Many of the gods and goddesses of Egypt had parts to play in the mortuary ritual, but some of them are specifically connected with the dead. Anubis the jackal-headed was the guide of the dead and the pa-tron of cemeteries and embalming; he was a kindly deity despite his predatory head. Wepwawet of Assiut and Khentiamentiu of Abydos were also mortuary gods. Chief of them all, ruler of the regions of the dead, was Osiris. Plutarch has given us the oldest complete version of his story. The Egyptians never wrote it down, but they referred to it constantly, and despite minor discrepancies, the Greek and the Egyp-tians agree on the main points.

Osiris was an ancient king of Egypt who brought his people out of savagery, teaching them the arts of civilization and ruling them with benevolent kindness. Everyone loved him, including his sister-wife, Isis, with one exception. His brother Set grew jealous and decided Osiris must die. Set and his adherents tricked the good king into lying down in a chest, which they promptly covered, nailed up, and threw into the water. The grieving wife, Isis, set out on a long and arduous search for her husband's body. Finally she found the chest at Byblos, where the sea had carried it, and brought it back to Egypt. In a lonely spot in the marshes she opened the chest and threw herself on her husband's body, weeping bitterly. The gods, pitying her grief, sent for Anubis to come and embalm the corpse. But first they revived Osiris sufficiently to impregnate his wife, so that she gave birth to a son called Horus. One day Set, out hunting, found the chest and its contents. This time he tore the body into fourteen pieces and scattered them up and down the length of Egypt. Patiently Isis set out again to collect them. She buried each piece of the body in the place where she found it; according to some versions of the story the head was buried in Abydos, hence this city became particularly sacred to Osiris. Other versions say that the god's entire body was buried there. Resurrected by the mercy of the gods, Osiris was set to rule over the dead in the Land of the Westerners, and his son, Horus, grown to manhood, fought his wicked uncle and regained his father's throne. The second sister of Osiris, Nephthys, often joined Isis in her search and in her mourning, despite the fact that she was the wife of Set.

Osiris belongs to a class which is well known, particularly in the Near East—the dying gods. His spiritual cousins are Tammuz and Adonis and Attis, fine young men whose premature deaths symbolize the annual death of vegetation, and whose resurrection is seen in the young green sprouts of the new crop. The appeal in the stories of Osiris and the other dying gods is obvious; here was a man who died, and who lived again. In his story there was hope for all men.

Osiris was not, however, the only king of the dead in Egypt. The withering of the grass suggests death, and so does the daily progress of the sun, which vanishes each night behind the western horizon. If the region of death is the west, then the east is, inescapably, the place of resurrection; for with the dawn comes the rebirth of the dying sun god, Re.

Two supreme gods of the dead, and two afterworlds governed by them, are not so terribly inconsistent in themselves. Different elements of the population might have held different beliefs. But knowing the Egyptians as—I hope—we have come to know them, we will not expect to find the situation so clear. And it is not.

We can only guess about the prehistoric religion of Egypt; by the time we get a fairly coherent picture of the cult of the dead we find the Osiris faith and the solar faith existing side by side. Not only is there official acceptance of two gods of the dead, but any inner consistency is missing. The heavenly realm governed by Re is somewhere up in the sky, but he also passes through the underworld, which ought to be Osiris's sole responsibility. Re dies in the west each night, but he is not "Lord of the Westerners"; that title belongs to Osiris, who borrowed it from an even older mortuary god.

There are hints in the Pyramid Texts, the oldest body of mortuary texts known, that Re and Osiris were not always so compatible. A few puzzling passages in that great compilation of magico-religious spells speak of Osiris as an enemy; other passages reject the east, the region sacred to Re's resurrection. But these elusive hints are the only evidence we have of what may have been, at one time, a battle royal between two opposing cults, and it is impossible to attribute one cult to one part of the population and one to another. Some scholars believed that the solar faith was that of the king and the court, while the religion of Osiris belonged to the people. Neat as this theory is, it cannot be proved. Osiris and Re together were guardians of the king and of his people. Either or both could guarantee eternal life in the west—or the east—or the underworld.

All three regions are mentioned as locations for the realm of the dead. Another possible direction is north; for here lie the circumpolar stars, which never set, and one fate the dead may anticipate is to join these starry immortals. This concept is rather remote and etherealized; the Egyptians enjoyed the pleasures of life as much as, if not more than, we do, and they were just as susceptible to a super-earthly heaven, well supplied with tasty haunches of beef, foaming jugs of beer, sweet northern breezes, and a nice little house with a garden.

All these pleasant things could be found in the most comprehensible of the Egyptian versions of Paradise, a place called the Field, or Marsh, of Reeds. It seems to be a swampy region, rather like the scenery of the ancient Delta. Some texts contain little maps of the Field of Reeds, with rivers and islands and towns. In this happy land the grain grew ten cubits high and other supplies were equally lavish.

Then there was a region known as the Dat, or Duat. Eventually this came to be located under the earth, but originally it was a typical Egyptian paradise in that it could have been almost anywhere. Water is a frequent feature of the afterworlds, in the form of rivers or lakes; the Lily Lake, in the eastern sky, had to be crossed by the dead before they could reach the court of Re, if that was their destination. Names for the next world were as numerous as they were poetic—the Land of the Westerners, the Beautiful Roads of the West, the Field of Offerings, the Land of Eternity.

Perhaps the Egyptian was not so much concerned with where he lived as with living itself. He would accept any place, any position, so long as he could win life thereby. The celestial circuit of the sun, which was sometimes viewed as a boat sailing the heavens, presented many possibilities for the dead man. He might become a rower in this boat of Re's, or carry a spear in order to fight the enemies of the god. If he was particularly fortunate, he would be invited to sit beside Re while other, less well-equipped spirits toiled at the oars. If he journeyed to join the gods in their abodes, east or west, he would take any job that was open—he would be the god's secretary or servant.

The Egyptians were generally cheerful souls; their versions of the hereafter, divergent as they are in geography, generally agree on one thing. The Land of Eternity is "just and fair, without troubles." The dead are the "transfigured spirits," whom their mourning relatives expect to join in everlasting bliss.

Now and again, though, we detect a sour note in the hymns of praise. The regions of darkness under the earth, where the dead are sometimes thought to dwell, are illumined by the sun god when he passes through them on his way to the eastern horizon to be reborn in glory; but his light gives no comfort to these dead, and they weep pitifully to see the waning of his splendor. In these dark realms the sun god's boat encounters fearful dangers—hideous serpents attack it, and demons must be fought off by force of arms. Here too, according to some references, there is a river of fire, where the souls of the enemies of Re burn in everlasting torment. And one text gives a discordant, and very poignant, picture of the land of the "happy and just":

> Deep and dark is the dwelling place of the inhabitants of the West. It has no door and no window, no light to brighten it, no north wind to refresh the heart. The sun does not rise therein; each day they lie in darkness. . . . Those who are in the West, they are set apart and their existence is misery. One is loath to go and join them.

One is loath indeed. "As I love life and hate death" is a common adjuration in ancient Egyptian; it is a candid expression of the fear and doubt that must have lurked, skull-like, under the bright face of faith. Nowhere, I think, are these doubts expressed more eloquently than in one brief sentence from an Egyptian text: "None has returned from there, to tell us how they fare." These simple words have always epitomized, for me, the doubts which are surely as universal as the belief, founded in desperate desire, in eternal life.

One interesting facet of the Egyptian language, which I suppose we could interpret as a psychological trait if we wanted to, is its reluctance to mention death. Ancient Egyptian had a word which meant "to die," but it was usually avoided in favor of any one of a dozen different euphemisms. When a king died he "went to join his father the sun," or "mingled with the gods," or "rested from life." In a land so dependent on water transportation, an image involving boats came readily to mind. Death was the time when "the mooring stake was driven in"—the final landing.

The ultimate proof of the Egyptians' fear of death is the mortuary cult itself—not only the time and money spent on tombs, coffins, and other paraphernalia, but the fantastically imaginative attention to detail, which anticipated any possible—and some impossible—dangers that might prevent the resurrection so urgently desired. Death was an enemy, to be fought and conquered. And sometimes the dead too were hostile.

The prayer we quoted at the beginning of this book is a prayer against malevolent spirits. Sickness, as all Egyptian physicians knew, could be caused by the hatred of a dead man or dead woman, as well as by other hostile agencies. Most fascinating of all our sources are the texts called "letters to the dead." Scribbled on rough pots, they were "mailed" by being deposited in a tomb. Here are excerpts from one of them, written by a man to his deceased wife:

> To the excellent spirit, Ankhere. What evil thing have I done to you, that I should have come into this wretched state in which I am? What have I done to you? What you have done is that you have laid hands on me! . . . I made you a married woman, when I was a youth; I was with you, and I did not put you away. I did not cause your heart to grieve. . . . When you became ill, of the illness which you had, I [sent for] a master physician. . . . I wept exceedingly, with all my retinue, before all my neighbors. And I gave you linen cloths to wrap you, and I caused many cloths to be made, and I neglected no good thing that could be done for you. And now, look, I have spent three years living alone. . . . And, look, I did it because of you. But, look, you don't know good from bad. It will be decided between you and me! And, look, the sisters in the house, I have not entered into one of them!

The writer's extreme mental anguish even affected his spelling; the original is full of careless mistakes. The poor fellow reminds his wife of his many kindnesses to her, including the services of a good doctor during her last illness. As is common in Egyptian texts, the unpleasant fact of death is never explicitly stated; but the husband says he grieved publicly for his wife and gave her a good burial. Furthermore—and this obviously preys on his mind—not only has he remained unmarried for three long years, but he has not even had relations with any of the women in the house. Yet in spite of his kindness to his wife, she has afflicted him with some unnamed but awful fate; and he threatens to call her up for judgment in the tribunal of the gods.

Obviously this man regards his dead wife as living on and as capable—in every sense of the word—of doing him an injury. They may have been as happy together as his letter implies; but catastrophic, undeserved bad luck could only be explained by the malice of some spirit.

It has been claimed that the Egyptians were not really afraid of the dead as a group. They feared only particular people who, having been unpleasant during life, might be equally nasty after they were dead. Yet the letters to the dead do not really bear out this theory. The afflicted husband, in the letter we have quoted, is outraged precisely because he had never given his wife cause to harm him and had no reason to expect her to do so. The argument that Egyptian tombs would not have been desecrated in such an efficient, wholehearted fashion if the robbers had been afraid of their occupants is not conclusive either; there are always people in any culture whose greed, or need, gives them enough intestinal fortitude to risk the sanctions the society sets up against antisocial behavior. We are supposed to have a healthy respect for the law and for policemen, but our jails are full of people who managed to rise above this inhibition. In many of the rifled tombs the mummies have been brutally hacked apart in a manner as shocking as it was unnecessary; but this ferocity is understandable if we assume that the robbers believed they could protect themselves against the revenge of the violated dead by dismembering their bodies.

So in the Egyptian faith we find, in addition to the inconsistency we have come to expect, a wide range of attitudes toward death and the dead. But we also find a unifying theme: the desire for survival in some, perhaps any, form. Let us go on to see how this survival was attained, and what a man had to do and possess in order to be "made into a living ba."

Fifteen

"MY BODY SHALL
BE ENDURING"

MUMMIFICATION—GENERAL

There is no more typically Egyptian object than a mummy, unless it is a pyramid; and both represent essential elements in the equipment for eternity. Mummies have often been the villains in modern horror tales and films—another illustration of the fact that we still find a dead body an object of fear. Many years ago, when I first became interested in ancient Egypt, my indiscriminate reading led me to a particularly ghoulish, true (?) mummy story. Thanks to several kindly readers, I was able to track it down, and I will now relate it to you.

The archaeologist-protagonist of my tale was Arthur Weigall, at one time Inspector of Antiquities for Upper Egypt, and author of a number of popular books. One day he and his crew found a tomb wherein lay a mummy. By evening, when his crew had gone home, Weigall was working with the mummy in the depths of the tomb, where he had descended by means of a rope. Absorbed in his task, he suddenly realized that the tomb had become very dark, and looking up, he was horrified to see a mass of black clouds obscuring the small square high above which led to the open air. One of the infrequent Egyptian storms had come up, as they do, with startling suddenness.

Weigall knew that by morning, when his crew came back, the tomb would be flooded. He was in no danger, having his rope; but his now-unwrapped mummy, for which he had apparently conceived an inordinate affection, would never survive a wetting. He had to get it up and out, or it would be lost.

He came to the conclusion that there was only one way out of the difficulty. He would have to sling the mummy on his back and climb the rope. The problem was, how to get it attached to him? He seems not to have had any extra rope, which was careless, but by no means fatally so. He decided to put the mummy's arms around his neck.

Painfully he inched his way up the rope, hand over hand and foot over foot. Above, the sky was ominously black; thunder rumbled distantly, like the remote roaring of an Egyptian lion goddess. All at once a bright streak of lightning cleft the threatening clouds; startled, Weigall slipped and slid down a few feet. And as he did so, the mummy moved. Its clasped hands slithered down over his breast and its head dropped; when he turned his own head, Weigall found himself staring directly into the withered eyes and fleshless grin of the old woman's face, which was now resting coquettishly on his shoulder.

The rest of the story is anticlimax; but even now, after an unmentionable number of years, I still think it's one of the best mummy stories I have ever read. Weigall wrote with flair and verve, and the only reason why I put a question mark after the word "true" is that he sometimes preferred literary effect to accuracy.

In one sense it is irrelevant to ask why the ancient Egyptian needed a mummy in order to survive death. He obviously thought he did, or there would not be so many mummies. We have already mentioned the principle of sympathetic magic as one explanation for the attentions paid to the corpse, but it is not necessarily the complete answer. Once again, we will understand the Egyptian methods better if we first look briefly at the techniques used by other people to dispose of their dead.

Although mummies have been found in many parts of the world besides Egypt, mummification as a method of disposal of the dead is comparatively rare. Leaving aside such exotic processes as exposure to birds of prey and ritual cannibalism, the most common techniques, by a large margin, are two in number: inhumation and cremation.

Modern scholars who like logical systems have tried to find some relationship between the type of disposal used by a particular culture and the contemporary views of the hereafter. Is cremation in itself a denial of survival after death? No. We have already agreed that the body does not live again, no matter how carefully it is treated; therefore, the destruction of the body need not affect the existence of the soul. But if the soul is freed by the conflagration which consumes the body, it ought to rise, on the lifting smoke, to a celestial paradise. Conversely, inhumation ought to imply a belief in a subterranean afterlife.

It doesn't work that way—possibly because ancient people were not as interested in consistency as the frustrated scholars who study them. Some cremation peoples believed in subterranean afterworlds, and some inhumators thought of paradise as "heaven." There seems to be no essential difference in dogma between cremation and burial in the earth. Cremation burials include such features as elaborate tombs, sumptuous grave goods, and food offerings. In both methods of disposal something of the physical individual is preserved; and after a few hundred years or so there is very little difference to be seen in the final results of the two processes.

Mummification, then, cannot be regarded as the ultimate development of inhumation—the preservation of at least part of the body—as opposed to cremation—the utter destruction of the body. Mummification is a separate, and a special, technique.

We must distinguish first of all between embalming and mummification, and between accidental and deliberate preservation of the body. Mummification, which is basically a process of desiccation, is only one form of embalming—the intentional preservation of the body from decay. Embalming by the injection of preservative materials is relatively new. Some attempts were made, in ancient and medieval times, to preserve tissue by the application of chemicals or vegetable substances, but most of the materials used by ancient embalmers were, in fact, quite useless for the purpose for which they were employed. In a few cases the embalmers hit on a substance which did preserve tissue; this was usually a desiccating agent, and the result was a mummy.

Mummies themselves may be deliberate or accidental. Perhaps the best preserved of all bodies—not really mummies—are products of a special environment: the peat bogs of Europe. These bodies are really remarkably lifelike; they have none of the wrinkled, withered look of a genuine mummy, but preserve the texture of clothing and the very expression on the corpse's face. (It is usually not pleasant.) The chemicals in the soil transmuted cloth and flesh into a leatherlike substance. These bodies are the remains of careless pedestrians who missed their footing, or of criminals whose bodies were tossed into the bogs to get rid of them, or of victims sacrificed to a god. They are accidentally preserved.

In classical and medieval times the bodies of royalty were often subjected to some sort of embalming. Some were successes, others were horrible failures. However, most of the successful examples must be viewed as accidental mummies, for they owe their survival to fortuitously favorable conditions of air or soil rather than to the materials which were meant to embalm them. Most of the bodies treated by the embalming techniques of olden times are in terrible condition today. Visitors to the catacombs of Rome are shown bodies of "embalmed" early Christians who, if they had known what they were going to look like two thousand years later, would have begged to be excused. A skeleton is beautiful by comparison.

We must now consider cases of deliberate, successful mummification. Since the Egyptian mummies are the finest of the type, and the oldest, it was once suggested that all other intentional mummies were cases of cultural transmission from Egypt. Mummies are found in South America, Australia, and New Mexico, among other places, so this would mean that the Egyptians and their friends really got around.

The foremost exponent of the diffusion theory was no amateur, but a very distinguished scholar indeed—Grafton Elliot Smith, one of the first qualified medical men to study the physical anthropology of the ancient Egyptians. His book on Egyptian mummies, written in collaboration with Warren Dawson—another doctor, and a disciple of Smith's theories—is still a standard work on the subject. Smith's name is honored in Egyptology, but I doubt if any reputable scholar today would support his diffusion theory. None of the attempts to prove contact between the Old and New Worlds in ancient times has been successful, nor is there any real similarity between mummies of Egypt and those of the Western Hemisphere—except for the fact that all of them were mummified. As we shall see, Egyptian mummies were treated in a distinctive manner.

Peruvian mummies, perhaps the best known of all the New World types, were surely not accidental; they were meant to be preserved. Although there is some evidence of evisceration, they are primarily the product of climatic conditions as favorable as those of Egypt—dry cold instead of dry heat. The Egyptian cadavers were usually extended, but the Peruvian cases are bundled up; they look as if they were huddled against the cold. Cold has also preserved some bodies from the northern parts of North America—the Aleutians and Alaska. In the south of the same continent, another unique environment "pickled" the bodies of Indians of New Mexico and Kentucky in the saltpeter mines of those areas. These mummies, though deliberately placed in the mines, were not eviscerated.

The use of fire to dry bodies is also known; but in Nicaragua, for instance, this preliminary mummification was only temporary. After a year the body was cremated. A good many of these mummification techniques preserved the flesh for a limited time only. In various areas of the Pacific, evisceration and embalming of a rude sort was known, but infrequent. The Samoan mummies lasted for only thirty years or so, and the Tahitian variety were only good for a few months. A common procedure here was the pricking of the skin in order to allow the fluids of decomposition to escape, which, so far as we know, was never done in Egypt.

The same procedure was followed with the mummies from the Torres Straits area between Australia and New Zealand. I have never seen one of these mummies—nor, to be honest, have I tried very hard to do so—but the photographs show them to have been fairly successful. They look vaguely like Egyptian mummies, except for the bamboo frames to which they are bound. It was on such frames that the embalming process was carried out; the body was raised and suspended from the bamboo. I will spare the reader further details; they make rather repulsive reading. By comparison, the Egyptian process is fairly antiseptic. Suffice it to say that the two techniques have nothing more in common than the aim of the process made inevitable. There are just too many difficulties in the diffusion theory, besides the fact that none of the other mummies show any important procedural resemblances to those of Egypt. Not only are the distances involved very great, but the time gap between ancient Egypt and the Pacific and American cultures is altogether too long.

In one case, however, the notion of mummification may have come to another society from Egypt. The Baganda tribe of Uganda mummify dead kings—or at least they used to; I can't see why they should have given it up, since it is no more bizarre than our mortuary techniques. Scholars who have studied the Baganda seem to think they exhibit other traits which resemble those of ancient Egypt, but whether the resemblance is more than coincidental, or, if it is, whether the connection lies in direct borrowing from Egypt by the Baganda ancestors or in a common "African" heritage, no man can say, nor I. At any rate, it is not impossible that the Egyptian and Bagandese embalmings are related.

Possible contacts between Egypt and the Canary Islands, where mummies were also manufactured, are hard to prove. The Guanches of the Canaries—who are, I understand, extinct—were of Berber stock, but it is unlikely that they left Africa, if that is where they came from, before the Egyptian mortuary cult faded out. According to reports, the Guanche mummies were preserved by the resin of a particular tree found in the islands. Resin was used in embalming by the Egyptians, and cedar oil seems to have preservative qualities. These mummies were extremely desiccated, some weighing no more than seven pounds. It seems unlikely, offhand, that resin alone could so dehydrate the tissue.

Obviously, preservation of the body is not so much a result of theological notions relating to immortality as of more or less fortuitous physical conditions. Most of the people who believe in a life hereafter— which includes just about everyone—are satisfied with burial or with cremation. The preservation of the body is not a necessity for immortality. When the climate was right, or when the tribe had a handy natural embalming workshop such as the saltpeter mines, then we get mummies. Really effective embalming techniques could not be developed until a certain level of physiological and chemical knowledge had been attained. Sometimes a culture might stumble on an effective desiccating agent; but even then it was necessary to keep the body in a suitable environment or, sooner or later, decay took place.

Egyptian mummies depend for their endurance on the hot dry climate of Egypt. Mummies in damp tombs often decayed despite the best efforts of the embalmer; other mummies began to deteriorate after they were moved out of their tombs.

Of course, the theological factor cannot be dismissed. Mummification in Egypt, as elsewhere, may have begun because of environmental conditions, but the complex profession we are about to study would not have developed if a need had not been felt. This need, as I have suggested, can probably be explained in terms of sympathetic magic. A man would live in Paradise as long as some part of him continued to exist in this world—but no longer. A statue, or even a name, could provide the necessary focal point for the spirit. But the best, and most direct, physical remnant of a man was his own body.

MUMMIFICATION—EGYPTIAN

Everyone seems to agree that the Egyptians probably got the idea of embalming their dead from seeing the accidentally preserved bodies of their distant ancestors. In prehistoric times the dead were buried in the sand, without coffins or wrappings. The dry air and the hot, baking sand preserved the fragile flesh, as they have also preserved cloth and wood and withered flowers. Laid in shallow graves, sometimes the dead reappeared. When Breasted was excavating in Nubia, he had to pass through a cemetery each day on his way to work, and, across his path, he saw the feet of a corpse which had been uncovered by the wind. They were as rough and callused as the feet of the living Nubians who worked at the excavation. As wind and time uncovered these remains for Breasted, so they must have exposed older specimens for the Egyptians of 3000 B.C., who lived at the time of the unification of the Two Lands.

The unification and the beginning of the First Dynasty mark the beginning of Egyptian civilization, as opposed to prehistory. Civilization means more complex ways of doing things. No longer were the dead shoveled directly into the sand. Graves were lined with wood, brick, and stone; bodies were wrapped in cloth or enclosed in coffins. This care defeated one of the ends for which it was designed. Stone and wood shut out air and sand. Protected bodies decayed.

Attempts at mummification go back a long way in Egypt, possibly further back than was once believed. The remains of bodies found at Hierakonpolis, one of the capitals of predynastic Egypt, show that some were wrapped and padded and that resin had been applied to the bandages. By the time of the Second Dynasty, more complicated attempts at preserving the body were being made. At Sakkara, James Quibell found the remains of a woman who had been carefully prepared for the grave. The body lay on its side in a flexed position, knees bent. (The extended position, more convenient for mummy wrapping, did not come into general use until later.) Within the elaborate wrappings of this mummy was a mass of corroded linen whose condition suggested that a material such as salt or natron had been applied to the surface of the body. The process did not work; only bones were left. But this example proves that a beginning had been made.

A few centuries later we are in the Pyramid Age, the time of the Fourth and Fifth Dynasties. It is a period of fantastic achievement in many areas, symbolized by the immense mass of the Great Pyramid. Mummification had not made the same strides as had tomb building, but the diligent embalmers had developed a new process which compensated, to some extent, for their inability to preserve the physical body. The corpse was treated with resin and wrapped in layer upon layer of linen bandages. While the outermost layer of bandage was still wet and sticky with resin, it was molded into the form of the body it covered, and the resin-soaked cloth set, forming a shell, or carapace, of stony hardness. The modeling was so exact that fine details of anatomy and expression are preserved. On one mummy, found at Medum by Petrie, the owner's neat mustache was reproduced in the linen, and the sexual organs were modeled with such care that we can tell that circumcision was practiced at that time. This mummy lay in the extended position, which was beginning to be the normal one. Its body cavity was packed with linen, and the head rattled when it was shaken (to such extremes does a passion for truth lead archaeologists!), probably with bits of desiccated brain. At this period the brain was not removed, though the abdominal organs were.

Mummification gradually improved during the succeeding dynasties. By the Middle Kingdom the technique of modeling the surface of the body in plaster or linen had been abandoned. The body was eviscerated and treated with resin or gum; linen was used to fill the abdominal cavity. Sometimes sawdust was used for filling instead of linen. The brain was not removed.

The classic style of mummification did not appear until the New Kingdom. A new advance had been made—the removal of the brain by means of an instrument which was inserted through the nostril and up, piercing the ethmoid bone, into the skull. The organs were removed from the abdominal cavity; the chest cavity was entered through an incision in the diaphragm, and all its contents were removed, with the exception of the heart.

The heart was the seat not of romantic yearnings but of thought and memory, so we can see why it might be left in place. The other organs, with the exception of the kidneys, which were sometimes left in the body, were treated separately and then placed in four canopic jars.

This method is described by Herodotus, whom I do not intend to quote. For an Egyptologist the value of Herodotus rests almost entirely in the joy of his delightful prose. He was sometimes right but just as often wrong, and his statements cannot be accepted without confirmation. He does, however, describe mummification fairly accurately, mentioning three different types. His first, and most expensive, method is the one just described. Methods two and three involve injecting cedar oil to dissolve the abdominal organs and cleaning out the intestines with a purge. I am informed by Dr. Salima Ikram, a top expert on mummies in general and animal mummies in particular, that the second method actually works if an oleo-resin resembling turpentine is used, so Herodotus was right about this. He also scores on the most important point of all. So far we have only mentioned the preliminaries of mummification; the all-important desiccating agent has yet to be discussed. Herodotus correctly identified the agent.

In the past there was some disagreement about this vital substance, but recent experiments have pretty well settled the argument. If we wanted to duplicate an Egyptian mummy—and it appears that some of us do!—we could.

The experts did not argue about what substance was used, but about how it was used. The substance is natron, a kind of salt whose dehydrating properties are very high. It is found in quantity in Egypt, particularly in the Wadi Natrun, one of the oases. There is no doubt that it was used in mummification; it has been chemically identified on many mummies and in canopic jars from as early as the Fourth Dynasty.

Herodotus says that the cadavers were placed in natron for a period of seventy days. Until recent times it was assumed that the natron was used in solution; so we had the novelist's gruesome version of an Egyptian embalmer's shop, with corpses floating in their salty baths. A thoughtful reader, however, might have found himself wondering. Baths? The aim was dehydration, wasn't it? Why add more water?

Herodotus used to be quoted as the authority for the natron baths, but here the interpreters, not the Greek, may be off the track. The word he uses is the word used to describe the salting of fish, which may be soaked, certainly, but which are often, in Egypt at least, preserved with dry salt.

One way of solving the problem was to try both wet and dry natron on tissue and see what would happen. This was done by Edward Lucas, the chemist who worked on the Tutankhamon objects, and the author of a definitive book on Egyptian materials. Another recent experimenter was A. T. Sandison of the Department of Pathology of the University of Glasgow. Neither man actually tried their experiments on a human body. Lucas used chickens and pigeons, and Sandison used human toes. Both experimenters agree on the essential points: that it took an extremely high concentration of natron in the liquid state to preserve tissue, and that the results did not resemble Egyptian mummies; but that dry natron did produce specimens resembling Egyptian mummies. Dry natron seems to be the answer. The process might be recommended to modern morticians, if preservation is what they want. Some of the Egyptian specimens have lasted quite nicely for over three thousand years, with the help of the admirable Egyptian climate.

The most interesting modern study of the matter took place a few years ago when an inquiring scholar named Bob Brier decided to mummify somebody. Brier cheerfully admits to having been fascinated by mummies since childhood, but his argument for carrying out the procedure was that we couldn't really know how the Egyptians did it until we tried it ourselves. It took him some time to convince a medical school that his proposition was a legitimate variety of research. Having finally obtained permission, and a cadaver, Brier and Ronald Wade, of the University of Maryland Medical Center, got to work. They used replicas of ancient embalming tools and the same preservatives the Egyptians employed, following procedures described and depicted in ancient times. In general, these worked just fine. The one major difference was in the removal of the brain. (Note to the squeamish: skip to the end of the paragraph.) Pulling out bits of it through the nose, using a hooked instrument, didn't really do a neat job. Brier found that using a kind of whisk and stirring the contents of the skull as one might beat eggs (I told you to stop reading) reduced the brain to a semiliquid, which could be poured out if the body was turned upside down. The cavity was then swabbed out, leaving it nice and clean.

The organs removed from the body were placed in canopic jars, and the body was then covered with dry natron, which Brier had brought back from the Wadi Natrun in Egypt. Within thirty-five days the corpse had lost eighty pounds in body weight, all of it water. Once it was properly dried the body was wrapped in Egyptian style. The remains were treated with respect and reverence—at least as much as a modern mortician would have given them—and Brier made sure that the proper amulets were enclosed in the wrappings and that the proper prayers and spells were written on the bandages. The anonymous individual who donated his body to science may be surprised when he wakes up to find himself sitting in the boat of Re. Personally, I wouldn't mind too much, considering some of the alternatives.

The "classic" method of embalming continued with minor changes for hundreds of years. It was quite a successful method; some of the mummies of this period, particularly those of Yuya and Seti I, are excellently preserved. Although the morticians could in many cases stave off the dangers of physical dissolution, there was one danger that threatened the mummy which they could not avert. Tomb robbers not only stole the goods buried in the tomb but often dismembered, mutilated, or burned the mummies themselves. During the Twenty-First Dynasty the situation got so bad that the pious priestly rulers of Thebes felt it necessary to restore and rebury the battered bodies of the ancient kings. The royal embalmers who picked up the pieces— quite literally, in some cases—had ample opportunity to view the results of the techniques they and their predecessors had practiced, and they may have decided that those results were not entirely satisfactory.

Tissue was certainly preserved, but the mummies did not look lifelike. The skin was wrinkled and shrunken, the cheeks hollow, the flesh sunken.

Physicians have adopted Aesculapius as their patron; perhaps morticians, who are always seeking to improve their methods, ought to adopt one of these Twenty-First Dynasty embalmers. They were not disheartened; they were stimulated to do bigger and better things. But the techniques they adopted were rather peculiar.

This period is considered, by those who know, to be the height of mummification techniques. We ought to pause to consider the methods in some detail. There is no use warning off the squeamish, as I did before describing a modern mummification. What follows will be no worse than what has come before.

The undertaker of the Twenty-First Dynasty received his patient in a workshop which was not a permanent building but a temporary booth erected for the purpose. The body was laid out on a wooden table or platform. An incision was made in the left flank, and all the internal organs except the heart, and perhaps the kidneys, were removed. The brain was extracted, and then the entire body was covered with dry natron and allowed to remain in it for a period which was no longer than seventy days. This is the length of time assigned to the entire procedure by various texts; probably a good portion of the total was taken up by the bandaging and other parts of the process.

The organs removed from the body were also preserved in pots containing natron. At the end of the designated period the body emerged dry and desiccated, with loosened skin. It was at this point that the Twenty-First Dynasty embalmer departed from the practices of his predecessors and rose to heights of creative power. (Or, as Winlock puts it, he resorted to an expedient of somewhat doubtful taste.) He stuffed the body.

The abdominal cavity had always been stuffed, but this was different. Through slits made in the skin, the mummy was padded out with sawdust, salt, ashes, and various other substances, rammed in between skin and muscle until the desiccated form took on a shape resembling that which it had had in life—or perhaps any form that appealed to the undertaker.

After the body was stuffed, it was painted. The face was adorned with cosmetics, the lips rouged, artificial eyebrows gummed into place. If the natural hair was thinning it was eked out by false hair elaborately waved and curled. As a final touch, false eyes were inserted; they were of black-and-white stone, or of linen with painted pupils, or, in some cases, onions.

The body itself being now prepared, the organs, which had been carefully preserved, were wrapped into seven packages, which were replaced in the body cavity along with small wax figures of four guardian genii of the dead. The incision was closed with a plug of paste or linen, or covered by a plate inscribed with magical figures.

The mummy was ready for wrapping. It was laid on wooden blocks for easier manipulation (modern archaeologists, when unwrapping mummies, sometimes use sawhorses), and a pile of old sheets, shirts, and shawls was placed close at hand to be torn into strips of varying width as they were needed—narrow ones for fingers, wide ones for the torso. Before the first bandages were applied the amulets and ornaments of major importance were placed around the throat or wrist or on the forehead. The fingers and toes were wrapped separately, with very narrow bandages; gloves or finger coverings of silver or gold, if the mummy was that of a royal personage, might go on the fingers first. Sandals have been found on the feet.

Bandaging a mummy took hundreds of yards of linen. It must have been a drain on the family linen closet. Perhaps the living saved old sheets and shawls toward the day of death, and extra supplies might be bought from temple warehouses or from thrifty individuals who had some to spare. We know, from the state of wear of much of the linen and from the worn, washed-out laundry marks, that most of the material was not made specifically for mummy wrappings. The marks weren't really laundry marks, of course, but they are reminiscent of ours, being little scribbles in one corner which give the name of the owner or the warehouse to which the linen belonged. One Eleventh Dynasty mummy used 375 square meters of linen in its bandaging; the coffin was filled with extra sheets, and these, with the palls used in the funeral procession, brought the total linen required to the staggering sum of 845 square meters.

After the first layer of bandages was applied other amulets might be placed on the body. Then came more bandages, in a prescribed order—first wound spirally around the body, then a sheet covering the whole form, then more spiral bandages. At one point the head was fixed in position by a strip of linen around the face and neck. The arms were fastened to the thighs, and the legs were bound together. Twice during the wrapping process the bandages were covered with warm, melted resin. This substance, which has been erroneously called "bitumen," or "pitch," sometimes had a deleterious effect. Tutankhamon's mummy had been stuck to the coffin by the resin poured over it, which had hardened into a stony mass. Even more destructive was the spontaneous combustion brought about by the decomposition of the unguents, which carbonized the linen wrappings and reduced the flesh to a cracked and brittle state.

Finally the mummy was formed by the layers of bandaging into a rigid columnar shape. The final sheet was then applied. Unlike the other bandages, it was made especially for the trade, being a sheet of coarse linen with a figure of Osiris drawn on its surface. This was covered by a piece of linen stitched up the back, and then a set of tapes was applied over the whole form. The mummy was now ready to be delivered to the family. The embalmers were through with him—almost.

Sometimes archaeologists have found deposits which seemed, at first glance, to be refuse—pots, some empty and some filled with rags, stained bits of linen, miscellaneous implements, bags of natron (used), and other odds and ends. We sometimes bury garbage, but the Egyptians were not so fastidious. It does not take much imagination to identify this particular trash as the residue of mummification and of the final funerary feast. None of it could be discarded; having been connected with the dead man, it partook to some extent of his essence, so it had to be given some sort of burial. Or, as Winlock cynically suggests, if a man wanted to be sure that all of him got into sacred ground, he would have to insist that even the sweepings of the embalmer's floor be gathered up.

There was good reason for such care. Some of the embalmers, certainly, were men of integrity. But in a number of cases posterity has caught them out, although their contemporaries were deceived. Even in carefully prepared mummies they sometimes slipped, letting bits and pieces of their equipment, or assorted small animals, be wrapped into a second or third layer of bandages. What difference did it make? The relatives of the dead man weren't going to unwrap him, and nothing essential had been left out.

More serious were cases like that of the woman whose inner workings had been lost or misplaced while the body was being mummified. The embalmer finally made up a set of organs out of a coil of rope and a bit of cowskin and some rags, bundled them up with the four sacred figures, and put them inside the lady. One would like to think that she encountered him later, in the hereafter, and told him what she thought of him.

The nastiest of all accusations, worse than carelessness or laziness, can also be levied against some ancient embalmers. The word is ghouls—robbers of the dead. Winlock describes one case which is an excellent example of archaeological detection—a process of reasoning which puts the blame for the robbery squarely and unmistakably on the shoulders of the men who had been paid to guard the mummy.

The mummies in question were those of two women. When Winlock first found them, they were lying just as they had been placed in the grave: tapes, outer sheet, and Osiris sheet were in place. But as the archaeologist unwrapped the bodies more and more confusion among the chest bandages became apparent. At last the bandages were off, down to the first layer of resin which had been applied; and there, in the hardened gum, was the imprint of the metal hawks which had once covered the ladies' chests. The hawks were gone. Around the torn bandages on the chests were fingerprints made by hands sticky with resin. The left hand of one woman had been laid bare in a search for finger rings. Winlock concludes somberly, "The mummies had been rifled before they were even completely wrapped; and that must have taken place in the undertaker's own establishment."

Despite such cases of corruption and carelessness, the mummies of this period probably represent the height of Egyptian skill in embalming. From this point on the technique degenerated and the carelessness increased. Some Ptolemaic mummies are very dark and hard and shiny, presumably from the application of resinous material directly to the skin. Poorly preserved mummies were kept intact by a long stick thrust through the body. Others can hardly be called mummies; they are only loose bones flung higgledy-piggledy into a framework of palm fibers bandaged into the shape of a body. As the embalmers' skill decreased, the wrappings became very elaborate; the bandaging sometimes looks like woven basketry. The elaboration of bandaging reached its peak during the Roman period, and the mummies were at their lowest point. They were so thickly coated with resin that the material formed a cast all around the body, and sometimes we cannot even tell whether evisceration was carried out. The process had made a complete circle, back to the technique used in the earliest mummies—a cast or carapace covering the entire body.

Mummies, it may be thought, are not only an unpleasant topic of conversation, but an even more unpleasant object of research. This attitude stems not solely from the squeamishness of our effete culture, it is a reflection of attitudes toward the dead which are a lot older than modern man. The other objects of an Egyptologist's study need no justification, but perhaps we ought to explain his interest in what may strike some people as a nasty business.

One reason for the study of mummification ought to be immediately obvious to any reader with archaeological know-how. The changes in embalming technique form a chronological sequence which can be pinned down by absolute dates. This means that otherwise undated mummies, and the contexts in which they are found, can sometimes be dated by means of this sequence, which was worked out so skillfully by men like Smith and Dawson.

The human remains found in some of the Old Kingdom pyramids illustrate how the sequence can be applied. In 1837 Colonel Richard

Vyse, an English explorer, was the first man in modern times to penetrate the interior of the third Giza pyramid, built by Menkaure. Vyse was several thousand years too late to find an undisturbed burial, but he did discover the king's sarcophagus and, in an upper chamber, scraps from a wooden coffin and from a mummy. It was only reasonable to suppose that the mummy fragments were the remains of the pyramid builder.

Another supposed mummy of the Pyramid Age was found in the tomb of King Mernere, near Cairo. The remains were found in 1881, more than four thousand years after Mernere had been sealed inside his pyramid.

But according to Smith's analysis of embalming techniques, the Mernere mummy is an Eighteenth Dynasty effort, coming from a period about a thousand years later than the pyramid in which it was found. The Mycerinus mummy is also later in date. Both were what archaeologists call "intrusive" burials—burials which made use of an already prepared tomb. Thus, the study of mummification can correct a date based on misleading circumstances of discovery. It can even correct a date based on what would seem to be unarguable evidence— an inscription naming the mummy.

Most of the royal mummies come from two caches discovered at the end of the nineteenth century. The kings, queens, and other individuals (a few were nonroyal) in these collections had been gathered together by priests of the Twenty-First Dynasty, after the original tombs had been robbed and the mummies violated—so grievously in some cases that the priests had to do a sort of ghoulish jigsaw puzzle with the pieces. Some mummies had been rewrapped; few were in their original coffins. The priests dutifully relabeled them, and when Maspero and Smith examined the bodies they accepted these identifications. There was only so much Smith, the anatomist, could do with these sad remains. X-ray techniques were crude, and since one can only tell the age of a body by the bones, Smith couldn't get at this information without defleshing the mummies.

So the situation remained until the 1970s, at which time a team of Egyptologists and physicians asked permission to reexamine all the royal mummies using more advanced X-ray techniques. They did it; and the results were extremely disconcerting. You see, the physical evidence didn't agree with the historical evidence. To put it in its most elementary form, a king who ruled for at least thirty-nine years and married a wife when he came to the throne had to be at least forty at death—probably older. If the mummy labeled with his name is that of a man in his early thirties, there is a problem.

Egyptologists scrambled to explain the discrepancies. There are only three possibilities: one, the anthropologists are wrong; two, the historians are wrong; three, the labels on the mummies and coffins are wrong. I favor the third explanation. So do a good many scholars, but trying to figure out who is really who has led to what Dennis Forbes, editor of *Kmt*, has called "Mummy Musical Chairs." According to one revision, the mummy labeled Seti II is really Thutmose II. The one labeled Thutmose II becomes Thutmose I. The former Thutmose I is an unknown earlier Thutmosid. The mummy accepted as that of Amenhotep II, though it was found in his tomb, in his sarcophagus, with his name on it, isn't Amenhotep II after all. He's really Thutmose IV.

Confused? So am I. Adding to the confusion is a methodology called cranio-facial morphology. According to the proponents of this procedure, the reason why Amenhotep II isn't Amenhotep II is that he can't be the son of the Thutmose III mummy (assuming that Thutmose III is really Thutmose III) because the measurements of skull and facial bones don't jibe. The reader has probably realized that this methodology strikes me as dubious in the extreme. Despite the technical terms involved, what it essentially comes down to is that two people can't be related because they don't look alike. No doubt I am being unfair, but the maternal contribution is never taken into account, since we don't have the mummies of the mothers.

I had better stop talking about it.

However, this may be an appropriate time to discuss modern scientific methods of examining mummies. One of the most useful is the CAT scan, which produces an extremely detailed and accurate model of the body without invading it physically. Medical endoscopy and complicated techniques of rehydrating dried-out ancient tissue have produced interesting results. One of the specialists in these techniques is Dr. Rosalie David of the University of Manchester, whose books will tell you all you want to know about them. But the letters that get some Egyptologists all a-twitter are DNA.

The discovery of the genetic code is surely one of the most astonishing scientific breakthroughs of all time. It is hard to simplify such a complex concept, especially when (as is the case with me) one doesn't really understand it. But I'll give it my best shot. These long strings of beadlike genes define each individual, determining gender, physical attributes, genetic diseases, and God knows what else. They are made up of contributions from both parents, so that matching the codes of a child and his parents, or more distant ancestors, can determine relationships. Mitrochondrial DNA, as opposed to the other variety, is passed on only in the female line. A boy-child has his mother's mitrochondrial DNA, but he can't pass it on to his children.

Since some of the most hotly debated arguments in Egyptology hinge on who was related to whom, scholars pounced on this breakthrough with shouts of delight. At last, they crowed, we can determine who the royal mummies really were! We will pry poor Tutankhamon out of his coffin again, scrape off a bit of him, and find out once and . for all whether his DNA matches that of various other mummies we think may be his kin.

It's a pity that it won't work. Again I am out of my depth here, but as I understand it, DNA deteriorates with time and other factors. With ancient remains it may not be possible to get enough of the stuff to make a definitive match. If we keep picking pieces off various mummies—teeth are particularly good—there won't be much left of them. So far I remain unconvinced by most of the DNA matches claimed by modern researchers.

Anyhow, it's much more entertaining to go on arguing, using the old methods.

One of the questionable mummies is the one labeled Amenhotep III; actually, there are several names on the label. This king dates from the Eighteenth Dynasty; he was the father of Akhenaton and—I think—the grandfather of Tutankhamon. This mummy had been stuffed; packing had been introduced under the skin. Now this process, as we have seen, was not begun until the Twenty-First Dynasty, some four hundred years after the age of Amenhotep III. When Elliot Smith examined the mummy he was unhappy about the attribution of it to an Eighteenth Dynasty king; he suggested, very tentatively, that the unique technique might be one of the heresies of the Amarna Period, which was generally iconoclastic. But we now have other mummies dating from about the same period, and they show no signs of stuffing. The mummies of Yuya and of Tutankhamon were prepared in the traditional Eighteenth Dynasty manner. We cannot firmly deny that this mummy is that of Amenhotep III on typological evidence; the trouble with a noninclusive series is that a new example may turn up at any time to upset the arrangement. But it is clear that this particular mummy should be labeled with a big question mark.

Tutankhamon's mummy furnishes other examples of the useful application of the study of embalming. Derry's investigation of the mummy turned up one interesting and curious fact which had to do with the skull measurements.

Tutankhamon's skull was unusually broad, as well as flat-topped (platycephalic), with a markedly projecting occipital area. The general shape of the head was strikingly like that of another skull—the one found in the peculiar little tomb KV 55, which was originally named "the Tomb of Queen Tiyi." Both Derry and Smith, who examined the latter skull, commented independently on the unusual breadth and flatness of the two specimens. A later investigator, R. G. Harrison, a professor of anatomy, confirmed the resemblance and praised Derry for the accuracy of his observations.

There seems to be no doubt that the owners of the skulls were related by blood, and this is a point of great importance. The most likely candidate for the occupant of tomb 55 is Smenkhkare, the son-in-law and co-regent of Akhenaton. If he and Tutankhamon shared that distinctive skull shape, they were probably brothers. It is barely possibly that Smenkhkare might have fathered Tutankhamon, though the likelihood is that they were too close in age to be father and son.

This is another useful fact to be learned from the study of mummies—the approximate age of the deceased. For example, Tutankhamon's age at death was somewhere in the neighborhood of eighteen years. Egyptian records give the number of years he reigned, so from the physical data we can deduce how old he was when he came to the throne. Smenkhkare—if the questionable skeleton is indeed his—was probably around twenty when he died. This would make him seventeen years old when he became king. Tutankhamon succeeded him; so if the two were brothers, Tutankhamon was the younger brother.

If you think there are a lot of "ifs" in that paragraph, just wait. If Tutankhamon was a king's son, as one inscription states, then Smenkhkare must have been a king's son too, for a commoner, whatever his age, would not have preceded a prince of the blood onto the throne. Only two kings qualify for the paternal role. If there was a long co-regency between Akhenaton and his father, then the latter monarch could have lived long enough to father Smenkhkare and Tutankhamon. If there wasn't a co-regency, the father must have been Akhenaton, because that king reigned for seventeen years and Tutankhamon was only nine when he ascended the throne after Akhenaton's death.

Well, we seem to be getting off the subject of mummies. We don't have Akhenaton's, and even if we did, we couldn't eliminate all the ifs. A close resemblance between his remains and those of Smenkhkare and Tutankhamon would not prove he was their father; he might equally well be their half-brother. But we would be able to find out how old Akhenaton was when he died, and skeletal remains would settle, once and for all, the old argument as to whether Akhenaton suffered from a pathological condition severe enough to produce the deformities seen in some of his statues and reliefs.

Those of us who are interested in Egyptology engage in this sort of guesswork all the time; it is going to be a blow to us if Akhenaton's mummy ever does turn up, because we enjoy our fantasies immensely, particularly when we label them "theories" and get into exciting arguments with other archaeologists.

We could go on listing the benefits to be derived from the study of mummies—the manner of death, the types of diseases prevalent, the state of medical treatment, styles of hairdressing and makeup, not to mention the all-important question of mortuary beliefs. Before I conclude our study of Egyptian mummies—which may have seemed, to the squeamish reader, inordinately long—I want to touch on one last value. It is the value of simple human interest. These poor scraps of mortality were once people; and if we have an ounce of imagination we cannot help wondering when we see them in the unaesthetic but actual flesh, what they were like. How did they live—and how did they die?

Most of the time the last question is impossible to answer. The vicera of almost all mummies were removed and many specimens were damaged by time or tomb robbers. Still, certain of the mummies have a story to tell. The two little mummies of the premature babies found in Tutankhamon's tomb suggest not only a father's disappointed hopes but the fall of a dynasty. (The suggestion that these fetuses represent an otherwise unattested religious ritual is extremely far-fetched.)

Detective story addicts who study the mummies mentioned in a book like Smith and Dawson's may be struck, as I was, by the apparent rarity of violent death. The great exception is the terrible mummy of King Sekenenre, who met an extremely violent end at the time of the Wars of Liberation, when the Theban rulers were beginning to object to the domination of the Hyksos invaders who had ruled part of Egypt. The wounds of ax and club can still be seen on the skull, and the expression on the face suggests that Sekenenre died painfully. Our fancy cannot lead us into overdramatizing Sekenenre's end; assassinated or struck down in battle, this man's death was dramatic.

Since I have a basically evil mind, I suspect that some other Egyptian kings did not die of old age. The histories of various nations, including those of the "enlightened" Western world, indicate that kingship was not the safest of all possible jobs. The royal mummies might not tell the complete story. Some were so badly battered that it is hard to tell whether they once showed signs of a violent attack; and poison, to name only one popular method of assassination, would not leave traces on the bones. It has been suggested that Tutankhamon was a victim of assassination, on the basis of a suspicious-looking hole in his skull. The most recent examination found no evidence of a blow to the head, or even a hole. Tutankhamon did suffer a serious injury to his leg, which might have resulted in infection and death. Not murder, but accident, possibly resulting from his being thrown from his rapidly moving chariot. Another dramatic plot gone west. . . .

Smith and Dawson cite a case of violent death in their classic book and reconstruct a reasonable, and very pitiful, story to explain it. The mummy was that of a girl about sixteen years old. It had not been eviscerated, so the doctors could tell that she was six months pregnant. The probable cause of death was a fractured skull, and both forearms had been broken before death. Drawing on parallel cases from modern times, Smith suggested that the girl was unmarried and that when her condition was discovered by her family, her male relatives proceeded to wipe out the stain on their honor. When she flung up her hands to ward off their blows her wrists were broken, and then the murderers proceeded to beat her to death. It makes a plausible story, although we must state, in all fairness to the ancient Egyptians, that we have no reason to suppose that they had stupid hangups about virginity.

The most mysteriously suggestive of all the mummies known to me was the body of a person who is still unidentified. It was found in 1872 when some lucky peasants stumbled upon a thieves' paradise. In a hidden cache in the cliffs near Thebes lay the bodies of the greatest kings and queens of Egypt, gathered from their desecrated tombs and secretly reburied, for safety, by the rulers of the Twenty-First Dynasty. For some time the happy tomb robbers, worthy descendants of forebears who had practiced the profession for generations, kept the secret of the discovery while marketing objects from their find, but they were eventually caught by the shrewd detective work of the Department of Antiquities, then headed by Gaston Maspero. The cache was opened and the royal mummies taken to the Cairo Museum, where they were examined by experts.

Among the mummies of the bluebloods was one which Maspero ignored at first. Enclosed in a plain white coffin, without name or inscriptions, it seemed hardly worthy of notice, except for the fact that it was "wrapped in a sheepskin of white wool"—an unusual feature. With the change in temperature and humidity, however, the mummy was adversely affected, and eventually it forced itself upon Maspero's attention. He decided it had better be unwrapped at once. At first everything appeared to be normal; within the sheepskin the mummy was wrapped in typical Eighteenth Dynasty style. But as the unwrapping proceeded, the horrified archaeologists realized that this mummy, the body of a young man about five feet ten inches tall, was unlike any other they had seen. The body had never been eviscerated; it was preserved solely by dry natron which had been skillfully distributed on the surface of the body. Everyone who was present at the unwrapping seems to have been powerfully affected by the sight of the face; and, according to Maspero, all assumed immediately that death was the result of a convulsant poison. Maspero even suggested that the wrapping had been begun before life was completely extinct. (This notion has inspired several modern horror novelists and filmmakers.)

It comes as something of an anticlimax to realize, on sober reflection, that perhaps Maspero and his examining physician, Dr. Fouquet, let themselves be carried away just a bit. Of course, there is no way of telling how this miserable wretch died. The faces and bodies of a number of mummies are distorted because of belated or careless handling by the embalmers. When mummy expert Bob Brier recently examined the Unknown Man, he found that the scrap of sheepskin was not large enough to have wrapped the body. Yet the circumstances— the plain unmarked coffin, the sheepskin itself, and the fact, unique among all other mummies in the cache, that the body was not disemboweled—all this does justify a question as to how the man died. There is a mystery, even if it is not a murder mystery. We cannot even put up a reasonable guess as to who the man was. He must have been of high rank or he would not have been included in the cache, and yet the cavalier treatment of the body suggests that he may have been guilty of some crime. Brier and others have theorized that the man may have been a son of Ramses III who conspired to take the throne from his older brother and was caught and condemned; but until now his fate and his identity remain a mystery that not even Sherlock Holmes could unravel.

Of all the qualifications necessary for immortality, a physical simulacrum of the deceased was one of the most important. If we had no other evidence of this belief, the long centuries of scrupulous attention lavished on the corpse would be evidence enough. Admittedly, mummification is a curious custom; and it is a bit disconcerting to travel three thousand years into the past and find ourselves staring at a distorted, but recognizable, version of recent American funerary customs. Although embalming did not disappear entirely until Moslem times in Egypt, some of the early followers of Christ saw the impropriety which seems to elude certain American Christians. St. Anthony, son of a noble Egyptian family, addressed the faithful followers who surrounded him just before his death in these words:

> Permit no man to take my body and carry it into Egypt, lest, according to the custom which they have, they embalm me and lay me up in their houses, for it was to avoid this that I came into the desert. . . . Dig a grave then . . . and hide my body under the earth . . . until the Resurrection of the dead, when I shall receive this body without corruption.

Sixteen

"A GOODLY BURIAL IN THE NECROPOLIS"

TOMBS AND MORTUARY TEMPLES

Once the Egyptian had his mummy, he needed some place to put it. Simpleminded as this may sound, it is the basic reason for a tomb—a place in which the body can be protected. Like Egyptian mummies, Egyptian tombs are the quintessence of the type. Nothing bigger in the way of tombs exists than the Great Pyramid; no ruler's mortuary equipment ever outshone the treasures buried with the pharaohs.

Like those of people everywhere, the earliest Egyptian graves were holes in the ground. The bodies, unembalmed except for the natural action of dry air and sand, lay on their sides with knees drawn up and hands folded before the face, in the attitude of a sleeper or a child in the womb, awaiting birth. (I've always wondered how the Egyptians knew about that last position. Logical inference? There's not room in there for the infant to stretch out.)

As time went on, the holes were tidied up, squared at the corners and lined with mats and planks and bricks. Over the grave pit the earth was piled up in a low mound. As all gardeners know, refilling a hole after you have planted something in it—tree or body—results in extra dirt. According to the accepted theory, this heap of leftover soil or sand came to represent the primeval mound, where the creator god Atum stood and did whatever it was he did to start things moving.

In the two elements, pit and mound, we see the constituents of the later tombs. Archaeologists call the pit the substructure; the superstructure is the part of the tomb that shows aboveground. At the very beginning of the dynasties the Egyptians had developed these two elements into a surprisingly complex and handsome tomb, all the more amazing because of its nearness in time to the prehistoric grave pits. First Dynasty royal tombs at Abydos have substructures consisting of several rooms, with the body in the central, largest room. Surrounding rooms were used for the storage of goods designed for the benefit of the dead. By the Second Dynasty the substructure had developed into an imitation house or palace, complete with bathroom and toilet.

The superstructure was of a type called a mastaba—a flat-topped, rectangular structure with sides that often slope in a bit as they go up. The earliest mastabas, some of which are as large as 180 by 90 feet, were made of brick, with complex niches all around the outside. Later the niching disappeared except for one recess, which developed into a mortuary chapel.

Up to the Third Dynasty there does not seem to have been any stylistic difference between royal tombs and those of the nobility. Djoser and his brilliant architect Imhotep apparently introduced the pyramid as the king's tomb. Djoser's tomb started out as a large mastaba. Several additions extended it out and up, into the first pyramid. It was built in steps, as were others of the period; later ones had the steps filled in to make a smooth-sided structure. The first true pyramid was built by Snefru, the first king of the Fourth Dynasty. Once he got started, he didn't seem to know when to stop. At least three major pyramids are

Reconstruction of niched mastaba

attributed to him, one at Medum and two at Dahshur, and he may have built several other, much smaller, pyramids scattered around Egypt.

It required a certain amount of experimentation to work out the problems of stress and weight that arose when such giant monuments were piled up. The Medum pyramid has lost its shape—it looks like a tower, in several stages—and one of Snefru's pyramids at Dahshur changes the angle of its slope halfway up, perhaps because it had begun to develop structural difficulties. (Maybe that's why Snefru built so many pyramids; it took him a while to get it right.) He and his architects finally succeeded with the second of the Dahshur pyramids, called "the Red."

There was probably a theological reason for the popularity of the

Giza mastabas

type. One of the most plausible theories is that both step pyramid and true pyramid were symbols of the ascent to the regions of Re, where the dead king hoped to go. The Pyramid Texts mention ladders and stairs as methods of ascent, and the step pyramid does resemble the hiero-glyphic sign for a staircase. As for the later pyramids, one ingenious explanation compares their smooth slopes to the slanting rays of the sun—another way of climbing to the celestial regions, according to the Texts. On a cloudy day at Giza the rays of sunlight streaming through rifts in the clouds may take on the appearance of a shining, transpar-ent pyramid of light, with the same angle of slope as those of the three great tombs.

Snefru's successor, Khufu (called Cheops by the Greeks), only built one pyramid, but it was a masterpiece—the largest such struc-ture ever constructed, one of the Seven Wonders of the World, the only Wonder still standing. The two other Giza pyramids belong to Khafre and Menkaure of the same dynasty; they are smaller, but still pretty big.

As we have seen, and will see, the various elements of the pyramid itself and its subsidiary structures had both practical and religious meaning. What they did not have was any relationship whatever to the continent of Atlantis, prophecy, visitors from distant galaxies, or modern mysticism. That is one of the few flat, unqualified statements you will find in this book; I've said it before and I will say it again, since theories of that sort keep popping up, with slight variations, every few years, and people still fall for them. They are like weeds, and Egyptologists feel like frantic gardeners; you can smack the little rascals flat with rational argument, but just turn your back and there they are again.

The pyramid was only one part of the king's funerary complex. The earliest royal tombs at Abydos had separate enclosures, some distance from the tomb, in which (presumably) the mortuary cult was carried on—offerings, ceremonies, and such. The Step Pyramid at Sakkara is surrounded by a complex of other structures that played a part in Djoser's spiritual survival. In its classic form the pyramid complex included two temples, one against the pyramid and one at the edge of the cultivated land, a causeway to connect the two, a small subsidiary pyramid (whose function is still being debated), and other small pyramids for the burial of the king's wives. Stone-lined pits contained huge boats. In 1954 an Egyptian archaeologist, Kamal el Mallakh, found one of these boats in almost perfect condition; it had been partly dismantled, but the wood of which it was built was still sound. These boats have been called sun boats, but it is likely that they have some other significance. The spirits of the dead needed such transportation, for the Land of Eternity had many rivers and lakes. Boat pits have been found in connection with First Dynasty mastabas, so they were not restricted to pyramids. Some rulers had a whole fleet of boats.

The substructure of the pyramid in the Old Kingdom was fairly simple. Like that of the Great Pyramid, it consisted of a shaft going down under or into the superstructure and leading eventually to the burial chamber. The same type continued in the pyramids of the Fifth and Sixth Dynasties, which resemble their predecessors in general plan but not in size or building technique. Rulers of the Fifth and

Sixth Dynasties moved from Giza to other sites near Memphis, notably Sakkara. Their pyramids are shoddy affairs of mixed stone or rubble,
held together by a limestone facing. When the outer layer of stone was
removed by scavengers, chief among whom were kings of later times,
the whole structure slid down into a limp heap. The late Fifth and
Sixth Dynasty royal pyramids are notable for one thing, however—the
famous inscriptions known as the Pyramid Texts on the walls of the
burial chambers.

The mastaba continued to be the most popular type of nonroyal
tomb during the Old Kingdom. One Fourth Dynasty king built his
tomb in this form. It has been suggested that this was a break with the
solar religion, of which the pyramid was the symbol, but we do not
have enough evidence to determine whether or not this theory is
right. At Giza mastabas were built by other Fourth Dynasty kings for
their friends and relations; they were laid out like genuine cities of the
dead, in neat rows, with streets between them. These private tombs
are stone-built and fairly simple, being smooth-sided except for the
enclosed chapel, and having substructures which consisted of a shaft
down into the ground, culminating in a tomb chamber.

The chapel, like the mortuary temple of the royal pyramid, represents the second reason for the building of tombs. The tomb itself
sheltered the body; the chapel allowed for contact with the soul. At
the far end of the small room was a "false door," shaped like a portal
but made of solid stone. The figure of the dead man which was painted
or carved on the door symbolized his coming forth into the regions of
the living in order to enjoy the offerings left for him.

The dead were also represented physically by life-size statues of
stone or wood, painted in vivid colors. The statue was kept in a tiny
room called the serdab, built into the superstructure and walled off
from the outside world except for a small opening high in the wall,
through which the statue could "see." The most famous of the Old
Kingdom private statues came originally from the serdabs. In some
Giza tombs are also found the so-called reserve heads. This idea, that
the heads were meant as "reserves" in case the statue was lost or destroyed, is now questioned; when you come right down to it, a decapi-

tated head isn't a very effective substitute for the whole body, but nobody has come up with an explanation for them that is entirely convincing.

At Giza we also find the first of a new type of tomb which was to become as important as the mastaba—the rock-cut tomb. In one sense, of course, all tombs were rock-cut in part; the substructure went down into the ground. But the real rock-cut variety has no superstructure, only a room or series of rooms cut into a cliff face. As the Egyptians were to discover, rock-cut tombs had one great advantage over the type with a superstructure. They were not so conspicuous. As far back as the Fourth Dynasty, when King Khufu buried his mother in a deep, unmarked shaft near the causeway of his pyramid, he and his associates must have been aware of the need for secrecy; it is thought (by some people, not me) that the queen's original tomb had already been plundered, and that this was a reburial. Khufu could not know that his pious undertaking would survive forty centuries untouched; the hidden tomb was not discovered until A.D. 1925. But it is hard to understand why he would have sought such security for his mother, and then have himself buried in a monument that was visible for miles in every direction.

It was almost a millennium later before the kings of Egypt learned the painful lesson that secrecy was preferable to bombast in tomb building. Even the earlier private rock-cut tombs sometimes defeated this advantage by adding porticos and courtyards and chapels—an "X marks the spot" for any interested tomb robber, of whom there were multitudes.

By the Fifth and Sixth Dynasties private mastabas had become very large and elaborate. You could get lost in the tomb of Mereruka, who served as vizier under King Teti of the Sixth Dynasty. Several rooms were added to serve the burials of his wife and son, and the walls were covered with beautiful reliefs. Not only are the reliefs aesthetically pleasing, but they offer invaluable information on Egyptian life, since they depict the activities in which a wealthy man of that period engaged.

During the First Intermediate Period the country broke up into a number of separate states. With the collapse of royal power the kings' tombs diminished so thoroughly that they have practically disappeared; they were still pyramids, but that is about all we can say of them. Conversely, tombs of local chiefs, or nomarchs, became more elaborate; some of the handsomest are the rock-cut tombs of Beni Hassan, with their fine pillared porticos. The reliefs of these tombs and others of the same period have given us some of the most delightfully animated of all scenes of daily life—children playing, vigorous dancers, and wonderful, lively animals—but the technique of painting and carving is sometimes crude compared with the delicate sophistication of the Old Kingdom reliefs.

When the reunification of the country was begun by the vigorous Theban rulers of the Eleventh Dynasty, the royal tombs adopted a new style. A great courtyard (called a saff) was dug into the cliff on the west bank of Thebes. It ended in a rock-cut facade surmounted by a small brick pyramid—no longer a tomb in itself, for the king was buried underground, beneath and behind the rock face. It was at one of these Eleventh Dynasty tombs that Maspero found the stela of Intef and his five dogs—the Cook Pot, Blackie, the Gazelle, and the others.

Very little remains of these tombs today, but one can still make out the badly damaged foundations of the greatest Eleventh Dynasty tomb, which was built by the first of the kings of this dynasty. His name was Mentuhotep Nebhepetre—the man who completed the reunification and brought all of Egypt under a single king for the first time in many years. It stood against the western cliffs of Thebes in the same bay of Deir el Bahri where Hatshepsut would later construct a bigger and better temple. Mentuhotep's structure was impressive and unusual, though, for its time; when it still stood, in all its glory, it must have been one of the handsomest buildings in Thebes. A courtyard, filled with the waving green branches of tamarisk and fig trees, ended in a ramp which led up to a monumental colonnaded portico. Atop this was another set of colonnades, and surmounting the whole a pyramid lifted up toward the sky. Or maybe it was a mound instead of a pyramid—there isn't enough left to be certain. The prevailing theory favors the latter, but by the time this book is published experts may have changed their minds again. The king's tomb was under the temple, and behind the pyramid another court and a pillared hall served his mortuary cult.

Mentuhotep buried several of his wives in or near the temple, so that they could accompany him into the West. The tomb of Queen Neferu, later a tourist attraction, was one of them, and six other ladies found their last resting places within the temple precincts. One of them was a rather pitiful case; within the big, adult-size coffin lay the body of a little girl only five years old, wearing the pretty necklaces with which she had dressed up during her brief lifetime. Her name was Mayet—"Kitty." But of the king, her husband—or, surely, husband-to-be—there was no trace.

Pyramids continued to be royal tombs during the Twelfth Dynasty. The "substructure," inside the pyramid now instead of under it, became infinitely complicated, a real labyrinth of corridors and hidden chambers. The Labyrinth itself, mentioned by Strabo and other Greek tourists, was perhaps the mortuary temple of one of these Twelfth Dynasty pyramids. It covered an area greater than that of the temple of Karnak, but nothing remains of it today except acres of stone chips on the ground. The Middle Kingdom pyramids were built, in part, out of stones pilfered from earlier royal tombs. The Twelfth Dynasty kings got what was coming to them; later generations treated their pyramids in the same way, and today there is not much left of the tombs—and nothing of the men who built them.

For private tombs, rock-cut types continued through the Middle Kingdom and Second Intermediate Period. In this latter period the country again fell into political anarchy, assisted, perhaps, by the mysterious invaders from Asia who are called the Hyksos. These people, whose origins are still debated, adopted Egyptian customs, including their burial habits.

The Eighteenth Dynasty marks the beginning of the New Kingdom, with another unification of the country under Theban kings, and with a dramatic change in royal burials. The lesson that should have been obvious centuries before finally sank in, reinforced, perhaps, by an increase in tomb robbing as a result of the breakdown of royal power—the failure of massive monuments to fulfill their major function, the protection of the royal body. The most logical conclusion would have been the practicality of a humble burial, without the gold and rich oils that tempted the poor tomb robbers. But royal majesty and human pride could not face such a decision. They strove to attain safety through secrecy.

There is something about royal tombs that grabs the imagination, even of us believers in democracy. Egyptian kings were buried in a number of different places, including some I'll bet you've near heard of—Zawaiyet el Aryan, Mazghuna, Tanis, Abu Roash, Abusir. However, the two biggies are unquestionably Giza and the Valley of the Kings at Thebes.

Actually there are two valleys, the East and the West. The East Valley is the one where the great majority of the tombs are located. It contains sixty-three tombs, the last having been located in 2005 by a team of American excavators. (Or, to be entirely accurate, sixty-three tombs have been discovered thus far; I agree with those who think the Valley still contains unknown tombs.) Not all are kings' tombs, and not all are decorated or even finished, but they include the burial places of the great pharaohs of the New Kingdom.

The architect of King Thutmose I boasted that he had excavated his king's tomb in secret—"No one hearing, no one seeing." A slight exaggeration, to say the least. The men who worked on the tomb—stonecutters, painters, draftsmen, sculptors—knew its location; so did their friends and families and anybody who wanted to look on. The idea that the workmen were summarily executed after they had finished the job is pure fiction. That would have been impractical, time-consuming, and a waste of skilled labor.

The tombs themselves are pretty much the same. Most Egyptologists would howl at that statement; they have produced detailed analyses of the orientation and internal arrangement of royal tombs. Ah, well, perhaps I had better go into more detail.

Except for the extraordinary tomb of "King" Hatshepsut, which burrows and squirms almost seven hundred feet into the gebel, royal tombs of the Eighteenth Dynasty are comparatively simple. (Compared to later tombs, that is.) A flight of stonecut steps led down to a series of passages and chambers dug into the cliffs. Some of the entrances to the tombs are easily accessible; others, like that of Thutmose III, are high up in the cliff and must have been reached by wooden stairs which were later demolished. The most famous of all the tombs in the Valley, that of Tutankhamon, is much smaller than the tombs of greater pharaohs and may have been taken over from another, nonroyal owner when the king died at the early age of eighteen.

It is possible that the young king had begun a tomb in the West Valley, where his grandfather (I'm sticking to that) Amenhotep III had excavated his own tomb. Tutankhamon's immediate predecessor, Akhenaton, started his own royal valley at Tell el Amarna, where his tomb may still be seen, if you fancy a three-mile walk or know somebody who owns an all-terrain vehicle. Except for minor variations, the plan resembles that of earlier royal tombs. There's nothing in it today. The theory is that after the court had moved back to Thebes the inhabitants of the Amarna tombs were also moved, for safekeeping.

Isometric plan of tomb of Amenhotep III

The only other finished royal tomb in the West Valley at Thebes belongs to Ay, Tutankhamon's successor. The Ramesside rulers returned to the East Valley. The most impressive tomb is that of Seti I. It is over three hundred feet long and is beautifully decorated with scenes of the king being welcomed and protected by various gods. Perhaps the most unusual tomb in the Valley is KV5 (tomb number five in the Valley of the Kings, that is), which appears to be a multiple burial of the sons of that industrious progenitor Ramses II. So far the excavator, Kent Weeks, has found over one hundred rooms, and he's still looking.

The Ramesside kings no longer attempted to conceal the entrances to their tombs. In earlier times the portals were closed by walls of mortared stone, and sometimes the entrance stairs and corridors were filled with rubble. Ramesside tombs closed the entrances with wooden doors and decorated the jambs and lintels.

Ramses II had so many offspring that he had to double (quadruple, sextuple) them up. Other princes had their own tombs, some in the King's Valley, some in the so-called Valley of the Queens. What about the queens? That's a good question. Some tombs, like that of Amenhotep III and the royal tomb at Amarna, have separate rooms, or suites of rooms, which may have been intended for the burials of the royal ladies, but Hatshepsut had a separate tomb of her own as queen, even before she took over the throne and dug herself another one in the Valley of the Kings, and the jewel-like tomb of Nefertari Merenmut, wife of Ramses II, was hers alone. It is in the Valley of the Queens, along with those of other royal ladies and princes of the later dynasties, but the burial places of most of the royal ladies of the Eighteenth Dynasty have not been located, and neither have the mummies of many of them. Egyptologists are still looking.

Even the hidden tombs were robbed, perhaps by the very workers who had constructed them. Only one survived the ages, and it did not go unmolested; there is evidence, in Tutankhamon's tomb, of two successive attempts by robbers who succeeded in making off with some of the contents. The only thing that saved it from being stripped was the fact that, in a later period, workmen's huts were built over it by a king who was constructing his own tomb nearby, and the location of Tutankhamon's last resting place was forgotten. However, the tomb robbers have recently found defense lawyers. Recent studies suggest that the final stripping of the royal burial equipment may have been done by priests of a later dynasty, under the direction of the king himself. This notion sheds a different light on the "pious priests" who tenderly rewrapped and recoffined the battered remains of earlier monarchs; they did, but not until after the last scraps of gold and other recyclable wealth had been removed to the royal treasury.

Since the hidden tombs in the Valley of the Kings had no external chapels, the kings' mortuary cults were served by separate temples, built on the edge of the cultivation near the river. Most of them are in ruins today. That of Amenhotep III survives only in the gigantic and sadly battered Colossi of Memnon, which once guarded the pylon gates. Like the humble chapels of the private tombs, the royal funerary temples served the cult of the dead and were as necessary for the dead man's resurrection as was his tomb. Here the offerings were made which would give him nourishment in the next world. The royal mortuary temples also served as homes for the gods. At Hatshepsut's temple there were shrines to Amon, Anubis, and Hathor.

Hatshepsut's temple is a masterpiece and, according to many, the finest of all Egyptian temples. It resembles the Eleventh Dynasty temple-tomb of Mentuhotep, having a series of colonnaded terraces which rise up in several levels toward the cliffs behind it. Comparisons are invidious, since most of Mentuhotep's complex is gone, but it's hard to believe his could have been as elegant as hers. The two structures, now more or less side by side, differed in function; Hatshepsut was not buried in her temple, though it has been suggested that she originally intended to push her tomb in the Valley of the Kings clear under the mountain, with its burial chamber under the temple. Maybe not. It was heading in the right direction, but the undertaking would have been impractical.

A more typical temple is the one belonging to Ramses III, which is now called Medinet Habu. It has the elements we have already described as characteristic of the standard religious edifice: pylon, enclosing wall, pillared courts, and sanctuary. The temples of Seti I and Ramses II (the Ramesseum) are of the same type.

After the Twentieth Dynasty the royal necropolis was moved from Thebes to Tanis, in the Delta. The royal tombs in this city were built within the temple precincts; they are sad degenerations of the great rock-cut tombs of Thebes, but a few of them went unrobbed until the twentieth century A.D. They yielded up an astonishing amount of precious metal in the form of coffins, vessels, and gorgeous jewelry. Much of it probably came from the burials in the Valley of the Kings.

Even before pyramids were abandoned by royalty they were, like other kingly elements of the mortuary cult, taken over by commoners. Some of the little mastabas of the Middle Kingdom at Abydos have diminutive pyramids of brick perched on top of them—how art the mighty fallen! Private tombs at Deir el Medina, the workmen's town of the New Kingdom, also had small pyramids. The Nubian pharaohs of the Twenty-Fifth Dynasty took the pyramid form back with them to Cush; the pyramid fields of Napata and Meroe are the last survivors of the form.

Deir el Medina tombs

Back in Egypt the rock-cut and free-standing tombs of the New Kingdom had become very elaborate, with courts and porches, all handsomely decorated. The king's official residence was at Memphis, and although he was always taken back to Thebes, to the Valley, for burial, many of his officials built large, temple-type tombs in one or another of the Memphite cemeteries.

Early in the nineteenth century some of these great New Kingdom tombs were discovered by Karl Lepsius, the indefatigable German scholar whose survey of Egyptian monuments was published in a series of enormous volumes. One has to give the man credit for being ahead of his time insofar as accuracy and thoroughness were concerned; but the museums of Europe were greedy for artifacts, and Lepsius had to satisfy his sponsors. He may not have been the one responsible, but by one means or another a number of beautiful carved blocks and statues from these tombs ended up in museums, and the tombs themselves were left to be buried by the ever-encroaching sand.

A hundred and twenty years later an English Egyptologist, Geoffrey Martin, observed large, rectangular depressions in the area south of the causeway of the pyramid of Unas at Sakkara. He was, of course, well acquainted with Lepsius's work, and he finally persuaded the Service des Antiquités to allow a joint expedition of British and Dutch scholars to look for Lepsius's lost tombs. One he hoped to find was that of Maya, Tutankhamon's treasurer, who was well known from other sources, including a magnificent, life-size dyad (double statue) of Maya and his beautiful wife Merit in the Museum of Leyden. Lepsius had made a map, but as the excavators were to discover, it wasn't as accurate as it might have been. When you are shifting tons of sand, being a few yards off can make quite a difference. Maya's tomb wasn't where it was supposed to be, but the excavators were not disappointed; they hit on the tomb of Harmhab, another of Tutankhamon's advisers, who built himself a royal tomb in the Valley of the Kings after he claimed the throne.

Maya's tomb turned up a few years later, by which time the excavators had found the burials of several other officials and princes. These great private tombs had burial shafts under superstructures consisting of chapels and colonnaded courtyards and pylons. Though piteously despoiled, they yielded fragments of carved and painted relief of breathtaking beauty. Some of the missing sections could be restored, using casts of the blocks that had been looted by Lepsius and others and given to various museums. There's always a silver lining. . . .

Martin believes that there are at least thirty-eight more great tombs out there under the sand. And that's just one part of one cemetery.

Theban tombs of high officials become very pretentious; that of a man named Pedamenopet is a miniature brick temple up above. The substructure, below the temple, contained a court, many rooms, stairs, and long corridors. During the Saite or Twenty-Sixth Dynasty, there was a curious development in decoration. So great was the admiration of the men of this time for the wonders of their country's past that they copied not only scenes but whole tombs of the Old and Middle Kingdoms in their own burial places. Some are done so well that it is hard to tell which is a copy and which the original.

The tomb builders of this period at some of the Memphite cemeteries came up with an ingenious solution for the protection of the mummy. A series of passages, vertical and horizontal, surrounded the sarcophagus chamber. After the burial, props were knocked out of the openings, so that sand flowed into the passages, completely filling them and the burial chamber. If a thief wanted to get at the mummy he had to excavate the whole tomb. Astonishingly enough, some of them did.

SARCOPHAGI, COFFINS, AND OTHER BARE NECESSITIES

One thing leads to another. As tombs got more elaborate, coffins and other equipment went from bad to worse—if we look at the process from the point of view that coffins are pure vanity.

Next to the tomb, the coffin itself was the most important piece of equipment. The oldest coffins are plain boxes of wood, just big enough to hold a body in the contracted position then in vogue. As the body was extended, so was the coffin; by the Middle Kingdom it had become a sophisticated piece of carpentry painted inside and out with pictures and texts. The Herakleopolitan coffins, from a period just before the Middle Kingdom, show how elaborate the type could be. One important motif was the pair of eyes painted on one side of the coffin opposite the spot where the eyes of the corpse would be as it lay on its right side. The texts on these coffins—called, logically enough, the Coffin Texts—now fill six fat printed volumes. Not every coffin had all the texts; each bore a sort of anthology of the owner's favorites. Ultimately the texts derive from the Pyramid Texts of the Old Kingdom, although some spells have been discarded and new ones have been added.

A new fashion in coffins came in during the Second Intermediate Period with the adoption, by kings and commoners alike, of the type now thought of as typically Egyptian—the anthropoid, or human-shaped, coffin. For men and women, king and humble scribe, the form was the same: that of a wrapped mummy figure with a linen headdress. The earliest anthropoid coffins are of the so-called rishi type; the word means "feathered," and it appropriately describes the decoration, which looks like wings spread protectively over the body. The rishi type died out, to be replaced by the coffin with bands of inscriptions and rows of miniature scenes or divine figures. These continued until late times, but the rishi type survived in certain royal coffins, such as those of Tutankhamon, where the delicately inlaid feathering takes on real beauty of technique and conception. The sweep of the wide wings, those of a protecting goddess, eloquently represents her tender care of the dead.

We would know very little about royal burial equipment were it not for the fabulous discovery, by Lord Carnarvon and Howard Carter, of Tutankhamon's tomb. From it we learn that kings of this period had not one but three coffins. Although they were made of wood, Tutankhamon's outer coffins are miracles of the jeweler's art, covered with sheet gold and marvelously inlaid. The innermost coffin had to be seen to be believed; it was 2,448 pounds of solid gold. That this incredible coffin was not unique we may deduce from late royal burials at Tanis. At this period royal power had declined tremendously, and yet Psusennes, an undistinguished pharaoh of the Twenty-First Dynasty, could still amass enough wealth to make his innermost coffin of solid silver. We must always remember, in assessing Tutankhamon's equipment, that it was that of a minor king who not only died young but who lived at a time when the imperial revenues from Asia were comparatively low. Sometimes I dream of the impossible and imagine finding the tomb of a king such as Amenhotep III still intact—the tomb of a king who had over thirty years to prepare his equipment and the resources of Nubia and Asia with which to pay for it. This can never happen except in dreams; the tomb of Amenhotep the Magnificent is rifled and empty, as are the other known tombs of the mightiest rulers of Egypt.

Tutankhamon's tomb not only demonstrates the incredible wealth with which pharaohs were buried, but it illustrates the Chinese-box character of these burials. The three coffins, nested one inside the other, were all contained inside a sarcophagus. The sarcophagus, as distinct from the coffin, was of stone—often wonderful stone such as quartzite and granite. Sarcophagi had to be big to hold a body and three coffins; they are so heavy, weighing in tons, that even the masterful tomb robbers of Thebes, who ought to be made patron saints of the burglaring profession, could not carry them off. I am sure they would have stolen them if they could have moved them; they stole everything else. The weight of the sarcophagi explains why we have a number of them with us today, while the coffins and the mummies which once lay within them have disappeared.

Few commoners could afford a sarcophagus; they usually had to settle for a coffin, and for only one of those. Royal sarcophagi go back a long way, at least to the Third Dynasty. In the earliest time they were plain stone boxes, with separate lids of equally heavy stone. One exceptional Third Dynasty sarcophagus had, instead of a lid on top, a sliding panel at one end. By the New Kingdom, sarcophagi were covered with bands of inscription and with carved figures of the divinities who protected the dead.

Tutankhamon had three coffins, a sarcophagus, and three shrines—seven layers of physical protection, not counting the walls of the tomb itself. Yet the physical protection of the body was only one part of the mortuary cult, and most of the objects placed in the tomb served another purpose.

Originally a tomb may have been just a hole to hold the body, but its walls came to be used for texts and pictures designed to equip the dead with magical substitutes for the objects he would need in the hereafter and to guide him through the prescribed rituals to various gods. A coffin could also kill two birds with one stone: enclosing the body and bearing still more magical texts. The anthropoid coffin itself was a simulacrum of the dying god Osiris, with whom the dead man was identified so that he could share in the death and glorious resurrection of the god.

Among the specifically funerary objects placed in the tomb, one of the most important was the structure which contained the viscera, removed from the body during the process of embalming. In the Late Period the embalmed entrails were replaced in the body, but before that, beginning in the Old Kingdom, they were put into four pots called canopic jars, which in turn were enclosed in a canopic box or shrine. The canopic jars have a characteristic shape; at first they had plain stoppers, but later these were superseded by lids in the form of portrait heads of the deceased. One of the loveliest sets of these lids was found in the so-called Tomb of Queen Tiye. It was first thought to be a portrait of Akhenaton, then of Smenkhkare; now scholars believe it is the head of a lady of the Amarna Period, possibly Akhenaton's eldest daughter, Princess Meritaton or—the latest idea—his wife Kiye. Whoever it is, he or she was very handsome.

Instead of "portrait" heads, the later canopic jars have the heads of the four mortuary genii, the sons of Horus—baboon, jackal, hawk, and human. Each of them protected specific organs of the body. The canopic shrine, in which the jars were placed, also had a standard shape, and as one might expect, the most elegant known is that of Tutankhamon. To me it is one of the loveliest objects ever found in

Canopic jars

Egypt, with its four protective goddesses standing with outspread arms on each side of the gilded box.

Food, shelter, and clothing, the three basic necessities, were provided for. The tomb gave physical shelter, and there was a formula which promised the spirit the means to build a house in Paradise. Tomb paintings of houses were another form of insurance. Middle Kingdom and First Intermediate tombs included house models, some of them delightful little miniatures of a rich nobleman's estate. As for clothing, we have seen the extent and richness of Tutankhamon's wardrobe. But if these could be provided for, why not other things that would make the next life even more pleasant?

ALL THE COMFORTS OF HOME

Jars of fine oil, perfumes, and unguents were highly desired gifts for the living and hence for the dead; they were also irresistible to tomb robbers, who sometimes brought little leather bags so that they could raid the contents of the heavy oil jars. All the amusements were provided for; a hunter had his bows and arrows, boomerangs and daggers. Women took into the tomb their elaborate toilet tables, complete with an extra wig or switch of false hair. More indolent men took their game boards along.

Human sacrifice died out in Egypt at the beginning of the dynasties. Since slaughtered servants were de trop, the Egyptians provided for their services as they provided for other necessities—by magical substitutes. In the Old Kingdom the wall paintings which showed scenes of daily life included multitudes of servants, making bread, reaping grain, carrying offerings, combing their mistresses' hair, and dancing for the amusement of their masters. In the First Intermediate Period and Middle Kingdom, when models came into style, we find charming little groups of miniature workers going about their chores. But the most enduring answer to the "servant problem" was one which has filled museum cases all over the world—the little human figurines called ushebtis or shawabtis or shabtis. They are made of all sorts of materials, from cheap faience to gilded wood, and represent all degrees of skill, from crude figures just recognizable as human to beautiful little statuettes. All were designed to satisfy the same need—the need to avoid doing any work in heaven. Written somewhere on the figure was a text, another of the standardized mortuary formulae:

O thou ushebti! If the deceased [So-and-so] is appointed to do any work which a man does in the necropolis—to cultivate the fields, to irrigate the banks, to transport sand of the East to the West—"Here am I!" thou shalt say.

This is really an admirable thought; I suppose the only reason it hasn't occurred to us is because we don't expect *anyone* to work in paradise.

Most of the objects placed in the tomb can be interpreted as pleasures the dead man hoped to go on enjoying. Some attempts have been made to find a symbolic meaning for each of them. The weapons represent the battle against the enemies of Re, the game board stands for the struggle between the powers of good and the powers of evil, and so on. Of course, we can find a deeper significance in almost any object if we try hard enough; I don't recall that anyone has explained the symbolism of the cosmetic box, but I feel sure it could be done. Even the little female figurines with the decorations emphasizing the pubic region have been described as "fertility goddesses," or, more ponderously,

"figures evocative of the female principle," which symbolized the rebirth of the dead man, procreated by himself.

Interpretations of this nature may do more credit to the fertile
imagination of the interpreter than to the speculative habits of the
Egyptians. In particular, the habit of finding fertility symbols scattered
all over the cultural landscape seems to be spreading from some
schools of prehistorians into Egyptology. The other day, while reading
a book on prehistoric religion, I ran across a statement which seems to
me to represent the ultimate absurdity of this type of argument. The
author denied, indignantly, that a certain object found in a Paleolithic
context could be a phallic symbol. Paleolithic man, said the author—
probably correctly—knew nothing about the male role in procreation.
How then, he demanded, could a phallus be an object of worship?

I am sorry to say that this naive statement brought an unladylike
grin to my face. Certain Christian doctrines insist that the procreation of children is the only legitimate aim of the sexual act; my prehis-
torian wants to go the theologians one better, by maintaining that it
is the only aim. Surely it is nonsense to suppose that this abstruse
doctrine was held by Paleolithic, or any other ancient, people. I am
not completely convinced that at some times and under some circumstances the little naked ladies were not "magical concubines." Every
other need and desire was provided for, why not that one?

Another magical object found in many tombs was the Osiris bed,
or "germinated Osiris figure," as it is called. A silhouette of the god
was made out of wood and filled with rich earth; seeds were planted in
the dirt and watered, so that when the figure was placed in the tomb it
was a green, living symbol of the resurrection of god and man. The
popular but erroneous notion of "mummy seeds" may have had its origin in these figures. Like the mummies of men and women, the seeds
found in ancient tombs have never known a physical resurrection.

It is literally impossible to describe all the objects found in the
tombs; the single burial of Tutankhamon included hundreds of separate items, and even private tombs of well-to-do persons were well
stocked with furniture, linens, and ornaments. We ought to mention,
though, some of the things found on the mummy itself. One impor-

tant object, in vogue from the late Old Kingdom down to Christian times, was the mask placed over the head of the dead man. Tutankhamon's mask was gold, and it is a gorgeous piece of work, like everything else he owned. Common masks were of the cartonnage type, made of layers of linen coated with plaster or stucco and molded while wet. They covered the whole head, not just the face. These helmet-type masks continued, off and on, into Ptolemaic times, along with other variations; but by the Roman period the three-dimensional mask was often replaced by a portrait painted on wood or linen.

The mummy was richly furnished with jewelry of various types—which led, inevitably, to the destruction of the precious body by hasty tomb robbers. The most popular piece of jewelry, in death as in life, was the broad collar made of beads or semiprecious stones. Not all the jewelry placed in the tomb had been worn; some was so fragile that it could only have been designed for the inactive dead. Bracelets, collars, and rings might be purely ornamental in purpose, but some jewelry had a specific religious meaning. The broad vulture collars symbolized the care and love of the goddess Mut, and various amulets stood for particular qualities the dead hoped to be endowed with.

The most important amulet was the heart scarab; after the Middle Kingdom all mummies of any pretensions had them. The scarab amulets are well known; they are still being sold to tourists, and 99.99 percent of them are modern fakes. The heart scarabs were bigger than the usual variety, and according to the magical texts, they ought to be made of a dark green stone. On the flat base there was a short inscription from the Book of the Dead.

There are dozens of other amulets, some made of metal, some of faience, some of stone. They were hung around the neck or tied to the wrist or to another part of the body. Some took the shape of Bes and Taweret, the hideous but beloved household gods, and others were made in the shape of hieroglyphic signs which signified life, stability, health, and other desirable attributes. A particularly vital amulet was the "Horus eye." It recalled the loss of the young god's eye during the battle against his father's murderer, and it was the symbol par excellence of offering to the dead.

FUNERARY RITUAL

But coffin, tomb, and sarcophagus were only necessary prerequisites to immortality. They were not sufficient in themselves. A soul had to be fashioned out of the dead husk of the corpse.

Perhaps this process began with the embalming, but we have only a vague idea of the rites performed during the process of mummification. The vital ceremony was part of the funeral service; so let us see what happened after the mummy had been restored to the sorrowing family.

On the day of the funeral, a long procession set out for the tomb. Leading it was the mummy, on a sledge topped by an open shrine and pulled by oxen. Friends and relatives of the dead man lent a hand on the ropes, and the chief female mourners—wife and daughter, or wife and mother—walked at the head and foot of the bier. Priests accompanied the hearse. Other mourners walked behind, and all of them, male and female, expressed their grief in dramatic gestures. The women, as they were expected to do, exhibited less self-control than the men; with garments torn and streaming hair, they poured dust on their heads and cried aloud. When there were not enough women in the family to make a goodly show, or when the survivors wanted to be pretentious, professional female mourners were hired. Naturally they outshouted the ladies of the family, and the reliefs show them with rows of symmetrical tears flowing down their cheeks onto the ground. One painted scene depicts a little girl apprentice among the professionals; she seems to have considerable aptitude for the trade, and she always makes me think of poor little Oliver Twist, who made such a handsome mute—especially for children's funerals.

Following the mourners came servants carrying food, furniture, and chests containing clothing and other grave-goods. Another small sledge held the canopic box, with the four jars containing the entrails.

In essence the funeral ritual was a recapitulation of the Osiris legend, and an identification of the dead man with the god. The coffin itself was made in the Osiris shape. The two mourning women who

The tekenu

accompanied the bier represented Isis and Nephthys, weeping for their husband and brother. However, there are several elements of the ritual which do not obviously fit in with the Osiris cult, and which are still mysteries.

One of them is the strange figure called the tekenu. In some funeral scenes it is only a muffled, ambiguous shape resting on a sledge drawn by two men. Other scenes show it more clearly—it seems to be a man wrapped in a cloth or skin, seated or lying in a doubled-up position.

What function does this peculiar personage play in the funeral ritual? No one knows exactly. To some scholars the pose suggests the fetal position and the tekenu represents the rebirth of the dead man into eternal life. Others see in it a symbolic survival of ancient human sacrifice—a shedding of blood to give strength to the strengthless dead—which may have been practiced in prehistoric Egypt. It has also been suggested that the bundle contains the leftovers from materials used to embalm the body, which were given a separate burial. The tekenu had a short period of popularity; there is no sign of it—or him—in the Old Kingdom scenes, but then these are not normally

Muu dancers

scenes of funerals. For the present the tekenu must remain one of those lost Egyptian mysteries that the occultists are so fond of.

When the funeral procession had toiled up to the desert plateau and reached the tomb, it was met by another unusual group—the muu dancers. These men were distinguished by strange crowns of reeds, whose shape and material strongly suggest the royal White Crown of Upper Egypt. There ought to be some clue in this as to the origin and function of the dancers; but in fact none of the theories suggested by it really sound convincing. The dancers performed a weird, jigging dance, something like a Highland fling with finger snapping.

After the dance the mummy was lifted from the sledge and propped up in a standing position before the door of the tomb. The ceremony of the "Opening of the Mouth" was about to begin. It was conducted by the Sem or Setem priest, with his distinctive leopard-skin mantle and shaven head. First, the mummy was sprinkled with water and censed.

Sacrifices of various animals were made. Then came the heart of the ceremony, the touching of various parts of the body with specially designed instruments which would restore the lost senses of the mummy. The mouth, as the organ of speech and of nourishment, was of particular importance. More censing and incense burning followed, and then the funerary meal was served; the dead man now had power to partake of it, and he was joined by his living relatives and close friends. It is significant that the "Opening of the Mouth" could be performed on a statue as well as on the mummy; as long as some physical representation of the dead man was operated on, his nonphysical aspect received the benefits of the operation.

A new soul had been born. The members of the bereaved family, turning away to return to their homes, must have felt a lightening of their sorrow as they thought of the newly hatched spirit, safely launched on the beautiful roads of the West, where they would one day join it—but not, they hoped, too very soon.

The act of rebirth was completed. But the newborn soul, like a newborn child, had to be kept alive. If we could visit the tomb once again, on the day after the funeral, we would find that the burial chamber had been sealed. But one part of the tomb was still accessible, and there certain activities were going on. Inside the painted chapel a priest deposited loaves of fresh bread and jars of water on the low altar. Every day of the year, from now to forever, the dead man was fed at this altar.

Food and drink were always buried with the dead. The poor man had a few jars filled with beer and some loaves of bread. The royal dead dined sumptuously—jars of vintage wines, haunches of beef, cakes, and the finest white bread were piled in heaps in the storage chambers of their tombs. But it was necessary to renew the food supply when it was used up, and so the funerary offering was instituted.

In theory the offering was made by the devoted son of the dead man, playing Horus to his Osiris, just as the son was responsible for all the other necessities of his father in the world to come. Some sons were as pious and dutiful about these responsibilities as they were supposed to be. In one inscription a man tells us that he caused himself to be buried in the same tomb as his father, not—and I love this touch of sinful human pride—because he could not perfectly well afford a tomb of his own, but because he loved his father so much that he wanted to be with him always. Still, human nature being what it is— and was—the wise Egyptian took steps to remove temptation from his offspring by providing for as many of his postmortem necessities as he could while he could. Among these necessities was a daily food offering, and this was arranged by formal contract.

The contracts were made with ka-priests like old Hekanakhte, whom we have already met; they agreed to substitute for the pious son, who naturally had no time to go traipsing over to his father's tomb every morning. Early in the game the methodical Egyptians formalized the problem of mortuary contracts, and some tomb owners had copies of them written on the walls of the tomb. The language of the texts is rather amusing, for its dry, legal tone seems far removed from the lofty business of immortality. Some contracts list not only the days on which offerings are to be made, but the precise number of loaves and jars which must be given. On festivals and holy days, extra food was provided.

A rich man might endow his tomb with five fields and their produce; a king could leave the riches of a dozen towns. The offerings themselves were not the only expenses involved, for the "wages" of the priest and his family also came out of the total. Such wages were paid in goods, since there was no money in pharaonic Egypt.

By now the economics majors among my readers are probably trying to calculate how long it would be before the entire national economy was sunk in tombs and tomb maintenance. It would not have taken long if the contracts had actually been honored; they provided for food "in perpetuity." Luckily for society, if not for morality, there was a constant redistribution of wealth. Time passed, families died out, and the contracts quietly lapsed. Or else there was a change in dynasty, or confiscation, and contracts were reabsorbed into the treasury. Another class of people helped to keep the wealth in circulation, although the kings who gobbled up old mortuary contracts would have resented being compared with them—the tomb robbers. Something good can be said about them after all.

The Egyptians were well aware of this process. They knew that if their tombs were maintained for a century they were lucky. So what did they do? If the actual loaves of bread stopped coming, they could be replaced by magical substitutes. The tomb paintings which show rows of comely young women carrying food were magical insurance against the failing of forgetful ka-priests; so were the loaded offering tables which are depicted on tomb walls, stelae, and funerary slabs. A second line of defense in case of neglect was a written list. This became a formula; it is probably the best known of all Egyptian texts to beginning students, who can rattle it off with their eyes closed or read it glibly off the wall of any tomb. I have often done this to impress my non-Egyptological friends; I don't do it for Egyptologists, because they know the formulae are all alike.

The offering formula goes something like this: "A boon which the king gives, to Osiris, Lord of Abydos [or some other god], that he give invocation offerings of bread and beer, oxen and fowl, alabaster and clothing, and every good and pure thing for the ka of the venerated [So-and-so]."

The process seems unnecessarily complicated; the king pays Osiris or some other god who then makes the offerings to the ka of the dead man. Occasionally the king's "boon" may have been a real offering, made for a favorite courtier, but by the Middle Kingdom these formulae are inscribed for all sorts of people, including "nobodies" whom the Lord of the Two Lands did not know existed. The term translated "invocation offerings" is extremely significant; it means "a going-forth of the voice," and it suggests that the boon is a purely magical offering, a supply of spiritual food through the power of the spoken word. Although the lists of offerings vary, they include the staples of the Egyptian diet, beginning with the basic bread and beer; and they end with one of the typically Egyptian "et ceteras" to cover anything that might have been overlooked.

There was a last line of defense against spiritual starvation, in case all the others failed. Some tombs carry an inscription which appeals to passersby—to any casual stranger who might be strolling in the vicinity of the tomb:

Oh you who live and exist, who love life and hate death, who
shall pass by this tomb: as you love life and hate death, so shall
you offer to me that which is in your hands. If there is nothing
in your hands, you shall speak thus: "A thousand of bread and
beer, of oxen and geese, of alabaster and linen—a thousand of
all good and pure things, for the venerated [So-and-so]."

Inscriptions like this fill me with mingled pity and admiration—pity
for the resigned acceptance of human frailty, which can visualize the
necessity for such a desperate last resort, and admiration for the deter-
mination which refuses to give up the ghost—or rather, the means of
maintaining the ghost.

Seventeen

"ON THAT DAY OF JUDGING THE DEFICIENT"

BOOKS OF THE DEAD

B etween the time when the newborn soul left the tomb and the moment when it settled down amid the comforts provided for it in the Land of Eternity, it had a long and dangerous journey to make. In order to reach the West the dead man had to cross water; for this he needed a boat. Perhaps there was a ferry; if so, the ferryman might prove hostile or indifferent. He would have to be bribed, or coerced, or wheedled into carrying the spirit across.

All along the way the dead man was beset by demons. If not properly handled, each and every one of these monsters—gigantic snakes, animal-headed monstrosities—could overpower and destroy the spirit. Supposing that he passed the demons unscathed and managed to cross the river, the dead man still had to face the gods. What if they

didn't know him, or refused to accept him? All these possible emer-
gencies had to be anticipated and prepared for. The whole process has
always reminded me of a child's game: "Suppose this happens! All
right, but then suppose that happens!"

The defenses against dangers of this kind could only be of one
sort. They consisted of magico-religious spells, and they make up several sizable collections. The oldest collection is the Pyramid Texts,
which were inscribed in pretty blue hieroglyphs on the walls of the
Fifth and Sixth Dynasty pyramids. These texts are a real hodgepodge;
if we find Egyptian religion contradictory, the Pyramid Texts are the
epitome of contradiction. There are spells invoking Osiris and spells
asking for protection against Osiris; spells hailing Re as god of the
dead and other spells naming Osiris. In one text the dead king humbly
accepts the job of secretary to the god; in another he threatens to
march in and eat Re and the rest unless they submit to his demands.

The contradictions are to some extent resolved if we regard the
Pyramid Texts as an anthology, made up of spells from different places
and times. And there is a unifying feature. Although a few texts are in
the form of hymns to the god, the great majority deal with practical
problems: how to reach the hereafter, how to live once one gets there,
how to control potential antagonists.

The Pyramid Texts as such were used for the royal dead, although
not all the privileges they claim for kings and queens were their sole
prerogative. By the Middle Kingdom the magical collection had been
taken over by commoners and written on the coffins of the dead. The
Coffin Texts were not just the Pyramid Texts in a revised edition and a
new medium but include many of the older spells and have the same
purpose. In the New Kingdom and thereafter the anthologies of magical
incantations, greatly altered and revised, were written on papyrus scrolls,
some of them handsomely decorated with miniature scenes, or vignettes,
of the life to come. We call these scrolls the "Book of the Dead," but
there were actually a number of different collections, for which the
Egyptians had other names—the Book of Gates, the Book of That
Which Is in the Afterworld, the Book of Coming Forth by Day.

The Book of the Dead is often mentioned in awed tones by various schools of occultists. However, if a reader has the fortitude to wade through the entire collection, he is left with an impression not of mysterious, occult power, but of practical, thorough organization. The books of the dead, all of them, are guidebooks to the beautiful roads of the West, including useful phrases, explanations of local customs, and hints on how to deal with the natives. A sampling of chapter titles gives some idea of just how thorough the compilation was:

CHAPTER OF:

- Not letting X be bitten by snakes
- Not dying a second time
- Not letting the head of a man be cut off from him
- Drinking water and not being burnt by fire
- Taking the form of a hawk of gold or whatever a man pleases
- Bringing along a boat
- Going into the boat of Re
- Giving funeral offerings
- Not allowing the body of a man to decay
- Not eating filth
- Making the ushebti figure do work

This is only the briefest sampling; there are hundreds of similar texts. It might be interesting to examine one in detail, to see how it works. If a man wants to avoid being bitten by snakes in the afterworld, he says: "Oh Serpent! I am the flame which shines on the Opener of hundreds of thousands of years, the standard of the god Tenpu."

Offhand, this may not strike us as very effective. But we are not attuned to this variety of magic. Underlying all the seemingly meaningless verbiage was the basic power of all spells, the power of the word. Even the spoken word had effectiveness; the written was even more powerful, and the very fact that the handsome, and costly, papyrus said, in writing, that these words would eliminate the danger from serpents meant that that danger was thereby eliminated.

Above all, the books of the dead, from Pyramid Texts to papyrus scrolls, decree life for the lifeless. In their affirmation of life, the texts deny death. There is a majestic power, even in our pedantic translations, of the rolling, constantly repeated demand for existence: "King Teti has not died the death! He does not die! This king lives forever!"

Affirmation of a desire or denial of a fear have magical potency in themselves. Some words had more power than others, and one of the most significant magical words was a man's name. Like his image and his blood and his spittle and all the other elements that resembled him or were part of him, his name contained the essence of his being. In many cultures the names of the gods were sacred, not to be spoken. This is not only respect, it is a reflection of the idea that the name was power. When Herodotus describes the rites of the Dying God in Egypt, he refers to the deity as "a god whose name a religious scruple prevents me from mentioning." Another example is the name of God which devout Jews refuse to pronounce aloud.

In Egypt, to know the name of a god or of any man or object was to have power over it. The magical texts are full of the phrase, "I know you, I know your name!" The dead man, confronted by the gods who might question his right to enter heaven, gives each of them his name and passes in, triumphant. There is even a spell to keep a man from forgetting his own name—tantamount to a loss of identity and, hence, of existence. The magical compilations were the final bulwark against "dying a second time." Not only did they protect the dead from danger, but they provided substitutes for necessities which might fail or be missing. And all this could be done for the price of a painted coffin or a written scroll.

Thus, the dead were guarded against possible neglect of their funerary cult and against purely spiritual dangers. Another peril had its magical defense as well. The Egyptians were painfully well aware of the industry of the tomb robber. Ancient tombs gaped forlornly in various abandoned cemeteries, thieves were constantly being punished by local or royal courts. Perhaps the best defense against these ghouls (or redistributors of wealth) was to die and be buried during the reign of a strong, ferocious pharaoh who would put up with no nonsense in the necropoli. But this was at best a temporary expedient; so, once again, the power of the written word was called in to defend the tomb and its occupant.

> As for any man who shall enter into this tomb in his impurity, and who shall do a thing evilly against it, or who shall damage any stone or any brick in this tomb, or who shall erase the writing herein, I shall seize his neck like a bird. . . . I shall be judged with him in the august council of magistrates of the great god. But as for any man who shall enter into this tomb, being pure with regard to it, I shall be his partisan.

From texts like these (the quotation is a composite) come the exciting but incorrect journalists' stories of "curses" in ancient Egyptian tombs. As our quotation shows, these texts were not so much curses as threats—not of ghostly ghastly attack, but of a lawsuit in the court of the gods! And the threats were not against visitors to the tomb as such, but against violators. In these terms, modern archaeologists should stand high in the favor of the ancient Egyptian kas whose tombs they discover, for most of them would rather cut off a hand than destroy a stone or a sign. They are pure with regard to the tomb. However, archaeology in the early days was not so scrupulous. The world's great museums include statues, pieces of wall paintings, ushebtis, and the mummies themselves, removed from the tombs. The original owners can be said to have attained a kind of immortality by being placed on display, but it wasn't publicity they were after. What about the poor soul (pun intended) whose body is in one museum, his canopic jars in another, and his Book of the Dead in a third? And what about the ones whose mummified bodies were ripped apart in the name of science, the protective amulets removed?

Neither threats of divine retribution nor physical barriers availed against the worst desecrators, thieves ancient and modern. Egyptian doctrine could not allow the only sure defense against despoilation—a burial so poor in worldly goods that no robber would waste his time on it. In Egypt you could take it with you. At least you could take your worldly goods as far as the tomb, and the chance that you might succeed in carrying them all the way into the West was well worth the effort.

But what about the men and women who had nothing to take, who could not afford even the cheapest type of embalming? It has been suggested that the poor in Egypt lacked the hope of immortality; there was no "pie in the sky" to make up for the conspicuous lack of that commodity on earth. The theory that the lowest classes gave their dead to the animal scavengers of the river and the desert instead of burying them is contradicted by hundreds of proofs—the graves of ordinary men, women, and children. We see today that people are willing to impoverish themselves to give their dead a "nice" funeral; the principle must have operated even more strongly in Egypt, where survival depended on the preservation of the body and where a cheap, accessible embalming material was available to everyone in the desert sand.

At all periods of Egyptian history the poor found the same grave— a hole in the ground—and they were laid to rest in the dignity of their own unembalmed flesh and bone. These people had no coffins; sometimes the survivors could not spare so much as a pot of food from the scanty household store. Yet the naked, hungry soul could have one hope of nourishment. As a beggar squats at a rich man's gate, the bodies of the poor were often buried near a nobleman's tomb, where they could catch the crumbs from his well-stocked offering table. This process reached its logical conclusion when the tombs themselves were invaded. Such intrusive burials, tucked cozily away in someone else's tomb, are common; even the pyramids were not exempt, and some tombs have dozens of burials ranging over many generations. Ironically enough, the poorest of the poor sometimes attained that physical survival which was denied the divine pharaoh. The coffins and sarcophagi, the very unguents used in the ritual of resurrection, helped to destroy the flesh they were designed to protect; and if time and decay spared the royal bones, the tomb robbers did not. There is a moral in all of this, of course; but perhaps we are in no position to sneer at the Egyptians because they failed to see it.

THE LAST JUDGMENT

Tomb, mummy, magic, food offerings—in all this there is one conspicuous omission—any reference to an ethical or moral requirement for eternal life. Some scholars believe it was actually missing, that anybody could get to heaven from Egypt if he could pay the price. Contrarily, other scholars have claimed for the Egyptians the "dawn of conscience," and the first demonstration of righteousness as a prerequisite for immortality.

The truth probably lies somewhere between the two extremes, as it so often, boringly, does. The phrase "dawn of conscience" comes from James Henry Breasted. His argument, presented with enthusiasm and elegance of expression, was very persuasive; today, however, most Egyptologists would qualify it almost out of recognition. And yet we cannot dismiss all of the Egyptian mortuary cult as magic. There was, for one thing, the Judgment.

On the walls of the Sistine Chapel, Michelangelo's masterpiece gives an unforgettable picture of the Last Judgment in Christian terms. Christ, enthroned aloft, is not the merciful Redeemer, but the stern Judge. With upraised hand He sifts the risen dead, lifting the blessed into Paradise and sending the wailing shapes of the damned to Hell.

The Egyptian judgment had its majestic aspect too, but it was the formal majesty of the law court, complete with judge and jury, recording secretary, prosecutor, defendant, and witness. Two of our common symbols of law were present in the courtroom—the scales of justice and the goddess of truth. They didn't mean quite the same to the Egyptians, but they strike an oddly familiar note.

In the Hall of the Two Truths sat the judge, the resurrected Osiris, with his wife Isis behind him. The jury consisted of forty-two personages instead of twelve, and all were gods. In the center of the hall, the focus of the scene, was a huge pair of scales. Thoth, the divine scribe, stood beside it, his pen poised and ready to record the judgment. Sometimes he was accompanied by the goddess Maat, Truth (or Divine Order); sometimes she was represented by a small figure or by the feather which was her symbol, occupying one pan of the scales. In the opposite pan was the heart of the man or woman to be judged. Near the scales hovered one other essential member of the court—a beast with the head of a crocodile, the midsection of a lion, and the hindquarters of a hippopotamus. Its name was "Devourer of Souls."

Into the court came Anubis Psychopompos, leading the defendant by the hand. The dead person was dressed in his best, just as he would be for such an occasion today. The dead ladies, in their finest filmy linen and curled wigs, irresistibly suggest the attractive females who try to explain to a sympathetic male jury why they felt it necessary to shoot their husbands.

The image of the feather in the pan of the scales is one I find very appealing. The feather was the symbol of truth, the goddess; but the idea that the heart of the dead man must be so light, so free of evil, as to balance the featherweight on the other pan of the scales is a modern interpretation rather than that of the Egyptians. It is still a significant symbol—the weighing of the heart against truth or divine order, that which was and should be. The scales must balance—and in the scenes of the Judgment, they always do.

The heart was the seat of the emotions and the organ of intelligence, memory, and will. With its accumulated memories of passions and deeds, the heart was the sole witness for or against a man in the case of his own salvation.

This was the Egyptian judgment in its developed form, known to us not only from descriptions in the Book of the Dead but also from the pictures with which such texts were illustrated. The idea of a judging of the dead goes back a long way, however, to a period before the papyrus scrolls came into use, and our knowledge of the earlier conception is not so clear.

The first judge may not have been Osiris. He is called the "Great God," and although there has been a lot of debate about his real name, we cannot be entirely sure who he was. His identity is less important than his function. Assisted by a tribunal of divine magistrates, he, like Osiris, judged the fitness of the soul for immortality on the basis of the defendant's plea:

I gave bread to the hungry, water to the thirsty, clothes to the naked. Never have I done anything evil against any man. I rescued the wretched man from one who was stronger than he. I judged two men so that they might be satisfied. I was respectful to my father, pleasant to my mother. Never did I take a thing belonging to any man. Never have I said anything evil against any person. I spoke truth, I rendered justice.

There is quite a contrast between texts like this, which were written on tombstones of the late Old Kingdom and First Intermediate Period, and the Pyramid Texts, which were used at approximately the same time. The truth or falsehood of the claims to virtue are immaterial, as is the possibility that the mere statement of them had magical import. What is important is that they state a moral code, and that a man's behavior during his lifetime had a bearing on what happened to him after he died. "I spoke truth, I rendered justice."

However, there has been a lot of debate in Egyptological circles about the key words in that last sentence. They are the same word in Egyptian—the word "maat." As we mentioned earlier, this word can be translated as "candor" as well as "truth" or "justice." It has also been read as "the divine order," that arrangement of the universe which was established by the god creator at the beginning of the world.

Our word "truth" means many things in different contexts, and it is clear that "maat" has no one meaning. The men whose tombstones claim that they spoke maat and rendered maat give a number of specific examples of the acts they thought of as just and true, and these are moral qualities—charity toward the poor, help for the helpless. If these were qualities established by the gods in the beginning, "the divine order," that order itself had what we would call moral standards.

Later in the First Intermediate Period a royal father, composing a series of precepts for the guidance of his son, had this to say about the day of judgment:

Perform maat while you endure on earth. Quiet the one who weeps; do not oppress the widow; supplant no man in the

property of his father; impair no officials at their posts. Be on
guard against punishing unfairly. . . . The council which judges
the deficient—you know they are not lenient on that day of
judging. . . . Existence yonder is for eternity . . . but as for him
who reaches it without wrongdoing, he shall exist yonder like
a god, striding freely like the lords of eternity!

This is, I think, an impressive statement. My omissions, represented by dots, give the text more coherence than it actually has; but
the development of the idea is really there.

At about the same time that King Achtoy wrote his Instructions,
the Coffin Texts were beginning to be inscribed. Once again there is
a distinct difference between the mortuary magic of the Texts and the
mortuary ethics of the Instructions.

After the Coffin Texts came the Book of the Dead; and by now we
have reached the judgment as it has been described, with Osiris as
supreme judge and all the trappings of the formal court. What about
the moral aspect of this version of the judgment?

I am afraid there is some excuse for the attitude of the skeptic, who
claims that even this noble concept degenerated into another attempt
to reduce all problems to those which could be solved by magic spells.
The Book of the Dead is quite wordy about the Judgment. Chapter
125 (the number is that of a modern classification) is the one dealing
specifically with the Hall of the Two Truths and what went on there.
It gives, at some length, the speech of the defendant to the tribunal.
The chapter in question used to be called "The Negative Confession"—
a well-turned but essentially meaningless phrase which has now been
replaced by other titles such as "The Declaration of Innocence." In his
peroration the dead man makes a statement to each of the forty-two
gods, denying that he has committed a particular sin. We find all the
Ten Commandments mentioned, except for the first two—Egyptian
gods were not at all jealous, and they were very fond of graven images.
In place of these there is a long list of crimes and sins. The dead man
tells the god "Dangerous of Face" that he has not committed murder,
and informs the "Devourer of Shades" that he has not stolen. Lying,

assault and battery, deceit, gossip, adultery, general violence, arrogant behavior, inordinate ambition—the list is much longer than the Judeo-Christian catalog of prohibitions, which, we must recall, is also negative in character.

As an implicit ethical code, "The Declaration of Innocence" is fairly impressive. A certain number of rather picayune ritual sins are mentioned, but in general the list compares favorably with any other morality statement I can think of. However, the shining air of virtue is sullied by the fact that this chapter forms part of a book made up almost entirely of magical spells. The format makes it clear that this is only another formula, another incantation against danger. The denial of sin negates the sin, and the gods can be mastered by telling them their names.

But the judge, Osiris, surely reaches his verdict through the evidence given by that impartial witness, the heart. Can the decision of the "Foremost of the Westerners" be subverted by a petty official armed with a papyrus scroll?

It could be; but there is an easier way out of the difficulty. The most disillusioning of all the spells in the Book of the Dead is Chapter 30, the text written on the base of the ubiquitous heart scarabs. Its intent, candidly stated, is to gag that one essential witness: "My heart of my mother! My heart of my mother! Do not stand up against me as witness! Do not create opposition against me as witness! Do not create opposition against me among the magistrates! Do not weigh heavy against me in the presence of the keeper of the scales!"

No, there is not much ethical content in this. It is said that there is more rejoicing in our heaven over a repentant sinner than over many of the faithful. The Egyptian did not even need to repent; all he needed was enough money to buy a scroll that *said* he had repented.

Yet it would not be entirely fair to see in the corruption of the Judgment a shift from primitive ethics to sophisticated cynicism. The Pyramid Texts are just as "magical" as the Book of the Dead, and the later literature contains statements which show not only a striving for moral virtue, but a new humbleness before the god and an awareness of man's sinful nature. "The Declaration of Innocence" is corrupt, but its content cannot be wholly ignored. To the literal sinner—a category not restricted to ancient Egypt—the magic of the written word might be assurance enough. To a more thoughtful believer, it might be a statement of a creed he had honestly tried to follow. In Egypt even the gods could err; and knowing human courts, the man preparing himself for the judgment from which there was no appeal might feel more secure in the knowledge that he had a written statement of the innocence he had tried to maintain. Perhaps the humble burials of the poor are themselves a testimonial to the enduring faith in the purity of the Judgment. If these men and women could hope for survival, without the aid of heart scarabs or magical scrolls, they must have had some spiritual claim to be included among the followers of Osiris.

There was no appeal from the Judgment; the sentence for the guilty was annihilation, that "dying a second time" which the Egyptians dreaded beyond all else. The little vignettes of the judgment hall always include a picture of the monster called the "Devourer of Souls." His name makes his role fairly evident, and sometimes he is so impatient for his prey that he stands on his hind legs, fairly drooling. I find this monster rather charming, myself, and it is possible that the Egyptians did not take him too seriously. Even in the scenes where he sits poised, hungrily watching his potential dinner, the dead man smirks and bows, fully confident that the judgment will be in his favor.

We do not find the Egyptian monsters very frightening; the neat crisp drawing and the conventional types reduce them to abstractions. But perhaps the Egyptians were not so blasé about them. It is not always easy to distinguish between gods and demons, for some of the gods were strange composites of men and beasts, and even they might be hostile toward an unprotected spirit. Serpents are among the commonest of the demons; the great enemy of Re, who attacked his boat each night in the Underworld, was a snake named Apophis. However, there is no real Devil in Egyptian theology. Set, the murderer of Osiris, was only evil in specific contexts. He represented the barren desert and the storm, forces of disorder, but he could sometimes be personable and agreeable, holding the ladder for the dead king to mount to

*Selected demigods and demons who might interfere with the dead man during his journey
to the hereafter (from a mortuary papyrus). Left to right: the Devourer of Souls,
a lion-headed god, "Turn-face" the ferryman, a great serpent.*

heaven and helping Re repel the threatening serpent. In the Nineteenth Dynasty, and perhaps in the Second Dynasty as well, he was
one of the patrons of the royal house.

Whether they feared their demons or not, the Egyptians did fear
death—the first physical death and that second death from which
there was no resurrection. They spent a good part of their lives fighting annihilation, and in so doing they built up the most complicated
structure of mortuary ritual any people has ever produced. We are the
beneficiaries of it, in terms of museum collections and scholarly books;
and perhaps we will not find the painted mummy cases and weird
amulets so bizarre if we see, beneath their extravagance, a common
human terror and a common hope.

Reading List

Since this is a list of suggested readings and not a bibliography per se, I have included only books in English that are up-to-date, comprehensible to a nonspecialist, and obtainable through booksellers and libraries. If you are really gung-ho you will find more comprehensive bibliographies in several of the books listed below. Articles in professional journals such as the *Journal of Egyptian Archaeology* and the *Journal of the American Research Center in Egypt* are, in general, too specialized to be of use to a lay reader. There are several popular journals; by far the best is *Kmt, A Modern Journal of Ancient Egypt*, which has, during its fifteen-plus years of publication, included informative and readable articles on every topic mentioned in this book. It is indispensable to any serious student. Look for it at the library or subscribe by writing the publisher at PO Box 475, Sebastopol, CA 95473-1475.

You will not find detailed information on the Internet here, since I am computer-illiterate. Just start with "Egypt, Ancient," or "Egyptology." You will find—I refuse to estimate—a *lot* of websites, of varying degrees of specialization, covering every sub-category from excavation reports to the lunatic fringe. I hope that by the time you have finished this book you will be able to tell the difference.

GENERAL

James, T.G.H. *Ancient Egypt: The Land and Its Legacy.* University of Texas, 1988.
———. *Pharaoh's People.* University of Chicago, 1994.
Janssen, R. M., and Janssen, J. J. *Growing Up in Ancient Egypt.* Rubicon Press, 1990.
McDowell, A.G. *Village Life in Ancient Egypt: Laundry Lists and Love Songs.* Oxford University Press, 1999.

Silverman, David, ed. *Ancient Egypt*. Oxford University Press, 1999.

Teeter, Emily, and Douglas Brewer. *Egypt and the Egyptians*. Cambridge University Press, 1999.

TOMBS AND SITES

Bierbrier, Morris. *The Tomb Builders of the Pharaohs*. Macmillan, 1995.

Davies, Vivian, and Rene Friedman. *Egypt Uncovered*. Steward, Tabori, and Chang, 1998.

Edwards, I. E. S. *The Pyramids of Egypt*. Penguin Books, 1991. Revised edition of a basic work.

Forbes, Dennis. *Tombs. Treasures. Mummies. Seven Great Discoveries of Egyptian Archaeology*. KMT Communications, 1998.

Lehner, Mark. *The Complete Pyramids*. Thames and Hudson, 1997.

Martin, Geoffrey. *The Hidden Tombs of Memphis*. Thames and Hudson, 1992.

Reeves, C. N. *Ancient Egypt: The Great Discoveries*. Thames and Hudson, 2000.

Reeves, C. N. and Richard Wilkinson. *The Complete Valley of the Kings*. Thames and Hudson, 1996.

Strudwick, Nigel, and Helen Strudwick. *Thebes in Egypt*. Cornell University Press, 1999.

LANGUAGE

Collier, Mark, and Bill Manley. *How to Read Egyptian Hieroglyphs.* University of California Press, 1998.

Davies, W. V. *Egyptian Hieroglyphs*. University of California Press, 1987.

Malek, Jaromir. *ABC of Egyptian Hieroglyphs*. Ashmolean Museum, 1994.

These are for fun. If you really want to learn the language—I don't recommend trying it without a teacher—the basic work is Gardiner's classic *Egyptian Grammar* (3rd ed., Griffith Institute, 2005.) A worthy (but equally difficult) substitute is James Allen, *Middle Egyptian* (Cambridge University, 2000).

WOMEN

Robins, Gay. *Women in Ancient Egypt*. Harvard University Press, 1993.

Tydesley, Joyce. *Daughters of Isis*. Viking Penguin, 1995.

Watterson, Barbara. *Women in Ancient Egypt*. St. Martin's, 1991.

And two catalogs, with gorgeous pictures and excellent articles:

The Royal Women of Amarna, Metropolitan Museum of Art, 1996.

Mistress of the House, Mistress of Heaven. Cincinnati Art Museum, 1996.

LITERATURE

Lichtheim, Miriam, ed. *Ancient Egyptian Literature*, 3 vols. University of California Press, 1973, 1976, 1980.

Simpson, W.K., ed. *The Literature of Ancient Egypt*. Rev. ed. Yale University, 2003.

RELIGION

Faulkner, Raymond, tr. *The Egyptian Book of the Dead*. Chronicle Books, 1994.

Lesko, Barbara. *The Great Goddesses of Egypt*. University of Oklahoma Press, 1999.

Wilkinson, Richard. *The Complete Temples of Ancient Egypt*. Thames and Hudson, 2000.

———. *The Complete Gods and Goddesses of Ancient Egypt*. Thames and Hudson, 2003.

MUMMIES AND MORTUARY BELIEFS

Brier, Bob. *Egyptian Mummies*. William Morrow, 1994.

David, Rosalie, and Rick Archbold. *Conversations with Mummies*. HarperCollins, 2000.

Ikram, Salima. *Death and Burial in Ancient Egypt*. Longman, 2003.

———. *Divine Creatures: Animal Mummies in Ancient Egypt*. American University in Cairo, 2005.

Ikram, Salima, and Aidan Dodson. *The Mummy in Ancient Egypt*. Thames and Hudson, 1998.

Partridge, Robert. *Faces of Pharaoh: Royal Mummies and Coffins from Ancient Thebes*. Rubicon Press, 1994.

Smith, G. Elliot. *The Royal Mummies*. Duckworth, 2000. A reprint of the classic 1903 edition originally published by the Service des Antiquités.

ART AND ARCHITECTURE

Aldred, Cyril. *Egyptian Art*. Thames and Hudson, 1983.

Robins, Gay. *The Art of Ancient Egypt*. Harvard University Press, 2000.

Russman, Edna R. *Egyptian Sculpture*. University of Texas Press, 1989.

Smith, William S., *The Art and Architecture of Ancient Egypt*, rev. by William K. Simpson. Yale University Press, 1998.

MISCELLANEOUS

Andrews, Carol. *Ancient Egyptian Jewelry*. Harry N. Abrams, 1991.

Brier, Bob. *Ancient Egyptian Magic*. William Morrow, 1980.

Malek, Jaromir. *The Cat in Ancient Egypt*. Rev. ed. British Museum Press, 2006.

Manniche, Lise. *An Ancient Egyptian Herbal*. University of Texas Press, 1989.

———. *Sexual Life in Ancient Egypt*. Kegan Paul, 1984. Paperback ed., 1994.

Muller, Hans Wolfgang, and Eberhard Thiem. *Gold of the Pharaohs*. Cornell University Press, 1999.

Nunn, John. *Ancient Egyptian Medicine*. University of Oklahoma Press, 1996.

Volumes in the Shire Egyptology Series are great buys—written by experts, inexpensive, covering such diverse subjects as textiles, warfare, furniture, and many other topics.

Sources of Quotations

Quotations from Egyptian and other ancient texts have been made more comprehensible to nonscholars by omitting symbols such as brackets and parentheses and by a certain freedom of rendering when the meaning of the literal translation is not immediately apparent to a modern reader. I believe I can claim, however, that I have not altered the basic sense of the texts. Those who want to check up on me can refer to the following sources.

With the exceptions noted below, translations of literary texts are derived from the indispensable three-volume work of Miriam Lichtheim or the revised edition of W. K. Simpson, *The Literature of Ancient Egypt* (see Reading List).

Unfortunately there is no equivalent modern source for historical texts. James H. Breasted's *Ancient Records of Egypt*, in five volumes, has never been supplanted, and although individual texts have been studied and revised, it remains a basic reference work. It has been reprinted by the University of Illinois Press (2001). A selection of Egyptian literary and historical texts can be found in the translations by John A. Wilson in *Ancient Near Eastern Texts Relating to the Old Testament*, edited by James B. Pritchard (Princeton University Press, 3rd ed., 1969).

My source for the Hekanakhte letters was H. E. Winlock, *Excavations at Deir el Bahri, 1911–1931* (MacMillan, 1942); the translations are those of Battiscombe Gunn, who unfortunately died before completing them. Complete translations are those of T. G. H. James, *The Hekanakhte Papers and Other Early Middle Kingom Documents* (Metropolitan Museum of Art, 1962), and, most recently, James P. Allen, *The Heqanakht Papyri* (Metropolitan Museum of Art, 2002).

The classic versions of religious texts are those of R. O. Faulkner, *The Ancient Egyptian Pyramid Texts* (Oxford University Press, 1969); *The Ancient Egyptian Coffin*

Text, 3 vols. (Warminster, 1975–78); and *The Ancient Egyptian Book of the Dead* (Chronicle Books, 1994). You can get a fancy new edition of the last, with a fake jewel on the cover (if that sort of thing appeals to you), from Barnes and Noble (2005), with an introduction by James P. Allen.

William Murnane, *Texts from the Amarna Period in Egypt* (Scholars Press, 1995), contains up-to-date translations of the restoration stela of Tutankhamon and other documents of the period, including Harmhab's Karnak stela.

There are a number of editions of Manetho. The one I use is the Loeb Classical Library version.

The only complete translation of Edwin Smith (in English) is by J. H. Breasted, *The Edwin Smith Surgical Papyryus*, 2 vols. (University of Chicago Press, 1930). A recent study, with interesting additions and emendations, is John F. Nunn, *Ancient Egyptian Medicine* (University of Oklahoma Press, 1992).

Translations of the Dream Papyrus and the calendar of lucky and unlucky days may be found in McDowell, *Village Life in Ancient Egypt* (see Reading List). McDowell's book, which focuses on materials from the workmen's village at Deir el Medina, includes letters, prayers, and related texts. An accessible source of magical texts is Bob Brier's *Ancient Egyptian Magic*, which includes translations of letters to the dead, the complete calendar of lucky and unlucky days, charms, and excerpts from the Book of the Dead and the Pyramid and Coffin Texts. Brier footnotes the original sources. The texts are discussed, but for some reason not translated, in Geraldine Pinch, *Magic in Ancient Egypt* (British Museum Press, 1994).

Arthur Weigall's mummy story can be found in his *Tutankhamen and Other Essays* (Thornton Butterworth, 1923).

Neugebauer's remarks on Egyptian mathematics come from his *The Exact Sciences in Antiquity* (Princeton University Press, 1952).

Sir James Frazer, *The Golden Bough*, is still of value for students of early religion and magic; volumes I and II of the complete edition (Macmillan and Co., 1913, 1920), *The Magic Art*, supplied much of the material I have quoted or mentioned. Another useful source is Bronislaw Malinowski, *Science and Religion and Other Essays* (Doubleday and Co., 1954).

More recent translations of various texts have appeared in articles in such journals as the *Journal of Egyptian Archaeology* and the *Journal of the American Research Center in Egypt*, as well as in journals in languages other than English. I leave it to advanced and/or obsessed students to track them down.

Index

physicians, 60, 218, 246, 247, 249, 250, 251, 252, 254–55, 256–57, 319, 333, 338–39
 see also doctors
Piankhi, 48
pigs, 48, 108
Pinkhi. *see* Piye
Pinudjem, xvi
pit, grave, 347–48, 382
Piye, 48
Plutarch, 288, 314
poems, poetry, 51–53, 55–56, 66, 128
poison, 45, 98, 211, 343, 345
polygamy, 62, 63
portraiture, 185–88, 365, 369
pottery, potters, 104, 106, 195, 196, 214, 215, 265
prayers, 127, 235, 274, 292–93, 332
priestesses, 286
priests, 80, 148, 213, 218, 219, 278, 286, 338, 359, 370, 372, 373, 374, 375
princess, "heiress," 67, 69, 73
professions, 124–25
promiscuity, 63
pronunciation, of Egyptian language, 135
property rights, 64
prose, 113–15
Psusennes, xvi, 364
Ptah, 25, 44, 45, 162, *261*, 262, 264, 266, 269, 292
Ptahhotep, Instructions of, 61, 62, 63–64
puberty, 49, 72
Puemre, 194
pulse, the, 256
punishment, corporal, 139
Punt, *12*, 242, 244
pylons, 25, 29, 279, *280*, *281*, 282, 285, 286, 359, 362
Pyramid Age, 246, 329, 338
pyramid complex, 351–52
pyramid mystics, 207, 232, 239–40
pyramidology, 207
pyramids, 153, 194–201, 226–40, 347–62
 see also specific pyramids
Pyramid Texts, 130, 271, 316, 350, 352, 363, 378, 380, 385, 387

quarries, quarrying, 25, 31, 34, 153, 154, 198, 229, 230, 240
 see also stone
quartzite, 35, 191, 230, 364

queens, 69–75, 91–92, 93, 98, 358
 position of, 73–74
 see also specific queens
Quibell, James, 15, 328

race, 18–19
Ramesseum, the, 279, 359
Ramses I, xvi
Ramses II, xvi, 14, 24, 26, 28, 29, 32, 41, 50, 53, 154–55, 161, 162, 164, 184, 358, 359
Ramses III, xvi, 160, 205, 218, 245, 345, 359
Ramses IV, xvi, 205
Rauser, 6–7
Re, 6, 7, 45, 54, 74, 114, 116, 162, 260, 262, 264, 265, 267, 269, 270, 271, 286, 290, 291, 315, 316, 317, 318, 350, 367, 378, 388
 see also Re-Atum
reading, 139, 140
 see also education
Re-Atum, 265, 288, 289
 see also Atum; Re
Red Crown, 22
Reddjetet, 6, 7
Red Land, 22–23, 33
Red Sea, 33, 36, 244
regents, queens as, 70, 72
Re-Harakhte, 25, 54, 262, 265, 271, 272
Reisner, George, 166
reliefs, 49, 53, 59, 87, 89, 121, 174, 176, 180, 184, 188, 189, 190, 193, 268, 283, 313, 353, 354, 362, 364, 370
religion, 202–3, 213–19, 226, 234, 246, 259–93
rituals, mortuary, 215, 278–88, 310, 318–20, 365, 370–76
Romans, Roman period, xvii, 98, 122, 185, 195, 221, 278, 337, 369
roses, 98
Roth, Ann Macy, 249

sacrifice, animal, 373
saff, 354
Sahure, xvi
Sais, 23, 289
Saite Dynasty, 121, 184–85, 362
Sakkara, 25, 56, 107, 194, 195, 196–97, 328, 351, 352, 361

Tjehenu, 38
Tjemehu, 38
toilet articles, 103, 104, 105–6
tomb robbers, 89, 104, 197, 235, 250, 320,
    332, 336–37, 343, 344, 353, 356, 358–59,
    364, 366, 369, 374, 380–82
tomb(s), 347–76
  of Amenhotep III, 357
  art in, 173, 174, 177–78, 190
  astronomy in, 225, 226
  boats and boat models in, 243, 244
  of Djoser, 194
  at Giza, 150
  intrusive burials in, 338
  mummies and, 327
  plan of, 199–200
  reproduction of, in Saite dynasty, 185
  rock-cut, 353, 355, 360, 361
  of Sakkara, 194, 195–97
  senselessness of, 310
  Twelfth Dynasty, 231
  of women, 65
  see also mastabas; *specific tombs*
tools, 23, 36, 102, 147, 172, 191, 227, 229,
    231, 297, 331
totemism, 269
"tourist trade," 120, 121, 122, 123
towns, town sites, 26, 94–96, 111, 167,
    374
toys, 41
trade, 37
training. *see* education
travel, 120–21
trumpets, 162–63
truth. *see* maat
Turin, Museum at, 34
turquoise, 36, 137, 138
Tutankhamon, xvi
  ascension to the throne, 179, 277
  death of, 71, 343–44, 357
  equipment of, 14, 46, 82–83, 90–91, 98,
    103–4, 105, 155, 156, 162–63, 331,
    365–66, 368–69
  father-in-law of, 27
  fetuses in tomb of, 71, 343
  Harmhab and, 164, 361
  mummy of, 335, 340, 341–42
  successor of, 71
  tomb of, 82–83, 104, 184, 357, 358–59,
    363–64

treasurer of, 361
widow of, 71
Twain, Mark, 305, 308
Twelfth Dynasty, 89, 90, 91, 153, 176, 231,
    271, 279, 288, 355
Twentieth Dynasty, 95, 159, 164, 245, 278,
    360
Twenty-Fifth Dynasty, 48, 184, 192, 360
Twenty-First Dynasty, 23–24, 107, 332–33,
    338, 341, 344, 364
Twenty-Second Dynasty, 18, 23–24
Twenty-Sixth Dynasty, 362
"Two Brothers, The Tale of," 115–18
Two Lands, 21–39

Unas, pyramid of, 361
Uni, 153
Unis, xvi
University of Pennsylvania Museum, 8
University of Vienna, 23
Upper Egypt, 147, 160, 164, 176, 240, 264,
    279, 296, 372
Userkaf, xvi
Usermaatre Setepenre Ramses Meriamon.
    see Ramses II
ushebtis, 367, 379
utensils, 106

Valley of the Kings, 15, 19, 29, 47, 95, 292,
    356–62
Valley of the Queens, 358
viziers, 31, 60, 80, 141, 146, 147, 148, 164,
    194, 353
Vyse, Colonel Richard, 337–38

Wade, Ronald, 331–32
Wadi el Hol, 138
Wadi Hammamat, the, 33, 34, 35–36, 244
Wadi Natrun, 37, 148, 330, 332
Wadjet, 264
Wahankh, 47
warriors, 37, 153, 154, 157, 159
Wars of Liberation, 343
Waset, 29
  see also Thebes
Wawat, 32–33
weapons, 155, 156–57, *158*, 160, 163, 309,
    366, 367
weavers, weaving, 60, 66, 76–77, 101, 128,
    178